8x(5|09)6|13

First Son

First Son

GEORGE W. BUSH

and the
Bush Family
Dynasty

BILL MINUTAGLIO

TIMES [T] BOOKS

RANDOM HOUSE

Library of Congress Cataloging-in-Publication Data

Minutaglio, Bill.
First son : George W. Bush and the Bush family dynasty / Bill
Minutaglio.—1st ed.
     p.   cm.
Includes index.
ISBN 0-8129-3139-4 (acid-free paper)
1. Bush, George W. (George Walker), 1948–   . 2. Governors—
Texas Biography.   3. Texas—Politics and government—1951–
4. Bush family.   5. Presidential candidates—United States
Biography.   6. Children of presidents—United States
Biography.   I. Title. F391.4.B87M56   1999
976.404'63'092—dc21   [B]   99-16462

Book Design by Mina Greenstein

SPECIAL SALES
Times Books are available at special discounts for bulk
purchases for sales promotions or premiums. Special editions,
including personalized covers, excerpts of existing books, and
corporate imprints, can be created in large quantities for special
needs. For more information, write to Special Markets, Times
Books, 201 East 50th Street, New York, New York 10022, or
call 800-800-3246.

To Francis Xavier, Tess, Holly, Rose, Nicholas

Preface

AFTER ELEVEN MONTHS of research and writing—and after some members of his family and staff consented to interviews for this book—speculation had given way to a sheer sense of inevitability surrounding Texas Governor George Walker Bush's run for the highest office. He was, as the title of this book suggests, "the first son" of President George Herbert Walker Bush. But now some said he was the first son since John Quincy Adams poised to follow his father into the White House. The transformation was almost breathtaking, even by today's political standards, and it obviously was occurring only a few years after the elder George Bush had left office.

My work began after George W. Bush had been governor of Texas for three and a half years. As the research unfolded it centered, in good part, on his evolution in a singular, influential American family that traces its roots to this country's earliest settlers and that spread from the Northeast to the Midwest to Texas to Florida. That fact simplified matters when it came to answering the many variations of an obvious question posed to me by a plainspoken, high-ranking Texas lawmaker: "Is your book pro or con?" I was able to answer the question about any possible biases by saying that the two people who had read my work in progress had said the book had led them to different decisions: one that he would vote for George W. Bush, the other that she would never vote for him. Their differing decisions, I think, were based less on party allegiances or ideological biases and more on how they viewed someone's private and public upbringing. Their decisions, I suspect, were based on how they viewed all the many things that lead to someone's being elected to high public office as opposed to what someone might do while serving in that office.

   This work is about a political person in what is obviously one of the most acutely political families in American history. Toward that end, and after twenty-one years in journalism, I knew that the same rules would apply in Texas as they do in Washington: some close family members and staffers were helpful to me, even when they recognized that other family members and staffers were less inclined to assist. I met with George W. Bush in his second-floor office at the Texas State Capitol on two highly insightful occasions in the summer of 1998 in order to convey my intention to do a fair, thorough book. Bush staffers told me eleven months later that he was still reflecting on whether to offer interviews. Though this book is not authorized, several close relatives—including his brother Jeb Bush, uncles (the siblings of President George Herbert Walker Bush), and cousins—agreed to free-ranging interviews. At work's end, more than three hundred other people had been interviewed, from his Little League coach to Texas oil wildcatters, from high-ranking officials in his father's presidential campaigns to one former employer who was finally tracked down in the Mexican Yucatán and who was now harvesting bamboo commercially. There was research done on the ground in deep West Texas, Houston, Dallas, Austin, Washington, D.C., Massachusetts, and Connecticut. With the assistance of federal and State of Texas officials, thousands of public papers—from White House documents to the governor's correspondence—were eventually released to me.

   In the painstaking months I spent on this book, the full breadth of modern political journalism, a methodology in the making constantly being redefined by each new revelation from the Clinton White House and the Office of the Special Prosecutor, also managed to reach directly to Austin, Texas. The culmination was a story in May 1999 on the front page of *The Wall Street Journal* that examined the evolution of the unfounded "rumors" surrounding George W. Bush's use of drugs—a story that, in essence, touched on the rumors about the prevailing rumors in Bush's life. The day the article appeared, I was told about it by Bush's old college roommate, someone I had contacted during my latest, extensive round of fact checking. This fiercely loyal friend from Yale, someone whose child is Bush's godchild, gingerly asked me "What's next?" and I understood it to be an inquiry into what I was planning to write about the rumors. I had already received legions of similar inquiries from Bush supporters, Bush critics, and unsubtle members of the media. My answer was easy: David Maraniss, in his biography of Bill Clinton, had once suggested that readers who were hungering for news on Clinton's sex life would have "to do their dining elsewhere." The same remains true for anyone looking for dollops of drug tales in this book.

Instead, this biography is meant to serve, in some way, as an introduction to and exploration of the place and state of mind called Texas. It is also meant to serve as an evenhanded attempt to examine what it is like to grow up with an influential family's ever-apparent legacy—and what it is like to both embrace the legacy and keep some distance from it. If anything, the first son was born into politics—in almost every sense possible.

Bill Minutaglio, May 1999

Contents

First Son

1

Reality Day

November 3, 1998

From inside the Lincoln Town Car, all blue-silver like the river snaking through Willie Nelson's smoky rancho deluxe, it's impossible to miss the cloud cover beginning to burn off over the Texas Hill Country. It's a little after 9 A.M. on a slightly chilly day, and as the clouds are erased there are the soft bumps and shoulders, the same loping country that LBJ retreated to, bouncing along in his own Lincoln on the banks of the capricious Pedernales River . . . in the same bit of Texas that Willie Nelson and his aging coterie of snaggletoothed mad-dog musicians like to claim as their outpost.

Sometimes the Midland good old boys remind him: Back in '75, back then his West Texas friends would yodel and snort when they saw him. Here comes the Bombastic Bushkin, George W., that SOB . . . *George Dubya!* Back then, one night, he and Charlie had had some beer and had finally decided, hell, that it would be all right, important really, to walk onstage at the Ector County Coliseum with Willie and his band. And all the while Willie was vaguely aware of something happening behind him, all the while Willie kept staring in his usual goggle-eyed way into the cosmic otherworld and the band was going to be playing *Whiskey River, take my mind.*

His Lincoln is in downtown Austin now, and it's slamming hard off Lavaca Street and straight onto a sloping driveway. Wheels flashing, it's surging just inches from the still-opening automatic wrought-iron gate. It's rolling right to the rear entrance of the faded white governor's mansion. The building, Greek Revival-meets-southern-plantation stately, is crawling with splattered, callused remodelers, many of them Hispanic, dressed in soiled jumpsuits and hanging from a cobweb of scaffolding. They're smiling. And they're nudging each other: "*Señor Suerte*" . . . "Mr. Lucky," whispers one of the admiring workers, nodding toward the Lincoln.

He's riding shotgun, his right arm is hanging out the window as if he's in the lead car in the homecoming parade in Amarillo, as if he's gone cruising downtown Fort Worth in a T-Bird, as if there's somebody out on the drag by the University of Texas whose attention he desperately wants to get, as if it's Midland in the 1950s or Houston in the 1960s and the smiling mothers on the baking sidewalk are halfheartedly shielding their curious daughters' eyes. George W. Bush's brow is doing a Lone Star two-step up and down. It's election day. He's leading by an extraordinary margin and projected to be the first Texas governor ever elected to consecutive four-year terms. The numbers are huge, and in the shadowy piney woods creeping toward the Louisiana border, a woman comes up to him at an old-fashioned political rally and presses a jar of fresh Henderson cane syrup into his hand. Outside the weathered Camino Real Hotel in El Paso, an elderly Mexican immigrant grips his shoulders and won't let go as he stares into his eyes. In the soul of the new high-tech Texas, in Austin, computer billionaire Michael Dell invites him to his yawning hillside manor one Saturday in January; on Monday, the first thing George W. does is write a note, just like his father trained him to do, carefully scribbling notes by the thousands, shorthand-scrawled missives suggesting an intimacy, a lingering friendship: *Dear Susan & Michael: Laura, the girls and I had a fine time Saturday at your party. We especially appreciated the tour of your home. It is great. I look forward to future visits. Sincerely, GW.*[1]

Looking out the car window, he can see the little army waiting for him outside the mansion. It makes him laugh, he can't help it, and it makes him want to scream something out the Lincoln: "Hey . . . welcome to Reality Day!"

The driver brakes the car hard just short of the porte-cochere. The governor of Texas bolts from the car and takes a few strides to the back door of the mansion. Up close, the 142-year-old refurbished building looks like any one of a thousand fraternity houses, one of those older homes that the family of an iron-willed nineteenth-century industrialist donated to the local university—all Ionic capitals and ribbed columns, all stately and ghostly, a witness to twinkling soirees, toga party chants, and pregame rallies. Bush shoots the cuffs of the white dress shirt under his gray suit. The rolling amoeba of coffee-clutching reporters that has been waiting all morning for him begins to tumble in his direction. CNN, *The*

Washington Post, Associated Press. He's winking at his boys, the fraternity of security detail men and the armed, white-hat-wearing Texas Rangers, who can't help but grin too as they line up outside the mansion's back entrance. The energy level out here is set at the usual, nice, rollicking pitch. He suddenly shrugs his shoulders.

"I'm glad Reality Day is here!" he yelps into the air. "Yesterday was Speculation Day. Today is Reality Day!"

He starts to bob in a bantam rooster strut across the hand-laid bricks in the circular driveway. His head is tilted back, all chinny defiance. He's done twenty-three press conferences in the last seven days: Dallas, Austin, Waco, San Antonio. His caffeine-sucking press handlers, saggy faces, bad skin, and droopy shoulders, are all dragging, but he's still up at 6 A.M., still crackling to jump on the King Air campaign plane: San Angelo, Wichita Falls, Sherman. There have been dozens of reality days, speculation days, one after another.

"Oh, it's been a long campaign!" he shouts, still beaming, still antsy.

FOR WEEKS, the first son had been on the phone, taking meetings in his cavernous second-floor office and debating the merits of the new slogan. It was, he and his advisers had decided, compact. Al Gore will deride it and the knuckle-draggers will complain, but it will really put some velvety distance between himself and Newt Gingrich, between himself and all those other soon-to-be defrocked bastards. And it was, though hopefully no one will notice it, the exact same slogan his father's closest aides had once devised to describe the elder Bush to Christian voters back when he was finally sure his 1988 presidential campaign was rolling forward: *Compassionate Conservative*.

This morning, the first thing was to call his father. They had been making these calls for decades, these election-morning calls. They talked about the same things they had talked about face-to-face several weeks before, during the annual, almost giddy August retreat at the ninety-six-year-old seaside family compound in Maine. In Kennebunkport, it was obvious. It was celebrative. The numbers *were* impressive. The crafty backdoor Democrats in Texas were still falling all over themselves for the first son. Jeb was going to win in Florida. His father had said he'd decided he would take Jeb's and George W.'s mother and go to Florida. He wouldn't be coming to Texas, where he had done all that grinding back-room muscle work to force the modern Republican Party onto its feet and out of that pockmarked landscape in oil-stained West Texas, out of that sickening humidity in Houston, every day his starched white shirt sticking to his chest like a moist blanket. He wouldn't be coming to Texas, where he had done all those things that had made it possible for his first son to become governor. More important, he said, that I go to Florida. The first son had agreed.

Exactly twenty-five years ago, he'd had a different conversation with his father. That night, he'd been drunk, and he was out driving with his fifteen-year-old brother, Marvin. After he had rammed through the garbage cans with his car and walked in the front door of the house . . . he was ready, if it was going to be that way, to fight his father. He was from Houston, Texas, he was beery, he had no real career, it was late, and for most of his life he, more than anyone in the family, had been measured against his father, his grandfather, the Bush legacy. That night, he'd stood in front of his father, in the den, and asked his father if he was ready to fight:

"I hear you're looking for me. You want to go mano a mano right here?"

Now, this morning, he was happy his father was traveling to Florida and would be with his younger brother. Through five decades, there has always been a Bush as governor, senator, congressman, or president. Since the early 1950s, there have been only rare, random interludes when a Bush hasn't been in a prominent political office. This one, for the first time, is one the first son is going to claim on his own without all those losers, all those *psychobabblers*, who pretend to know him, who want to analyze him, who waste their time looking for some deep-rooted angst, some inner, complicated undulations . . . all those soothsayers from the Northeast . . . all the weak-willed products of the 1960s, the people who fell for all that claustrophobic, indulgent William Sloane Coffin guilt at Yale and Harvard . . . the ones who whisper that they can always see his father's shadow hanging, nagging, pacing off to the side.

ALL YEAR, the extraordinary poll numbers have been delivered to that second-floor office at the State Capitol, the one with the collection of 250 autographed baseballs neatly arranged in a dark-wood display case, the Western painting with the lone rider that his Midland oil buddy Joe O'Neill III . . . *Spider!* . . . had loaned him, the rows of framed photographs on the counter behind his chair, the photos, staring at his back, of his stern grandfather and his misty-eyed father. All year he has led by pneumatic numbers in every poll, including the national prepresidential ones that say he's more popular than Colin Powell, Steve Forbes, and Al Gore. All year in Texas it's speculation squared: He had already made the calls to set Newt Gingrich's resignation in motion, hadn't he? Larry Flynt was investigating him, wasn't he? Hasn't a Texas reporter called up his press office and asked if the governor ever killed anyone?

Six years ago the *Houston Chronicle* ran the wrong picture of him. It was on a Sunday, the final day leading up to his carefully scheduled official announcement that, without ever holding any other elected office, he was going to run for governor of Texas. Of course, by mistake, the newspaper had run a picture of his father:

> "In some copies of Sunday's State section, the wrong picture was used in a story about George W. Bush's address to the Texas Federation of Republican Women."[2]

He said it didn't bother him. But whenever the extended Bush-Walker clan assembled for their annual meetings at Kennebunkport, they watched him, as they always did, because they wanted to see what he would do or say next. He was the oldest, most incendiary, of the five kids, but he was always more than that: *Primus inter pares*, as his erudite, wordy Uncle Bucky liked to harrumph. First among equals, maintained Bucky.

His uncle, especially, loved to watch his nephew, wondering how he would turn out. He could see the patterns emerging, even when he had taken him to his first ball game at the old Polo Grounds, watching the New York Giants play the Cincinnati Reds, and even later, sitting in box seats at Shea Stadium, keeping tabs on the New York Mets, one of the baseball teams the Bush family would own a piece of over the years. Bucky saw the way Jeb, Neil, Marvin, and Dorothy deferred to Little George . . . no one ever called him Junior, unless he allowed them, unless it was someone he knew very well. Bucky saw the way the three younger brothers stepped out of his way, just the way they stepped aside for their mother. Little George, Bucky liked to tell people, was "as close to being the boss as you could be. I mean . . . they looked up to him and respected him and were . . . maybe . . . a little afraid of him from time to time."[3]

Now the glum Texas Democrats, truth be told, knew what people had said inside the walls of the Democratic National Committee offices in Washington after he first got elected: "The guy is a fucking giant killer," said one normally soft-spoken, level-headed DNC researcher. The Bush clan had assumed that Jeb was going to be elected to high office first. Jeb was the ideologue, Jeb's face wasn't going to wash over with anger, with rage, as his older brother's was prone to do. There might be a time for George W. Bush, but not in 1994, not in Texas, not against Ann Richards.

He would raise his profile, establish his own identity, but he wasn't going to beat the high-haired populist incumbent with the splendid approval ratings . . . the way she pounded the Bushes, sounding like rusty nails at the bottom of a coffee can when she went on the national talk shows. What about the cover of *Texas Monthly*, the photo of her sitting on a motorcycle? Don Henley from the Eagles loved her. So did Steven Spielberg. They gave her $50,000 each. She got money from Robin Williams, Annie Leibovitz, Linda Ellerbee, Gloria Steinem, Willie Nelson, Marlo Thomas, Rosie O'Donnell, Donald Trump . . . *Donald Trump!* She'd ladled Texas acid on George W.'s father at the Democratic National Convention; the one-liner, about George Bush being born with a silver foot in his mouth, was one for the ages. In 1994, she'd done it again, unblinking and over and over again, serving it up as pointed as an ocotillo, talking about an anemic link at the tail end of a gilded Bush dynasty. Her family had grown up desperately poor, on hardscrabble Texas farms in hamlets called Bugtussle and Hogjaw. She had been raised as an only child in a microscopic town outside of Waco, the small city sometimes called the "Heart of Texas," and her relatives survived from paycheck to paycheck provided by her grandfather's job driving trucks with Humble Oil. And Richards called the New Haven–born Bush the Little Shrub.

As the campaign between the most popular governor in America and the most powerful political family in America ground forward, Bush was confiding to a friend in Dallas that he was worried that Texans would never see him as a "real person"; that he was in his forties and that when they heard his name, they still simply thought of his father.

Early on, his chief political adviser ordered him to avoid the media, to avoid all the people wanting to talk to him about his father, about a modern American dynasty. The strategy, instead, was to carry around four ideas, four issues, only four campaign issues—education, crime, welfare and tort reform—to one more town hall meeting in Waco, one more 4-H show in Abilene, one more rusted-out cotton gin in faraway, forgotten Lubbock. The strategy was to make him more Texan than Ann Richards and also to extinguish any anger. He was always moving, wrapping his lean arms around the Luby's cafeteria lady, her cheeks slathered with dollops of hopeful rouge, and posing for a picture in some population 600 Texas town, or he'd go to the high school in Sherman, not far from the Red River, insisting to the fidgeting juniors and seniors, *I have no ill will or feel negatively toward Ann Richards. . . . I find her to be an interesting soul.*

That was exactly when the family thought that maybe, maybe, something had happened to him. His favorite cousin, Elsie Walker, couldn't believe it: Little George, the turbulent cosmos inside every family gathering in Maine, the combustible brother who doled out what he liked to call "behavior modification" to the wandering, disenchanted members of his father's White House staff? Now, somehow, he was holding it all back, holding on to it "like a dog with a bone," said a vaguely worried Elsie. She immediately sent off a telegram to Barbara after she saw the way Richards was working him over in their debate, trying to get him to snap and he wouldn't . . . not this time. Elsie's telegram to his mother began this way: "WHAT HAS . . . WHAT DID HE DO?"[4]

He was supposed to buckle and erupt. His sister, Dorothy, knew he was still wrestling with it. They all watched him, his brothers and the cousins—Elsie Walker, John Ellis, and the others—who swirled around him every summer at Kennebunkport.

"Then he just kicked the living shit out of Ann Richards!" yelled Ellis.[5]

HE KNEW what Richards's closest friends were saying: *She really doesn't want the job anymore.* Pinpointing the weak spots was almost easy. Concede the Austin version of Texas, that version of Texas that might be Easy Texas without all the hassles—without the urban anxieties, the rural paranoia, the suburban fears. Concede that part and instead take the four issues and deliver them to the federal-loathing outbacks of Texas, places filled with wistful, charged affection for the days when Texas was its own republic. Take them to the Petroleum Clubs, the private clubs with the drowning-pool-deep carpets and all those regulation-hating oilmen that you could find in almost every downtown in West Texas—the clubs with white-gloved waiters and Charles Russell paintings or thick blocks of burnished oak mounted with yet another Frederic Remington sculpture. Take them and deliver them to the endless stretches of block-long Chevy Suburbans in Dallas and Houston that were toting the soccer mothers hell bent on Family Values; to the religious right, all the antiabortion Southern Baptists shoulder to shoulder inside the massive cathedrals that look like Graceland at the side of Interstate 35; to the quiet but omnipotent Dallas Citizens Council, the one that had elected every mayor in the city for decades before and after John F. Kennedy was killed, the one that blacks still gingerly called the Dallas *White* Citizens Council.

This is what he grew up with when his father was working the rooms, never standing still, first in Midland and then in Houston. These were the same people he knew from his time living in and jetting out of Washington, crisscrossing the country in service to his father. But right up to the end, his friends didn't think it would happen. They knew that, deep inside, even he had his doubts. He'd lost his first race, a bare-knuckled congressional race out in West Texas, when the Democrats finally played those dynasty and carpetbagging cards on him, when they reminded all the wheat, cotton, and sorghum farmers up on the South Plains of the Panhandle that he was from a soft carpet in Connecticut, that he had spent nine years of his life in the three most exclusive schools in America. They hammered him just as they'd hammered his father during his father's first run for office in Texas: *Tool of the Eastern Kingmakers.* One of his intimates, Pete Laney, the Democratic Speaker of the Texas House, knows for a fact that Bush surprised himself when he finally won a race in Texas.[6]

NOW, all of 1998, it's not just another new round of speculation, it's the millions of campaign dollars rushing in from every direction, so much of it that he has reminded his deep-pocketed contributors not to forget the fact that his brother is running for governor in Florida. There's been really only one fractional, microscopic glitch on the road to gubernatorial reelection against his Democratic opponent, Garry Mauro, an earnest sixteen-year veteran of state politics with a cottony voice and the intellectual, well-intentioned demeanor of Al Gore: the Debate.

At Team Bush staff meetings, they talk about the assets, the liabilities. Even the people who know him well, are saying it's no good, it's going to be shades of Dan Quayle and Lloyd Bentsen all over again. They can practically hear it now, the unsubtle invocation of the Texas political saints: *Governor Bush, I knew Barbara Jordan, and you, sir, are no Barbara Jordan.* He finally agrees to a single debate, but his people make sure that it is scheduled to be held in remote, isolated El Paso—practically in Mexico and the hardest city to get to in Texas. They make sure it will be moderated by just one El Paso newspaper reporter, and everyone else who could truly hurt him, from CNN to the Baltimore *Sun,* is banned from the actual debate room in the television studio. They make sure it's held on a Friday night in the middle of high school football season, when the entire state is consumed by the narcotic, religious addiction of Texas high school football. "I don't have to do this," Bush tells people all week on the cramped King Air campaign plane. "People told me not to do this, but I'm gonna do it."

The debate unfolds with few hitches, and after it, Bush is in the hallway, wiping the moisture from his upper lip and rocking on his heels again. The next morning, on the Southwest Airlines flight back to Austin, one of the Democratic candidate's top aides is pulling his own bottles of beer out of his coat pocket and waving them around. The flight attendants are glowering, are circling him, huddling with one another. They demand that he step to the front of the plane for a stern lecture on airline regulations. Some of Bush's top aides are on the same plane, watching quietly, smiling quietly, pretending not to smirk as they peek over the *El Paso Times*. It has been like this all year, the uncomplicated campaign and uncomplicated, Reaganesque messages. And, all year, best of all, nobody from the national media seems to even want to know who the Democrats are sacrificing, who the poor political lifer is, and he keeps getting visit after visit from Bill Clinton, Hillary Rodham Clinton, and Al Gore.

Ten, twelve, finally fourteen times the Clintons or Gore show up. Meanwhile, the Democrat's mother has been manning the back door of the Democratic campaign headquarters that party activists have been forced to set up in a ratty, wires-hanging-from-the-ceiling downtown building in Austin, a building scheduled to be gutted. In the drought-plagued summer, the guy's *mother* is the one signing for the UPS deliveries, picking up the dozens of sticky, half-empty Dr Pepper cans, sidestepping the Himalaya of oily pizza boxes tossed in the falling-down hallway. No way Bush's mother is coming down from Kennebunkport to give her signature to the UPS driver in a building that should be condemned.

Through each droning-with-heat summer day, each week after week as the temperature squats above 100 degrees, the incestuous little group of Texas political spin doctors swears they have never seen anything like it. Over platters of chicken-fried steak and okra at the Scholz Beer Garden, or over bowls of gut-wrenching hot stuff at the Texas Chili Parlor, they're marveling at the message discipline and the money: Bush has been burning cash in the last few weeks by, of all things, running Spanish-language ads on prime-time TV. He wants something his father and his grandfather never got when they were elected to office, something the Republicans never get in Texas: he wants Hispanics to vote for him; he wants African Americans to do the same.

In every speech he has begun using the line about "living life on the sunshine side of the mountains"—so often that it sounds like the Great Communicator talking about "Morning in America." In Austin, at least one bookie is handling the Bush-minority-vote projection in between bets on the Dallas Cowboys and the University of Texas Longhorns.

As the campaign skips along from one blistering hot day to the next, his dough-skinned chief political adviser, his personal, private spin doctor, can't help himself. Everybody must have a nickname, and the spin doctor has a quality nickname, *Turd Blossom*—as in wherever-he-goes-something-is-sure-to-pop-up.[7] Turd Blossom finally blurted out a week before election day what everyone else knew but wasn't saying: "Yeah, you're right, the governor's race is over."[8]

HE'S STILL bouncing by the Lincoln, deciding whether to go inside the mansion. A reporter in the driveway wants to know by how much he will win. The projections have crested at a possible 70 percent of the vote. "Foxy," begins Bush, staring off at some distant point, tugging on his tie, and using his favorite nickname for the reporter, "one vote would be good."

He waits a second, a country-fried, good-old-boy pause preferred by people in the heart-arresting oil business in Texas. It's something he picked up from all those 1970s nights of worrying about dry oil wells and drinking with his friends from that broad, conflicted wildcatter's patch out in Midland and Odessa.

"I think I may be able to get sixty percent," he trumpets, his head still cocked, his face still shiny. He's winking now, moving closer to the herd. A decade ago there was the day he pulled all of his business partners aside, the investors who had allowed him to be part of their seventeen-member group by giving him 1.8 percent of the Texas Rangers baseball team, and said he would do all the talking. He'd be the out-front guy: *I know how to handle the press.*

In Austin, in Dallas, in Houston, when the political lifers heard what the young Bush had said, when the people who'd seen this kind of thing before in Texas heard what he had said, they couldn't help but smile. They remembered what LBJ, the Colossus of the Hill Country, had said on one hot, hot day in mid-July 1965: *The press helps me. . . . The press is one of the best servants I have.*[9] For all of 1998, this is how it will go, using all the lessons learned about the national media when he served in Washington as his father's loyalty monitor, his media monitor, and his direct arm to the hard Right, the Christian Right. He was headquartered in his father's 1998 campaign command post, in his little office in the Woodward Building, working next door to his mentor Lee Atwater, the founding prince of wicked political spin. And what was it Mary Matalin, Atwater's heir, had admiringly called the first son? A "political terrorist."

Now all of them, each reporter intrigued by the next phase of a Bush dynasty, would be escorted onto the plane in 1998. Each would be brought to his side for a few minutes, the setting overriding the issues, until there would be similar stories and columns and quotes and datelines and headlines (THE SON ALSO RISES), one after another, in every other national magazine and newspaper: SOMEWHERE OVER TEXAS—*With the prairies of Texas unfurling below, Gov. George W. Bush stared out the window of his airplane and remarked at how surprised he was by all the ceaseless speculation. "I feel like a cork in a raging river," he admitted.*

Months ago, a national columnist wrote that the Democrats were hoping that he would just run for reelection unopposed.

SOMETIMES it's easy to remember, he tells people he can see it, the first details from those years after his father packed the family and carted him at the age of two from tree-lined Connecticut to the unpaved moonscape of West Texas. Out there, in the Saudi Arabia of the Southwest, he fell right in with all the other bored sons and daughters of the displaced Yankees from Nantucket, Martha's Vineyard, Kennebunkport—from Connecticut, New York, New Jersey, Maine, and Massachusetts—who had followed the money trail to the sandy, oil-coated outbacks of Midland and Odessa. He was called Little George by the extended clan of Bushes and Walkers in the Northeast, and now he was the eldest son in the First Family of Midland. Everyone knew his father, knew that he was a war hero and the first Yankee to make a million dollars in Midland.

Everyone knew his grandfather, the grave, impossibly tall senator from Greenwich, Connecticut, who would alight in the desert and receive the awed West Texans. Everyone knew "Little George," who rounded up boys on bicycles, who patrolled the tiny city built on top of an ancient dinosaur graveyard known as the Permian Basin. Nobody blinked when he tossed a football through his West Texas elementary school window or came to class one day made up like Elvis. His Little League coach never said a word about the lousy-hitting kid, especially when the coach thought to himself, *Jeez, I'm coaching the only Little League millionaire in Texas.* That was, they'd say, searching for just the right name to distinguish him from his father: Georgie, Little George, George W. . . . *George Dubya!* . . . anything but Junior.

At Phillips Academy in Andover, Massachusetts, he was the head cheerleader and people fed off his energy, the way he was always just there, always remembering people's names, birthdays, habits, parents, brothers, sisters. He wasn't very good at baseball, his father's sport at Andover and Yale. When he got onstage with a rock band back at the prep school, he wasn't very good at singing, unlike his august, bow-tied grandfather, who liked to croon masterfully with the other members of the Whiffenpoof Singers at Yale. But he memorized everyone's name the instant he met them, and it pleased them that he did. It was something he did even better than his father and grandfather. Ten, twenty, hundreds of names, he could recite them all, total recall, minutes after meeting them. And everyone, even if it took him a while to figure it out, got a nickname: If a guy was huge and ugly, he became "Rodan," after the Japanese movie monster. If a guy was breaking him down on the tennis court, someone who was all angles, arms, and limb, he became "Spider." Of course, he liked it when his running buddies in high school called him "Tweeds," as in Boss Tweed—probably better than what they called the three or four Asian, Mexican, or Italian kids at the boarding school: "Chink," "Spic," "Dago" . . . it said so right there alongside their pictures in the yearbook.[10] Now, at fifty-two, he still liked to sling the nicknames, it made things immediately intimate, like writing those notes his father had taught him to do. The reporter who won't go away: *Mononucleosis*. His head press person: *The High Prophet*. The barrel-shaped chief of staff with the crew cut: *Big Country*. Even the eggheads, the ones down the line at the State Capitol, get nicknames:

"Tree Man, get up here," he giggles, snapping his fingers, during the otherwise somber July press conference: He wants the arboreal wonk overseeing the Forestry Service in Texas to explain forest fires to the scribes, to explain why the whole damn state isn't spontaneously combusting in the middle of the eighteenth straight day of over-100-degree heat, why that heat has killed at least eighty people so far. As he stands to one side and listens, he sticks out his tongue and makes his funny blowfish face, winking at the *Newsweek* writer who has come down to Austin, again, to write about Bush as a Presidential Possibility. An aide slips him a note. He pulls his reading glasses out of a suit pocket and, without unfolding them, uses one hand to press them to his face. He scans the room mock seriously, still peering through the folded glasses, holding them with one hand as if they were opera glasses. His staffers, their eyes trailing his every move, are chuckling, and Tree Man is still droning on. "Welcome to Texas . . . feel our pain!" the High Prophet shouts merrily when she spots the *Newsweek* writer at the back of the drought conference.

RON KAUFMAN, his father's dogged, loyal aide . . . a Good Man . . . a Friend to the Bushes . . . *an FOB* . . . had carefully described his father to the evangelical Right as the Compassionate Conservative in the late 1980s.[11] Now it's the new name the first son is borrowing and trying out all over the New Texas, trying out across the country. He's the Compassionate Conservative, not the fraternity president answering inquiries from the cops, not the Yale senior answering inquiries about branding pledges with hot metal. He's not the National Guardsman stranded in an officer's club in deep Georgia, with everyone knowing he was the chosen one whom President Richard Nixon was sending a government plane for—the one who was actually going to be allowed to leave the godforsaken base and be whisked off to Washington for a date with Nixon's daughter. He's not the unproved oilman in the flimsy black slippers he brought back from China, padding around all the tobacco-chewing West Texas ranchers and wildcatters with their sweet-looking $2,000 hand-tooled cowboy boots. Not the one who told people he had something better than an office—he had a great name—while he was living in and working out of a trashy back-alley apartment and saying that a good week was when he made $150 . . . from playing cards. Not the bored assistant trainee with the doomed agricultural company his father had hooked him up with, all those months pretending to be interested when his collar is sweating and he's sitting in yet another meeting with yet another Texas farmer worried about some city boys from Houston who want to buy him out.

Not the one that all the 1998 Team Bush insiders agreed was the best surrogate presidential candidate to send out around the country, the one who most looked like his father, actually moved his arms and head like his father. Not the one always quietly, willingly going below deck to mess with the oily, roaring mechanics of that uneasy relationship between his father and the media . . . between his father and the hard Right, the Christian Right.

Not the self-described loyalty "enforcer" for the president of the United States, the one who quietly flew to Washington to personally confront the White House chief of staff and returned to Dallas satisfied, knowing his words had been heeded, knowing that the White House chief of staff would soon be gone.

"OH, I think people like the fact that I can see a better future for Texas," he says, shifting back and forth on the balls of his feet. Out here, under those angelic, spread-out wings from the mansion's ancient live oak trees, he really does have this one tucked away. Chuck Norris . . . *Walker, Texas Ranger* . . . is coming to the election-night parties. Just five days ago, in Waco, in the sometimes unforgiving Baptist buckle of the Texas Bible Belt, where they still debate about dancing on the local college campus, there was a young black child at the campaign stop. He spontaneously stooped and scooped the child up and held him up in front of the cameras: "There is a role for government, but government can't make people love one another. I will tell you this: I would sign the law, I would sign the law, or I'd spend all the money it took in our budget to cause people to love one another. I wish I knew the law that would make people love one another . . . 'cause we'd pass it in Texas."[12]

His press handlers and security men stared at him. The people who had been watching him for years—the ones who knew he had once drunkenly challenged his father to a fight, the ones who knew he had cursed at the *Wall Street Journal* editor dining with his four-year-old in a Dallas restaurant[13]—just stared at him. After he put the kid down, after he talked about love, after he used it exactly thirteen times in his remarks, different reporters couldn't help but scoop that same little boy up too. Nobody, especially reporters, ever scooped up little black children in his father's wake.

Now, the door to the mansion is swinging open. His wife, Laura, an ex-librarian from Midland, steps outside.

"C'mon, Bushie," she whispers.

They married three months after they met. He was thirty-one and a bachelor with a reputation in the middle of a race for Congress—*By then, I'd lived a lot of life, and I was beginning to settle down*—and they never had time, really, for a honeymoon. They began campaigning the day they got married. People at the Midland Country Club, at the Midland Polo Club were shaking their heads. It had always been a truly funny parlor game: guessing the name of the woman who would marry the Bombastic One.

As she steps outside the mansion, from somewhere inside the old house comes a tangy, muscular aroma of coffee and aftershave. Back in the 1800s, chickens used to skip out of their coops and sometimes skitter across the flat grain planks made from the pine trees chopped down in the pristine woods of nearby Bastrop. Immigrant German farmers who had driven their wagons up from hamlets that would become New Braunfels, Niederwald, and Weimar used to stop sometimes and stand in the mud out on what is now Colorado or Congress Street. If they were lucky, they'd get to see Sam Houston, the frontier legend and ex-president of the Republic of Texas, trudging determinedly around the grounds.

Laura links arms with her husband. She smiles. Her eyes have, as usual, a perpetually alert, wary look. She has nursed her husband through a hangover at the Broadmoor Hotel in Colorado Springs, willed her way through a dangerous pregnancy, and delivered their twin daughters at the big-city Baylor Hospital in Dallas, even painfully learned to speak a few words in public after he promised her in 1977 that she would never have to—even after the first time, when she stepped in front of a small audience in Muleshoe, Texas, standing on the courthouse steps and knowing that she was running out of words, her speech dwindling down to nothing.

They stroll. She tilts her head up to her husband as he begins the speech, the one in which he introduces the new slogan that he has been delivering the last few weeks:

"I believe my philosophy is conservative and compassionate," he says. "I feel great," he adds as he turns to look at Laura. "We know how to run an incumbent's campaign." She nods and whispers something. Her face is shiny, too. They are almost leaning on each other. Without anyone asking, with his hand slipping into Laura's, he's suddenly thinking out loud about his father. For the first time all morning, he's still. He stares out over the heads of the reporters:

"I checked in with my mother and father this morning. They're the ones sweating it," he slowly begins. "We love our dad. He taught us the definition of quality time with his children. There was his love and counsel."

He lets it settle in. That's enough. Jeb knew it, there were days when their father wasn't there. While they were growing up in Midland, their father was on the road, out late, cooking oil deals, calling another YMCA planning meeting to order, registering Republican voters, going off somewhere else to shake hands at some PTA meeting, speaking to the Exchange Club, addressing the library board, finding more people to add to his Himalaya of address books, building a network, never standing still.

He begins angling for the street, the same one his Lincoln Town Car has just driven up. He and Laura are aiming for the voting booths in the old county courthouse just down the street, just outside the gate. For a second, he stops. The rolling amoeba has shifted, it's blocking his path, the security guards are whispering into their mouthpieces. Karen Hughes, his press secretary, the High Prophet, the daughter of an Army general who was the last governor of the Panama Canal Zone, is lurching forward, moving fast in a flanking maneuver. She looks like him sometimes, with her squared-jawed glare. Taller than any of the reporters, she is always positioned fifteen feet away, usually toward his right or left, never his centerline of vision. Now the High Prophet is feverishly waving her arms. She's herding the sheep, trying to prevent them from leaving the grounds of the Governor's Mansion, trying to trap them in old Sam Houston's barnyard. "No, no!" she booms. "Only pool reporters are allowed out of the gate!"

Hughes, whose father trained at West Point, spreads her arms out. She is wielding a legal pad as the governor of Texas pauses to watch. He's grinning, his eyes look like blue Sweet Tarts . . . reporters trapped inside the gates of the Mansion: "Well, we've got the voting mob scene!"

The reporters are frozen when they hear him; they're not sure if they're *allowed* to leave the grounds of the Governor's Mansion and walk onto the public sidewalk and then the street. His path is clear, he's moving now, out from under the canopy of oaks. People are shouting questions at his back, he's smiling, and it's just like Reagan blithely and steadfastly disappearing toward that voice-drowning whir of the helicopter. Karen Hughes is still frantically waving her arms as she blocks anyone from leaving. She has a long reach. She has slightly angled the top half of her body over, a good offensive lineman's trick, giving her more power and stability. No one can edge around the High Prophet. No one gets to the quarterback, and he's glowing as he sneaks a peek at the scene unfolding over his shoulder. He's shouting again: "We're gonna need traffic control!"

He slips his arm around Laura's waist and they glide together, almost as if they were dancing. Suddenly, still trapped inside the gates of the Governor's Mansion, Charles Zewe, the serious, erudite correspondent from CNN, is screaming. "Bullshit!" he thunders. "That's a public street!"

Zewe is bloodred. He pushes his cameraman forward. Hughes, stoop-shouldered, has advanced to the sidewalk now. She has one eye on the first son and Laura. She takes one last hard look at the press pool. She freezes the pool with a glare, spins, and wobbles into the street. Lately she has been openly bristling at anybody who thought all that Compassionate Conservative business was just some late-breaking mush to court all the people who somehow still supported Bill Clinton: "What part don't you like?" the High Prophet would eventually demand. "The Conservative part or the Compassionate part?"

Now the gates are wide open, but no one instantly chases the first family of Texas. Then, finally, the reporters begin to slowly pad outside the gates of the Governor's Mansion by ones and twos. By then he's moving too fast, he's too far ahead to catch. Up on the scaffolding, the remodelers have taken a break to watch the commotion. They're smiling as they watch him walking west and occasionally turning to look at the commotion in his wake. If he kept pushing forward, he'd just disappear into the rolling soul of the Texas oasis.

2

Deep Money

After being raised and educated in New York City and New Jersey in the latter half of the nineteenth century, the blunt Samuel P. Bush moved to Ohio and eventually built a sprawling, landscaped estate at Bexley outside the city of Columbus. Samuel, a steel and railroad industrialist and George W. Bush's great-grandfather, was a leader of the National Association of Manufacturers and a charter member of the United States Chamber of Commerce—among the country's most muscular lobbying groups. In addition to being a director of the Federal Reserve Bank in Cleveland, he emerged as a close adviser to President Herbert Hoover, who would appoint Bush to a special Depression-era commission to "deal with problems of business and unemployment relief."[1] Samuel, president of Buckeye Steel Casting Company, was also credited by family members with starting the Ohio State University Buckeyes football program: "It was he who introduced football to the state of Ohio and was the first coach of football at Ohio State," said one of his grandchildren.[2]

Samuel's son Prescott—George W.'s grandfather—was born in 1895, and grew up in the Bexley mansion, and then was shipped east to St. George's preparatory school in Newport, Rhode Island. Prescott proceeded to Yale and was a varsity baseball player, a football player and a remarkable golfer who would later bag a record-setting round in the U.S. Seniors Championship. His Yale classmates, including the handful of other members of the secret Skull & Bones society, were dazzled by Prescott's amazing ability to memorize names. He had a voice that sounded like he was perpetually speaking from the bottom of a deep well.

Prescott Bush was also a close-harmony man, the irrepressible head of the Glee Club, and the second bass in The All-Time Whiffenpoof Quartet at Yale. As a member of the Connecticut National Guard, he had hoped to see action on the Texas-Mexico border in 1916 at about the same time Pancho Villa was weaving his complex mythology. Instead, he eventually was commissioned as an army captain, assigned to a field artillery unit and shipped to the front lines in France during World War I. After the war, he easily gravitated to Wall Street and a partnership with his father-in-law's investment house. For years, Prescott Bush was also usually the tallest man sitting in the U.S. Senate or on the boards of Yale, Prudential Insurance, Pan American Airways, CBS, and Dresser Industries.[3]

In the summer of 1919 Prescott announced his engagement to Dorothy Walker, whose ancestors had settled in Maine in the 1600s and, generations later, moved to St. Louis and developed an influential national dry-goods business. Dorothy Walker's father, George Herbert Walker, had been named in honor of George Herbert—a seventeenth-century graduate of Cambridge, a poet, a "public orator," and the brother of the Baron of Cherbury. George Herbert Walker, George W.'s great-grandfather, would co-found Brown Brothers Harriman, the oldest and largest private investment house in the history of Wall Street; he was also a redoubtable political adviser and among the twelve men who had gathered at a private meeting in the early 1930s to insist to New York Governor Franklin Delano Roosevelt that he run for the presidency. New Yorkers said that George Herbert Walker was often best defined by the potency of his Manhattan addresses: His office was at One Wall Street and his home was at One Sutton Place.[4]

He was known to demand athletic excellence from Dorothy and his other children, and the Walker family eventually lent its name to the Walker Cup, considered one of the truly prestigious international golf events. The Walker family's interest in sports led to their financing or overseeing the creation and operation of Madison Square Garden, the Belmont Race Track, and eventually the New York Mets baseball club. Beyond their interest in politics, Wall Street, and sports, the Walkers spent some of their fortune building a seaside mansion on the rocky shoreline of Walker's Point in Kennebunkport, Maine. Meanwhile, the Walkers developed an estate on Long Island in New York and another retreat on the 10,000-acre Duncannon Plantation near Snelling, South Carolina. According to family members, every year the Walkers would fill a private train car with family, friends, and servants and travel to the plantation to celebrate Thanksgiving, Christmas, and other holidays.[5]

• • •

IN 1921, Dorothy Walker and Prescott Bush, George W.'s grandparents, were married at the Church of St. Ann in Kennebunkport, and for decades, various descendants of the Bush-Walker family would also be married in the church or would attend services during the annual summertime retreats at the family's seaside compound. The couple eventually settled in Greenwich, Connecticut, and raised five children in an eight-bedroom, three-story house with maids, cooks, and an expansive porch on tree-lined Grove Lane. After Alec Chodaczek, the Ukrainian chauffeur the family had nicknamed "Chowderhead," dropped the children at Greenwich Country Day School, he would steer Prescott to the train station as part of the daily routine through the Depression years. Commuting to Wall Street, Prescott was a hard-to-miss mass of a man. He had a teardrop-shaped countenance, a sagging face that his relatives would suggest to friends was really like Gary Cooper's. He was 6-foot-4, he punished the scales at close to 250 pounds, he had a slightly hunched carriage, and impossibly long fingers that looked like fluttering stems on a live oak tree.

Prescott and his wife Dorothy labored to instill a sense of unbridled competition in the children—George, Prescott Jr., Jonathan, William or "Bucky," and Nancy. Under the strict supervision and encouragement of Dorothy Walker—"the most competitive living human" according to her daughter-in-law Barbara Bush[6]—the family was always uncorking another marathon of games, challenges, and contests. "Listen, our family's middle name was games. Oh, we used to have tiddlywinks championships! Oh, wild tiddlywinks championships! We'd play, oh, just about every kind of game you can think of, from Parcheesi to tiddlywinks to Go Fish or Sir Hinkam Funny Duster," said Dorothy's son Prescott Bush Jr.[7] For years in the Bush-Walker household there would be an endless series of measuring moments, codified by what was sometimes called "The Rankings," an oft-debated statistical grid that placed various children and grandchildren at different levels of expertise in everything from running to horseshoes.

Prescott Bush liked children, he wanted his children and their children to compete in every sport imaginable, but he also refused to suffer their disturbances. "Their father wasn't crazy about that, so Dottie would sneak them up the back steps so they wouldn't bother him," remembered Dorothy's sister Mary Walker.[8] At home, at the summer place, on the train, Prescott exhibited the same brisk, sometimes intransigent demeanor as he did in his penthouse office at Brown Brothers Harriman, where he had been a partner since 1931. He preferred precision, neatness, and accountability, plus jackets and ties at dinner.[9] He always had the grave bearing, the formal, august, and sometimes intimidating way of filling up a doorway. "My father was a very strong, big man . . . and very much sort of the eastern business establishment," said his son Prescott Jr.[10] "He had an amazing ability to make little boys behave. Nobody misbehaved around Prescott Bush. Oh, he was a scary man, lemme tell you," recalled his son Jonathan.[11]

One Friday morning, many years later, Prescott's grandson Jeb, then the newly elected governor of Florida, paused as he let that same image of his grandfather assemble and then well up in his mind: "He was a stern, righteous man." And he was someone who would suggest, at dinner, that "I want you to call me 'Senator.' "[12]

PRESCOTT BUSH'S slim and agile second son, George, named after his prosperous maternal grandfather George Herbert Walker, had been dispatched to the finest preparatory school in the country, Phillips Academy in Andover, Massachusetts. Poppy, as he was later called, graduated in 1942, and the eighteen-year-old immediately enlisted in the Navy. The stories about his career as a fighter pilot, about his fifty-eight missions, have been written so often they have taken on an almost uncomplicated tone, but his defining moment remained an extraordinary one: being shot down by antiaircraft fire during a raid in the Bonin Islands southeast of Japan and later being plucked from the sea by submarine, events that were rewarded with the Distinguished Flying Cross. Back in the Connecticut suburbs, he enrolled at Yale, following the same path as his father and older brother, Prescott Jr., and mixing easily with the all-male student body culled from the most important families and private preparatory institutions in the country.

Like his father, Poppy was a zealous overachiever who had also played first base on the varsity baseball team and been a sure-handed star and captain. He was an economics major, a Phi Beta Kappa, a member of different honors organizations, an instrumental fund-raiser for the United Negro College Fund. He was also, for a while, chapter president of his Delta Kappa Epsilon fraternity. And, like his father, he had been tapped, summoned, into the Skull & Bones, the exclusive, fifteen-member secret society at Yale that had its roots in the gilded classes of nineteenth-century Germany. The Bonesmen met in a triple-padlocked, windowless mausoleum on High Street that was filled with the same sorts of burnished knickknacks, skulls, brass candlestick holders, yellowed books, and worn leather chairs found in the old societies and clubs at English universities. Bonesmen were required to leave any room if they ever heard the words

"Skull & Bones" uttered by strangers. Bonesmen were forbidden forever even to say the name in conversation with people who weren't Bonesmen. And sometimes they were required to undress, lie down in a coffin, and, with their chums standing near, talk about their most intimate sexual histories. It was not the kind of existential moment the Bushes or Walkers were accustomed to; nothing they would ever become accustomed to.

Public self-analysis, public self-reflection were always aggressively discouraged in the Bush-Walker household: "It goes against how we were . . . it's just, we are not . . . it's not natural for us, for, uh, I think I can speak on behalf of all the family, to get into, to be, to turn on this reflective mode and somehow spill our guts," offered Jeb Bush one day in a slow voice. "We were brought up to basically do the exact opposite . . . and so I think, naturally, it's an uncomfortable thing."[13]

GEORGE BUSH and Barbara Pierce met in 1941 at a Christmas dance at the Round Hill Country Club in Greenwich and went gliding across the floor to Glenn Miller tunes. The rolling-lawn, orderly, affluent community had become synonymous with the Bush-Walker clan. Pierce lived in the nearby thoroughbred city of Rye, New York, and was the daughter of the polished president of McCall Publishing Company as well as a descendant of the fourteenth president of the United States, Franklin Pierce. It was in some ways a meeting of powerful equals. He was an unflaggingly formal boy with an argyle sensibility, someone related to the crowned heads of Europe and a thirteenth cousin of Elizabeth, the future queen of England.[14] Barbara Pierce was a Manhattan-born debutante educated at the Ashley Hall finishing school in South Carolina, a young woman who had returned home to find that life in the three-story, five-bedroom Pierce home was still being orchestrated, in part, by the two live-in Chinese servants who tended to the gardens and the artificial pond. The third of four children, Barbara, along with her parents, was wedded to a cycle among some Rye residents: being admitted to the Social Registry; taking up "civic causes" such as working to outlaw traffic on certain streets and ordering baskets of flowers to be hung in public spots; volunteering in local book circles; organizing bridge tournaments; staging charity golf matches; taking the children to Miss Covington's Dancing School or for tennis lessons at the Manursing Island Club.[15]

After marrying in January 1945, the Bushes eventually moved into a small house at 281 Edwards Street in New Haven, Connecticut. George Bush continued his studies at Yale, and the couple awaited the birth of their first child. On a warm, humid day early in July 1946, Barbara Bush's mother gave her daughter a dose of castor oil, hoping to expedite the delivery of the baby.[16] Then, according to the official papers the hospital was required to file with the Connecticut State Department of Health's Bureau of Vital Statistics, the family checked into New Haven Hospital at about 12:30 A.M. on July 6, 1946. At 7:26 A.M., with Dr. Margaret Tyler as the attending physician, George Walker Bush was born.[17] The family called him Little George or Georgie, and sometimes they were quick to remind strangers that he was not George "Junior" or George Bush II.

The New Haven Evening Register for that day had these front-page headlines: "First Phase of Atom Plan Nearly Ready"; "Truman Healthy After 14 Months; Strength Likened to Roosevelt's"; "Baby Is Born in Japan with 2 Faces and Bodies."[18] The new father asked William Howe Jr., a New Englander and old friend from both Andover and Yale, to serve as his first son's godfather. When Poppy had returned to Yale from World War II and begun playing first base, Howe had been in right field. Howe was happy for his old friend Poppy, and he thought then and for years later that the boy looked very much like his father.

At home in New Haven, there were both a christening and a lawn party. Soon after, the family moved into another apartment, inside a sprawling house at 37 Hillhouse Avenue; their next-door neighbor in the comfortable neighborhood was Yale President Charles Seymour. Dozens of Yale classmates and Bush-Walker family members arrived to see the infant. And the newborn's grandmother, his mother's mother, sometimes couldn't stand being in the same room with the baby. She said that if she took her eyes away from him, if she weren't looking directly at him, if she weren't aiming her full attention at him, George Walker Bush's face would twist into a hurt, pained expression.[19]

AFTER THE WAR, the Skull & Bones Society had evolved, above all else in the sometimes uncertain times, into a business network—a ready resource for big investment capital and a source of stock-buying advice and management jobs. So Prescott Bush once again spoke to Neil Mallon, his friend and fellow Bonesman. Bush had always considered Mallon to be the brightest young man of their Yale class, "a very able fellow," and he hand-selected Mallon to serve as head of Dresser Industries, an oil conglomerate that the Bush family and its investors controlled. Mallon was a *Good Man*—the highest praise in the preferred Bush lexicon, a good fellow, stiff-backed, of quiet resolve, competitive of course. Prescott Bush always treasured what Mallon embodied: consistency, loyalty, order. And for twenty years, Prescott Bush was at Mallon's side: "I was Neil Mallon's chief adviser and consultant in connection with every move that he made."[20] Mallon really was almost a member of the Bush-Walker family, a trusted adviser and manager of the family's investments, and he said that a trainee job was waiting for George at the International Derrick and Equipment Company, a Dresser subsidiary, in Odessa, Texas . . . in the soul of the Permian Basin, the nerve center of the new deep-money pools of oil gurgling up in Texas. By 1948, Dresser was selling more portable oil rigs than anyone else in the world. Mallon had a proposal: Poppy would eventually be allowed to try his hand at almost every aspect of the oil game if he moved to Odessa with his wife and child. George broke the news to a skeptical Barbara Bush. "I've *always wanted* to live in Odessa, Texas," she replied.[21]

With $3,000 in seed money and a new red Studebaker, Bush drove to West Texas the day after graduating from Yale in the spring of 1948. He knew he wasn't going to Texas alone; he had the entire Bush-Walker network invisibly attached to him: "If I were a psychoanalyzer, I might conclude that I was trying to, not compete with my father, but do something on my own. My stay in Texas was no Horatio Alger thing, but moving from New Haven to Odessa just about the day I graduated was quite a shift in lifestyle."[22]

His wife and two-year-old son arrived a week later after a twelve-hour propeller plane flight. In Odessa, the clouds on bad days sometimes looked like dirty, airborne ashtrays. The air could be sluggish, thick with the bitter smell of oil. There were few flowers, and the place was remarkably free of trees. The land was unrippled, endless. And there was a stillness that made the sandstorms all the more profound when they finally came, like a silent wall of brown dust from the desert floor to the clouds. Each of the sandstorms was given a name, just like a hurricane—Eli, Kinsey, Leo, Farouk—pushing and pushing from New Mexico, from Antelope Ridge, from the Monahans Dunes, from Alkaline Marsh, from Loving County— the least populated county in the United States—from all that emptiness around Gyp Hills, from the Apache Mountains, until the rolling, gritty fog simply made houses, cars, and people disappear.

The Bushes moved into a small one-bedroom duplex apartment set on a fifty-foot lot at 1519 East Seventh Street in Odessa. They had the only refrigerator on their block, and they shared a bathroom with an outgoing couple, Valta Ree and Jack, who had moved to West Texas from Oklahoma. When Valta Ree and Jack left, they were replaced by a mother-and-daughter prostitute team who kept odd hours and received many male callers. Meanwhile, at work one day, somebody wanted to know if Bush was a college kid.

Bush replied, "Yale."

The man said he had never heard of it.[23]

IN WEST TEXAS, the Santa Rita No. 1 oil well had blown on a day late in May 1923, eighty miles from Midland-Odessa in Reagan County. When the well was first being dug, some Catholic investors had laughed and suggested that it be named after the Saint of the Impossible. Santa Rita was the well, its top suddenly transformed into a fluttering, Salome's veil of oil, that truly opened up Midland and the rest of endless, empty West Texas, adding to the already mammoth splurges of oil that had been uncorked twenty years earlier on the eastern side of the state. The Saint of the Impossible was the thing, the constantly recited mantra, that made the idea of years in this part of West Texas bearable. Santa Rita No. 1 was also the well that began to force the wickedly strained marriage between the uneducated ranchers turned oil field owners and the hundreds of soft-palmed Yale, Harvard, Princeton, and Dartmouth graduates who would bring their East Coast money and connections to one of the remotest places in the United States.[24]

Over time, much of what Santa Rita inspired was run from Midland-Odessa, the geographical center of a great 200-million-to-300-million-year-old dead sea inside the Permian Basin. Midland, at its formation as a stop on infamous stock manipulator Jay Gould's Texas & Pacific Railroad, had first been known as Midway. It was nothing more than a stopping point between Fort Worth and the Rio Grande. With the oil boom, Midland became the convenient, centrally located place where deals were cut and investors came in to fund the shallow but lucrative wells. It was where the hotels were built, the contracts were signed, the company headquarters were stationed, and the ledger side of the oil game was played. Overlooking it all was the unlikely twelve-story Hogan Building, a tan-colored skyscraper, a Midland minaret, built in 1929 by a former senator from Montana.[25]

Odessa, the sister city a few miles farther west, evolved into a city where the oil field suppliers would set up their warehouses, their welding shops, the blue-collar side of things . . . where the roustabouts, roughnecks, and pipe layers moved into what was politely called manufactured housing. Odessa was the hardscrabble, hard-drinking, honky-tonk underbelly of West Texas. And it was wet, which was what people said about a place in Texas where you could buy a drink and bend the edges on that emptiness.

But in Odessa, anybody who had an iota of East Coast pretensions really wanted to be twenty miles down the road in white-bread, white-collar Midland, even if Midland County had outlawed liquor sales.

Everybody knew the slogan: *You raised hell in Odessa, you raised your family in Midland.*

INTO THE early 1930s, the miracles were disappearing at the same time the Depression had reached the Permian Basin. At the outset of 1932, West Texas oil was selling for ten cents a barrel. Water, said some ranchers, was more expensive. In the mid-1930s, a third of Midland's population was unemployed, and the symbolic center of the city—the twelve-story "skyscraper" built by the ex-senator from Montana—was virtually empty. Some of the West Texas rigs were torn down or were left to bake and erode in the unforgiving desert. Like a painful, predictable sorrow, the oil game in the Permian Basin was stumbling—until, that is, a few explorers decided to try to go deeper in the late 1930s and the 1940s, until the war jump-started a thirst for oil and Howard Hughes's blessed invention had taken hold—his gift to Texas, the triple-toothed, cone-shaped drill bit with the insistent, satisfying, whirring sound, like a million copulating insects, that let the oilmen go farther into the high-pressure gas formations, into beds of salt, all the way down to the fossil fuels from the Pennsylvanian Reef and into the Devonian, Fusselman, Simpson, and Ellenburger geological zones deep below the Permian Basin. That's where the new oil boom had to be, another 4,000, 5,000, 10,000 feet below the old shallow pools of oil that people had been tapping in West Texas since the 1920s.[26]

Meanwhile, because some of the older oilmen thought it would draw attention to the city, they worked hard to make sure that one of the largest bombardier training sites in the world was created, in midwar, in Midland. In 1942, hundreds of pilots moved in and out of Midland's Army Air Force Bombardier Training School, practicing runs over the sandy void. Through January 1945, 1,245,107 bombs were dropped onto the Permian Basin. During one period in 1943, one bomb went off approximately every forty seconds. Some of the earliest transplants to that part of West Texas, the ones who had left the North and the East to head down the oil trail, would say that the desolate Permian Basin was almost too perfect—that parts of it deserved to be bombed.[27] Finally, in November 1945, crews from what veteran wildcatters said was a "fly-by-night" outfit named Humble (later Exxon) first sucked something out of the Pennsylvanian Reef in Midland County, when they uncorked the No. 1 Mrs. O. P.

Buchanan well in Section 32, Block 37, W. M. Baldridge Survey. Right away, everyone else followed them down.

Deep money was there for everyone, said the gnarled West Texas natives, including all those stuffed-shirt Yankees in their blazers and sweaters, the ones who started sweating instantly as they stepped from their planes onto the baking tarmac, blinking at the aching endlessness of it all. After the war, thousands of oil-hungry families were flocking to the unpaved, arid, godforsaken area. In 1940, only 9,000 people lived in Midland. Eight years later, there would be more than three times that many, and throughout the postwar invasion by outsiders, no one was kidding anyone. "Midland was the ugliest place on the face of the earth. The only reason to be there was because they had oil under the ground," remembered Randall Roden, one of George W. Bush's first childhood friends.[28]

The deep money was out there, and anyone could get lucky, even the real West Texans, undercapitalized septuagenarian ranchers who had signed away the mineral rights to their land for royalties . . . native Texans with mushy faces turned the reddish purple of a cactus pear from spending too many hours under a hot sun, the ones who liked nothing better than to crank up their prewar Harleys, strap on their welding goggles, snort hard-to-find whiskey courtesy of the liquor man Pinky Roden, and scorch across the crunchy desert sands at 120 miles an hour.

Hell, even they could get to like the rich Yankees.

BY THE BROILING summer of 1948, there were three thousand wells being drilled in the Permian Basin. People were chasing the oil into Hale County and something called the Matador Uplift, and they were heading as far west as Chaves County in New Mexico. Close at hand was one of the true defining moments in Texas oil history, the ungodly splurge that would erupt in the Spraberry Field just outside of Midland. Barbara Bush was adjusting, raising her only child and writing back home to her parents that "we find some West Texans are . . . Eastern-prejudiced."[29] In the spring of 1949, the family was temporarily moved by Dresser to California. The elder George Bush had become a salesman for the company, hawking drilling rigs and traveling a thousand miles a week.[30] *"In addition to the Super 7-11 rig, Ideco offers The Self-Propelled Drive In Rambler and the Two Trailer Dual Rambler. . . . Of Course, Ideco Also Offers Air-Controlled Torque-Converter Rigs. Air Friction Clutches. Full-View Masts."*[31] For a year, the family moved up and down California: first to Whittier, then to Ventura and several months living in the Pierpoint Inn, then to Bakersfield, and finally into a narrow box of a building in Compton. Then, five days before Christmas 1949, there came a second child, Pauline Robinson, named in honor of Barbara's mother, who two months earlier had died in a car accident. The family simply called the girl Robin.

A few weeks later, the family was transferred permanently back to Texas and Midland-Odessa. The elder George Bush scouted around and found a Main Street motel in Midland called George's Courts. He still woke at sunrise and drove off to tout drilling rigs, the Connecticut Yankee stepping out of his car in Big Spring . . . in Wink, where Roy Orbison was born . . . *Hi, my name is George Bush, with Ideco.*[32]

One day at George's Courts there was a horn-blaring commotion when Poppy put on his Bermuda shorts and went out for milk. Men didn't wear Bermuda shorts—or any shorts—in West Texas. Poppy made a mental note never to show his legs again.[33] He also finally found a home where his son could play in a yard, a place at 405 East Maple Street in an especially desolate part of north Midland called Easter Egg Row.

The area was on the banks of the parched Scharbauer Draw, a hopelessly dry slough that fills with muddy water only after a rare, lingering rain and whose nine-foot-high flood-stage measuring pole looked like a mockery, like seeing a 'No Swimming' sign in the middle of the Sahara. The new Easter Egg Row neighborhood was an orderly series of small, $7,500 wooden bungalows, each painted one shade of pink, green, orange, red, or blue. Every 847-square-foot home was exactly the same, with four boxy windows facing a twenty-foot-deep patch of yard. There were no trees, and it looked as if the homes had been airlifted into the desert. Easter Egg Row quickly filled up with house-hungry independent oil operators, wildcatters, and junior management petroleum executives who had been sent to Midland by out-of-state firms. *Yuppieland West*, George Bush would say later[34] . . . all the orderly houses filled with children the same age as his son, George W. Bush.

"There were a lot of people coming here who had connections in the East, Midwest, West Coast, Oklahoma, and so on. One of the Getty boys was here. One of the members of the Mellon family. People whose parents were running brokerage houses. There was some feeling against them, there was some jealousy at first. You know, people in the South, since the Civil War, have not always embraced the Yankees. Pretty soon, the animosity disappeared. Out here we were isolated, and we all got to know each other," said John Younger, a Midlander who watched the price of oil for almost sixty years.[35] Those Yankees immediately formed a Harvard Club, a Yale Club, a Princeton Club with thirteen members; and the old-timers talked about that tall fellow George Bush and the others who defiantly held martini parties and struggled to keep the insidious, dusty sand from blowing through every crack in every house; how the Yankees woke up in the morning with outlines on their beds from all the brown dirt circling their bodies; how they had to build, everywhere in Midland, giant, repulsive cinder-block walls surrounding their lavish houses just to keep the damn dust away.[36]

The fever caught on in Hollywood, and even Bob Hope and Bing Crosby hit it real fine, investing $160,000 and then pocketing $5 million each, with their holdings deep in Scurry County. Jimmy Stewart wanted in, film directors wanted in, and nervous oil brokers were waiting for phone lines to free up in Odessa as they placed calls to movie sets and hotels in California.[37] And throughout that second oil boom in West Texas, there was a unifying, collective thought running through the minds of the tight-knit wildcatters, brokers and money men who were scrambling to cut handshake deals on the handful of paved streets in the Permian Basin: You could win the game on your own, the government wasn't going to do it for you, you had to sell your deals, raise your own money, work the angles, punch holes in the ground. The money, the oil, was out there; you just had to go get it, and you had to go deeper to get it.

In the early 1950s, now that the deep money oil trough was overflowing, in the homes on Easter Egg Row there was the giddy belief that there were now three things to do instead of two in the basin, in this ancient ocean turned desert that covered more than 100,000 square miles and fifty-four counties.[38] Now there were three things to do in the desert, where tumbleweeds literally tumbled and the spiky bundles pressed against the front doors and the windows, scratching on the screens, latching onto the underneath of your car: *You raised hell in Odessa . . . you raised your family in Midland . . . and you drilled for that deep money.*

SOMETIMES POPPY would take Little George and his friends out into the howling maw of the oil patch. One night, on one of those trips, Little George and Randall Roden were drifting in and out of sleep in the back of the station wagon while waiting for Big George to check on a series of wells. Roden's grandfather had been an early-century Texas cowboy, nothing at all like his friend's grandfather. One time, Roden and Little George had been taken to Washington to visit Little George's grandfather. At dinner one night in the Connecticut senator's impeccable Georgetown home, young Roden drank out of one of the finger bowls. Senator Bush stared at his grandson's little friend from Midland and then ordered someone to bring the West Texas boy some water in a glass.[39]

In West Texas, listening from the back of the station wagon, the unnatural clanging of the oil field equipment and the eternal nodding and bobbing of the pump jacks were the only sounds rising up out of the night. For the two children, peeking from a window of the car, it was like staring into a mechanical dream of pipes, towers, and lights.

There was a gurgling, more noise, stabs of flame. It was like a Thomas Hart Benton painting, George W.'s first friend from kindergarten thought many years later, with all those callused souls in the middle of all that dangerous, hulking machinery. "There was an oil boom. It was like winning the lottery, it wasn't a model of how the real world works," remembered Roden. "It was a risky enterprise, using other people's money. There was guilt. If you succeed, you're a hero. If not, you're a villain. You either make people rich or you break 'em . . . or you break yourself.

"Midland is probably where he [George W. Bush] first got the mistaken idea that doing well in business is the solution to America's problems, that is, what's good for business is good for America. 'Opportunity and business fortune for all' isn't really true for everyone," said Roden. But, he felt, "it was for them [the Bushes]."[40]

ON SUNDAY, all of them, the poplin-wearing, college-educated "carpetbaggers" such as George Bush and the tobacco-spitting rednecks who had never graduated from high school, would dutifully troop their children into the aisles of the First Methodist, Baptist, Presbyterian . . . take your pick. This hard-to-reach part of West Texas was too small for them to avoid one another. Their reference points, their gathering points, were the same. Everything was connected. Everyone was connected.

The money people needed the land people, and the land people needed the crews to punch and stab the land even deeper. And there they would all be on Sunday, the members of that uneasy alliance, trying to iron out the exact same Saturday-night wrinkles they had all picked up at the Ace of Clubs or the Black Cat Pavilion or someplace where the beer flowed and the jukebox played Bob Wills and the Texas Playboys.

On other numbing mornings, everyone, rednecks and carpetbaggers alike, would also quietly, dutifully gather with their families at other churches—Agnes's restaurant or the Rendezvous or the coffee shop in the six-story, 250-room hotel the Scharbauer family had built in the desert. They'd stare down at their runny eggs, fiddle with their toast, huddle under a cumulus of cigarette smoke, and draw a little closer in their fraternity, talking about the only thing that mattered: the deep money. The twenty-four-hour anxiety in the Permian Basin didn't just *want* company.

It *needed* company. It was as if there were no doors. It was almost tribal, the way everyone would lean over and confess both their successes and failures—even the starchy ones such as Bush who wore ties to the First Presbyterian Church, even the Catholics, damn strange Papists who had become friends with the Bushes, including Joe O'Neill, a hard-nosed Irishman and ex–FBI agent from Philadelphia who had come to Midland to make sure an old Notre Dame buddy wasn't being swindled in the Texas oil game. Like all the others from up North, back East, he wound up staying when he saw the way the money was sometimes there for the taking. There were a hundred more like him, hundreds more coming, just like the Liedtke boys, who would go on to form Pennzoil.

And through that decade and into the next one there were stories that portrait artists were being flown in to capture the newest millionaires and their families on canvas. There was the Midland Country Club miraculously planted in the desert, its magical green rug of grass rolled right across the baked earth and obsessively watered, watered, watered, until it somehow took root in the sand—and where the green grass ended and suddenly gave way to the desert, it looked exactly like the sharp side of a felt-covered table. But those were the obvious extravagances.

The real indulgences were behind the closed doors of the sometimes surprisingly modest-looking homes that were being built toward the west side of Midland—modest, as if there had been some unstated agreement to understate the fact that the instantly rich were stacked up next to one another, one after another, in the tightly bunched clusters on Humble Street, Gulf Street, Sinclair Street, Harvard Street, Yale Street, Princeton Street—all those low-slung brick concoctions surrounded by industrial-looking cinder-block walls. Inside, though, you never knew what was being planned or what you would find: $25,000 mink coats slumped in a languorous heap; the rarest of mounted game—polar bears, grizzly bears, and elephant's feet turned into ottomans; priceless pieces of Fabergé next to the Frederic Remington paintings. Years later there would be word from one edge of the Permian Basin, heading toward Abilene, that a determined oilman was funding expeditions to raise the *Titanic*, to find Bigfoot, and to photograph the Loch Ness Monster. There were group trips to Kentucky to purchase and bring home the offspring of prizewinning thoroughbreds. The 20,000-acre ranches, usually located in more verdant parts of the state, would be stocked with oryxes, wildebeests, and impala. Some people said there was also one tall-ceilinged home in Midland with a stuffed giraffe.[41]

And whether at Agnes's or elsewhere, people took their turns at the collective catharsis, complaining about the federal regulations, more than convinced that the big hits, the big strikes, the gushers were going to be delivered to the wildcatter who hustled the hardest. Anyone could do it on his own, and not because the government was ever going to help. At Agnes's, at the Petroleum Club, in the Wildcatter's Room, people's faces would turn into open books, and they would brag about how everything was on their shoulders, how they had thrown all that damn money down that damned dry rat's nest near the Three Bar field, near the Sweetie Peck field, near the Dollarhide field. The heated Texas myths and tall tales would be punctuated by a slogan: *No guts, no blue chips.*

The wildcatters chortled over the bittersweet saga of the two long-suffering Midland oil boys with the 1949 Mercury that was as beat to hell as one of Agnes's frying pans. Every day, the partners did nothing but drill and drink. Dry hole after dry hole, the 105-degree heat pressed down on their necks like a hot hand. They slept in the Mercury. They drove the car from one barren, tumbleweed-choked piece of leased land around Midland and Odessa to the next, checking geological maps, setting up their raggedy little rigs with their raggedy, unpaid crew of roustabouts.

Then they hit something outside Midland. A core sample showed traces of oil. Then, like a dream, as in the movie *Giant*, the caked sand cracked open and out gushed a spray of black liquid. The boys were drunk. They were dancing. And right there, they set fire to that crappy, battered Mercury. But suddenly, as the flames went higher, the spray went lower. It sputtered as the fire in the car blazed. The two good old boys sprinted to their Mercury, their only asset, sank to their knees, and began flinging handfuls of the Permian Basin sand on the burning car.[42]

"You think they fucked up good? You heard what happened to those other boys?"

Two other sons of the oil patch had hit it flush. They had fourth-grade educations, enough to convince themselves that they weren't going to waste their money on any stuffed giraffe. Or one of those acorn-sized diamonds that the traveling jewelers from Houston were hawking out of black bags from one end of the Permian Basin to the other. Or one of those forged paintings like the ones that Algur Meadows, the Texas oil-man who had scored big, had wound up buying later . . . dozens of fake masters, including some alleged Picassos, Gauguins, Bonnards, and Chagalls.[43] They were going to Dallas, where things had a certain decadent order, where they could treat themselves to Kansas City yearling steaks and rooms in the rococo-on-the-prairie Adolphus Hotel, just down the block from Neiman Marcus, the most famous store in Texas.

At the Adolphus, the waiters and elevator crew were Negroes ordered to dress like genuine Moroccan genies in turbans, billowy pasha pants, and harem slippers with upturned, curled-back toes, like some dizzy Texas version of *The Arabian Nights*. The West Texas wildcatters hired some whores and drank whiskey, both of which they picked up in Oak Cliff, the conflicted side of town where Jack Ruby lived and where Lester "Benny" Binion, who owned the Horseshoe Casino, had allegedly once paid off the police as he ran numbers and, some say, had ties to dope dens and Texas contract killers. The Midland boys went shopping in the Jewish pawnshops on Elm Street—the zone was nicknamed Deep Ellum—where the Texas blues were born, where Blind Lemon Jefferson and T-Bone Walker used to play on the corners, where the pawnshop keepers learned to take inventory every time a gang of sticky-fingered gypsies came to town, where you could easily buy a gun (the way John Hinckley bought one in Deep Ellum years later). The Midland boys peeked in the army-navy stores that had sprung up after World War II, places owned by hustlers who had come to town from New Orleans, Kansas City, and Chicago, places offering all manner of surplus combat gear that had somehow mysteriously been obtained from the military bases in San Antonio or the docks in Houston and Galveston.

In the middle of the gas masks, bayonets, and canteens, one of the Midland oil boys found a Luger, a nice-looking one that had come home with some GI from Europe. Back at the Adolphus, the oil boys handed the keys to a new Cadillac to each of the girls and told them to never come back. And as they drank some more and fiddled with the Luger, they argued about shooting it out the window, from five floors above Commerce Street, somewhere in the general direction of Sol's Turf Bar ("Serving David Berg's Famous Corned Beef") or the Unique Steak House, with the glass-paneled phone booth right in the middle of the room and a line of men, toothpicks stuck in their mouths and *Racing Forms* under their arms, waiting to make a call. The wildcatters argued about shooting the Luger into the mattress. They drank some more and argued about shooting into the curtains as thick as blankets. Finally, they agreed: they'd shoot it into the toilet. And when they did, the whole thing exploded. They laughed, pressing towels into the water, until they finally passed out. The next morning, they woke up in a sea of water. Temples bulging from hangovers, they laughed some more as they dropped cash onto the front desk and stuffed silver dollars into the palms of the turbaned Negroes.

They got into their own Cadillac and followed the sun west, aiming straight for the endless desert and Midland in the dead center of the parched cup called the Permian Basin.[44]

ONE DAY over a backyard barbecue, the elder Bush was talking to John Overbey, a University of Texas graduate who had moved to Midland in 1947 to become an oil and gas lease broker. Overbey lived across the unpaved street at 406 East Maple, he and his wife baby-sat George W. when the Bushes needed a hand, and the two men talked about the possibility of forming their own oil company. Hundreds of people were starting their own oil companies, and Bush told Overbey he had money from the Northeast, he'd call relatives, especially an uncle with connections to Wall Street, Herbert Walker, who had already agreed, along with some investing friends from London, to supply $300,000 in start-up funds. Prescott Bush would also throw in some money, as much as $50,000. In 1950, the Bush-Overbey Oil Development Company, Inc., dedicated to buying and selling oil-drilling royalty rights in the Permian Basin, opened offices in the Petroleum Building across the street from the Midland County Courthouse.[45]

The concept was simple: Bush-Overbey would purchase the mineral rights on land adjacent to other pieces of property where someone was planning to drill. If the company doing the drilling hit oil, the value of the mineral rights on the nearby land would soar in value. Instantly, Poppy was spending even more days away from George W., traveling from San Angelo to Abilene . . . *now's when your ears have to be wide open, now's when you have to talk to fifty people a day. He was out for hours, trying to make* something happen, *gotta meet somebody at the Scharbauer* . . . gotta talk to Rosenelle Cherry, the all-knowing county clerk at the courthouse who for forty-eight years handled all the handwritten deeds and records she knew who was looking at that land north of the city, she knew who had a hunch about something in the desert.

Meanwhile, Poppy was teaching George W.'s friends at the Sunday school at First Presbyterian. He was rounding up the fathers of George W.'s friends and trying to convert them to the Republican Party. He sat on the planning sessions for the YMCA, he visited the Midland Reporter-Telegram and became best friends with the conservative, influential publisher Jimmy Allison. Jimmy, always a good man . . . he'd make a good Republican. Inside the broadening pool of easterners, George W.'s father was the most prominent, the most visible bridge to the native Texans, who were still suspicious—even bitter, sometimes—about all those Yankees who had arrived like well-heeled anthropologists and Egyptologists ready to cart away the only resources in the desert.

Big George was on the local cancer board, he directed the chamber of commerce, he helped draw up the papers for the Midland Commercial Bank and Trust Company.[46] Of course, he was also there on the weekends, playing tennis with the other members of the Yale Club, ready to rush the net, and sometimes taking George W. with him. And there was another good man, another FOB—*Friend of the Bushes*—Earle Craig Jr., the Yalie who had arrived in August 1950 but who also enjoyed golfing "on island" in Nantucket or hunting in Scotland.

Behind Craig's back, George W. and the other kids in Midland were already nicknaming the New Englander with that impossibly nasal way of speaking, that powdered wig of a voice, the Earl of Craig. When he had arrived, Craig was sometimes dissatisfied with the state of the Midland Country Club on Cutbirth: its caliche tennis court, its nine-hole course, its little kitchen, a phonograph but no records. Little George's friends liked to talk about how, one day, Craig had been walking through one of the rare parks in Midland and someone had let a dog loose. Irritated and perplexed, he had thundered out words never heard in West Texas: "Tether that beast!" There was solace in meeting the Bushes, and he would always remember the first time he saw them all together; he would always be able to picture the four-year-old "Georgie," the way he was "hanging on to the perambulator which his mother, Barbara, would push at the time. . . . Robin was in the pram, and Georgie was hanging on."

Like many people in West Texas, Craig called Georgie's father Big George, and he told people what they already knew, that the Bushes were the first family among the displaced Yankees in the Permian Basin—that Big George "was always the quarterback of the football team, he was immediately in charge and it was so clear that he was the leader of our group, socially and intellectually."[47] Among families like the Craigs, Big George and the children were now truly comfortable. Big George could begin to memorize all those names—*must send those Christmas cards*—to what seemed like everyone living on every block from Big Spring Street to West Ohio, *must take the kids to that fund-raiser for the Midland Community Theatre*, joining any board that asked him, sidling next to anyone, everyone, at the JFS Ranch House. There were hamburger cookouts in the Bush backyard all the time, with the men huddled around the grill and talking oil deals, and if one of the patties accidentally dropped in the sand, Big George would smoothly pick it up, dust it off, and grin: "Give it to the kids." There were deacon's meetings at First Presbyterian. After work, he,

Barbara, and Little George were off to volunteer activities with the Midland Memorial Hospital and the Community Chest. And Barbara, of course, was the leading light in the Junior League and the Midland Service League, and all the while huge boxes kept arriving from her relatives in Rye, New York, the ones packed with delicacies, groceries, and other supplies they assumed were foreign to a place like West Texas.[48]

BY MID-DECADE, there were 30,000 people and 215 oil-related firms in Midland, including dozens that were nothing more than one-man shops with white-suited salesmen in short, wide ties who spent their waking hours knocking on the door of every desolate ranch house within a two-hundred-mile-radius. These were the land men, the deal makers, the middlemen. Growing up in Midland, George W. couldn't avoid the land men.

They were always there, sometimes on Easter Egg Row, bobbing together in little groups, quaffing bottled Cokes, smelling better than most people in the oil game, and, when a young woman went walking by, they would doff their foppish, pinched-front fedoras with the two-inch brims made by the Resistol Company in Dallas, the company that had perfected that secret Texas technological thunderclap: *"Now . . . Our Leather, Interior, Headband . . . Actually . . . RESISTS . . . sweat . . . prevents the hat from compressing onto the forehead."*[49]

The land men were really just salesmen who talked to the geologists, found out where the oil might be, and then spent hours in the bowels of the Midland County Courthouse, trying to figure out who owned which bits and chunks of the unmarked, unfenced Texas desert. The land men deciphered the handwritten deeds to see who, if anyone, was entitled to what lay underneath the sand. The land men locked in on the mineral rights: who had them, who would sell them—even when they really didn't want to. Finally, the land men would arrive, uninvited, on someone's doorstep, already jawing about the weather, about that damn dust, about what fine, big kids the rancher had. *Yes, I'd love to stay for some iced tea.*

A land man wasn't a rainmaker, but he was the one who told the rainmakers where the rain was likely to fall. A land man wasn't a geologist, he wasn't the one who leavened his science, his core samples, with intuition and vision. George W. couldn't avoid the land men. His father would work as one for a while, on the side. And people in Midland would say that some day it would be the perfect piece of the oil patch for his first son.

3

The Core

Big George's mouth was often hanging half open in a pleasant, engaging kind of way, and he was becoming an *über*-citizen in a city where civic pride was transmogrifying into a competitive sport. His younger brother Jonathan took a break from his investment banking business on Wall Street and decided to visit West Texas, and he could see it, he could tell that his brother had become the Prescott Bush of Midland; Jonathan loved it, he relished the way his older brother was "the king of the roost."[1] Jonathan had always admired his brother for leaving the Northeast, the way he had struck out for the Texas wastelands to make his millions instead of following the more predictable family connections to Wall Street, banking, and railroads. He also knew that Big George was traveling away from the family for days on end, pitching proposals and visiting prospective financiers in Houston to talk about the big-gain business of exploring for oil in the hurricane-prone Gulf of Mexico. "He was hard-running, away from home a lot," Jonathan said.[2]

And when he and Barbara were away together, the Overbeys were still there to watch the children. Or sometimes the ever-patient company secretary, Anna Williams, would care for George W. and Robin. There were also Julia May Cooper and Otha Fitzgerald Taylor, black maids in a city that was, by and large, white and prosperous. The African-American population in Midland was almost nonexistent; the Hispanic population was small, and most of its members were employed, out of sight and out of mind, as ranch hands or in the service industry.

In west Midland there was always a gaggle of children, usually led by George W., a knot of kids rolling from one house to the other, patiently enduring the no-cruelty-to-animals lectures when they were summoned to the home of the elderly, childless neighborhood fixture whose husband ran the Honolulu Oil Corporation: *Now, children, we must respect all living creatures.* Up and down Ohio Street, over on Kansas, seemingly every home was planning a pregnancy. Young couples with children or ones on the way were everywhere. The average age in Midland in the 1950s was twenty-eight. If the couples had still been in the Northeast, they would have been moving easily among the postwar families populating the many suburban communities in Connecticut, north of New York City, or outside Boston or Philadelphia.

On Sunday mornings the desert stillness was underscored by the fact that the entire town was in church, and the First Presbyterian was ideal for the Bush household, for the Bush Yankee brand of Manifest Destiny. In the official history of Midland's First Presbyterian were the words: "Presbyterians are a determined people. Hardships and discouragements do not stop them. Because of their nature, they often turn stumbling blocks into stepping stones. [The] history of the Midland Presbyterian Church is splendid evidence of that traditional spirit and experience."[3] As in every small Texas town, the church served as a civic center, and Big George became a church deacon and then a church elder; loyal family friend Earle Craig was chairman of the board of deacons. Sometimes on Sunday afternoons after church, the touch-football Martini Bowl would be reprised— *the Martini Bowl!*—with Big George at quarterback calling the plays and the Midland Misfits lining up against the Lubbock Leftovers while the wives socialized and rocked the baby carriages and "Little George" scrambled alongside the high school field watching the adults play.

In 1952, the family moved from northeast Midland into a house on a paved street on the west side of the city, onto West Ohio at its intersection with H Street. The L-shaped wooden building with a slab foundation, a small concrete porch, and a big front yard was a quantum vault in surroundings, in neighborhoods, from Easter Egg Row. Even with its dirt alleyway, the three-bedroom house at 1412 West Ohio put the family closer to where the crackling wealth was concentrated. The neighborhood had a fistful of oak trees, small green patches that passed for lawns, and it wasn't anything even remotely like the shaded Tudor mansions in Highland Park in Dallas, the nouveau southern plantations in River Oaks in Houston, or even the German-castle confections in the King William neighborhood in San Antonio—each of the neighborhoods florid, in construction and landscaping, with what stands for wealth in Texas. Outwardly, west Midland was, if possible, simultaneously rich and frugal.

Now the family was closer to everything: all the important houses of worship, the newly designed country club just a few streets away, the schools, Sam Houston Elementary and San Jacinto Junior High. And it was amid all the places where the endless civic battle plans were being mapped out: the cancer fund-raisers, the YMCA expansions, the Little League teams, all of them spearheaded by "those who can." The people in west Midland were, George W.'s father would one day say, "a thousand points of light." With surprising quickness, a sense of order, postwar entitlement, and noblesse oblige began to set in. The native West Texans talked openly about it: the appreciative ones said it was about time the outsiders began giving back; the critical ones said it was pretentious, condescending. There were games proliferating that hadn't been played much in this part of Texas: golf, croquet, badminton, tennis. There was a dress code, especially among the easterners, who were wearing coats and ties to meetings, to church, to the electric train races at the YMCA—and there was the photo in the *Reporter-Telegram* the day after one of the races, Big George carefully dressed in a suit and kneeling on his hands and knees alongside his son, Big George's tie getting in the way of the model train tracks, and the first son's picture appearing in the newspaper for one of the first times in his life, and with him incorrectly being called "Junior"—a pattern of nagging description that would linger for the next forty-five years: *"Electric Car Enthusiasts, George Bush and his son, George Jr., participated in the electric train races for Midland children and their fathers.... George Jr. won first place in the races."*[4]

At the end of the workday, Midland's handful of downtown streets was rolled up and put away. There was an unambiguous rhythm, a quickly rooted consistency, and, as one West Texas writer put it, a "prevailing elitism, modified by the Western concept of egalitarianism, and a shrewd appreciation of reality. Around five o'clock on work days and weekends, the skyscrapers and offices downtown become deserted, and life moves to the elegant residences and the country clubs. Here Midlanders, in closely knit relations, familial and friendly, enjoy the fruits of their success, while planning for the days immediately ahead."[5]

SENATOR PRESCOTT Bush began the first of a series of regular visits to Midland. He had failed in a Senate race in 1950, running for the office without lengthy political experience other than having presided as the regular moderator of town meetings in Greenwich.[6] In 1952, he won a special election to fill the seat left vacant by the death of Connecticut's senior Democratic senator, Brien McMahon. In Midland, Senator Bush's arrival was always a cause célèbre, an event that warranted a fete, a formal gathering at the Bush household. It also set into motion a series of frantic ripples foreign to West Texas. One day, with the full knowledge that the senator was wending his way to Midland, Earle and Dottie Craig remained locked in debate about the merits of formal attire at the Bush household—*the blue shirt or the white shirt for the senator?*—and, meanwhile, around the city, maids were alerted to extra duty and plenty of highballs were to be made available for anybody who needed a cool beverage.

Senator Bush, taller than anyone else in the room, mingled and impressed with his gravitas. He would remain in office for a decade, and in time he became the one man Eisenhower would call when the president wanted to escape to the Burning Tree Country Club and play the best linksman on Capitol Hill. Too, even though he was never entirely comfortable on a golf course, then Vice President Richard Nixon would also seek out the Connecticut senator to round out a foursome. Prescott Bush considered his rounds of golf to be somewhat inviolable. "Nobody who plays golf with the president ever talks about it. Any other questions?" Senator Bush once lectured a reporter who asked exactly what was discussed on the links.[7]

Prescott Bush was widely regarded as an adequate caretaker, certainly not an arching ideologue, someone who diligently defended the prevailing Republican dogma: attacking communism, gingerly promoting internationalism, supporting the interests of big business.

He developed a reputation among his peers as the embodiment of a certain antique senatorial tenor—a solemn man whose reverence for a steady demeanor exceeded his reverence for the arcane nuances of public policy. One of his better-known legislative proposals was to ban his colleagues in the Senate from interrupting proceedings by pointing to the visitors' gallery and announcing the presence of certain guests.[8] One evening in Bridgeport, Connecticut, he encountered Joseph McCarthy, the lone member of the senatorial fraternity whom Bush had decided was veering too heavily toward corrupted comportment. Bush quietly pulled McCarthy into a hotel bathroom and lectured him, for more than an hour, about the embarrassing way he was conducting his infamous anti-Communist inquiries. McCarthy listened as Prescott Bush sternly warned that he was going to vote to censure the impolite, overbearing Wisconsin senator.[9]

In Midland, Senator Bush would sometimes find time to play a game of golf with his son and, of course, to talk politics. It was good that he was here; in 1952, Big George was attempting to organize Republicans in the heart of a one-party state, in the middle of a still-suspicious, inflexible

Texas–Old South Democratic stronghold dominated by Lyndon Johnson and Sam Rayburn. The family back in Connecticut could only imagine the work: there was Big George, knocking on office doors downtown, trying to scare up some money for the Eisenhower-Nixon ticket, and that night, when he held the first GOP precinct meeting, there were only three people at the meeting in the back room of the West Texas Office Supply Store—and two of them were Big George and Barbara Bush. Bill Collyns, the editor of the *Midland Reporter-Telegram*, a newspaper afflicted by all the usual political tugs in a small city, could tell that the Bushes were inventing something in West Texas. "Dad [George Bush] brought Republicanism to Midland in the late 1940s. It was strictly Democratic back then," observed Collyns.[10] At the Midland County Courthouse, the county clerk, Rosenelle Cherry, who knew all and saw all when it came to the comings and goings of the oilmen, was ready to switch parties after she met George Bush and his family: "We didn't have a GOP here then. Elder Bush was one of the first precinct chairmen. He won us over because we're just a real friendly bunch of people."[11]

In the moments when Midland seemed awed by the presence of a Connecticut senator, by the Ivy League stories, by the seamless, energetic brio of George Bush, it was as if the Bush household had succeeded, more than any other in West Texas, in re-creating its Long Island Sound–Greenwich–Rye genus in the heart of the ancient dead sea. To maintain their ties to the family, they continued to take George W. to the compound in Kennebunkport, Maine. But by the 1950s, the Bushes and Walkers were no longer gathering for the holidays at their other family estate, George Herbert Walker's 10,000-acre Duncannon plantation in South Carolina. For years the main house at Duncannon, an eight-bedroom, five-bathroom wooden structure, had been a beloved destination for George W.'s grandparents, parents, uncles, and aunt. George Herbert Walker, a millionaire by the turn of the century and someone who moved among the Vanderbilts and Astors, had also had a mansion on Long Island with marble floors, butlers, and two Rolls-Royces, but the Duncannon estate was clearly the Bush-Walker family favorite. On the plantation grounds and in surrounding communities, there were skeet shooting, polo matches, dove hunts led by the dog keeper, and, as George W.'s aunt once said, "the most wonderful black servants would come into the bedrooms early in the morning and light those crackling pine-wood fires."[12]

But after World War II, the family decided to sell Duncannon, and

Prescott Bush and his wife, Dorothy Walker, eventually found a new winter retreat for some family members, including the grandchildren, in the exclusive Hobe Sound–Jupiter Island enclave north of Palm Beach, Florida. For the next generation of the Bush-Walker family, Jupiter Island would almost become the modern Duncannon. Eventually five hundred homes were built on the fifteen-mile-long island, many of them occupied by the most influential families in American politics and industry: the Mellons, Doubledays, Fords, Roosevelts, Whitneys, and Vanderbilts. Averell Harriman, the statesman and head of the investment house that the Walkers and Bushes helped run, would also be a regular on the island.[13]

For years, it was simply understood that the Texas wing of the Bush-Walker family—Big George, Barbara, and George W.—would be making regular journeys from West Texas and Houston to Kennebunkport, Jupiter Island, and the other places in the Northeast where the family kept apartments or homes. The family, especially George W.'s uncles, would listen eagerly to the tales from the Texas desert and the bawdy legends about the nouveau-riche wildcatters who were packing pistols, buying racehorses, and making carefree trips to the big city of Dallas. It was obviously different from the way most members of the Bush-Walker family had made their money on Wall Street. And it was no doubt clear that, in Midland, the rocketing race toward prosperity was occurring in an uncomplicated vacuum, a place minus haunting, annoying urban realities. If there were stumbling blocks in West Texas, the key, always, was to keep moving, keep talking, borrow money from your friends but not the government, keep drilling, and win the lottery.

ON FEBRUARY 11, 1953, the second boy in the family, John Ellis Bush, was born and immediately nicknamed Jeb. Weeks after his birth, it became increasingly clear that there was something hauntingly wrong with three-year-old Robin; she was too dreamy, too weary, and there were surprising bruises on her body. Barbara consulted with the woman whom everyone in Midland took their children to, Dr. Dorothy Wyvell, a legendary figure in West Texas pediatric circles. The tentative diagnosis was the still-unknown, unusual leukemia. The elder George Bush called his uncle John Walker, the president of the prestigious Memorial Sloan-Kettering hospital in New York; John Walker was Dorothy Walker's brother.[14] The next day the parents and Robin quickly embarked on the first of a series of specialized tests and treatments at Memorial Sloan-Kettering, often staying at the spacious Walker family apartment on Sutton Place, nine blocks away from the hospital. Dorothy Walker also decided to dispatch Marion Fraser, one of the Bush-Walker family nurses, to Texas to live with and watch over seven-year-old Little George and infant Jeb.

For the next seven months, George W.'s parents were frequently out of town, either on business or traveling with Robin to New York on board private planes loaned to them by Texas oilmen. Little George was ordered not to play with his sister when she returned from her hospital stays; his parents were worried about roughhousing, about the bruising. The two children had been growing closer, more interdependent, and their time together was radically curtailed. That year, and especially how it ended, would become the first vivid memory of childhood, of life, for George Walker Bush.[15]

The same month his daughter was diagnosed with leukemia, Poppy decided he had to seize the business moment. In 1953, the oil boom was cresting, and he and Hugh Liedtke, an Oklahoman descended from Prussian immigrants, began meeting and talking about yet another independent oil operation. Liedtke, whose father served as Gulf Oil's head counsel, had been educated at Amherst, the University of Texas Law School, and the Harvard Business School.[16] The law partnership he ran with his brother, William, was on the same downtown Midland street as the Bush-Overbey outfit.[17] Liedtke and Bush, two Navy veterans, settled on a one-shot gamble: Bush would go to various Bush-Walker investors, especially Uncle Herbert Walker, and perhaps raise up to $850,000 to buy eight thousand acres; then they would begin drilling in the West Jameson Field, seventy miles east of Midland.[18] They were convinced there was a chain, a web of oil pools spread across the property: hit one, hit them all. Liedtke and Bush had seen the Elia Kazan–directed film *Viva Zapata!*, just released in 1952 and with the original screenplay penned by John Steinbeck. In an unlikely move, considering the pedigree and political tendencies of the filmmakers, they named their new oil venture after a movie exploring the life of a populist revolutionary. The Zapata Petroleum Corporation's entire resources were sunk into West Jameson, and the Bush-Walker family members diligently waited for reports from Texas.

Poppy spent days, weeks on the road, while Barbara shuttled to the hospital and the neighbors and maids spent time with the other children. After a year, Zapata had drilled seventy-one wells and none of them was dry. There were 1,250 barrels of oil every day, $1.3 million worth a year. Zapata was literally exploding with oil. It was the kind of moment, aside from those comfortable and placid rhythms of Midland, that kept everyone, *everyone*, wedded to the city, to West Texas. It was here . . . *finally* . . . the deep money was here.

ON OCTOBER 11, 1953, after lingering for seven months and after some last-minute surgical attempts to save her, Robin died in New York. The only extended visits she had had with her older brother had been during the annual summer gathering at the Bush-Walker compound in Kennebunkport. Still in New York, the family decided against a funeral; her body was donated to science. The day following Robin's death, Barbara Bush's father suggested a round of golf. Barbara and Big George drove to Rye and immersed themselves in playing a round. The next day, following a brief memorial service, they began preparing to return to Midland. They braced themselves: they hadn't told George W. the full details about his sister's condition. The autumn she died, her older brother was enrolled in the second grade at Midland's Sam Houston Elementary School.

It was the middle of a school day, and George W. was struggling down a covered walkway at the small school, weighted down by a Victrola that he and his friend Bill Sallee had been ordered to carry to the principal's office. He turned to watch his parents' car as its wheels crunched over the gravel parking lot and pulled up close to the school. There were children everywhere, the noisy, organized chaos of an elementary school. George W. stared expectantly at the car, assuming, hoping that Robin was there. For a second, in his mind, he could see his sister in the back of the car. He sprinted ahead to his teacher and blurted, "My mom, dad, and sister are home. Can I go see them?"

He had had no idea that his sister was dying. With her death, he was suddenly seven years older than the next child in the family. For days, months, the extended family watched him carefully. Sitting in the Memorial Stadium stands at a Friday-night Midland Bulldogs football game that fall, George W. suddenly turned to his father and his father's oil company colleagues: "I wish that I was Robin." Awkwardness pushed down, and finally his father asked him why. "Because I bet she can see the game better from up there than we can here."

George W. would press his father, wanting to know if "my sister was buried standing up or in a prone position . . . because the earth rotates, they said so at school, and . . . does that mean that Robin is standing on her head?"[19]

At home on West Ohio, Barbara Bush listened hard from her bedroom as she heard George W. at the front door talking to one of the other kids in the west Midland pack. "I can't come over to play because I have to play with my mother," he said. "She's lonely."

Barbara Bush would think about the impact, about how she wasn't sure that she and her husband had handled it very well at all: "You have to remember that children grieve. . . . He felt cheated."[20]

When his friend Joe O'Neill's six-month-old brother died of pneumonia, George W.'s memories of Robin were brought to life again. George W.'s favorite cousin from the Northeast, Elsie Walker, knew what it all meant to him. She had always felt a special kinship with George W., something that transcended bloodlines, something she always thought of in spiritual terms. "Barbara always says, 'Oh, Elsie, you overexaggerate it all,' " she said. "But I do think that the death of Robin had a big effect on George. I think it's very, very difficult for a young child to see his parents suffering. And so I think he tried to be lighthearted. I also lost my sister, and I think that is another thing that George and I have in common. You know, we're both clowns. I think kids who lose a sibling often try and find ways to, you know, make things easier in the family."[21]

Big George's brother Bucky had visited the Bush home in Midland, and he had seen the interchange between the children. Bucky was the youngest uncle, the one who came closest to being an older brother to Little George. He was almost surprised at how profoundly Robin's death influenced Little George, surprised at how his nephew was showing an adult range of emotions. "He was really struck with it. He was hurt by it, almost as if somebody had taken something away from him that he had cherished very, very dearly . . . he was that young and had that kind of an adult reaction to losing a sibling."[22]

Lud Ashley had been a close Yale classmate of the elder George Bush and, maybe more important, a loyal fellow Skull & Bonesman. Robin died two years before Ashley embarked on a long career as a Democratic congressman from Ohio. He knew the way the girl's death was affecting the first son: "His mother was away a lot during the illness. George Sr. was back and forth, he was in New York on weekends and then back, you know, running the kids and his business during the week, and that went on for month in and month out. I mean, at six, you remember those things."[23]

One night, not long after Robin's death, his parents had decided to let their usually insouciant first son have a sleep-over with his friend Randall Roden. Relatives in the Northeast worried that there was too large an age gap between the younger George and Jeb, that the first son would grow up almost as an only child. Throughout the night with Roden, the first son was engulfed in constant nightmares. Finally, Barbara Bush arrived to comfort her son. Roden was watching, unsure what was happening to his friend. Finally Barbara pulled him aside and quietly explained about Robin's death. "It was a profound and formative experience," Roden believes.[24]

Poppy seemed to mellow in some way after Robin's death. He had never really been an ardent disciplinarian anyway, he had rarely exploded in anger. If his first son committed transgressions, he imparted the image of the Disappointed Elder, whose shoulders slumped with the weight of his son's unreliability. Barbara, meanwhile, was asserting herself in almost the same way her husband had done from one end of Midland to the other, joining everything . . . *"and didn't Bar's Caesar Salad recipe always turn out better than anyone else's?"*[25] She smoked, enjoyed a cocktail, and moved outside the self-regulating Greenwich-Rye code. Here, in West Texas, it was easy to develop an edge, a blunt tongue, to become, in some ways, like one of the oilmen sharpened by repeated defeats. Barbara Bush, some relatives noted, was the one most markedly changed by her unshackled experiences in the Permian Basin. And she was the one who spent most of the time with her eldest child, the one known as the Little League Mom at every Midland Cubs game.

George W. could see the way she had reacted to Robin's death, the fact that she had worked with George W., smothered him. He later told people that "Mother's reaction was to envelop herself totally around me. She kind of smothered me and then recognized that it was the wrong thing to do."[26]

IN 1955, flush with the money generated by the dozens of wells on the West Jameson Field, Poppy had new plans for the family. They were moving again, this time into a three-thousand-square-foot brick home at 2703 Sentinel with a pool and a cabana, on a lot backing up to Cowden Park in west Midland. It was good, it *looked* like prosperity, on a gently curving street, and everyone had to come over because all the Little League games for all the sons of the oilmen were uncorking in Cowden Park, the backyard cookouts would be held poolside, and there would always be people around; the family would never be alone.

William "Bucky" Bush, George's youngest brother, was also back in town. Bucky had come down to West Texas with Fay Vincent, a friend of his from Hotchkiss, the prep school. They lived in the Bush house and took summer jobs that Big George had cooked up for them in the oil patch. Barbara was always complaining about how the pool was just no good after the two of them had been in it—too much oil and grease floating around in it after they went swimming. At night and on weekends, Bucky would umpire his nephew's baseball games; years later Vincent would become commissioner of Major League Baseball.

The West Jameson Field was a cash cow. At Agnes's and especially at the country club, the Liedtke boys and Big George Bush were the talk of Midland. They were rocketing so hard, so fast, that they were up to 90 wells, 100 wells, 127 of them, and each of them, sweet Jesus, was yielding oil. Earle Craig was aware of it, like everyone else, trying hard not to be envious, because that wasn't the way to do things, but it was so obvious, really, the way things were happening so fast for the Bushes . . . "the first to become worth a million dollars, which, in those days, you apply a factor of six or seven, and it was quite impressive to us."[27]

When Big George and Barbara went to New York or Connecticut together, Anna Williams would move in again and watch Little George along with the two regular maids: Julia Cooper, who arrived before anyone woke up, and Otha Taylor, who came during the afternoons and evenings. With Zapata planning to drill offshore, the elder Bush was out of town even more, heading to Houston for strategy sessions. Williams and the maids measured the first son against the father; they also measured him against the other children, including Neil Mallon Bush, born in 1955, and Marvin Pierce Bush, born in 1956. Little George was fast, thought Williams: "George had a quick wit about him, just the little remarks he'd make."[28]

Alone with the children, Taylor saw it too, and she always told people it had everything to do with his father being away from home so often, chasing the oil business into bruising, big Houston. Little George and his mother were always colliding, the maid thought, because they were together so much—and because they were so much alike. "They would squabble a lot. You know how kids and parents that are just alike will get? He was definitely like his mother, they were exactly alike, even their humor was alike."[29]

One day, Barbara Bush told Taylor that she was going to read stories to George W. and that it was okay for the maid to head home an hour early. The next afternoon, when Taylor came back to clean the house, Mrs. Bush nervously pulled the maid aside: "Mr. Bush came in last night, and he was saying you weren't there. . . . 'Where's Otha? She's supposed to stay here until her hour is up, regardless if she has anything to do or not.' "

Taylor simply stared and said, "Oh."

Later that day, when her brother came to pick her up at the big brick house on Sentinel, the family maid was livid at the elder Bush: "He's a really mean man. He was telling his wife not to let me go." Throughout her life Taylor thought about what had happened that day, all her days as one of the two maids in the Bush house. She liked the family, but the Bushes, she sometimes thought, were the kind of people who believed in teaching lessons.[30]

GEORGE WALKER BUSH, in Miss Austine Crosby's third-grade class, threw a football through a window at Sam Houston Elementary School one rainy afternoon when all the students had been ordered to stay indoors at lunchtime. "That was a surprise," Miss Austine liked to say in her deadpan way. Sometimes he was one of the children bragging about the fact that he had his swimsuit on underneath his blue jeans; pools were still a novelty in Midland, and the kids who wore swimsuits to school let everyone else know about it.[31] In fourth grade, a teacher ordered him to Principal John Bizilo's office after he had created a disturbance. Bush had been laboriously marking his face with a ballpoint pen, crafting a mustache, goatee, and long sideburns. Bizilo stared at Bush and then registered that he was imitating Elvis Presley, who had done concerts in Odessa. Bizilo issued a warning and sent Bush back to class.[32]

At home, his mother increasingly became the more frequent morality gatekeeper, and Joe O'Neill III, like a lot of the children, began moving around her more warily: "There's no question about it, she's the one who instills fear."[33] She was the ethical checkpoint, the one who did more than threaten her son by saying he would have to stay in his room and contemplate the fact that his father was on his way home from Houston, toting that unrelenting sense of disappointment . . . *you haven't been a Good Man.* "My mother's always been a very outspoken person who vents very well—she'll just let it rip if she's got something on her mind. Once it's over, you know exactly where you stand and that's it," George W. would say later.[34]

And his mother, whose hair had begun turning gray as she cared for her dying daughter, would interrupt the fights between twelve-year-old George and five-year-old Jeb: "They'd get into big fights, and their mother would wade into the middle of it and their father never would, never would get in—well, maybe he did, but he was always working pretty hard. . . . But Bar would always get in the middle of those fights and bust them up and slap them around," said George W.'s uncle, Jonathan Bush.[35]

SOME DAYS the sample bags, stuffed with promise and the size of a loaf of bread, were too much for Joe O'Neill III and Little George, out on their bikes in the early morning and making their rounds on the handful of downtown streets, the ones dotted with the always implausible office buildings rising out of the sand. Midland had begun promoting itself as the "Tall City of The Plains" or "Headquarters City of The Vast Permian Basin Empire." The streets that ran east–west were named after states: Louisiana, Michigan, Tennessee, Ohio, Illinois, Texas, Missouri, Indiana, Kentucky. The ones that ran north–south were named after all the little towns in West Texas that you reached once you ventured into the desert: Big Spring, Weatherford, Baird, Pecos, San Angelo.

Every night somebody would drive back from the general direction of all those smaller towns, carrying trunkloads of sample bags. The cloth sacks were crammed with core samples, disintegrated bits and bones from extinct species of horse, camel, mammoth, peccary, wolf, and sloth, and pieces of fossilized human skulls, ribs, and hand bones, such as the skeletal remains a pipeline welder first stumbled across in 1953 on somebody's oil lease, a disintegrating pile of ancient life, the oldest skeleton in North America, that paleontologists named Midland Minnie. The oilmen would jot their names on the bag tags, write down the depth the core sample came from, and fling them, like messages in a bottle, onto the doorsteps of the geologists who could study the contents and determine whether they had been plucked from a place atop an ocean of oil.

Sometimes Spider and George W. would reach down and scoop up the sample bags as they cycled off to meet their friends at the Ritz movie theater, Agnes's, or the Rexall drugstore. Everyone they knew had a nickname; another neighborhood kid was Big Chief, and one more was Rodan—he was always huge, Japanese-monster huge, running like a creature on four legs, picking up girls and slinging them over his shoulder. And the sample bags were good ammo, they were good make-believe bombs, the cloth equivalents of water balloons.

"Oh, it would really play hell with someone's information by stealing those things," O'Neill remarked.[36]

LITTLE GEORGE'S parents were leaders of the PTA in 1958, as if there were anything left in Midland that they hadn't joined or been in charge of. And as the decade neared its close, the population of Midland had increased by 186 percent since 1950. There were 40,000 new residents. There were 750 oil companies. There were even a few more Republicans, many of whom had signed on owing to the visits of Senator Prescott Bush, who had been reelected in Connecticut in 1956.

As the elder George Bush immersed himself in Zapata, in Republican politics, his first son was trying to memorize the starting lineups of every major-league baseball team, collecting baseball cards in a shoebox, and mailing the cards to players who might autograph them. One day, his mother took him to see Little League coach Frank Ittner. The gruff-voiced Ittner had moved to Midland in the early part of the decade and quickly become a community fixture as coach of the successful Midland Cubs. Ittner, like everyone in town, knew the Bushes, and he knew that the first son's father had been a college star at first base back east. Ittner settled the son at catcher: "He wasn't playing first base, he wasn't that talented. . . . Well, actually, he wasn't a good hitter." Ittner noticed that the first son's mother was always there, but no one else from the family: "I don't think his father ever showed up, I don't think that Big George ever showed up that I can remember."[37]

One afternoon, Ittner told the mother that the first son needed some extra help, some one-on-one baseball tutelage. Ittner had seen the boy at the plate, constantly slipping into a habit that he wouldn't break no matter how many times Ittner yelled at him: "He was stepping into the bucket. If a ball came over the plate, he would step back instead of stepping forward." Ittner threw pitch after pitch, but the results were the same. And the coach said to himself that the kid would never master the science of the game but "because he was a catcher, he'd be in on every play."[38]

One evening, Ittner went to a meeting of the Exchange Club. The elder Bush was giving a lecture about the first experimental, multimillion-dollar offshore oil rigs that Zapata was developing to use in the murky waters in the Gulf of Mexico. Bush had some literature, including copies of the company prospectus offering $1.5 million in stock. Ittner pored over the prospectus. A thought ran through his head: *He was probably coaching one of the richest Little League catchers in the world.*

By the late 1950s, the West Texas oil boom was beginning to shift into a lingering down cycle. Zapata, ahead of the trend, was positioned to move offshore, first along the Gulf Coast and then around the world, with five newly designed rigs worth as much as $6 million each. The elder Bush's official title was CEO of Zapata Off-Shore, which operated under the umbrella of Zapata Petroleum. He began to spend even more time in Houston, commuting back and forth, meeting with the Liedtkes and other founding members of Pennzoil and sometimes taking George W. with him to pose for a promotional picture in front of an oil rig. By 1958, it was obvious the family would have to move to stay on top of things. It was impossible to run an offshore venture from Midland, and Baine Kerr, a trusted lawyer with Houston's Baker & Botts and the future president of Pennzoil, found 1.2 acres for the family in an almost surprisingly verdant zone inside Texas's largest city.

The Bushes ordered a custom-designed house for the lot in Houston. The Bushes were never going to stay in Midland; the deep-money opportunities were slipping, the political possibilities were still stunted by the decades-old West Texas Democratic machinery. In August 1959, the last child in the family, Dorothy Walker Bush, was born. That same month, the Houston house at 5525 Briar Drive was completed. The homestead's oversized lot would later be used for five new houses.[39]

The Bush home was close to the Kinkaid School, which many people considered to be one of the most exclusive private schools in Texas, maybe in the South, second perhaps only to another Houston preparatory institution named St. John's. Friends of the family in Houston were saying that young George had applied to St. John's, had not been admitted, and was now headed toward Kinkaid. Meanwhile, Poppy began exploring the possibilities of having his first son eventually transfer to his old school, to Phillips Academy in Andover, Massachusetts. Of course, going to Andover meant going to Yale, as most people in the Bush family did. It meant following the exact path of his father, his grandfather, his uncles, Neil Mallon, and dozens of the closest members of the extended Bush-Walker clan.

4

Style

The stated mission was there on the Kinkaid logo: LUX PER SCIENTIAM, "Light through the science of knowledge." John Cooper wouldn't have minded if it had been changed to "Light through style." When the private school had opened at its new, sprawling location in the late 1950s, Headmaster Cooper had given a speech in his usual, measured manner:

> First, I would see Kinkaid as a school which will develop in its students a sense of style—which I take to be the understanding and practice of those qualities which make for the first-rate in any endeavor. Such a sense of style depends, I believe, upon the individual's capacity to attain his goal without wasteful and irrelevant effort.
>
> The second and equally basic objective to which I would see Kinkaid dedicated is that students will discover, in our example and in our teaching, evidence that this is an order-founded, God-oriented universe.
>
> An education which develops the best in the student, which seeks to give him a sense of style . . . will be in harmony with and will provide vigorous support for the best in America.[1]

The school dated to the turn of the century, when the city had needed new institutions, ones catering to the nouveau riche who had recently been relocating to Houston, "Bombay on the bayou," to take advantage of the oil booms on the eastern side of the state. On January 10, 1901, the great Texas gusher at Spindletop had erupted three miles from

Beaumont and began producing between 75,000 and 80,000 barrels of oil a day, 3.2 million barrels a year. By 1904, oil wells were also producing in Humble, and the state's annual oil production was headed toward 28 million barrels. Houston, especially, would be awash in cash, construction, and outsiders who would later launch into other parts of the state looking for oil. Three years after Spindletop, Margaret Hunter Kinkaid started a school in her cottage at San Jacinto and Elgin Streets; it was the oldest nondenominational private school in the city and one of the oldest in Texas.

Kinkaid, a short, auburn-haired woman whose father had been a gold prospector and a Confederate soldier, was an advocate of style but also of science, of the logical sequence of things. "Serpentology is a perfectly suitable field of study for young ladies," she would defiantly say when parents came to her, complaining about the fact that girls at the coeducational school had to handle the hog-nosed snake that the school had in its collection. Throughout Mrs. Kinkaid's tenure she remained fascinated by the place, the ranking, of each child in each family. She saw it as a key to understanding the future success of the affluent children of Houston, and when parents would arrive she would ask them about the child's place in the family hierarchy: "Now, where is he in the family? Is he the middle child, the oldest, the baby of your family?"[2]

By 1959, with Headmaster Cooper at the helm, the school had moved to a prime location on a forty-acre tract in the Tanglewood-Memorial area, a tree-laden zone that was considered to be leaning toward the country but with easy access to paths that paralleled the sluggish, café-au-lait-colored Buffalo Bayou as it ribboned toward the skyline of downtown Houston, and the collection of private petroleum clubs with uniformed servants, where the most profound and sometimes troubling business and civic decisions in Texas were made. When Headmaster Cooper had taken control of Kinkaid, he had strengthened the school's ties to Houston's business and political oligarchy, and it had begun to attract the children of prominent families. Cooper and Kinkaid's other leaders would proudly announce each new victory—"The First Completely Centrally Air-Conditioned College Preparatory School In The United States . . . The Third Largest Endowment Of Any Day School In The United States"—to the businessmen on its founding board of trustees: Robert Lee Blaffer, who had co-founded Humble Oil, which would become Exxon; Burke Baker, chairman of the board of American General Life Insurance; Harry Carothers Wiess, chairman of the board of Humble; James A. Baker Jr., whose family had helped start the Baker & Botts law firm and whose son would serve as secretary of state and White House chief of staff; Will Clayton, undersecretary of state and one of the authors of the Marshall Plan.[3]

That year, Houston was the largest city in Texas, with 938,000 residents and almost as many societal tectonic plates, each of them shifting and jostling one another, each of them segregated by sharp class boundaries. The most complex city in the state, Houston was wrestling with its southern heritage, its western ties, its growing foreign-born community, a clamorous anti-Communist movement spearheaded by the John Birch Society, racists on the police force, powerful and strident evangelicals, and simmering tensions in the less prosperous Third, Fourth, and Fifth Wards. Finally, there was the constant infusion of people from every corner of the United States, all of them hell bent on coming to this part of the Texas Gulf Coast, willing to endure the energy-sapping humidity for the chance of a direct or indirect encounter with the money oozing out of the oil sector. Those newcomers provided the bedrock of support for what was, compared to Midland, a more organized Republican Party, and, more important, a Republican state of mind: people who were tolerant and even attuned to the Northeast, limousine conservatives, people who could trace a personal line through the Rockefeller wing of things, the patrician side, the internationalist side.

It was a strange city for someone newly arrived from Midland, but a comfortable one once the Bushes realized that there was at least one place in Texas that had the same societal boundaries, circles, and layers as the Northeast. Midland had been, almost, a simple way station where one could make instant friends and instant money. Houston was a place that offered the same possibilities, plus one more: the prospect of true political opportunity for the entire Bush family.

FOLLOWING the recommendation of friends in Midland, in July 1959 the family had begun a summertime tradition of sending energetic George W. to the selective Longhorn Camp in the upper portion of the meandering Highland Lakes chain that fanned out to the north and west of Austin. The camp was run by Julian William "Tex" Robertson, a former Olympic swimmer and water polo player from Michigan who was also an inveterate promoter of his operation. Longhorn was a magnet for wealthy families around the state, and it was an incubator, a training ground for that unyielding Teddy Roosevelt–style verve, that ceaseless competition on which Dorothy Walker Bush spent her waking moments in Duncannon, Jupiter Island, Greenwich, or Walker's Point.

In a solemn moment at Longhorn, George W. was declared a

"Campfire Lighter," a special, almost operatic honor bestowed upon a camper who was handed a match and asked to ignite the nightly fire that would illuminate the skits put on by each cabin. Everyone would tilt their heads back and roar to the web of stars: "Oh hail, oh hail, to the campfire lighter." Slipping into the icy waters of Inks Lake, not far from the Longhorn Caves, where Confederate troops had once secretly manufactured gunpowder, Bush swam the traditional mile. He suffered abuse when word leaked out that his parents usually spent their summers in a foreign place called *Kenny-Bunk-Port*. Meanwhile, Tex Robertson's favorite phrase was "Aterwaytogo!"—something that everyone—campers, parents, counselors—was required to yell whenever something really good, monumental was happening. Tex knew that the Bushes understood the whole idea, even Little George: "He was a Campfire Lighter. . . . He went in for the Aterwaytogo stuff."[4] In time, George W. and another camper, future Texas Senator Kay Bailey Hutchison, would be inducted into the Camp Longhorn Hall of Fame.

After camp, there was an August family vacation, traveling through Scotland,[5] and then, even though there was a waiting list for almost every grade, George Walker Bush was allowed to set foot on the shady lanes at Kinkaid. The grandson of the Connecticut senator was one of 104 eighth-graders in a school with 889 students, and now he was also in the hands of Headmaster Cooper, a transplant from Rockford, Illinois, the father of six children, and the husband of a Latin teacher. The elder George Bush liked Cooper instantly. There was something about Cooper that reminded people of Prescott Bush. Cooper was obviously a stickler for comportment; he believed that life was defined, to a large measure, by your personal sense of style. But there was something else. Like Prescott Bush, Headmaster Cooper was an astounding singer, someone who had helped found the Houston Gilbert & Sullivan Society and who would break into tunes from *The Pirates of Penzance* right in front of people. It was all very stylish, all the G and S songs and shows. Some people in Houston said that was the real difference between Kinkaid and St. John's: "Kinkaid is where the kids who can't get into St. John's go. Fashion versus intellect, Kinkaid versus St. John's."[6]

George W. Bush was known mostly for participating in baseball and other sports. "He was very popular, he was very good-looking—he wasn't what I would call incredibly handsome, but he was popular," recalled Charles Sanders, who taught at the school for decades. There were speech and debate tournaments. Bush learned the fundamentals, and the debate team supervisors recognized him as someone who wasn't "set off in the corner. He was a real joiner."[7] His history teacher simply saw a heightened intensity in the way he related to people, something that struck the teacher as being more in line with his mother than his father. "His father had a definite influence on him, but his general relationship to people was more like his mother's. He was very intense. He inherited a lot of that from his mother," remembered Art Goddard.[8]

HIS FATHER was still frequently on the road, away from his office in the stately Houston Club Building, meeting with Uncle Herbert Walker, the Liedtke brothers, and other investors and keeping them advised on the family's multimillion-dollar investments in Zapata. Pushing Zapata's business interests even further, and through his uncle's international connections, the elder George Bush traveled to London, The Hague, Mexico, and Trinidad.[9] At the same time, he was making regular trips to the Northeast, visiting Washington and Republican leaders, including Prescott Bush's friends on Capitol Hill. "Even when we were growing up in Houston, Dad wasn't at home at night to play catch," Jeb remembered. "Mom was always the one to hand out the goodies and the discipline. In a sense, it was a matriarchal family."[10] In a way, it was similar to the days when elder George Bush had been growing up in Prescott and Dorothy Walker Bush's house on Grove Lane in Greenwich, Connecticut. "Dad taught us about duty and service. Mother taught us about dealing with life on a personal basis, relating to other people," the elder George Bush said.[11]

Doug Hannah was a neighbor and the son of a prominent real estate developer who would, in typically unbridled Houston fashion, eventually go into the private space rocket business. Hannah always wanted George W. to come outside, to hang around on Saturday afternoons in 1960. It would have to wait for three hours; the first son was inside in the study with his mother, as she held up the ten flashcards with the new vocabulary words he had to learn that particular weekend.[12] The more Hannah became friends with the family, the more he spent time at the Bush house . . . he and George W. stealing cigarettes from Barbara . . . taking dips in one of the only pools in Tanglewood . . . walking from the cabana and through the living room and watching as Neil Mallon and the Old Man were in there, huddling, talking about that new offshore initiative: "Sit down, Hannah! Talk to Neil Mallon!" And when everyone's parents were caught up in the swirl of activities that the Bushes had embarked upon, as if this part of Texas that they moved in was really just an extension of life back in Greenwich, Rye, and Midland, Hannah was marveling at what set his new friend apart from all the other young people in Houston society circles.

At the parties celebrating the launch of another one of the Zapata rigs, at the backyard barbecues, at the gallery shows, the fund-raisers, the GOP socials, the younger Bush would work the room, obviously not running for any office but working it hard anyway. It was unlike anything Hannah had seen, the way George W. seemed to be directly emulating his father, winding his way from one side of a party to the other, mingling, shaking hands, making sure he said hello to everyone in the room when he walked in, making sure to say good-bye to everyone on the way out. Hannah knew that Bush "was always more political. He has always been a political person. He would walk in that room and work it. Even as an eighth-grader, and that's pretty foreign to a juvenile—to even think that that is important."[13]

In the city of transplants, the upper ends of society were defined, bounded by the River Oaks Country Club, debutante balls, Museum of Art functions, the Bayou Club, and private parties celebrating the annual Houston Livestock & Rodeo Show, the rodeo being a thunderous and momentous spectacle that married the grisly realities of the Old West cattle barons with the champagne tendencies of the Stetson- and tuxedo-wearing urban cowboys. George W. Bush began spending more time with people who had ties to the more exclusive St. John's School; in his circle were Doug Hannah, Lacey Neuhaus, and Cathy Wolfman, children of oilmen, clothiers, jewelers, business leaders, and socialites. And at the seemingly endless string of functions, the young Houstonians moving from one to the next, he was even more impossible to extract, inserting himself and always moving, mixing, approaching people, just as his father did but with a bit more bluster, like his mother.

IN 1961, after he had been at Kinkaid two years, his parents summoned him and said that they would like him to attend Phillips Academy at Andover. Andover was really his parents' choice, and he went along with it. His close cousin John Ellis, six years younger, knew what was happening: "I don't think George chose to go to Andover because his father went to Andover. I think George went to Andover because his parents said, 'You should go to Andover, that's a good school, that's a good place to go,' . . . and he was fifteen, and he thought, 'Shit, why am I leaving Texas? OK, I'll try it, you know, I'm game. What the hell.' "[14] Ellis, like the other third-generation kids in the Bush clan, the ones who gravitated to George W. at Kennebunkport, bored by whatever business and political deals the grown-ups were hammering out, always knew this: "George got it, you know what I mean? He was on top of it. He got the joke, he got the deal."

Andover, nestled in rural New England twenty miles north of Boston and also twenty miles west of Salem, was the oldest incorporated boarding school in the nation, and its endowment and library were larger than the ones at many American colleges. Founded in 1778 during the Revolutionary War, Paul Revere created its engraved seal and George Washington wanted his young relatives, including nephew Howell Lewis and eight grand-nephews, to enroll. The five-hundred-acre campus fanned out from rolling Andover Hill and was dotted with carefully landscaped quadrangles and more than a hundred buildings, many of them built in the early part of the nineteenth century along gently curving lanes bordered by towering elms and maples. America House, the dormitory on Main Street to which George W. Bush was eventually assigned, was built in 1825 and was considered part of the "Rabbit Pond Cluster" of faculty and student residences.

In 1832, Samuel Francis Smith penned "America" ("My Country, 'tis of Thee") in a ground-floor room near the front porch of America House. Other significant bits of history and culture were omnipresent across the campus village, including Harriet Beecher Stowe's marker in Chapel Cemetery, the seventeenth-century atlas in the library's collection, the Robert S. Peabody Museum of Archaeology, and the Addison Gallery of American Art with its works by Whistler, Homer, and Hopper. The gallery's founder, Thomas Cochran of the class of 1890, had once said that "if Andover students could be surrounded by beautiful things, their lives would be immeasurably enriched."[15]

One of Andover's founding mottoes is *"Finis Origine Pendet"*—The End Depends upon the Beginning—and the school's original charter states that "goodness without knowledge is weak and feeble; yet knowledge without goodness is dangerous." Oliver Wendell Holmes attended the school, as did landscape architect Frederick Law Olmstead, Dr. Benjamin Spock, Alfred I. du Pont, photographer Walker Evans, Humphrey Bogart (though he was expelled for "incontrollably high spirits"), telegraph inventor Samuel Morse, artist Frank Stella, future Yale president and baseball commissioner Bartlett Giamatti, Secretary of War Henry Stimson and Chinese Ambassador to the United States Sir Chentung Liang. Holmes, who graduated in 1825, wrote "The School Boy," a poem about life at Andover and how similar an experience it was to Eton, that most famous of English schools and one that dated to the fifteenth century:[16]

> The immortal boy, the coming heir of all
> Springs from his desk to "urge the flying ball,"
> Cleaves with his bending oar the glassy waves,
>   With sinewy arm the dashing current braves
> The same bright creature in these haunts of ours
> That Eton shadowed with her "antique towers."

When Bush arrived on campus, the school had just completed a $6.75-million-dollar construction campaign overseen by forty-nine-year-old John Mason Kemper, the headmaster with a square face and absorbing eyes. One of Kemper's ancestors had commanded a brigade at Gettysburg and served as governor of Virginia. Kemper had passed up a standing family offer to pay for his education at Princeton and Harvard Business School in order to enroll at West Point. He later earned a master's degree in history at Columbia University and spent several years assigned to Army intelligence units, compiling the ongoing combat history of the U.S. armed forces during World War II. Colonel Kemper resigned from the army in mid-June 1948 and took over Andover two weeks later. His uncompromising philosophy of education was punctuated by his insistence on the importance and the superior nature of at least one thing: style.

The regimen he had devised at Andover and, by the 1960s, perfected was proving to be an immense attraction to parents who were fidgeting over the way postwar certainties were unraveling at the edges. In a shifting world hallmarked by an Irish Catholic in the White House, revolution in Cuba, the Red Menace, Andover was in the precise hands of John Kemper. Visitors to the campus on the day General Douglas MacArthur died could see that the flags, under orders from Kemper, had been lowered to half-mast; on the day Eleanor Roosevelt passed away, the flags remained at full-mast.

Life at the school in the early 1960s was an ordered, structured world that allowed for little variance from Kemper's West Point edicts. Breakfast, chapel, or a school assembly were held early each morning, with demerits sometimes handed out to anyone who was even a few seconds late. Kemper had decided to allow students no more than seven minutes between classes, and the same demerit system was in place for anyone who was late to class. School was in session through early afternoon; then there were sports and organized activities for two or three hours and finally late afternoon classes running to 6 P.M. Variations of the cycle were repeated on some Saturdays, and every day there were unsubtle suggestions that everyone do something . . . belong to something . . . join something. In a precious few minutes, usually at night and sometimes on weekends, students were finally left to their own devices, left to reflect on where they were. One student in the 1960s wrote an essay about the Andover experience, about how it was

> almost like "Lord of the Flies" . . . physical ability and cultural conformity were at a premium and pressures were extreme. . . . A boy in my dormitory stayed up all night cutting himself with a razor blade, and we, his dorm mates, stayed up all night trying to stop him, and no one went to the house master for fear the boy would get kicked out. . . . Anyone who believes that sexual activity can be sublimated into creative activity could find great support for the theory in our P.A. years. . . . We were dynamos. We had to meet other people's expectations. We had to live by other people's values.[17]

GEORGE W.'s father, of course, had preceded him at Andover and had graduated nineteen years earlier. From the Bell Tower to the Vista to Rabbit Pond to George Washington Hall to the paths leading to Samuel Phillips Hall, amid all of it, the portraits of Andrew Jackson and the original works by Winslow Homer, amid it all was the legacy of George Herbert Walker Bush. In the pages of the annuals, it was spelled out along with the fact that George W.'s father had been named "Best All-Around Fellow" at Andover: there were twenty-three distinctions for his father, including president of senior class, captain of baseball team, secretary of the Student Council, captain of the soccer team, treasurer of the Student Council, John Hopkins Prize. In the changing times of the early 1960s, the elder Bush was an omnipresent checkpoint for students sequestered on the tight-knit campus, a reminder of what Kemper always wanted, what Andover wanted, what was expected of you.

In Benner House, students would hang out, smoking, eating hamburgers, and staring up at an impressive black-and-white photograph of George Bush: "I remember on the wall there was a picture of George Bush Senior, must've been taken when he was a senior at Andover, and he was in his baseball uniform. Everybody knew that this was the guy who'd been captain of the baseball team and who had gone up to Secretary of War Stimson at graduation and said, 'I don't wanna go to Yale right now, I wanna fight for my country.' I mean, everybody knew about it."[18]

Among the 264 members of the class of 1964, there were three black students. Coats and ties were required at all appointments and at morning chapel. Among the members of his all-male class, Bush saw a familiar Texas face: Randall Roden, his kindergarten friend from Midland. There were also people whose fathers and grandfathers were immersed in important things or, like George W.'s father, poised for important things: D. D. Pei, son of the architect I. M. Pei; Glenn Greenberg, son of the immortal baseball player Hank Greenberg; Torbert MacDonald, godson of U.S. President John F. Kennedy.

Bill Semple, an affable hockey player who had come to the school with his twin brother from Grosse Pointe, Michigan, remembered seeing the grandson of the Connecticut senator in Williams Hall: "There were the untouchables, there were groups of people, big men on campus. But they weren't necessarily the jocks. But George was always part of a small group of seven or eight guys who were really, well, you'd have to call them the big men on campus. He was one of the cool guys." When you walked into the study hall, the pecking order at Andover was clear: if you sat on the right, you sat with the serious students, the intellectuals, the young men who were either steadfastly getting good grades or focused on them. Everyone else was on the left, and "George would more or less be on the left."[19]

Semple, a self-professed jock with no political ax to grind, began to marvel at the breezy, uncomplicated student from Texas:

He rose to a certain prominence for no ostensible, visible reason. First of all, he was an attractive guy, very handsome, he had a presence to him, he had a cool look. He had a way about him, and he fit easily in. You know the cool guys? They didn't go out of their way to pay attention to you if you weren't part of their crowd. He really came as "to the manner born." The problem is that you don't know if that is arrogance or if, ultimately, he is a shy guy. Some of these guys who are very public are essentially very shy people, and that, you know, whether he was actually arrogant or he was just, in a manner, quiet . . . I couldn't say. He just never seemed very warm. He didn't wear anything on his sleeve, but you know, in some way he kind of sailed through the time incognito to some of us. In a way, it's interesting: they consider Clinton to be the Teflon Man, but Bush went through high school sort of the same way—nothing ever stuck. Obviously, he inherited some extraordinary political skills. I have to say, I found it a shock, it amazes me, on a certain level, that here he is, a viable candidate for president, and you know, he may just win. and yet I don't ever remember him saying anything profound. I never knew what his passion was, I never thought of him as a passionate person. And yet he got there. How does that happen? He was always just there. He just didn't let people get to know him, whether he did that by design, I couldn't say. He managed to get himself in the right place at the right time.[20]

AT ANDOVER, the Texans drew close together, especially Bush and Clay Johnson, a tall, lanky public school student from Fort Worth whose father had been involved in various ranching and business ventures in North Texas and Oklahoma. Andover students would huddle at night and talk about military-style "drownproofing," the way some physical education teachers would tie up students, toss them into a twelve-foot-deep pool, and tell them to figure out some way to stay afloat. They talked about Dean of Students G. Grenville Benedict, an intimidating man with an oblong Eisenhower-like countenance. They talked about the teachers, about how Tom Regan looked like Ichabod Crane and how he would throw chalk into your mouth if he caught you yawning. They talked about the demanding Tom Lyons, the teacher who taught the American history class that was the pinnacle of the entire program at Andover, a college-level course crafted for years with a custom syllabus and frequent tests and sometimes taught in terms of the evolution of Supreme Court decisions. Too, there was mention of Josh Miner, the teacher who had helped bring the Outward Bound program to the United States and who championed a certain Andover code of self-reliance and physical ability.[21]

By the end of his first year at Andover, in 1962, Bush had played junior varsity baseball and junior varsity basketball and was a member of the Spanish Club, an outgrowth of the total-immersion language classes at Andover: nine hours a week in class with English banned.

For his first English class assignment, Bush was asked to write about a soul-stirring, emotional experience in his life. He decided to write about the death of Robin and its impact on the Bush-Walker family. He struggled to find the right words and reached for a thesaurus his mother had given him as a going-away present when he was leaving for Andover. She had told him to avoid using the same words over and over again; she had urged him simply to look up other possibilities.[22] Bush wanted to say that "the tears ran down my cheeks," but he had already used the word "tears" several times. He looked up "tears" in his thesaurus and then wrote, "And the lacerates ran down my cheeks."

When his paper was returned, he was given a failing grade, and it was also marked "Disgraceful" and "See me immediately." Bush was worried, scared . . . his father had been at Andover. He asked friends, "How am I going to last a week?"[23]

He confided in Johnson, one of eighteen students from Texas, and they talked about their ongoing, bittersweet relationship with the intellectually and historically intimidating Andover. Through their time together, the pair would bemoan the long winters in the Northeast and how, beyond the climate, there were strange, intellectual walls separating some of the Texans from the other people who seemed to thrive on the academic rigors at Andover. Johnson could see it, and Bush would talk to him about it for years—how the younger Bush had begun to see his self-professed mission at Andover, how he had decided that his legacy at Andover was going to be, maybe out of necessity, entirely different from his father's. His father was one of the most famous student athletes in the history of the then 185-year-old institution; the younger Bush had decided that his own legacy at Andover was, as he said later, to "instill a sense of frivolity," either directly or inadvertently. He and Johnson played second string on the basketball team under the tutelage of an Andover stalwart, Frank DiClemente, who had also coached the Old Man. During the last few seconds of a tense game against archrival Exeter, someone stage-whispered, "Bush, get in there!" Bush bounded up from his usual seat on the bench, falling for the practical joke, and almost sprinted onto the floor while everyone else started laughing.[24]

Bush's core group was forming: Clay Johnson; Doug Brown, a hockey player from Waterville, Maine; John Kidde, a lacrosse and football player from Pasadena, California; Mack Thompson, a tennis player and wrestler from Fort Worth; Tory Peterson, a soccer player from Old Lyme, Connecticut; James Lockhart III, a sailing club member from Saint Paul, Minnesota. Absorbed into the Bush-Walker circles, some of them were the ones who would get to stay at George W.'s grandmother's house in Rye, New York, for the big prep school tournament called Rye Tennis Week. Sometimes Bush would also invite friends to Kennebunkport for weekend or summer getaways under the watchful eye of the housekeeper and wait staff. The Old Man would order everyone out of bed—"C'mon, let's go!"—and they would all go down to the rocks and jump into the cold water, like a ritual, and then it was time for baseball and then something else, until the sun was setting over Maine.

IN THE SUMMER of 1962, the Old Man arranged for sixteen-year-old George W. to take a $200-a-month job as a messenger and runner with

Baker Botts Sheppard & Coates, a prestigious Houston law firm in the Esperson Building that was affiliated with the family of James A. Baker III, the young attorney who would faithfully serve the elder George Bush in several national capacities over the years. Baine Kerr, the attorney who had found the property for the Bush home three years earlier and would soon serve as the president of Pennzoil, also worked at Texas's most influential law firm. It was a typical summer for the Bush family, who divided their time at Camp Longhorn and Kennebunkport, dealing with the steady stream of friends and family in and out of the Houston house.

And in the early fall, commuting back to Boston and then traveling on to Andover, George W. knew that his cousin Kevin Rafferty would be joining him on campus. Shortly after his return, people on campus were scrambling from dorm room to dorm room holding a copy of the October 25, 1962, *Time* magazine. The headline read, "Excellence and Intensity in U.S. Prep Schools." On the cover was a sobering image of John Kemper—the headmaster told people that he thought the image made it seem as if he were about to bite someone.

According to the article, Kemper, more than ever, was unwaveringly committed to shoring up the sense of style he demanded in the people at Andover. But he was also beginning to worry "about the lucky-me attitude that affects many Andover boys." Kemper said he had been struggling with how to maintain the academic diligence at Andover while struggling to "teach them a sense of humanity and public service."[25]

In the article, the venerable Emory Basford, chairman of the English Department, who had been at the school since 1929, was more blunt in his belief that Andover was now more about advancing students to a good college and not to a life furthering noble ideals: "The spirit of man is neglected in this school. This has become a strange, bewildering, killing place."[26]

BOB MARSHALL, a soft-voiced student from Bronxville, New York, had invented a game, a way literally to pass the time inside the codified world of Andover. He would time his walks to Cochran chapel, almost flirting with the rules in a quiet kind of way, listening to the bells ringing, calling out the five-minute deadline for an assembly. If he timed it just right, he would be entering through the chapel door with just one second to go before it was locked. He was, in a way, courting disaster. A student who missed chapel accumulated black marks. Anyone with enough black marks got expelled. Rushing to beat the increasingly insistent bell, students such as Marshall could sometimes see Bush and others in the doorway, hands on the door, ready to slam it shut. Some upperclassmen had been assigned the task of closing the door on anyone who was late, trying to catch anyone outside and then scurrying to close the doors . . . and there was nowhere else to go on campus when the doors slammed.

Bob Marshall's resolute affinity for Andover would last through the years, and it would be manifested by his diligently taking time out from his law career to compile the "class notes" for the Phillips Class of 1964. He remembered Bush:

> I'm sure he took some things seriously, but he was more interested in social standing than what grades he had to get in order to get into Yale. By the time I got there, there was an in crowd, experienced or pretending to be experienced with girls, with liquor, with driving, with all the things associated with being adults. They would walk around with a certain confidence, bravado, a little swagger . . . wouldn't include others at their table or at their group or their activities. Everyone else in the group had some other thing going for him that was useful, so-and-so was a good basketball player, so-and-so was a good hockey player. There wasn't anything else that George was known for or could do, so that's why he identified with that cool-guy image. He wasn't a scholar, he wasn't a leader, he wasn't a good athlete. He would call people names, derogatory nicknames. Other people would use them behind people's backs, but he was more open about it.[27]

In the pent-up environment of Andover, sarcasm became almost a common method of communication: "The Andover atmosphere of sarcasm was sort of the language we spoke. When anybody did something good, the first comment was always something bad. Just to sort of even everything out. It was always sort of all done in kidding. Certainly George shared that with the rest of us," said dormmate James Lockhart III.[28]

BUSH TOLD people that he had decided to devote himself to two principal extracurricular activities, and they would become the roles that most of his fellow students would remember him for: head cheerleader and "high commissioner" of a popular intramural stickball league. The cheerleaders were an eight-man aggregation who carried megaphones to the Andover-Exeter football games while fluctuating between perfect prep school passion and perfect prep school cynicism. "We were a pretty cynical crowd back then. I would say they were probably not emblematic of school spirit—maybe the embodiment of some otherworldly spirit," suggested

Henry Hobson III, whose grandfather was president of Andover's board of trustees.[29] In the Andover yearbook there would be the requisite photos: Bush as the head cheerleader, leading his squad in the traditional prank of stuffing themselves into a telephone booth; Bush and his cheer squad posing, in a row, as they straddled a tree limb. In the free-form narratives that frequently fill the pages of high school yearbooks, there would be mention of *"Bush and his gang. A Heck of a lot of spirit from them."*[30] His friends, including Doug Brown, felt that Bush had found his perfect métier: "It was a role, it was perfect for him.[31]

But during the holiday and spring breaks back in Houston, it was not something that Bush would bring up very often. Friends rarely heard him mention cheerleading, and years later, many of them were surprised when they learned he had been a cheerleader, though some were not surprised to hear that he had been the head cheerleader. "Texans have a hard time relating to male cheerleaders," he would say.[32]

One day, the entire student body was ordered to assemble for another football game pep rally, and Jeff Stripling, a reflective, intellectual student from Fort Worth who had grown up with Clay Johnson, was wondering what Bush had planned. The room was buzzing, and finally Bush burst through the gymnasium door and across the floor dressed as a mop-top version of one of the Beatles. There were, thought Stripling, only a few people at Andover who were apt to do the same thing—who were as apt as George W. Bush to sprint through his years at the school immersed in the "process" of being a student. "That's the thing I remember most about him. I was more interested in the subject material, and he was more interested in the process. It's very hard to get below the surface of George, he is so facile and so personable. . . . He was already who he was, but being at Andover gave him a chance to hone his skills."[33]

AT THE END of the 1962–63 school year, his father and mother had told George W. that they had had summertime plans for him: they were sending him to the Quarter Circle XX Ranch in the middle of the high Ponderosa Pines in northern Arizona, eight miles southeast of the small town of Williams, about thirty miles west of Flagstaff. The XX Ranch was in the hands of the family of U.S. Senator John Greenway and his wife, U.S. Representative Isabella Greenway. The Greenways, who had accumulated an Arizona copper-mining fortune, had once consulted with Prescott Bush's investment firm in New York. And their son Jack had been a faithful, albeit competitive, roommate of the elder George Bush at Andover, someone who seemed to consistently place just ahead of the elder George

Bush in the internal student polls over who was really the most influential student at Phillips Academy.

Jack Greenway and the elder George Bush had also attended Yale together and had remained in close contact, even as Bush began charting ways to move beyond Houston and follow Prescott Bush into the U.S. Senate. Bush and other friends from Yale and Andover frequently asked if Greenway would take their children off their hands for the summer and let them stay at the ranch, a place that Greenway liked to use as a cool-weather getaway from his businesses in Tucson. Through the Greenways' Ivy League and political ties, the ranch had attracted visits from various senators and from President Franklin Delano Roosevelt and Eleanor Roosevelt—the first lady was especially close to Isabella Greenway. Pictures commemorating the Roosevelts' extended visits were prominently displayed at the main ranch house.

The plan was to have George W. work at the 225-square-mile spread, set at an elevation of almost seven thousand feet, close to Red Horse Wash and the San Francisco Mountains, helping to build fences to corral the nine hundred head of cattle and do anything else that ranch foreman Thurman Mays ordered the $200-a-month dude rancher from the eastern prep school to do. George W.'s roommate that summer in the woods near the Kaibab National Forest was the imperturbable Peter Neumann, a nephew of Jack Greenway and someone who came to the XX for five summers. They shared a small room in one of the ranch's two cottages, which stood a quarter mile away from the main house. The wood-sided bunkhouse had four bedrooms; other ranch employees, including Jack Greenway's chauffeur, lived in the other rooms.

Neumann quickly realized that the sixteen-year-old Bush had never had any real experience riding work horses. To Neumann, Bush was an easterner, not a Texan. "He was an easterner, really. He was, you know, a preppy," said Neumann. "He was smart enough to not be a snob."[34]

Each morning the two would get marching orders from Mays, who had worked on the ranch for four decades. Mays, who had grown up on a spread in New Mexico, had had very little formal education but was a dignified, expert ranch hand who left most people with the impression of a self-formed Renaissance man. Neumann, in awe of the almost ambassadorial cowboy, was amazed to hear Bush shouting, *"Hey, Thurman, what's your cousin Willie Mays like?"*[35]

Neumann knew that Mays and the other working ranch hands treated summer visitors with a light touch. The mood would soften, especially in the evenings, when family members, visitors, the chauffeur, and the ranch hands would gather for dinner in the main house. After the meal, some would retire to chairs by the fireplace and join in songfests. Neumann thought of it as a quaint, old-fashioned Victorian atmosphere, different from the times when he and the Andover student drove into the small town of Williams, with its maybe 2,000 residents, and "hung around and raised hell. Went to a movie, hung around, tried to get served illegally in the local bar, whatever."[36]

One day, out on the trail, Neumann killed a rattlesnake and cut the rattle off. Before going to sleep, he placed the rattle on a side table next to his bunkhouse bed. In the middle of the night, a field mouse approached the rattle, grabbed it, and began skittering across the floor. It sounded almost like a rattlesnake moving in the night. "George just went right through the roof. He woke up and thought his end was near. I mean, his life flashed before his eyes, I guess. All his plans to follow in the footsteps of his father . . . oh, he just said a lot of expletives. I went back to sleep, but the next morning he hadn't gone back to sleep yet. He was so scared. He thought I was a son of a bitch for having that on my side table. He just had a fit."[37]

That summer, Neumann felt that "it was clear—he idolized his father. I think he wanted to do everything he could to be just like his dad. He wanted to play baseball just like his dad did. He wanted to go to Yale, just like his dad did. And he was the first son, that was important, and so he was going to do just like his dad. And his dad wanted him to." That summer of 1963, Bush also confided to his roommate that his father's goal was to be president. Neumann was well aware of the extensive political history surrounding the ranch, the way that senators, congressmen, and even a president had made it their getaway.

It was fitting, in a way, that the young Bush's father had presidential aspirations; maybe the young Bush also had his own political ambitions. Neumann felt that he already knew enough about the Bush family after meeting the first son sent from Andover to Arizona. "My impression was that he [the elder Bush] wanted the status but . . . wasn't an active ideological animal. I think his son's the same way."[38]

BACK AT SCHOOL in the fall of 1963, Bush settled into America House, where he was appointed the proctor, essentially an upperclassman designated to be the student representative of the elegant, old dormitory. He was still distinctly absent from many on-campus political groups or debates. His wide-faced roommate was John Edgar Kidde, a football-playing Californian whose Andover nickname was "Moondoggie." With Bush, the two linked up with the Torques, a popular on-campus rock band that played loose versions of fraternity garage-rock tunes, highlighted by Henry Hobson III, grandson of an Episcopalian bishop, barking out the nonsense lyrics to the Trashmen's hit novelty tune "Surfin' Bird": *The bird is the word.* Bush wasn't a full-fledged musician; he was one of the leaders of the Torques Clappers, the people onstage who provided background rhythm and who were invited to a photo session at Logan Airport in Boston—one of the Torques had convinced his father, a pilot, to make arrangements for the band to be photographed standing on the wing of an airliner.

That senior year, there were sedate school mixers, with prep girls from nearby Abbot Academy lined up across the dance floor and the punchbowls filled with what somebody said was treacle. Johnny Mathis records were outlawed because they might lead to groping on the shadowy margins of the mixer. The joke was that either the men at Andover were gentlemen or they didn't remember. Back in the dining halls, dressed in coats and ties, the Andover students were putting pats of butter on their silverware and flipping the yellow rockets onto the ceiling so they would eventually fall onto someone's head.

In 1963, at the invitation of politically interested students, Barry Goldwater came to the campus to speak at a special evening assembly; many students walked away impressed that Goldwater wasn't as rabid as they had been led to believe. In America House, Kidde was stunned to see Goldwater's strident warning shot to weak-limbed Republicans, *The Conscience of a Conservative*, sitting on his roommate's desk. When the Californian confronted him about it, Bush said that the elder Bush had told him to pick up a copy.[39]

That fall of 1963, the basketball team had a game scheduled against the Amherst College freshmen; the starting players on most of Andover's sports teams were good enough to compete with those of area colleges. One of the Andover guards was injured, and Coach DiClemente, who had always known that the elder George Bush was a better athlete than his son, finally said, "George, looks like you're going to start today." George W.'s face lit up. He played, as usual, with energy. After the team stepped off the bus, back at Andover, his parents were waiting in the parking lot. "Well, your kid did a helluva job today," DiClemente said.

"Well, what did you expect?" replied Barbara Bush.[40]

That fall, the assassination of President John F. Kennedy, coupled with ongoing nuclear concerns, pierced some of the staid walls of Andover—though his friends and acquaintances later said that young Bush hadn't mentioned the events and they hadn't seemed to affect him as deeply as some of the other students: "I was playing squash, and someone leaned over the fence and said he'd [Kennedy] been shot," said Jose Gonzalez-Inclan, who had spent time with Bush at Grandfather Pierce's house in Rye, New York, during the prep school tennis tourneys. "I had nightmares about nuclear bombs. I woke up at night. We were all young. It felt like the world was ending."[41]

By the end of the fall semester, Bush was back home in Houston, and on New Year's Eve he went to a party with the reassembling old friends who had taken their breaks from St. John's and Kinkaid. Doug Hannah instantly gravitated toward Bush's side and watched him work the room, as always. Hannah kept insisting that they leave; the high schoolers had reservations for an early-morning flight from Houston to Dallas so that they could watch the annual Cotton Bowl football game. As usual, thought the impatient Hannah, Bush had to enter and exit a party like a politician. There was something else, thought Hannah and some of the other people in Bush's Houston circles. With college on the horizon, several of them were unclear what the young Bush was expecting or leaning toward later in life. "I don't think he spent a lot of time discussing 'what I want to be when I grow up.' I don't think he sat down with a big circle of friends and had any introspective talks," said Lacey Neuhaus, a stockbroker's daughter who had met George W. right after the Bushes had moved to Houston and whose family helped oversee the exclusive Bayou Club.[42]

AT ANDOVER, in America House, on the cheerleading squad, in the stick-ball league, it was simply assumed that George W. was eventually going to be admitted to Yale: his grandfather sat on Yale's board of trustees and his father had essentially left a legacy at Yale the equal of the one he had left at Andover in the 1940s. But a story also circulated that one of the Andover officials, perhaps Dean of Students Grenville Benedict, had summoned George W. to his office and talked about collegiate choices.[43] It was reportedly suggested to Bush that he think about applying to, and perhaps attending, a school other than Yale.

In the spring of 1964, he saw those same Houston friends during the school break. He ran into the ubiquitous Hannah, the person who always seemed to be ready to enjoy the moment with Bush, and they talked about where they were going to college, where they were going to be admitted. In George W.'s circles in Houston, Yale enjoyed a cachet, and several of his friends were openly expressing the same thought being voiced at Andover: that he was destined for the exact college that his father, grandfather, and many others in the Bush-Walker family had attended. But George W. kept insisting to some Houston friends that he wanted to be a "Longhorn"—he really wanted to move to Austin and attend the University of Texas. It was the same thing at almost every spring break party, Bush talking about his ardor for the state university. Hannah was suspicious, wondering if Bush was worried whether his career at Andover had spiked any chances of going to Yale. "The most amazing thing about George is that he was a master of hedging every single thing he did, which is kind of a stockbroker's ability. When he was getting out of Andover, he wanted to go to Yale but he hadn't been accepted yet. So, at spring break, he talked up the University of Texas, saying it was his first choice and where he wanted to go, what he wanted to do, because I don't think he thought he would get into Yale. And I knew it was all bullshit. He really wanted to go to Yale."

Once he was accepted at Yale, Hannah "never heard him mention Texas again."[44]

AT ANDOVER, there was an outlet for the bottled-up energy in those final few months in the form of the springtime stickball league, "a loose confederation of lesser athletes."[45] The largest student-devised activity on campus, it was a semiserious, elaborate series of stickball games held after classes let out. Bush's cousin Kevin Rafferty, a son of Barbara Bush's sister Martha, thought it was all painstakingly elaborate: "The way to think about it is that this league, this activity, had no official connection to the school, but it was very important. We used broom handles, fungo bats, whatever, and it was taken very seriously, but there were also lots of baroque additions. The uniforms were very creative, and the accouterments were all taken quite seriously. The commissioner was like the czar. It wasn't a democratic kind of thing."[46]

In time it evolved into a quasi-official activity with dozens of teams, different rankings, statistics, and categories—all intentionally lampooning the bloated aura of Tammany Hall. Bush was named the high commissioner of the stickball league, and at the mock meetings, he presided in a stovepipe hat and doled out decisions, favors, and rulings. People began calling him "Lip" and "Tweeds"—as in Boss Tweed, the infamous grand sachem and patriarch of paternalistic corruption during the days when the Democratic political machine was using New York as a personal banking account. "You could tell he was destined for leadership. It was a very political position. Unless he got the rules right, we didn't play," said classmate Henry Hobson.[47]

Each of the Andover dormitories fielded teams, sometimes several teams, including one squad named the Crotch Rots and another named the Stimson Steamers, an irreverent nod to Secretary of War Henry Stimson and the way fresh dog turds steam in the snow. On occasion, Bush's assistants would carry him to rallies or out on the field on their shoulders. Then Bush would stand up and "speak some nonsense at the school assembly. It wasn't heavy lifting, but it was a socially important role," said Bob Marshall.[18] "He sort of liked to be a little bit of a showman. He liked being liked, or getting people to like him, and it was one of those things where everybody in the whole school would know who you are," remembered Tory Peterson. "I guess sarcasm was the chief method of saying things for people in the class in general, but he was fairly good at it."[49]

Randall Roden, his childhood friend from Midland, thought the seemingly silly position of high commissioner—what it meant, what it implied—said many things about George W. Bush, and even about his father. His involvement as high commissioner was really the thing that defined him for some people at Andover: "Being stickball commissioner revealed Bush's personality. He was a figurehead, well suited to deal with a diverse group. He bridged and brought them together. Bush was slightly impulsive, it was hard for him to bite his tongue and keep from saying something that would get him in trouble. It was a completely different heritage than his father's. His dad was from an oligarchic background. GWB was a prankster, mischievous."[50]

AT GRADUATION in June 1964, some students were fully aware that other seniors had thought about putting faculty members' cars inside the Copley Wing of the library. It was glass-enclosed, so the cars would be visible from the outside. The books for the grinding precollege American history course were inside the library. It would be, thought some students, an inevitable, symbolic prank. The library, with the cornerstone tomes of an Andover education inside, would look like an auto showroom, complete with French Professor Markey's 1964 Mustang.

The graduating yearbook in the library that year had two mentions of George W. Bush, including one joke reference to the phantom, rarely seen publication called *NELM:*

> Commissioner Bush and Umpire Hight . . . were instrumental in enabling NELM (the New England Literary Magazine) to maintain its high standard of non-existence, although they spent most of their time in corrupting the League.[51]

And:

> We had some hot athletes, but much credit goes to Bush and his
> gang. A heck of a lot of spirit from them. . . . I remember those Bea-
> tle skits.[52]

Kemper, of course, had prepared carefully for the June graduation.
The students, including Seth Mydans, a future foreign correspondent for
The New York Times, wondered what Kemper's final words to them would
be after they had followed the class officers in double file from Flagstaff
Court through the Commons and past the Bell Tower to the steps of
Samuel Phillips Hall, before which the seniors, alumni, and faculty took
their seats. Eighteen new members were inducted into the Cum Laude
Society. Then Kemper stepped to the podium. He honored two retiring
teachers, suggesting that they were men of style. He also offered to define
exactly what he meant by style, by what he meant when he wished that Andover men would be known for their sense of style. "It has to do with distinction in manner and bearing, with excellence and originality in all sorts
of expression," he said. "You are a proud group in a proud school. That
pride will be sustained if you take with you a sense of style."[53]

Years later, Mydans would remember that day, the final speech that
George W. Bush and others would hear, and how there seemingly had not
been much mention of principles or convictions.[54]

AFTER GRADUATION, the students were on the way, by and large, to Ivy
League schools. There were forty-nine going to Harvard, thirty to Yale,
twenty to Princeton, and several more to Columbia, Dartmouth, Brown,
and Penn. Clay Johnson told his friend that he would be joining Bush at
Yale, and they talked about the possibility of being roommates. But immediately after the graduation ceremonies, the younger Bush was scheduled to return to Houston. In 1962, Prescott Bush had announced to the
family that he had decided to not run for reelection to the Senate and that
when he stepped down in 1963 he was going to spend more time playing
golf, traveling, and sailing with Dottie and other Bush-Walker relatives in
Connecticut, Maine, or Jupiter Island, Florida. "Fortunately, we have able
younger men available," he said when he made his decision.[55]

At almost the exact same time as Prescott Bush's announcement,
George Herbert Walker Bush decided to enter politics in Houston by
running for the chair of the Harris County Republican Party—and in a
move that would exactly parallel a later event in his own son's political life,

a Houston newspaper promptly ran a photograph of "George Bush" that was, in fact, a photograph of someone else. By the time Prescott Bush officially left his Senate seat in early 1963, the elder George Bush was committed to making the dramatic move from his county GOP seat to his own run for the U.S. Senate. The heady leap from being a fledgling county overseer for the GOP to becoming a Senate candidate in Texas was never openly questioned by Prescott Bush or many others in the Bush-Walker network. Prescott had vaulted from town moderator to U.S. senator, and now the arching sense was that this was the same, appropriate window of political opportunity—especially in a less rigid state where the Bushes had achieved so much in little over a decade.

And with his first son graduating from his old preparatory school and eventually headed to Yale, the elder George Bush wanted him back in Houston, at his side, on his first full-time campaign trail, traveling into the complexities of Texas.

5

The Arrogance

By the summer of 1964, Secretary of Defense Robert McNamara had returned from South Vietnam, recommending a stepped-up military presence; Ho Chi Minh called the statement "sheer stupidity." National Guardsmen had sprayed tear gas on blacks protesting a visit to Maryland by Alabama Governor George Wallace. The Congress of Racial Equality announced major plans to demonstrate at both national political conventions, to "combat poverty and despair." Nelson Mandela was given a life sentence in South Africa. In Texas, the state's first GOP presidential preference poll was won by Senator Barry Goldwater. And in the small Texas Hill Country town of Johnson City, President Johnson delivered the commencement address at the school from which he had graduated in 1924. He was in the bosom of rural Texas and Old Democrat country. He talked about the future, one in which "every child will grow up knowing that success in life depends on ability and not on the color of skin or the circumstance of birth."[1]

In July 1964, just after his birthday, George W. embarked on his first full-fledged political foray when he boarded a bus caravan called "The Bandwagon for Bush." The elder George Bush told friends he wanted his eighteen-year-old first son by his side; the other children, starting with the next oldest, eleven-year-old Jeb, were too young to accompany him. At home, the family was also especially concerned about Neil's dyslexia, diagnosed two years earlier. Under the campaign direction of Midland attorney Martin Allday, the Bushes were taking their rolling parade to forty cities in Texas, from Houston to Quanah to Abilene, places without any deep Republican roots and where longtime, lockstep Democrats kept a cautious eye on newcomers to the state.[2]

It was George W. Bush's first introduction to extended Texas, not just the strange hybrid in Midland, where so many families had profited and succeeded in reinventing good chunks of their former lives in the Northeast, and not the urban mix in Houston, the biggest and most international of Texas cities. That summer, in the energy-sapping heat rising up in town after town, George W. dutifully listened as his father announced that he was actively opposed to LBJ's civil rights bill, to the Nuclear Test Ban Treaty, to increases in foreign aid, and to "wildly spending money on antipoverty programs"—and that he supported a war in Vietnam, a Cuban exile government, and a U.S. withdrawal from the United Nations if China were admitted. At one stop, his father described Martin Luther King Jr. as a "militant" whose civil rights movement had been bankrolled by union money.[3] The confident, well-funded road show crisscrossed the prairies and plains of Texas, and sometimes the gangly, grinning Bush would reluctantly step to the front of the stage with the Bush Bluebonnet Belles, a coterie of cheerleading Republican women.

In the mid-1960s, Texas was in a wary, precarious mind-set, unsure how to distance itself from the lingering impressions left behind by Lee Harvey Oswald, Jack Ruby, and all the other players and scenes that had emerged several months earlier on Commerce Street, in the Texas Theatre, inside Parkland Hospital in Dallas. Blame for the Kennedy assassination was being laid from one corner of Texas to the other, and there was also an emerging, palpable sense among many Texans that the entire state was being cruelly stigmatized and stereotyped, especially by the national media and its representatives in the Northeast. Into that uneasy environment, George W. took his first public political turns within a transplanted family of easterners. Many voters were more than alert to the presence of outsiders arriving in the state and presumably bent on easy analysis, and some of those Texas voters were also craving uniquely xenophobic Lone Star allegiances and assurances.

In the great Texas tradition, mastered by flamboyant Governor W. Lee "Pappy" O'Daniel, of having big-time musical caravans push across the state, the Bush campaign had the Black Mountain Boys, romping through C&W tunes for the rambling entourage, oozing old-style politicking at stop after stop across the heart of Texas, with the Bush Bluebonnet Belles crooning, *"Oh, the sun's gonna shine in the Senate someday! George Bush is going to chase them liberals away!"*[4]

• • •

IN THE Bushes' two-story brick house, campaign material was stacked everywhere, and Bush's many friends from Houston, the people in that extended network of private school students, were helping out, hanging around, amazed at the family's organizational tendencies—staring into the room where Barbara Bush had already stacked, in June, dozens of carefully wrapped Christmas presents. At the Zapata Off-Shore office in the Houston Club Building, it was almost the same scene, people coming and going, the elder Bush moving, calling, occasionally upsetting the lower-rung employees who wanted him to sit still, to study the big oil industry picture. People were continuing to wash into Houston from the Northeast, and the city solidified its deserved reputation as the brawny, snarling petrochemical command post of America. Houston entered the ranks of America's ten largest cities, and the southwestern suburbs of the city filled with more people who seemed dissatisfied with and often suspicious of the entrenched, old-style Southern Democratic political machinery.

The Texas version of the Democratic Party was, many newcomers conceded, probably conservative in terms of family values but maybe not entirely supportive of business interests. Worse, it was prone to occasionally giving lip service to the new crusades spurred on by the labor unions and civil rights activists. Moving the Bush-Walker political fortunes beyond Connecticut and getting started in Republican politics in Houston in the mid-1960s was easier than it had been in Midland in the early 1950s, even though Texas nominally remained a one-party state. Houston was a place of spiraling growth where even zoning rules were frowned upon as unnecessarily regulatory, as confining, as almost something antithetical to the U.S. Constitution. In Houston, by God, if somebody wanted to build something, a skyscraper if he pleased, he should be able to do it anywhere, in the middle of any damned block imaginable. Houston was also a place where the John Birch Society could and truly did prosper. Most important, it was a city effectively dominated by big-oil interests that were fiercely resistant to the twin ogres of taxation and regulation. There was, without question, an unbridled belief in the downtown hierarchy that what was good for big oil, what would make it grow and prosper, would have a salutary trickle-down effect for everyone. Houston was also a city with pronounced racial undertones exacerbated by a yawning economic disparity; it was a sometimes fearful, polarized place that was ripe for a conservative Republican looking to raise funds for a Senate campaign, especially against liberal Senator Ralph Yarborough, who could be portrayed as a rampaging leftist consumed by dangerous inclinations in unpredictable times.[5]

GEORGE W. knew that his father had wanted to run for office, that, as he had told Peter Neumann, his father had aspirations beyond being a senator from Texas. And the family, even the extended clan in the Northeast, recognized that Houston and, broadly speaking, Texas represented the best opportunity for his father to immediately follow Prescott Bush to Capitol Hill. Texas GOP pioneer John Tower had been elected in a special election in 1961, taking over the Senate seat that LBJ had abandoned on his way to the vice presidency. Republican Jack Cox, though he had lost, had performed well in the gubernatorial race against John Connally in 1962. Republican prospects were improving, keeping pace with Texas's growth. But the Texas political landscape grew complicated when Johnson took office after the Kennedy assassination. LBJ, if he could win the presidency on his own, would probably lead a sweep against Republicans all over Texas. Republicans braced for a backlash from people who linked the polarized times to Goldwater, to intolerant right-wingers disguised as GOP candidates. The trick then in Texas, as it would be for years, was to continue to pander to the Right but to court the moderates. Some Republicans, such as Barbara Bush, wished that Kennedy's assassin was from the far Left and not the far Right. Years later, she wrote in her memoirs, "We are hoping that it is not some far right nut, but a commie nut."[6]

The elder George Bush, courteous, insistent, and without any elected experience, had developed enormous resources in the extended white-collar business community that stretched into the Houston Country Club, the Bayou Club, the Ramada Club, and even the Episcopalian congregations. One key ally was Robert Mosbacher, the Houston millionaire oilman and family friend who would serve the elder George Bush over the years as finance and general campaign chairman in presidential elections and as secretary of commerce. He was somebody the elder George Bush really liked, could really relate to, the way Mosbacher had rolled the dice and come to Texas from the Northeast, even though he had all those deep social connections to the Newport yachting scene.[7] Mosbacher was fascinated by the Bush family, by the older George Bush's sense of style, and now it was impossible to ignore the political possibilities in the younger George Bush: "He was always very quick to catch on, very willing to be a part of it," he recalled.[8] George W.'s teenage friends saw it too, the way he was behaving around his father during the campaign. "He was very discreet. I never heard him confide things that shouldn't be confided. He had his father's confidence because he handled himself judiciously," said Lacey Neuhaus, who volunteered to work on the Bush campaigns.[9]

As the first son regarded his father's ascension in Midland, in Houston, he felt that it was easy to describe him, even to draw an accurate portrait of what his father must have been like when he was his age. His father, he told people, was always better at what he was doing than almost anyone around him, starting from when he had been a much younger man: "He was a star. He was a young man with a reputation for being considerate and polite but at the same time a person of tremendous abilities."[10]

IN THE FALL OF 1964, George W. entered his first year at Yale and was assigned to a room reserved for freshmen in the historic cluster of buildings known as Old Campus. Owing to their Andover ties, his two roommates were lanky Clay Johnson from Fort Worth and Robert Dieter, who had played football at Andover and was the son of a small-town physician from Eustis, Florida. Their first days together, while Dieter and Johnson set about divvying up the space, Bush headed out of the room: "out on the campus meeting people. Within three to four days a big percent of the people knew who he was."[11] Dieter, sometimes nicknamed "Kraut" at Andover, had played junior varsity football with Bush at their prep school, and they had gravitated toward each other because they were comfortable with their ties to small towns far beyond the Northeast and because they felt "outnumbered and overwhelmed culturally."[12]

The Yale campus was filled with constant, almost daily reminders that George W.'s father was immersed in an ideological tug-of-war in GOP politics, meshing Prescott Bush's and Nelson Rockefeller's moderate tendencies with Goldwater's harder edge. The *Yale Daily News* was also dominated by front-page stories about campus debates, forums, and lectures that were spilling beyond the usual arenas in Washington and consuming other universities and households: the conflict in Southeast Asia, civil rights, nuclear proliferation. Well-publicized announcements went up on campus that there would be high-profile visits from Senator Hubert Humphrey, from Republican vice presidential candidate William Miller's family, from several other Senate or congressional candidates. A week before George W. left New Haven to return to Houston in order to help his father in the last days of the Senate contest, the *Yale Daily News* also prominently displayed the results of a comprehensive on-campus poll. It showed that 73 percent of Bush's freshman class favored President Johnson over Barry Goldwater. The news that the campus was tilting away from the GOP and Goldwater, who had traveled to Texas along with Richard Nixon to support Bush's father, caused an immediate stir: "The generally held theory is that a freshman comes to college with a conservative orientation in his personal life, and then is influenced by a liberal faculty and friends and thus becomes more liberal," Richard L. Meritt, assistant professor of political science, told campus reporters. "Our figures are in direct contradiction to this and that's why I find the data so fascinating."[13]

On election day, the student newspaper presented a lengthy list of minibiographies of the many Yale alumni who were running for high office, including George Bush, Thomas Dodd, George Murphy, William Proxmire, Stuart Symington, Robert Taft, John Chafee, and Winthrop Rockefeller. The first biography listed on the front page of the *Yale Daily News* was about George W.'s father: "Mr. Bush is young, energetic, and very conservative, and a victory over liberal incumbent Ralph Yarborough would make him a power in the GOP. And a victory is quite likely."[14] Also on the front page of the student newspaper were the "Yale Results of Senate Contests." Each of the dozen dormitories, or colleges, had voted in its own mock Senate elections, and his father's fate was played out before his eyes, on campus, in the newspaper. In Davenport, the dormitory he would eventually move into, 89 students voted for the elder Bush, 59 for Yarborough. Several other dormitories were staunchly in favor of Yarborough, but the final campuswide totals showed 1,218 for Bush and 1,127 for Yarborough. In his first weeks at Yale, his father's name, his father's future, were impossible to avoid in the newspaper, in the trophy cases, in the photos of Yale's nationally known baseball teams, in the membership rosters at Skull & Bones. His grandfather's legacy as a student was not as fresh in many minds, but many people on the all-male campus recognized Prescott Bush as a Yale trustee and as the long-time senator from Connecticut.

IN NOVEMBER, George W. took off for a long weekend, returning to Houston and taking on the job of monitoring the election-night returns. Yarborough, leery of the surprising bustle within the Texas Republican ranks, had been launching broadsides in late summer and early fall. His attacks were, by definition, attacks on the Bush-Walker house, stretching to George W.'s father's brothers, to Herbert Walker on Wall Street and directly to Prescott Bush, whom George W. had come to view as almost larger than life, as the dignified, symbolic heart of the family. The Yarborough strategists had decided to also play to the antigovernment, antiregulatory passions in Texas and to simultaneously portray the Bush family as the consummate gilded clan from the Northeast, the quintessential insiders who had recently arrived in Texas and made it their financial and political playground. The Bush campaign was clearly unfamiliar with and unprepared for the populist onslaught, especially when its candidate and the Bushes and Walkers were described as "carpetbaggers"—"tools of the eastern kingmakers," with easily traced roots in northeastern money circles, in private schools such as Andover and Yale, in the society quarters of Greenwich, Rye, Kennebunkport, and other places far away from Texas.[15]

Through the final week of the campaign, the Lone Star Democrats continued to make repeated references to the fact that George Bush and his family had prospered well beyond the Red River; with these came sometimes unsubtle suggestions that the Bush family was somehow part of some shadowy, omnipotent cabal of Washington- and New York–based industrialists and internationalists. Yarborough pushed the stereotype hard: *"Elect a senator from Texas, and not the Connecticut investment bankers."* George W.'s friends knew that he and his family were caught off balance and had been virtually immune to the initial, occasional bits of resistance from the suspicious and sometimes jealous natives in West Texas. In the isolated, small city of Midland, the Bushes had been able to grind down most of the animosity toward the Connecticut Yankees, and the rest of it had withered away when everyone, both the native-born and the easterners, focused on the common denominator of the oil patch. Now, in a statewide race, George W. heard the family name, what the family stood for, being savaged as elitist, as foreign, just as his mother had once described it when she had written home in the late 1940s that West Texans could be "Easterner prejudiced."[16]

Yarborough also attacked the elder Bush's relationship to the Liedtke brothers and the massive Pennzoil Corporation, the oil conglomerate that had absorbed Zapata Off-Shore Petroleum the year before. The merger netted the Bush family a windfall in stock, and it allowed Yarborough an opportunity to tell Texas oilmen that Bush was linked with an international firm that was simply out to undercut the true, independent Texas wildcatters. Traveling into the East Texas oil fields, Yarborough asked a crowd in Gladewater if they were ready to vote for *"a carpetbagger from Connecticut who is drilling oil for the Sheik of Kuwait."*[17]

On election night at the Hotel America, George W. finally stepped to a board to pin up the returns for the growing crowd, including dozens of friends who had driven for hours from Midland. Each time he displayed another set of numbers, he knew his father was losing. By 11:30 P.M., it was clear that Yarborough was surging ahead and on his way to a crushing

300,000-vote victory margin. Closer to midnight, his father assembled the family and the handful of Texas oil millionaires who had funded his campaign and told them he was ready to concede. The campaign visits by Goldwater hadn't been enough to put him in office, and more than a few people in Texas suggested that they had in fact added to the lingering portrait of him as a handpicked opportunist dispatched by the northeastern establishment. Texas had clearly offered singular political problems for the Bush campaign, especially the fact that its candidate hadn't understood the uniquely Lone Star brand of provincialism. The voters rejected Bush because of who he was, what the Bush-Walker family symbolized, not precisely because of what he proposed. It was an extraordinary revelation, one that would linger with the first son through his college years and through each of the five political campaigns he would aggressively explore in Texas.

Standing with the relatives that night in Houston, George W. listened to his father, who said: "I have been trying to think whom we could blame for this and regretfully conclude that the only one I can blame is myself."

He also listened as the candidate tried to salvage some meaning from his first enormous failure, one that paralleled Prescott Bush's first public defeat when Prescott had abruptly abandoned his position as town moderator in affluent Greenwich and embarked on his own Senate race in 1950. His father pointed to the large Republican turnout, more than 1.1 million voters, which was, at the time, the biggest GOP showing in state history. He had lifted the hem of the political tent a little higher in Texas, opening it for the Republicans coming to the state and the ones who would flock to it from the Democratic ranks for the next two decades. With John Tower he had essentially aided a resculpting of the Texas political model, chiseling room for the nonstop influx of politically disenchanted transplants to Texas, the ones arriving with Republican tendencies and a distrust of populist politics. He had helped prod the Republican Party onto its feet in Texas, and when he did, he made sure it would remain standing for future Republican candidates running for office in Texas on a deep cushion of cash from like-minded oilmen, globally concerned executives, and all the conservative women organizing in the big cities and the suburbs. The support of Earle Craig, the Liedtke brothers, Robert Mosbacher, and all the other millionaire investors who had also descended on Texas and made fortunes in the oil patch would be invaluable to furthering the political interests of the Bush family through the next three decades.

That night, as relatives consoled the candidate, George W.'s eyes began to water. A close friend in Houston, Doug Hannah, knew that George W. had truly wanted his father to follow his grandfather into the Senate. George W. was, said Hannah, embarrassed by his father's defeat. The next morning, George W.'s father was on the phone all day, calling people, keeping the network alive, still moving. Barbara, tears streaming down her face, made a date to play tennis . . . tennis, golf, that was what she told people she did when confronted with tragedy. George W. was headed back to Yale, a freshman whose oilman father had lost a race for the Senate to one of the last fiercely liberal and populist lawmakers to emerge from Texas.

ON CAMPUS after his return, the Friday edition of the *Yale Daily News* had the lead headline "Professors Feel GOP at Its Low."[18] For weeks, Yale faculty and students were openly engaged in soul-searching arguments and postmortems—in the Yale Republican Club, on the editorial pages of the paper, at open-forum gatherings scattered around the university. It was news that was hard to ignore, it was news that resonated on a campus beginning to gurgle with activism and the occasional public confrontation. Strolling across the Yale grounds in the wake of his father's failed bid, Bush recognized the increasingly famous William Sloane Coffin Jr., the university chaplain who had also been a member of the secret Skull & Bones Society and who had been granted the rare honor of being "tapped," or summoned, into the ancient society by the elder George Bush and others in 1948. The New York City–born Coffin, who had served in World War II and whose uncle was head of the Union Theological Seminary, had been growing vocal in his support of peace movements here and abroad, something that had received more than usual notice owing to the fact that Coffin had once worked for the CIA after graduating from Yale. Now Coffin was developing a reputation as an intellectual pacifist, someone who could bend the symbolism of Yale and become an effective ivory-tower emissary, a flexible voice from deep inside the old-guard firmament. Leaders in the student movement eventually saw him as a powerful and useful presence, someone who would be instrumental in bridging the Ivy League's gaps to the antiwar movement, to the critics of nuclear proliferation, to the leaders of the civil rights movement, especially Dr. Martin Luther King Jr.

That day, when he spied the chaplain, George W. made a point of approaching him and introducing himself. This was a man his father had helped induct into one of the most fraternal bonding societies at any university. That, by definition, made him a *Good Man*. The perpetually buoyant Bush, who was deliberately uninvolved in campus political circles, waited to hear what Coffin had to say.

The Yale chaplain would have recognized the Bush name. Yarborough's victory in Texas was seen by hopeful liberals as a solid sign that both the GOP moderates and the Goldwater extremists, the whole John Birch wing of the party, had been headed off at the pass. Yarborough's victory, Bush's loss, had been well documented and chewed over by dozens of students and professors at Yale.

"Oh, yes," Bush heard Coffin say. "I know your father. Frankly, he was beaten by a better man."[19]

Inside, Bush was roiling, shifting between shock and anger. Here, at Yale, things weren't supposed to happen this way. This was Yale, not some yahoo outback in the middle of Texas filled with sonofabitch hardball-playing Democrats who didn't know any better than to paint his father as a slave to Goldwater, a minion of John Birch, or even a Rockefeller Republican. This was Yale. His grandfather and father were Bonesmen—*Good Men*—just as Coffin had once been, just as Neil Mallon, just as all the Bush family members and friends. "God, Country and Yale" was the old slogan, and it could have been written about his father. Plenty of people on campus knew about the famous photo from his father's days as a Yale first baseman, the one where he was standing alongside a visiting Babe Ruth. On campus, there were plenty of faculty members, trustees, and students who knew about his father's war record, his Phi Beta Kappa record, and Coffin, of all people, should know about his father, his uncles, the Walkers.

For the next thirty-five years, that encounter with Coffin would resonate in Bush's mind. It was a moment when he was forced to confront the fact that he was following the exact same path as his father and grandfather but that the path was narrower and more complicated, filled with people who questioned what his parents and grandparents had seen as the natural, entitled order of things. It was maddening. He was infuriated by the intellectual arrogance.

"What angered me was the way such people at Yale felt so intellectually superior and so righteous," said Bush years afterward. "They thought they had all the answers. They thought they could create a government that could solve all our problems for us. These are the ones who felt so guilty that they had been given so many blessings in life—like an Andover or a Yale education—that they felt they should overcompensate by trying to give everyone else in life the same thing."

He was repulsed. He wanted to get away—"away from the snobs."[20]

Decades later, after hearing that Bush was telling people about a confrontation on the Yale campus, Coffin would send Bush a carefully typed, four-sentence letter from his home in Strafford, Vermont. Coffin said that he didn't remember the incident but that if he said it had occurred, he believed him and was sorry about the way it had turned out. He wrote, in part, *"I have a hard time imagining my saying to you—and with the utmost seriousness—'your father was beaten by a better man.'"* Coffin ended his letter by asking Bush "to forgive what you cannot condone."[21]

Two weeks after he received Coffin's letter, the first son scratched out a short, handwritten reply: *"I believe my recollection is correct. But, I also know time passes, and I bear no ill will."*[22]

HE HAD enrolled in English, philosophy, political science, geology, Spanish, and astronomy courses. Political Science 13B, with Professor H. Bradford Westerfield, was a "study of competitive co-existence, the Communist challenge and the Western response—military, economic and political. The diplomatic significance of weapons systems and war strategies since 1940. Trade and economic aid, propaganda and subversive intrigue in underdeveloped areas," according to the college catalog. "He took it in the second term of freshman year along with hundreds of other students, and he did not perform well in the class," said Professor Westerfield. "He was, I would think, probably about the twenty-fifth percentile up from the bottom of the class. He was just getting his feet on the ground, so to speak, on the campus. I would not want to have the impression left that I think he's a fool. Quite the contrary, he was quite bright to go as far as he has subsequently, and he may indeed have accomplished a lot while he was still a student at Yale."[23]

Early on, Bush realized something about his academic life, something that he thought also applied to his sister, Dorothy, and his brothers, Jeb, Marvin, and Neil: "I was never a great intellectual. I like books and pick them up and read them for the fun of it. I think all of us are basically in the same vein. We're not real serious, studious readers. We are readers for fun."[24]

Robert Dieter always felt as if he could understand Bush's academic tendencies; he reminded Dieter of some people Dieter had grown up with in the Deep South. "Some guy might go to Yale and say I got the greatest book-learning education. I think George really thrived on people and thrived on the environment. He was the kind of person who knew what was going on, he wasn't the kind of person who was over in the library trying to perfect his paper on the British revolution of 1420," he said.[25]

Dozens of Yale classmates, including future New York Governor George Pataki, future Deputy Secretary of State Strobe Talbott, future White House Counsel Lanny Davis, and future Massachusetts Senator John Kerry, would immerse themselves in the politics-and-journalism subculture on campus. Several groups held regular meetings, among them the 160-member Young Republicans Club, the Young Democrats, the Political Union, the Yale Civil Rights Council, the Calliopean Society, the Republican Advance, the Alternative, Young Americans for Freedom, the Conservative Club, and the Socialist Union. Various graduate schools, including the law school, also had their own Republican clubs. There was the well-organized Ripon Society, an organization of young Republicans based in the Boston area but with extensive ties to Yale and New Haven. The university was obviously no different from many other major campuses; the number of students attracted to the political organizations rose in direct proportion to the complexities unfolding in Vietnam, Watts, and Alabama. If there was a difference at Yale, it was the fact that the university, almost a factory for producing future politicians, already had an extraordinarily varied set of forums in which to debate the issues of the day.

Bush instead signed up for an intramural football squad and the Social Council. He played club rugby. He learned that a soccer team star was grieving over his mother's death; Bush didn't know the player very well, but he went through Old Campus getting people to sign a condolence card. At Thanksgiving, on his way to New York with James Lockhart III, another old friend from Andover now at Yale, George W. was unusually serious. He turned to Lockhart: "I want to make something out of myself at Yale," he said.[26]

Meanwhile, Clay Johnson continued to look for visible signs that his roommate was despondent over his father's well-publicized defeat for the Senate seat. But he was the same as when he had come back to Connecticut from that long weekend in Houston. There was still not a single mention of the defeat, just as there had been no discussion about his father's ambitions for the Senate and maybe the presidency. At Yale, his roommates rarely discussed politics. "I guess there were some people in college who had an interest in the Young Republicans or the Young Democrats or the Political Union, but George was never involved in any of that. George had expressed no interest in it and had no involvement in it," said Clay Johnson.[27]

In the spring of 1965, Bush tried pitching for the freshman baseball team, but he was a self-described "junkball" pitcher and it was instantly clear that he wasn't going to play at the same level as his father. It was the last university team he would play for.

IN HOUSTON, his father had thrown himself back into Zapata's offshore oil deals and also into an aggressive plan to keep his Senate campaign network alive by shifting it into a run for Congress. He also told George W. that he had arranged another summer position for him: he wanted George W. to get a taste for the same type of ground-level work in the oil kingdom that he had been exposed to when Prescott Bush had funded his own trip to Odessa, Texas, in the 1940s. The Bush family had some friends from south Louisiana, oilmen affiliated with a drilling company, energy industry veterans who said their insurance was handled by George W.'s uncle Prescott Bush Jr.

The nineteen-year-old Yale sophomore was being dispatched to work on an inland barge operated by Circle Drilling Company, based in Lake Charles[28]—an isolated blue-collar oil town that was essentially the Odessa of deep south Louisiana. Circle Drilling was a subsidiary of a petroleum network owned by two postwar fossil fuel giants, Mordelo Vincent Jr. and L. Lee Welch, a pair of occasionally over-the-top oil czars who cast a merry glow over much of the netherworld running along the Gulf coast from Houston, through Pirate Jean Lafitte's old hiding spots, and straight into New Orleans. Delo was a civil engineer out of the wild and woolly town of Tampico in northern Mexico, along the Gulf coast; Lee was a mercurial geophysicist from Texas. The first independent oilmen to drill offshore in the Gulf of Mexico, they were known as "the Thundering Herd" by admiring friends and relatives.

Companies such as Zapata that wanted to take a crack at offshore drilling knew enough to seek out Circle Drilling. It had been charting and mapping the coastal waters since 1945, and the old hands at the company knew more than almost anyone else about sucking oil from the Gulf floor—and also about the way hurricanes could unsettle everything. The Thundering Herd's reputation stretched all the way from their headquarters in Louisiana straight into the soothing, air-chilled hallways of the Petroleum Club in Houston. When Delo and Lee were in Houston, they would rent the entire second floor of the elegant Warwick Hotel, and the music and liquor would be like an insistent little bayou coursing up and down the hallway; Delo and Lee had a private plane, a DC-3, and as a joke someone once decorated the interior of the plane like a bordello; Delo and Lee had gone to Mexico together, had had too much to drink, and had had to be rounded up and taken to the airstrip in an ambulance; the pair had a standing invitation to every grand opening of every new Princess hotel in the world.[29] Delo and Lee flew government officials around free of charge in the DC-3, and when they heard that the Lake Charles Country Club was slipping into bankruptcy, they bought it and gave it back as a favor. Delo was, some people suspected, the only person from this part of south Louisiana whose obituary would eventually show that he had been elected to the Chevaliers du Tastevin, a French order of wine connoisseurs.

Every summer, Circle Drilling would hire a crew of college boys, usually as a favor to oilmen whose business they were courting. In 1965, Circle Drilling foreman Shelby Prather's inland barge—a small platform oil rig anchored in sixteen to twenty feet of water—was settled offshore and not far from Mud Point, Redfish Point, Rabbit Island, out where the French pirates could get lost and where Carlos Marcello's crime family could hide the bodies driven out from New Orleans. The tightly packed crew was composed of fifteen men. There were college students and sons of oil executives. There was a cook. And there were year-round roustabouts who had driven from southern Alabama, from southern Mississippi, from all over Louisiana, attracted by the $400 paychecks and willing to suffer the boredom, bugs, humidity, rancid smell, and mechanical clattering.

The crews worked what were called ten-and-ten or seven-and-seven cycles: ten days of work followed by ten days off or seven days of work followed by seven days off. At the end of a cycle, paychecks were distributed, and some crew members immediately headed for the nearest beer joints along the highway running from Lake Charles west to Houston and east to the French Quarter in New Orleans.[30] Sometimes on the downside of a seven-and-seven, Bush would hook up with Doug Hannah, his old friend from Houston, and, according to Hannah, "we would hit spots up and down the Gulf Freeway. . . . He was making four hundred dollars in ten days, and that was a lot of money. You couldn't spend it fast enough back then."[31]

Bush's commitment to Circle Drilling was from June through August. Back home in Houston, during his week-to-ten-day breaks, he fit back in with the roving gaggle of friends bound, in part, by the private schools, the Houston Country Club, and the River Oaks Country Club. He played tennis, hung out at poolside, and talked, for the first time that anyone could remember, about what he wanted to do in life. He talked, Hannah said, about being a stockbroker, making big money, going to Wall

Street, where Prescott Bush, George Herbert Walker, Jonathan Bush, and other members of the family had prospered or helped to found Brown Brothers Harriman.

The cycle, the juxtaposition of the hardworking underbelly of south Louisiana and the soigné summertime habits of Houston, lasted several weeks. Seven days before his commitment was scheduled to end, he walked off the barge and never came back. He told friends he wanted to be in Houston. Word was relayed to his father. After George W. got back to the city, he was summoned to his father's office in the Houston Club Building downtown. The successful oilman stared at his son, the prodigal roustabout. But it was like all those times after Robin's death, whenever his father had wanted to discipline him. He showed his disappointment; he made George W. feel guilty. "You agreed to work a certain amount of time, and you didn't," George W. heard his father intone. "I just want you to know that you have disappointed me."[32]

The first son fled the office. He had failed his father in some way. His mother was always more precise, more operatic: "I would scream and carry on. The way George scolded was by silence or by saying 'I'm disappointed in you.' And they would almost faint."[33]

Two hours later George W.'s phone rang. It was his father. Enough time had passed. He wanted to know if George W. wanted to catch a Houston Astros game. But George W.'s father's disappointment that day in the Houston Club was something he remembered for years. "Those were the sternest words to me, even though he said them in a very calm way," George W. later told a close friend. He wasn't screaming and he wasn't angry, but he was disappointed. When you love a person and he loves you, those are the harshest words someone can utter. I left that office realizing I had made a mistake. . . . [H]e has never held a grudge against his kids. He has never been the type of person to put our failures in the context of his life and all that he has achieved. It's our failures in the context of our *own* lives."[34]

WHEN George W. returned to New Haven for the fall semester in 1965, he was registered to live in the two-story Davenport College, one of twelve dormitories, or "colleges," at the university. Each residence had its own libraries, study halls, social areas, and dining facilities; the walls and stairways of the Davenport complex had replicas of the college shield and photographs of the distinguished intellectuals and athletes who had once lived there. By the mid-1960s, Davenport had also earned a "reputation";

some wry students said that Davenport was, from the outside, clean and Georgian—but increasingly chaotic and flamboyantly Gothic inside. In principle, the older traditions were still intact: students were only allowed to eat in the expansive dining hall, under a chandelier, if they were dressed in coats and ties. During the day, they studied at one of the burnished, wooden tables in the second-floor library or tossed a ball in one of two courtyards. There were also a squash court, darkroom, and laundry room. Sometimes a student was at a piano. Eventually, the Davenport house parent would be Horace Taft, son of Senator Robert Taft and grandson of President William Howard Taft.

In his Davenport suite, George W. reunited with his two Andover colleagues and freshman year roommates, Bob Dieter and Clay Johnson. A fourth student was assigned to their room. Collister "Terry" Johnson Jr. had grown up in Far Hills, New Jersey, and was also the son of a Yale alumnus. One of George W.'s first orders of business was to gain admission to his father's old fraternity, the one his father had served as chapter president, Delta Kappa Epsilon. A short walk from Davenport, the DKE house was one of a half-dozen fraternities at Yale. It was known as the jock-and-party fraternity, the place where the big men on campus would hang out, where the best traditional beer-soaked socials were unharnessed. DKE was not a residential fraternity; it was an after-school way station, and almost everyone on campus knew that it had the biggest bar on campus . . . the biggest bar in New Haven, really . . . maybe the biggest bar in Connecticut.

The four roommates—Bush, Terry Johnson, Bob Dieter, and Clay Johnson—signed up for rush week and then found themselves at the elegant, antique fraternity house being hazed by upperclassmen. The thin, tall Clay Johnson was ordered to stand up, and he heard one of the senior members of the fraternity barking at him: *"You are all pieces of garbage. You don't care about each other, you don't deserve each other. You, Johnson, you piece of horseshit, quick, how many of these people do you know? Stand up and name everyone else in this room, name all these pledges."*[35]

Johnson slowly named four or five people and then slumped into a chair, very worried. Two other pledges were called up to do the same thing; each named four or five people. The fourth person picked was Bush. One by one, efficiently, he named all fifty-four people in the room. Johnson and the others were floored. Bush returned to Davenport knowing he was a shoo-in, probably leadership material at his father's fraternity. He received a letter a week later, on October 12, telling him he was admitted. He would continue to live in Davenport, but the fraternity quickly became the epicenter of his Yale experience, the place he devoted his unbridled energies to, the one thing he protected from outside attacks by the arrogant intellectuals and even the national media.

IN GEORGE W.'s dormitory, a small group of budding student journalists were mimeographing something called *The Felon's Head*, an intermittently published, irreverent diary of life inside Davenport:

> Davenport is called the Jock College. We dance, we mix, we drink and play sports with a new intensity. The crux of Davenport's identity crisis is that we seem to strive, just as intensely, to denigrate and stamp out academic endeavor and intellectual activity. Our University scholastic rating is well known. Our Philistine-like approach is effective in removing plays, recitals, literary anthologies . . . from meaningful discussions in Davenport life.[36]

His three-room suite, composed of two bedrooms and a living room, had become a gathering place for anyone who needed to know what was on the campus social calendar. Bush knew where the card games were, what girls' schools were holding dances, who had a car, who had the beer, what time the football game started, how to get there, who was going. Dilapidated couches, worn rugs, hockey sticks, rugby equipment, and baseball mitts were strewn about the room. His roommates liked to say that "Topic A" was sports. Then girls. Then the all-night poker games. The quartet roomed together for three straight years, but the gregarious Bush rarely talked about his father's—or his own—political or intellectual aspirations. "He was not—none of us who roomed together were—particularly an intellectual. I think that people would say, objectively, that we were reasonably intelligent but that we didn't spend a lot of time reading poetry in coffeehouses," said Terry Johnson. "George liked, more than anything, to be with people. Whether it was an all-night poker game or it was at the fraternity or it was going to sports—hockey games, football games, basketball or baseball, you name it—you'd find him there."[37]

George W. dressed in whatever was handy and zoomed across the carpeted floors, past the paneled walls and bay windows, out onto campus, shouting nicknames and unabashedly introducing himself to strangers. The already overheated political climate was bubbling, and the opportunities for political involvement were multiplying. The Yale Republican Club announced that Barry Goldwater, Richard Nixon. George Murphy, Jacob Javits, Gerald Ford, William Scranton, and John Lindsay were coming to campus to field student inquiries. And beyond the boundaries of Yale's political clubs, there was now a plethora of smaller, informal groups springing up: shade-tree seminars and dialogues run by earnest conservative and liberal ideologues alike.

During the spring, said a fellow Yale student, Bush was involved in the "crew races," a kind of beer-chugging, mock Olympics held every year for the amusement of students. Crowds would begin gathering early for a front-row sightline to watch teams of six students lining up on the grassy quadrangle. Someone would blow a whistle, and the first team member would chug a beer and toss the bottle. Then the next member of the team would chug a beer and toss the bottle. The beer relay would continue until the first six-man crew finished. "George was a prominent crew racer. Everything had a heavy male overtone. There was a lot of testosterone going around. The DKEs were primarily jocks, known for their wild and gross parties," said Davenport resident Craig Bolles.[38]

That April, close to the frothy crew races, George W.'s grandfather was prominently featured in a lengthy interview on the front page of the campus newspaper. The story included an older portrait of the somber-looking Prescott Bush staring from his desk in his old Senate office, with the Capitol looming outside the window behind him. His grandfather told the students at Yale that he took particular offense at the suggestions that the Senate was actually controlled by an inner club, that it was lorded over by a select few members of an "establishment" group: "It's almost like any organization where leaders gravitate toward the top. Men who have been there a long time tend to have more influence than newer men."[39]

BY SEMESTER'S END there was another summer job waiting for him, working as a $212-a-month sporting goods salesman at Sears on Main Street in Houston. But more important, he was growing closer to Cathryn Wolfman, someone he had first dated during Christmas break of his sophomore year. She had family roots in the Texas-Mexico border city of McAllen, and she lived with her mother and stepfather in the same prosperous, shaded Houston neighborhood as the Bushes. Like George W., she was a fixture in the fluid swirl of young daughters and sons of the city's influential families. Her stepfather ran Wolfman's couture store, and the short-haired, ebullient Cathryn had been considered one of the brightest student athletes back at Saint John's School in Houston. She moved to Smith College in Massachusetts, returned to Houston after a harrowing skiing accident, and eventually enrolled in Rice University, the school nicknamed the "Harvard of the South." Among the young women in that

River Oaks–Tanglewood world, Wolfman was considered a level-headed star, someone with definite presence and energy. She was, friends said, someone to know amid all the other college-age socialites and the crew-cut-wearing, budding playboys in their Corvettes. "I didn't know anyone who didn't respect her and like her. She was more than just popular. She had a lot to her," said her friend Lacey Neuhaus.[40]

That summer, George W.'s father was already quickly marching into his second extensive political campaign. This time, the effort was being run by Jimmy Allison, the deep-pocketed newspaper publisher his father had met in Midland, as well as Harry Treleaven, a Nixon media adviser and Madison Avenue advertising wizard with the J. Walter Thompson agency. It had been just a decade since his father had seen the money tumbling in from the oil patch, and, concurrent with his new campaign, the forty-two-year-old elder Bush was able to sell his stock in Zapata, emerge as a bona fide Texas millionaire, and completely commit his resources to politics and the eventual pursuit of the presidency. Senator Yarborough had once used the Bush-Walker connections to the Middle East oil fields to whipsaw through parts of Texas that the Bush campaign had mistakenly considered to be possible friendly territory; that wouldn't be as much of a problem for the Bush campaign in 1966.

Unlike his Senate bid in 1964, the congressional race was also a safer crapshoot in a 90 percent white district on the affluent western side of Houston, a place filled with wealthy registered Democrats looking for an easy reason to lean toward the GOP. Too, it was a place filled with oilmen and executives unsettled by the city's increasing racial tensions. The elder Bush applied the same campaign principles, again with George W. by his side, that he had used in 1964, but in a smaller, more predictable, easier-to-negotiate world. He worked the district hard, feverishly, out every day at sunrise, walking almost every block in the Seventh District, dripping with perspiration and telling people that he cared—but, as one writer suggested "about what was never made clear."[41] When pressed about what he stood for, he said that the War in Vietnam was Southeast Asia's last chance at freedom; he supported sending marines to land on the shores of Santo Domingo; and, in a clear nod to the people who had voted against him in the Senate campaign, he promised to dissolve big, regulatory government "excesses" perpetuated by career politicians in the Northeast.

AFTER GEORGE W. arrived back in New Haven in the fall, it was by almost unanimous acclaim that he assumed the headiest, most conflicted role of his career at Yale. When he was named president of the DKE house, it struck many students as a simple inevitability: it had been his father's fraternity. He spent even more time at the brick building where some fraternity brothers were rounding up willing victims for "squockey," a meandering mishmash of squash and hockey played with hockey sticks and a tennis ball. Jason or Ivy, and any of the other black former railroad porters who had gotten jobs as house managers and janitors, were usually on hand. Friends said Bush was the first to mention the idea of a toga party; the charismatic president conferred with Clark "Sandy" Randt, the DKE social chairman, and other brothers about the rock acts—Ben E. King, Jerry Lee Lewis— they could book for parties. Inevitably, at those parties, some sodden attendees would fall to the floor and do the Alligator—facedown, and moving fast in time to the music. "We all drank a ton in college. It was absolutely off the wall. It was appalling. I cannot for the life of me figure out how we all made it through," said classmate Gregory Gallico.[42]

At DKE, there were also opportunities to verify the theory that more than two hundred Lucky Strike cigarettes could easily be fit end to end on top of the justly famous bar. One frat brother also remembered George W. having a seemingly endless supply of clothes for the frat functions, including a suit that he would fish out of the clothes heap in the corner of his room. "He was the best at egging other people into schemes, like Tom Sawyer. We took road trips to find dates on weekends. He wanted me to help him steal the United Way sign in New Haven. We never did, but I went along. He's the great sun around which a universe revolved. He radiated star quality, but never in an unapproachable way," said Robert Beebe, a DKE brother.[43]

Years later, Beebe and Bob Dieter met each other in Colorado and decided to see the movie *Animal House*. When they walked out, Beebe and Dieter were laughing and saying the same thing: Bluto—the John Belushi character, the fraternity dervish with the fulsome appetite and the unsteady devotion to books—was George W. Bush.

THAT SEMESTER in *The Felon's Head*, the dormitory newspaper, there was an account of the Davenport Skittles Championship. "In the consolation match for third place, a somewhat inebriated George Bush beat the reluctant Jack Morrison 940–820. . . . [P]rizes will be awarded tonight by the Master at a cocktail mixer."[44] He was everywhere and almost everyone in the fraternity gravitated to his energy, his spontaneity: "Always in the middle of things, whatever group activity was going on, whatever pranks might be going on. He had natural leadership. He wasn't afraid to look foolish. He didn't care. He had an exuberance. Nobody experienced those feelings better than Bush," said Edgar Cullman, heir to the General Cigar fortune.[45]

His junior year transcript[46] reflected the fact that he had declared history as his major. History 35a and 35b were broad survey courses on "politics and American culture in the twentieth century." History 54a and History 54b were overviews of "European diplomacy in the nineteenth century." Philosophy 38b had the all-encompassing title "Nature, Man and God" and was described as "a systematic study in the basic dimensions of nature, the essential features of man." City Planning 10a was listed in the catalog as an "introduction to urbanism," American Studies 59a was a survey course in twentieth-century American literature, Anthropology 25a was a "survey of our prehistoric past."

Outside the classroom and just as Bush was assuming his most visible role at Yale, the broader fraternity system was slowly beginning a widespread decline. Many students and Yale officials, including Coffin, were beginning to condemn the fraternities as hoary symbols of misdirected priorities and runaway testosterone. And DKE was the essence of the once-prestigious fraternity experience at Yale, both for those in it and those who were beginning to loathe it. When Bush had attended an organizational meeting for DKE in his sophomore year, more than four hundred students had shown up. At the organizational meeting in his junior year, only two hundred possible recruits did so. Worse, there were rumors in the fraternity that some of the big-time jocks, Brian Dowling and Calvin Hill, were thinking of going somewhere else. But with Bush's insistent prodding, the name-brand jocks still came.

Even with some better-known students joining, DKE had no relevant status for more and more people on campus—certainly nothing approximating its stature during the time George W.'s father had been at Yale. "By being head DKE at Yale, Bush put himself somewhat off in a corner. It was an extremely liberal campus. There was little interest in fraternities. The DKEs were the jock frat. Jocks weren't necessarily the kings of the hill. A lot of people could've cared less," said Bob Wei, one of the quiet intellectuals at Andover who had also gone on to Yale.[47] Increasingly, almost all of the Ivy League fraternities were being accused of becoming mindless anachronisms—isolated, exclusionary, sexist. By the late 1960s, the Yale yearbook would headline the fraternities as "The Benign Irrelevancy."

The cornerstones of George W.'s Yale experience were beginning to twitch and convulse at the same time his father seemed on the verge of winning a seat in Congress. His years at Yale were the cusp years, a collapsing bridge between a predictable Bush-Walker pattern that had stretched back for decades and was now symbolized by Chaplain Coffin's judgmental arguments against the exclusionary things Bush's father and grandfather and great-grandfather had worked for, had felt they were entitled to. Bush would think about this, for years, about what he liked to call "the heaviness" on campus and how he was determined never to let it press down on him, never to let it destroy his turn at the lengthy Bush-Walker legacy in New Haven. It had begun at Andover, that sense of being displaced, that sense, as he would put it, of something "strange"—and now, at Yale, he knew he was struggling to find his own way, "to reconcile who I was and who my Dad was, to establish my own identity in my own way."[48]

Prescott Bush, for one, had seen Yale as a place to be taken very seriously. He once told his fellow Yale trustees: "It has become one of the greatest centers of learning and one of the greatest character builders in America. It has trained great leaders of church and state, leaders in teaching and the other learned professions, leaders of the press and of American industry."

One day, George W. was ambling across campus with a frat brother named David Heckler. Heckler lived in Morse College, and Bush was headed back to Davenport. Heckler had enjoyed thinking about the other DKE members, analyzing them a little, the way they sometimes easily fell into categories. He thought he had a firm handle on many of the people he had watched or gotten close to in the DKE house. Some of them were joyously unfettered—in a word, lunatics. And then there were some who, even when squarely in the middle of the beer-soaked madness, held something back. Maybe they were worried. Maybe they were simply being detached.

Now, Heckler and Bush were actually having a serious conversation: about the world, about the way the country was turning in the 1960s. Heckler was stunned to hear Bush speak about his father . . . about how much, right then, in that strained period of the 1960s, he had a deep sense of respect for his father. Heckler was amazed to hear him talk about his father, amazed to hear anyone, at that age, talk about *respecting* his father—his father the politician. The moment stuck with Heckler for decades.[49]

6

The Heaviness

In November, Bush left Yale for another long week-end home in Houston, and another in the long series of what some people in the family would begin to call Reality Days—those days when the constant, ongoing, horse-race Speculation Days finally ended and the actual votes were counted. Again he took on the job of posting the election returns for his father. At the campaign headquarters on Richmond Avenue, the family was in and out, including his uncle Jonathan Bush, who had only just flown down from New York. Each new return that George W. hung on the oversized board was better than the last.[1] As usual, his Houston friends said he was irrepressible and demanding during even these final campaign moments in the Seventh District. He was frequently that way: quiet in his father's presence, swinging to another extreme when his father was out of distance. His cousin Elsie Walker had seen it all before, his deference to his father, the way he tried to control himself around his father. "Young George—his father's quieter and gentler in a way—sometimes was sort of sensitive to the fact that he was too coarse or, you know, rough-edged for his father," said Walker.

For years with his mother, sparring and slinging arrows, he would spin and bounce on his feet, leaning forward, bursting out of his skin to ridicule something, almost to the point of black humor, making a mockery of the fact that her treasured dog had died. "Doggone it!" he would yell and whoop until they both started choking with laughter. His father would be half smiling, rolling his eyes exaggeratedly, making a show of groaning and suffering under the weight of what his son had just said.

With his father, the family said, he learned just never to push that far—but he sometimes went twice as far when the elder Bush wasn't there.

His father easily defeated Harris County District Attorney Frank Briscoe. The conservative Democratic opponent had decided to play even harder to the barely suppressed racial fears in the white neighborhoods on the west side of the city, and, almost by default, many voters had begun perceiving the affable Bush as the more moderate but somehow still conservative alternative. Briscoe was easy to paint in harsh, definable colors; candidate Bush's stripes were less clear. And Bush campaign media manager Harry Treleaven was exultant at the way his candidate had emerged as a "new" political commodity—how there was potency in the "haziness about exactly where he stood politically."[2] The lessons of that campaign—the way George W.'s father had achieved victory by reworking that initially devastating perception as a *"tool of the eastern kingmakers,"* the way he had somehow snatched victory as the less strident but still conservative option—would serve as a political signpost for the father and his children for the next three decades.

Bush returned to Yale knowing that his father was finally following his grandfather to Washington. He left Houston almost reluctantly; he was comfortable there, and his relationship with Cathryn Wolfman was deepening. He was ready for the inalterability of the fraternity he was running, but he confided in friends that there was something out of sync at Yale and in the Northeast, something too closely paralleling the shifts around the country. He later found a name for it: "I saw an intellectual arrogance that I hope I never have."[3]

IN DECEMBER, twenty-year-old Bush and a handful of his Yale brothers left campus, and the laughing, loud crew descended on the Christmas-bedecked streets of New Haven. Patrolling downtown, Bush spied a wreath on a storefront and reached out to take it. Almost as soon as he planned his escape, New Haven police officers pulled him over. The newly elected congressman's son was questioned, arrested, and charged with disorderly conduct. Years later he remembered it as a harmless college prank; he "might have had a few beers" and "we didn't make it very far. We probably were making a lot of noise, laughing."[4] The incident served to amplify a feeling that George W. was the untamed one, the resisting one, the Good Time Charlie in an unlikely family. "George was quite outrageous for many years. Pop off, hilarious, imitate people, very, very broad. I mean, he got away with it because he was so funny, but if most people tried what he would try, they would fall flat," remarked Elsie Walker.[5] News of the arrest and the criminal charges filtered through the Bush-Walker clan. So did news that twenty-year-old Bush had decided to become engaged at the same age his father had been engaged.

Cathryn Wolfman was entering her junior year at Rice, she was a member of the Elizabeth Baldwin Literary Society, and she and her parents were still embedded in the revolving band of people who attended private school reunions, fund-raisers, lawn parties, and onboard meetings for the Houston Museum of Fine Arts, the Houston Symphony, and Rice University. She was witty and well read, someone who would fit in well with the extended Bush-Walker clan in spite of the occasional misguided whispers in Houston society circles that the Episcoplian young woman actually came from a family of "merchants"—that thinly veiled reference to the possibility she was Jewish. Some close friends even suggested that the young woman was intellectually much older than her years, that she was a peer of her parents and other adults in Houston. The fact that she was committed to George W. Bush engendered a certain degree of jealousy among other potential suitors in Houston. It was, they said, almost too perfect that Cathryn Wolfman, the star of her class, was with the congressman's son. "She was the pick of the litter. George was really headstrong, and I think that was his thinking there. If George was a trophy hunter and that was his goal, that might have been what he was going for," said Doug Hannah.[6] In the past, his father had liked to suggest dates for his son. But he hadn't suggested Wolfman. She was someone George W. had gravitated to on his own, without his father's input. His parents told people that they loved Cathryn and that they didn't oppose a marriage; in fact, as some people in Houston remarked, it would have been duplicitous for them to resist it. "I don't know how they could have, in good conscience, start preaching to him about getting married in college, which is what they had done," believed Hannah.[7]

There was now something else, said friends, in the relationship between the father and the son—the son who was now planning a marriage at the same age and stage of life as his father's marriage. It was something, people close to the family also said, that underscored the generational differences between the Calvinistic father and the leash-tugging first son, something that pointed to an occasional awkwardness in their relationship. Relatives speculated that George W. had spent so much more time with his mother as a young man and that he had absorbed her piercing bluntness, her withering stare, her needling humor, her ability to deliver a crystalline retort. When his mother delivered a sharp line, it was expected;

when his father did so, it was almost treasured because it was so unexpected. And, family and friends said, so much of what his father expected from the first son was implicit, assumed, never articulated. Jeb had always suspected, sometimes even seen, the barely hidden pressure for his brother to emulate their father: "There might be more to it for him than the rest of us, because he is the oldest and it is his namesake, and he more directly followed my dad's path. If he was openly honest about it, he might say that it had some effect, that it might define him in some way. I learned a while back, my estimation of my father is so powerful that if I felt like I had to follow his footsteps and follow a path that he has set for me, I would fail. I came to grips with that a while back. A lot of people who have fathers like this, or moms, who have lived such extraordinary lives, feel a sense that they have failed because they haven't reached the same level of just being a human being as their predecessor—and it creates all sorts of pathologies."[8]

Jeb and George W. have both always used the same word to describe their father: "beacon." "He was just a beacon that simplified life tremendously, by his actions, not by his words," said Jeb.[9] For George W., it was also more than some stoic ideal, it reinforced his belief that his father was bashful, remote in a way that his first son never was: *By his actions, not by his words.* There were things left unspoken, merely an outline of what his father expected of him as an adult, even about the facts of life, about using contraceptives, a "raincoat." "Dad was shy," said George W. "We never had 'the talk.' He never told me to wear a raincoat or anything. I never had any sense of what his ambitions were for me."[10]

THE MONTH Bush was arrested and charged with disorderly conduct, he returned to a muggy, cold winter in Houston and began shopping for an engagement ring. He took along his friend Doug Hannah, who was home from college in Colorado. The two traveled downtown to hallowed Neiman Marcus, the sine qua non of high-society shopping in Texas. It was the week before Christmas. Hannah knew Bush and Wolfman had been spending a small fortune in long-distance phone bills. He also knew that his friend was plunging ahead, and he understood how serious it was when they stepped past the elegant store's doors. Hannah saw that Bush had brought money and was lingering over "a monster ring." Hannah was flabbergasted. "George, this is absolutely insane!"[11] he blurted.

Two weeks later, on New Year's Day, the *Houston Chronicle* ran a story and announcement by Society Editor Betty Ewing, the sage observer of the dizzying Gordian knot known as Houston high society: " 'Cupid

Hitched a Ride on Santa's Sleigh': The votes are in and it's Cupid all the way for the title of Man of the Year in these columns. He outran successful political candidates. . . . George Walker Bush, son of Congressman-elect and Mrs. George H. W. Bush of Houston and Washington will take pretty Cathryn Lee Wolfman as his bride." A veteran photographer was dispatched to shoot the couple as they posed in front of a fireplace with what looked like a ring bearer's pillow between them. No wedding date was announced.[12]

The charges against him from the Christmas incident were dismissed, and he returned to New Haven for his spring semester, still placing long-distance calls to Wolfman in Houston and administrating his increasingly ostracized DKE fraternity. In March, the Yale Republican Club announced that it would organize a model GOP National Convention under the guidance of Representative George Bush from Texas and with financial support from Robert Taft and Gerald Ford. But that spring, while the young Yale Republicans were making their plans, Bush was more concerned with the possibility of once again exactly following his father's and grandfather's tradition.

He assumed he would be invited to join the exclusive Skull & Bones Society, founded in 1832 and the essence, probably the epitome, of the elaborate secret society system at the university. The university's societies accepted only males and, beginning in the 1950s, only a handful of blacks and Jews. There were seven societies, including Book & Snake, Scroll & Key, Elihu, Berzelius, and Wolf's Head. But the Bonesmen always seemed to lure the biggest, most powerful names over the years: Dean Witter Jr., Henry Luce, Potter Stewart, Alfred Cowles of Cowles Communications, Harold Stanley of Morgan Stanley, Frederick Weyerhaeuser, Henry Stimson, Bush family business partner Averell Harriman, McGeorge Bundy, William F. Buckley Jr., and President William Howard Taft. The roster of Bonesmen was a profile in power, with many lesser-known but equally influential members moving on to join the federal intelligence community, or the upper administration of Yale, Capitol Hill, or Wall Street.

Skull & Bones, sometimes simply called "The Order," would swear its members to secrecy once they entered the doors of its mausoleum on High Street behind Jonathan Edwards College. Inside were faded, dark portraits of ancient Bonesmen, wooden intaglios with nods to the society's Teutonic heritage, walls covered with dark red velvet, shelves and tabletops adorned with skulls and bones. For years, the chairman of the San Carlos Apache tribe in Arizona would clamor for serious investigations into whether Prescott Bush or some other marauding Bonesman had taken possession of Geronimo's missing skull, maybe Pancho Villa's skull, maybe the skulls of other legendary renegades, and delivered them back to the dark tomb. Each year fifteen new members were admitted—or "tapped"—and each new Bonesman resolutely managed to skirt suggestions that his oath of allegiance had been administered by senior members in skeleton costumes and that the initiates were forced to recline in coffins while reciting their most intimate sexual histories. Too, they had played down the widely held belief that, in the 1960s, each new Bonesman had been awarded $15,000 and extended an invitation by the Russell Trust Association, the corporate entity behind the society, to visit the trust's hidden, wooded retreat on Deer Island in the Saint Lawrence River.[13]

The initiation into Skull & Bones, sometimes referred to as a process of dying and being reborn, was considered a passport to adult privilege, "converting the idle progeny of the ruling class into morally serious leaders of the establishment."[14] All the trappings were there: The preppy-voodoo iconography; the clubby Medieval nods to secret meetings, numbers, and names. The Skull & Bones experience added up to a certain muscled-up seriousness for the impressionable people involved, a sense that the Lost Fraternity Boys were growing into Society Men, into Good Men. Skull & Bones literature was filled with news about being a Good Man, that preferred Bush slogan, that Bush measurement. *Boni* meant "good men" in Latin—"And good men are rare," according to the Bonesmen's mottoes. The whole process, the burnished oddities and lights-out rituals, inspired loyalty, a perfectly codified level of Round Table–Arthurian kinship that settled well with generations of Bushes and Walkers. Prescott Bush George Herbert Walker, Jonathan Bush, George Herbert Walker Bush, and his cousin Ray Walker had been Bonesmen. So had family advisers Neil Mallon, the head of Dresser Industries, and Lud Ashley, the congressman from Ohio. The latter two men were like uncles to George W. Bush. He would frequently say that they were . . . *Good Men.*

ROBERT REISNER was a politically minded DKE brother who knew very well that George W.'s father had finally achieved elected office, taking his turn after Prescott Bush had retired. He also knew that George W.'s father had returned to Yale as a bona fide war hero and that, unlike his personable son, he had probably been more focused on keeping his nose to the academic grindstone. George W., thought Reisner, was focused more on his friends than on the grindstone. On the last Thursday night in April, Reisner ran into the young Bush outside the Yale cooperative. It was Tap Day, the famous day on campus when, after the bells in the Harkness

Tower rang at 8 P.M., black-suited senior society members, some of them carrying ominous-looking attaché cases, would sprint from one residential college to another, summoning—*tapping*—selected juniors for admission. All week long, the process had been building, with unsubtle hints, phone calls, and solicitations from the societies to the juniors. The campus newspaper was reporting rumors that prominent alumni, from Henry Luce to John Lindsay, were heavily involved in the process. The newspaper had also mentioned that George W.'s father was planning to visit the campus, ostensibly to speak to one of the Yale Republican groups.

Reisner, a hardworking student who considered George W. a good friend, stopped to talk outside the cooperative. Bush told him that he was expecting, that night, to be summoned into another society in addition to Skull & Bones. The other society wasn't one of the truly exclusive ones; most people on campus knew it didn't take itself too seriously. And it seemed as if George W. was at a crossroads. Reisner understood the implications for someone like George W. Bush, whose life was constantly being weighed against his father's, his grandfather's, the entire Bush-Walker legacy.

"What are you going to do?" asked Reisner, who had heard that the society in question was an "above-ground" society called, of all joke things, Gin & Tonic—a society that operated in the sunshine, that didn't have tombs, thick traditions, a weighty sense of responsibility.

George W. told his friend that he was maybe ready to depart from his father's career and the Bush family path, that this was something truly different. As Reisner listened, Bush seemed almost philosophical, affirming that he was going to go his own way but that it was OK, he would be OK with it. "This is what is going to fit me," Reisner heard Bush say. "This is the way it is going to work for me."

Reisner knew this was an important moment for his friend, but he didn't know if his fraternity brother was making the best of it or getting comfortable with it. The friends went their separate ways, the hour-long whirlwind of Tap Night ended, and over the next few days, students and Yale faculty began learning the names of the people who had decided to enter the various tombs and secret societies. Reisner and others learned that George W. Bush was going to enter Skull & Bones after all. And a story circulated that at 8 P.M. on Tap Night, at the moment the bells were tolling in Harkness Tower, there was a knock on George W.'s door at his room in Davenport. When he opened it up, his father, the U.S. congressman, was standing outside, asking that his first son do the right thing and join Skull & Bones—*become a Good Man*.

Owing to the surprisingly resilient nature of the secrecy surrounding Skull & Bones, Reisner and other friends never knew exactly who it had been outside their fraternity brother's door that night. For Reisner, the symbolism of the story is what is really important, the very possibility that George W. Bush's father might have personally urged the hesitant first son to stay the Bush-Walker course, not to veer from his legacy, his destiny. "To me, that was sort of symbolic—of the tradition and the sense of Walker's Point and the history that he had to live up to in his life. The idea that your father was that kind of presence in your life, as a mentor, as a guide," said Reisner.

Reisner knew that George W.'s Yale experience was defined by his father, by his grandfather, by the extended generations in the Bush-Walker house. In the end, Reisner also speculated, it was his father's lingering presence on campus and in the Yale newspapers that had something to do with the first son's wholesale rejection of political involvement. "The presence of his father is an important factor as to why he might have been understated about that, why he wouldn't have necessarily been a political figure in those days," Reisner said.[15]

EVEN AS he was ceremoniously escorted through the usually padlocked doors of the Skull & Bones mausoleum and finally inducted into his father's and grandfather's society, it wasn't hard to sense the same rejection, suspicion, and ostracism that he had felt with the fraternity. The day following Tap Day, *The New York Times* called the Yale secret societies "hotly controversial on the campus"; Chaplain Coffin, who had once been a Bonesman, had told the newspaper, "It's an awful indictment that you have to disappear into a tomb to have a meaningful relationship."[16]

Meanwhile, the Yale newspaper reported that "even social prestige is declining as a reason to join a society. . . . [T]he number of undergraduates who regard society members with suspicion rather than fear and admiration has been growing." If the fraternities were considered exclusionary in the late 1960s, the societies—which had always been by definition cryptic, mysterious, closed—were being assailed as antediluvian monstrosities. And now Bush was at his tomb every Thursday and Sunday night. Some fraternity brothers went in with him, including *Life* magazine cover idol and Olympic swimmer Don Schollander. There were also Gregory Gallico, who would become a nationally known plastic surgeon and assistant professor at Harvard Medical School; future prominent Los Angeles defense attorney, Donald Etra; Muhammed Saleh, a Jordanian student and future vice president for the Timex Corporation, destined to be head of the Yale alumni board; and Rex W. Cowdry, future deputy director of the National Institute of Mental Health.

On campus there was some parlor game speculation that Skull & Bones was slipping in prestige to Scroll & Key, that it needed a prominent boost—something that adding a congressman's son and an Olympic gold medalist could give. There were two Jewish members and one black student; no women were allowed. All members would remain inflexible about protecting the inner workings of the society. "Well, we generally don't discuss what goes on in there," said Roy Austin, the soccer team captain from St. Vincent who was the only black member of Skull & Bones that year. Bush "certainly never spoke politics," even though Austin also obviously knew that his father was a congressman.[17]

"He was not obsessed by anything, or a cause. He didn't have an agenda, a timetable, a program," said Saleh. "We were in the Vietnam era, it was a big subject, and the big thing about George is that really he was not doctrinaire about anything. You would think, coming from a political family, that he would take strong views."[18] Britt Kolar was one more Good Man, another loyal Skull & Bonesman that year. "Despite the tumultuous times in the sixties when we were in school, not all of us were radicalized by any means. I don't think it changed him at all. I think his values have been consistent from the word go, and these are the values that he learned from his family, that you make your commitments and you keep your commitments. Despite his upbringing, he is, I think, one of the least pretentious people I've ever met," said Kolar. But his friends also thought that being in Skull & Bones, a steady way station in the cusp years, had brought him closer to his father, his grandfather, and all the other Bushes and Walkers who had passed through Yale. "It just kind of crystallized his value system," Kolar added.[19] There was a return favor: Skull & Bones exposed students from more modest backgrounds, such as Austin, to a way of life that had previously been alien. "George, because of what we thought to be his patrician background, was a valuable asset," Bonesman Ken Cohen would later say. "He gave us insights into a way of life to which we'd never been exposed."[20]

AFTER THE spring semester in 1967 he was back home in Houston, and by now fourteen-year-old Jeb, especially, was in awe of his unbridled twenty-one-year-old brother. Jeb was trying to gauge George W.'s place in time, in the buildup to that famous halcyon summer of love and drugs in the Haight-Ashbury district in San Francisco. In a way, the year was the final bridge between the nascent Deep South stirrings over racism and that ongoing merger of the antiwar and counterculture movements. Rosa Parks's decision not to abandon her bus seat one day in December 1955 in Montgomery, Alabama, had later segued into the bloody, harrowing Freedom Rides into the South—and the freedom riders began attracting more northerners to the civil rights movement. The Students for a Democratic Society, founded by representatives from eleven colleges at a 1962 meeting in Port Huron, Michigan, had stated its mission in its charter statement: "We are the people of this generation, bred in at least modest comfort, housed now in universities, looking uncomfortably to a world we inherit."

On the heels of SDS, the Free Speech Movement at the University of California at Berkeley in 1964 and the 1965 explosions in Watts pushed the national debates to extraordinary levels. And beyond the pointed protests, there was also a fountain of influential, often-debated social policy taking shape—frequently as a cautionary response from lawmakers to the fledgling "movement." LBJ's War on Poverty, Medicare, the Clean Air Act, the Clean Water Act, the National Traffic and Motor Vehicle Safety Act, the Civil Rights Act, and the Voting Rights Act were all put in motion. Apart from the legislation, there were dozens of groups coalescing and emerging as perennially influential forces, among them the National Organization for Women, the Environmental Defense Fund, and the Consumer Federation of America. And on a broader, shifting level, college administrators and faculty were revising curriculums to include dozens of courses on Hispanic or African-American history and culture, women's studies, and pop culture.

Jeb was destined for the University of Texas in Austin, the only school he wanted to attend and really the only university and city in Texas where the new political tendencies were openly encouraged. Jeb always felt that his older brother "misbehaved like most people did; it wasn't like he was an angel." Jeb felt that he and his older brother understood the unsubtle cultural shifts in America, but he was sure of something else: "Boy, he wasn't a hippie or anything like that." For Jeb, his older brother was just funny—the funniest person he knew—"really funny."[21]

George W. told his family that being at Yale had reinforced his feeling that if he were ever asked where he was from, he would say Texas instead of Connecticut. "He was always saying, you know, Texans are so friendly and nice, you know. He's very at home there, and he's not at home in the more intellectual, very intellectual . . . more intellectual and more cerebral. Texas is more relaxed," said his cousin Elsie Walker.[22] His closest relatives, the ones who knew him best, could tell he had had bitter, unexpected moments at Yale. "It was very uncomfortable for him, as the son of his father, to be at Yale when there was so much antiwar and so much antiestablishment . . . and he comes from a very establishment, or *we* come from quite an establishment family. And his is the most establishment within our family. He felt a real conflict and a real loyalty to his family, and I think it was very hard to come from a prominent Republican family," continued Elsie Walker.[23]

Back in Houston, he was clearly at ease. "When he came back to town, it was the signal that the parties began again. People wanted to do things with him. It was worthwhile to spend time with the Bushes, and I think George acknowledged that and knew what a benefit that was," said his friend Doug Hannah.[24] During the day, George W. worked as a $250-a-month bookkeeper for Rauscher, Pierce Securities. In Houston, the college kids who were reassembling for the summer liked going swimming at the Bush house; they'd also take turns sitting in what they assumed was Prescott Bush's old Senate seat, the one he had had shipped down to Houston.

Unlike most of his friends' parents, Bush's mother frequently insisted on coming along, especially if golf or tennis were involved. Playing golf one day with his mother and Hannah, George W. started fuming and cursing at the first tee. By the second hole, his mother had had enough. "George, I'm not going to put up with this. Do it again and you are *done,*" a worried Hannah heard her demand. George W. promptly misplayed another stroke on the second hole and immediately starting fuming and cursing again. His mother stared at her oldest son for a moment and then ordered him to sit in the car until she was through playing.

When she found out that George W. smoked, she was furious. His father sauntered into the conversation: "Barbara, who are you to tell your son he shouldn't smoke as you so deeply inhale your Newport?"[25] Through it all, the long Houston summers took on a languid, fluid quality. Hannah said it was a standing arrangement that every weekend Lacey Neuhaus or another friend would have a party. At night at those parties, Bush would sometimes talk to his friends about what he wanted to do after Yale: "He wanted to be rich. He wanted to possibly be a stockbroker, because his great-uncle and uncle were stockbrokers," remembered Hannah. "He wanted to be around people who were important, simply because it was fun. George and I would sit around in the summertime, in the evening, and dream about opening up our own stock brokerage firm. We all wanted to be partners."[26]

Hannah knew his good friend's background, with all the wealth spread through Wall Street investment houses. He also knew his friend was good at hedging bets, as when he had been talking up the University of Texas in case he didn't get accepted at Yale. Hannah felt that he knew his friend better than most; he felt that George W. always had a "stockbroker's ability."[27]

BY EARLY FALL, Bush and Cathryn Wolfman were still engaged, but friends began to wonder if they would ever get married. The Rice student, some friends said, was given to surprising bursts of independence. Some even said she was simply a more serious student than George W., better read, ready to question assumptions. Their friends said that Wolfman wanted to wait until after graduation, maybe even longer. She returned to Rice and her deep interest in art and literature; he returned to Yale. On campus, the political environment continued to heat up, and amid it all there was news that any budding stockbrokers could join a Yale investment club and play the market as a member of something called "The Fund."

INTO OCTOBER 1967, the politicization of Yale's campus was still ongoing, sometimes attracting a handful of faculty members and sometimes outpacing other burgeoning campus movements around the country. The War in Vietnam was omnipresent, of course, as was the draft. Strobe Talbott, a classmate of Bush's and future deputy secretary of state, had written in the campus newspaper that "since the war in Vietnam became a killing and dying war for Americans, college students should have faced a new and deceivingly clear-cut responsibility. This responsibility is one of confrontation and self-examination. . . . [M]uch of the undergraduate sentiment about the draft is still divided between complacency and panic."

It was the last year at Yale for an all-male student body. At the impossibly long bar in the DKE house, Bush still avoided any soul-baring chats about the Vietnam War. One fraternity brother remembers one notable departure from Bush's almost apolitical presence at Yale: as he was standing shoulder to shoulder with him at the bar, Bush began railing about how the nation's oilmen were being strangled by some suggested tax-break variances in the oil depletion allowance. The college fraternity brother remembered George W. growing heated as he built his argument in defense of the oilmen in Texas.

October was a fitful month for the defenders of the campus status quo: Phi Gamma Alpha, one of the six Yale fraternities, was slamming shut because of dwindling membership and rising debts, faculty members were accused by concerned alumni of straying away from stringent, conservative politics, and William F. Buckley Jr., who had graduated seventeen years earlier, defiantly declared that he was running to be elected to the Yale Corporation, the 266-year-old body that governed all of the school's policies, because of "liberal bias" at the university and because "students simply don't have access to the conservative point of view." Buckley, whose father had gone to the University of Texas, testily added that Yale had ceased to be "the kind of place where your family goes for generations. The son of an alumnus, who goes to a private preparatory school, now has less of a chance of getting in than some boy from P.S. 109."[28]

University president Kingman Brewster blasted Chaplain Coffin as "strident" for spearheading on-campus draft protests. Finally, that same month, Federal Bureau of Investigation agents began combing through Yale, pinpointing and questioning students who had sent their draft cards to an antiwar protest in Washington, D.C. When military recruiters came to Yale that month, they were met and challenged by antiwar protesters.

For some, the all-male 1968 class simply still represented that final link from decades-old traditions to a different, easily more complicated, future. Bob Wei, who had gone to Andover and then to Yale, said, "The tradition was for the freshmen to get the seniors to buy them liquor. By my senior year, the seniors were getting the freshmen to buy them marijuana. We were the last of the preppies."[29] It was something that Bush and the embattled DKE house especially felt. As DKE brother J. P. Goldsmith put it, "We were the last vestiges of the rich man's school. A coat and tie was required for meals. A large percentage of the students were private school graduates. The world was good. We didn't know it, but it was about to get a lot worse."[30]

Bush continued to be a fixture in intramural sports. He spent two nights a week meeting in the Skull & Bones tomb. He disliked the direction the Beatles were taking; he had liked the early version with the three-chord beat, the mop-top version that he had imitated so ardently at Andover, but now even that was souring. Later he would say, "The Beatles went through that kind of a weird, psychedelic period, which I particularly didn't care for."[31]

At Yale Bush was always uneasy with cultural ambiguity, said his friends. He was, as one friend on the rugby team said, "a good old boy before his time—or out of his time." DKE brother Dan Begel, who sat next to him on the way to the rugby matches, noted, "He was not political, because in that time, to be political meant to protest. I don't know if it was because he was conservative or because he wanted to not jeopardize any future political ambitions."[32] In the fraternity, in Skull & Bones, in his circles in Davenport College, there was still that increasingly prevailing sense that a Yale era was coming to a fitful close. "It was really the last of those old days. We were right at the end, everything really happened after we left. It was really the end of an era. DKE was stuck in the fifties," remarked Franklin Levy, the DKE house chairman.[33] "It wasn't until senior year that really the world began to intrude in a big way," added Bush's roommate Terry Johnson.[34]

Except for a survey course on "Japanese literature in translation," his senior year work centered on the requirements for his history major. His transcript shows History 39a, listed in the Yale course catalog as "the history and practice of American oratory from John Edwards through FDR; analysis of oratory and instruction on speaking." His transcript also shows History 85, "Problems in Eighteenth-Century American History"; History 56b, "Germany 1871–1961"; History 36b, "The Antebellum South and the Civil War 1815–1865."

BUSH ALSO again devoted his time to his secret society and his fraternity—it was time to prepare for the new pledges—and he was instantly at the center of a controversy that found him defending his fraternity against stories that first appeared in the campus newspaper and that would eventually spread to *The New York Times.* The first Friday in November, the *Yale Daily News* published a special supplement charging the handful of fraternities with widespread physical and psychological abuse. The paper noted that school officials had sought to outlaw onerous hazing, but that the fraternities, especially Delta Kappa Epsilon, were guilty of excesses: "Despite Yale's Ivy sophistication, pledging a fraternity at Yale is often a degrading, sadistic and obscene process."[35]

The newspaper alleged that the DKE house hazing lasted a week and culminated in burning a half-inch-long Delta insignia onto a pledge's back.

> For some, after the beating that had gone before, the branding was almost a relief. "By that time," one pledge says, "my body was so numb that the iron felt good—like a match being held close to my body." On that final night, each pledge was forced to sit with his head between his legs, motionless, for two to five hours. If he coughed, raised his head or talked he was kicked by an older brother. The room was completely dark. Noise from the more violent parts of the DKE rites penetrated into the Drama School Theatre, where the audience was watching the second act of "'Tis Pity She's A Whore." A sophomore, walking past DKE after the

play, heard through a window someone yelling, "The poor baby. He's crying. Let's leave him alone." Much of the rest of the DKE initiation is degrading, but not violent. One pledge who dropped out recalls, "Guys would tell me to get them seconds in the dining hall. If I didn't, it was understood that I'd get beaten up in the next meeting."[36]

The allegations were picked up by *The New York Times* on November 8 in a story headlined "Branding Rite Laid to Yale Fraternity." It apparently marked the first time the younger Bush's name appeared in the newspaper: "George Bush, a Yale Senior, said that the resulting wound is 'only a cigarette burn.' "[37] The newspaper's disclosures appeared on the same day as front-page stories about dramatic election results around the country, including the groundbreaking victory of the first black mayor in a major city, when Carl Stokes was elected in Cleveland, Ohio. *The Hartford Courant*, Connecticut's largest newspaper, ran a story about the fraternity allegations on the front page alongside the other swirling news events of the day: Three American prisoners of war had been released by the Viet Cong after "sincere repentance"; Muhammad Ali had come to the state to give a speech about black nationalism; in North Carolina, 1,200 armed troops had been called out following the worst racial disturbances in the state's history.

On campus, emergency meetings were held between Yale's deans and fraternity leaders to discuss the well-publicized charges against DKE. Some Yale students said the DKE house was using heated-up coat hangers to brand people. The next Tuesday, there was another article in the campus newspaper. The congressman's son and his roommates had decided they would be the ones to publicly defend the fraternity against the allegations: George W. Bush, 1968, the past president of DKE, called the branding "insignificant." Stating that there is little pain, Bush said, "there's no scarring mark, physically or mentally. I can't understand how the authors of the Friday article can assume that Yale has to be so haughty not to allow this type of pledging to go on at Yale."[38]

His roommate Terry Johnson, someone who would later ask Bush to serve as his child's godfather, also wrote a defiant letter to the student newspaper:

> Threats of beating are so much hot air. There just is simply very little paddling. Hot air never hurt anybody. The News can print pictures of my backside all day if it wants to, and will find no mark or

scar attesting to my undying and lifelong allegiance to DKE or any other such nonsense. "Branding" at DKE is equivalent to a mild cigarette burn. The backs of this year's DKE pledges will be no different from mine in a month from now. The rest of DKE's initiation is personal, and I do not care to discuss it. But I can assure you one thing: after coming out of the initiation I was mentally, not physically, exhausted.[39]

Seven days later there was another set of high-profile stories saying that Yale's fraternity-governing board had unanimously voted to fine two unnamed fraternity houses an undisclosed sum of money. "All types of initiations which . . . might be detrimental to the best interests of the fraternities or of Yale are strictly forbidden," the governing body said in its official statement. Reverend William Sloane Coffin, for one, was watching the backlash against the fraternity system. "E. B. White was asked, 'What's the opposite of a fraternity?' He answered, 'Fraternity.' To take an illiberal student and put him in a fraternity is like taking a wino and putting him in a wine cellar," said Coffin many years later.[40]

A WEEK after the fraternity was penalized and he was defending the DKEs in print, Bush was again picked up by the police, this time by law enforcement officials in Princeton, New Jersey. He had traveled there with his fraternity brothers for the Yale-Princeton Ivy League championship football game on November 18. Yale had been ahead the entire game and finally won 29–7. Brian Dowling and Calvin Hill, loyal DKEs, had had their usual stellar day on the field. Just as the game ended, a fractious crowd gathered at one end of the field. Photographs in the *Daily Princetonian* show a throng on the field reducing the venerable wooden goalposts to, as the paper described it, "a twisted wreck."[41] The police quickly moved in to control the scene, to make sure that there were no fistfights, no further violence or property destruction. Newspapers reported scuffles, and there was at least one report of someone allegedly being assaulted and having his clothing stolen. According to Princeton police records, Bush was detained, questioned, and issued a warning. Information about the case was turned over to school authorities for any future investigation.[42]

"Somehow they picked him out," said Donald Ensenat, a best friend and a loyal fraternity brother from New Orleans. "The police came along, and somehow he got collared. I think I've learned since that the record reflects that he was told to leave Princeton. He had until sundown to leave campus."[43]

• • •

IN THE SPRING of 1968, the political fervor and the pitch of the intellectual arguments over racism, the war, and economic disparities had reached levels unprecedented in the history of the school. Yale's Black Student Alliance made national newspaper headlines by embarking on a two-day boycott of classes "to express our feelings of alienation from Yale, and of outrage and anger at the treatment routinely meted out to black people in this city."[44] There were an estimated ninety African Americans among the four thousand students at Yale. Author Daniel Yergin, one of Bush's classmates, would later write about 1968 as a time when "an alienation and suspicion of American purpose in the world had become common in our generation."[45] Students in the class of 1968 were obviously going through changes; future filmmaker Oliver Stone had already dropped out and would serve in Vietnam. And the outside events that spring were watershed moments in American history.

It began with the militarily debilitating and psychologically unhinging terror of the Viet Cong's Tet offensive in February. It culminated in a fateful seven-day span in April that began with President Johnson's stunning decision to abandon Washington for the Texas Hill Country and his televised announcement that "I shall not seek, and I will not accept the nomination of my party for another term as your president." Johnson's additional declaration to the 70 million viewers that he was halting the bombing of North Vietnam added up to a wild leap in the stock market and almost a collective sigh of relief around campuses, corporations, and households. A few days later, Dr. King was assassinated in Memphis and the United States was almost instantly engulfed in the most violent, chaotic racial outbursts in its history.

Washington was rocked to its core, with Stokely Carmichael and other black activists appearing in the impoverished neighborhoods ringing the seats of power and threatening revenge on "white America": "Go home and get your guns . . . when the white man comes he is coming to kill you." An order was quickly handed down to have squads of federal troops, many of them wielding rifles and bayonets, dispatched to guard the White House grounds. Other troops set up a machine-gun post to stave off any attackers who might storm up the steps of the Capitol. There were troop callouts, riots, or fires in 130 American cities; there were at least 20,000 arrests, and almost 70,000 military personnel activated to confront the domestic disturbances. There were more than a few people at Yale who felt that the entire scope of the cultural and political departures was somehow aimed squarely at what Yale embodied. William Sloane Coffin Jr. was going to trial, along with Andover and Yale graduate Dr. Benjamin Spock, in Boston's Federal Court Building on charges of conspiring to "counsel, aid and abet" young men interested in defying Selective Service laws. During the trial, Yale reappointed Coffin to the post of university chaplain. Elsewhere in New Haven, there were also stirrings—signs of Bobby Seale's strategy to expand the Black Panther Party from five to forty-five chapters across the country.

Finally, all semester, the members of the last all-male class at Yale were busy exploring, debating their ominous postcollege options, including the fact that student deferments were about to expire. For many, the obvious bottom line was avoiding going overseas. "Everybody did something: medical school, Naval Officer Candidate School. You either got drafted or flunked your physical," said Bush's classmate J. P. Goldsmith.[46] His other friends at Yale wondered if Vietnam was on Bush's mind at all, since he hardly ever spoke about it. He rarely talked about the nuances of the war, the stances his father and grandfather were taking, the military strategies, the roiling student protests, the way it was all rattling the highest levels of government around the world. Around him, his fraternity brothers were constantly debating—and the debates usually centered on the fact that so many of them, like Bush, had parents and grandparents who had had distinguished military careers. "Our parents had been in the military, and it was just something that was accepted," said James Lockhart III, the DKE brother who would later head the Pension Benefit Guarantee Corporation in the Bush administration. "The Army was not the spot to end up. . . . The general opinion was to get into a branch of the service that if you'd be sent to Vietnam you had to volunteer to get there rather than just be sent."[47] Even Bush's fellow Bonesman, world record swimmer Don Schollander, had announced that he was opposed to the war and to the draft, but that "I'll serve if I'm called."

Bush had registered with Texas Local Board No. 62 in the Selective Service System's Federal Building in downtown Houston and was still classified II-S, "registrant deferred because of activity in study."[48] In a rare expression of his feelings, he told one fraternity brother that he had been upset by what he thought was knee-jerk opposition to the American military's arrival in Southeast Asia: "He was upset by unthinking opposition to the war, just for its own sake," said Robert Beebe.[49] Back in Houston, Bush had also talked briefly with his summertime friends about the alternatives after his student deferment would expire. "George and I used to talk all the time that there has to be a better alternative than being a lieutenant in the Army. We didn't know people who were killed in Vietnam. We lost far more friends to motorcycle accidents than we ever did to Vietnam," said Doug Hannah.[50]

There was also speculation among Bush's closest friends about what the congressman's son would do—for himself, his family's reputation, his father's obvious designs on the Senate and the White House. In the end, it was another decision made as much for his father as for himself: "He felt that in order not to derail his father's political career he had to be in military service of some kind," said Roland Betts, one of his most faithful colleagues from the DKE house.[51]

In Houston, the sons of the most powerful political families in the state—the Connallys, the Bentsens, and the Bushes—were learning about precious slots available in the National Guard. Bush met with a Texas Air National Guard commander from Houston and enlisted twelve days before graduation, ensuring that he would return to Texas once his student deferment was taken away. "I was not prepared to shoot my eardrum out with a shotgun in order to get a deferment. Nor was I willing to go to Canada. I decided to better myself by learning how to fly airplanes," said Bush.[52] "I don't want to play like I was somebody out there marching when I wasn't. It was either Canada or the service and I was headed into the service. Somebody said the Guard was looking for pilots. All I know is there weren't that many people trying to be pilots."[53]

ON JUNE 9—three days after Robert F. Kennedy's assassination, a week after thousands streamed into Washington for the Poor People's March, a month after 720 student activists had been arrested in the takeover of Columbia University's administration building—Yale President Kingman Brewster Jr. gave the annual baccalaureate address to history major George W. Bush and the other 954 seniors assembled in Woolsey Hall. Brewster's oldest son had recently received a draft exemption as a conscientious objector. Brewster dedicated much of his speech to what was on his son's mind, what was on the minds of almost every student. The draft system, he said, had created a "cynical, evasive gamesmanship. . . . [M]any feel that they have no choice other than to approach the problem of military service in much the same spirit as a tax lawyer. They are left to weave their way down the narrow line which divides proper avoidance from improper evasion."[54] Brewster conferred various undergraduate awards, including the Snow Prize to Strobe Talbott for doing "the most for Yale by inspiring in his classmates a love for the traditions of high scholarship." (Years later,

Bush would harshly criticize Talbott on national TV, accusing him of being part of a conspiracy in the national media to keep his father from the presidency.)

The day after the baccalaureate ceremony formal graduation exercises were held under a slate gray sky. It was "a solemn outdoor ceremony heavily laced with reminders of the war in Vietnam."[55] There were 2,402 degrees to be conferred, including 14 honorary doctorates given to, among others, Cyrus Vance, then the deputy chief of the American delegation to the preliminary Vietnam peace talks in Paris; Sigmund Freud's daughter, Anna Freud; Robert Lowell, the poet who had been jailed for refusing to be drafted during World War II; Chester Bowles, ambassador to India; and Robert Lehman, president of the Metropolitan Museum of Art.

That day freshly printed copies of an antiwar petition circulated. It was signed by 312 of the 955 graduating seniors and outlined, in part, "opposition to our nation's unjust and destructive policies in Vietnam." Bush had not signed the petition. At Yale, he had aggressively avoided the weight, the intellectual gravity, the ambiguity unfolding before him—all those questions being asked about hazing, about women being admitted, about fraternities, secret societies, jocks, Vietnam, the government, big business. Years later, he was certain about his aversion to all of it: "I don't remember any kind of heaviness ruining my time at Yale."[56]

There was no commencement address. In the invocation given by Right Reverend Paul Moore Jr., a Yale trustee, he prayed for Chaplain William Sloane Coffin, the man George W. had unhappily encountered his first year on campus and who was now in Boston and still on trial for helping draft resisters. It was Coffin, more than anyone else, who symbolized for him the way Yale was changing—all that strangling, cultural kudzu that he could see blanketing what the school once stood for. "We pray for Yale's chaplain in the vocation of service which keeps him from us today," said the Yale trustee who was giving the invocation.

During graduation, Bush's friends were shocked to see his father, the U.S. congressman, on campus. He was rarely spotted, except when his name was on the front page of the student newspaper. He stayed for two hours, said a friend of George W.'s, and then left. And after his father was gone, Bush spent the rest of graduation weekend with roommate Clay Johnson's family, as if, said a friend, they were his surrogate parents.

"My father doesn't have a normal life. I don't have a normal father," Johnson heard Bush say. Johnson looked at his old Andover classmate and Yale roommate. He knew and he could see that Bush felt that he didn't have "normal access" to his father—but that he wished he had.[57]

7

Flying

Right up until his last day on campus, students and faculty seemed to turn their backs on the Bush-Walker touchstones. The fraternity system, the secret society, and the Yale administration and trustees, including Prescott Bush, were increasingly under suspicion. The inviolable things you were buying when you bought a Yale diploma, things like the unswerving loyalty of Bonesmen like William Sloane Coffin—"supposedly the guy that was there to comfort students," said an obviously bitter Bush[1]—even that was changing. He reiterated what he had been saying in the last few months at Yale. "He was very strong identifying himself as a Texan, maybe because of being at Yale and in Connecticut. It seemed a given that he'd go back to Texas," believed a Davenport resident.[2] Leaving the Northeast, Bush said, was all about leaving guilt behind. And, it was about returning to a state with an incomparable tendency to embrace every one of its most profound, flamboyant moneymakers.

He told friends that he was tired of suggestions that he should feel guilty about the family's far-flung fortune and influence. Upon graduating from Yale, he was convinced, more than ever, that his family, especially his father, had simply worked harder, run harder, moved faster than anyone else to make their fortune—and that living in West Texas, in the Permian Basin, where he had watched his father emerge outside the daily presence of the family network, was proof that making money was, as he would one day say, a matter of "free will." He was tired of all those Yale people, including Garry Trudeau, the Davenport resident and future *Doonesbury* cartoonist, who, he later concluded, were tending toward some naive idealism and sagging under the weight of an enormous, self-created guilt complex about their station in life.[3] "I saw this at Yale University," he later said. "People who felt guilty about their lot in life because others were suffering, or people who felt guilty because they happened to inherit a whole bunch of money and they hadn't done a dang thing to deserve it, but therefore felt guilty about it. There was this whole period of 'Well, I'm going to dedicate my trust fund to whatever, whatever, whatever,' and 'You're at fault.' "[4]

GEORGE W.'s father had been the youngest commissioned officer in the navy: shot down, rescued at sea by a submarine, sent home with medals. It was impossible to escape his father's war record. It had been brought up in the Senate campaign and in the congressional campaign, and it was a convenient reference point whenever he heard his father being interviewed or speaking at debates about the war in Vietnam. It was also there in the manner his father had perfected, the way he was so consistent about keeping himself and his family in touch with his military experience, with those other people who had gone to war with him. In the family scrapbooks and photo collections, Bush had seen the pictures of his father wearing shades and grinning back from the cockpit of his Avenger torpedo bomber—the one with *Barbara III* stenciled on the side—and the black-and-white picture of his father being fished out of the ocean by the submarine crew.

There were other portraits, dozens of them, shot after shot of his father in his crisp Navy lieutenant's uniform on the brisk winter day in January 1945 when he had married Barbara. George W. and the other Bushes and Walkers also knew this: in the Navy hymn, the third verse was always his father's favorite. It was the one that made his eyes well up, hit him in the core: "God bless the men who fly . . ." In the family, people knew that the Old Man had never seen Prescott Bush cry until the day at Pennsylvania Station in New York when the Old Man was being shipped out on a troop transport train for combat training in North Carolina. Back then, Barbara believed she knew what was on her future husband's mind, what was on the mind of everyone in the Bush-Walker clan: "When you're that young, you don't really consider death as a possibility," she said.[5]

Bush's father had come close to dying on September 2, 1944, the day he was shot down and finally rescued by the submarine crew on the USS *Finback*. In the sub, he talked with the sailors about how he had tasted fear, about the adrenaline-laced terror as the *Finback* had dived underwater and waited for an unseen Japanese attack. It had scared him more than flying in combat. "Many of the *Finback* officers said that they would never want to be a pilot, because you were too vulnerable as a pilot, and if you got hit, it was all over. Yet here I was, living proof that you could fall out of the sky and live to talk about it."[6]

ON MAY 27, 1968, Bush had talked with Lieutenant Colonel Walter "Buck" Staudt, the salty-tongued, cigar-gnawing, gravel-voiced Air Force veteran who was now commanding the 147th Fighter Group with the Texas Air National Guard in Houston. Staudt was one of the higher-ranking officers entrusted with the task of meting out the valuable slots in the Texas Guard. Staudt had told the congressman's son that there would be a battery of written exams and interviews administered by officers. Finally, Staudt asked the question he really wanted—needed—to have answered in a year when all the usual rules were being upended and so many people were looking for safer options than being drafted and instantly shipped off to war.

"Why do you want to join the Texas Air National Guard? What's the real reason?" Staudt, whom most people said was a ringer for Patton, had asked him.

"I want to be a fighter pilot because my father was," Staudt heard Bush say.[7]

Bush told his Houston society friends he was going to like the Guard, that it was all about living in the moment, especially if you were going to fly alone in a jet. Flying was simple—mechanical, really, in contrast with the way other things in the United States were evolving. Several years later, he talked about the late 1960s and how "the sharp contrast between right and wrong became blurred. . . . [W]e went from accepting responsibility to assigning blame. We became a nation of victims."[8]

Now that his draft status was simplified, now that he was based in his hometown and in the National Guard, there was something elemental about lighting the burners on a jet and flying around Texas. "For me it was much more practical. I am not very good at psychoanalyzing myself, but I learned to fly," Bush said to a writer for a National Guard magazine. "I remember telling people everywhere I went that it didn't matter where you've been, where you were going or what you were doing, when you put a burner on you are focused on the moment."[9]

The 147th Fighter Group had been founded as the 111th Squadron in 1923, and had enjoyed an honored combat record. Its airmen had flown in World War II and Korea, but in 1958 the group had been reorganized as an Air Defense Command Support Group. Its stated mission in the Cold War years, the era of nuclear proliferation and Fidel Castro, was to "defend" the Gulf coast and South Texas against ostensible attacks from the Soviet Union or anybody else who might decide to move up from Mexico, Central America, or South America. One of its airmen earnestly and simply said, "We were to shoot down Russian bombers if they came across our borders."[10]

It was an unofficial rule that most people joining the 147th in the mid-1960s would not be going to Vietnam. Subsequently, slots in the 147th were increasingly rare. There were ninety-eight officer slots authorized for Bush's unit, and seventy-two were already assigned when Bush enlisted, according to Texas Guard historians. Of the twenty-six remaining slots, five were set aside for pilots, and those were divvied up according to age, whether an applicant had a college degree or not, and how well he performed on the written and oral tests. Some Guard officials maintained that in fact there were no slots available and that there was a waiting list: "We were full," said Major General Thomas Bishop, who was the state's adjutant general in 1968. "There were definitely waiting lists. There wasn't any question about that," said another Guard official.[11] "There was a five-hundred-man waiting list prior to 1972, so there was not much recruiting. When someone left, you went to the next guy in line. I don't think his family got him in. There were rigorous qualifications, a battery of tests. I have no idea how long they had to wait on the list," added Joe Briggs, a retired chief master sergeant who served with the 147th from 1957 to 1993.[12]

In the early 1990s, there would be ceaseless speculation that somebody had pulled strings to help George W. get in. The allegations included suggestions that then–Texas Speaker of the House Ben Barnes might have been instrumental in Bush's application: "I had a lot of requests," Barnes recalled. "With the National Guard being an agency of the state of Texas, it obviously helped for the governor, lieutenant governor and the speaker to be recommending you." But Barnes said he couldn't recall whether or not he had helped the congressman's son, though he had aided the children of other influential Texans. "Nobody ever could [recall], and my staff was divided if I did or did not."[13]

One thing was still clear: most men entering the 147th Fighter Wing were under the impression that they were not going to Vietnam. Nationally, according to *The New York Times* and other publications, only 15,000 of the total of 1,040,000 Guardsmen and reservists would be sent to Vietnam.[14] In Houston, the sons of prominent families were enlisting in the Guard; some people later called it The Champagne Unit. Lloyd Bentsen III, son of the future senator and vice presidential candidate, had met Lieutenant Colonel Staudt at a friend's party in Houston and was also on his way into the same Guard unit. Bentsen had just finished his MBA at Stanford, and at the party Staudt told him that he was looking for men to fill the handful of remaining officer slots and could use someone in the Guard's accounting division. "His job was to go out and recruit people and guys like us who had just graduated from college and were willing to go off and be officers," said Bentsen.[15] Buck Staudt swore both him and Bush into the Texas Air National Guard, and they were then introduced to the other unit members. Bush was facing eighteen months of basic training, officer candidacy, and flight training before he could earn his pilot's wings. Staudt filed his paperwork on Bush and wrote, "*Applicant is a quiet, intelligent young man who has the interest, motivation and knowledge necessary to become a commissioned officer.*"[16]

It was, in some way, a reunion for people who had known one another from private clubs and the extended whirlwind of Texas's two premier private schools, Kinkaid and St. John's. "I tell you one thing, if they had done a story about our unit, it would have been just unbelievable. You had all the sons of the leaders of Houston," said Guardsman John Adger, whose father was an influential Texas oilman. Adger, like others, heard the accusations that the unit was really a home away from home for country club scions. "I looked at the alternative of being over in Vietnam. We sure didn't do anything that was beyond the law or anything," said Adger, who went on to buy and sell racehorses, flying between Texas and Kentucky.[17] Also in the unit was John Daugherty, whose father was an oil field pipe supplier who had a long-term business and social relationship with the elder Bush and yachtsman-investor Robert Mosbacher. "Most of us were members of the Houston and River Oaks country clubs, and we would see each other," said Daugherty.[18]

As usual, the elder George Bush refused to publicly draw any parallels between himself and his first son; he declined to say anything that could even be remotely construed as a comparison with his own war record. In 1987, he wrote his autobiography with help from his speechwriter, Vic Gold; the book was intended to promote Bush's 1988 campaign for the presidency, and in it he wrote that his son had been in the Air Force: "Now 'little' George was flying jets in the Air Force. Barbara, the other kids—Jeb, Neil, Marvin, Dorothy—and I were in a Waldorf suite overlooking the East River."[19] Barbara Bush was more specific. "What was wrong with that?" she demanded, talking about the National Guard. "Lloyd Bentsen's son was in the National Guard. George Bush's son was in the National Guard. And we're damn proud of him."[20]

• • •

BY NOW it was clear that Bush's engagement with Cathryn Wolfman would be called off. When they were planning their future, they had talked about getting married prior to his senior year at Yale. But the exact wedding plans kept getting pushed back to some uncertain future date, probably after graduation and maybe sometime in 1968. Friends in Houston speculated that it was because Wolfman and her family were having second thoughts about the burden of her marrying a man who was carrying his father's legacy on his back. "That whole process of getting engaged as a junior, which was just duplicating what his father had done—I think she realized at some point that George was just trying to do exactly what his dad did. She didn't want to be the next-generation duplicate, so she said, 'Let's wait.' They stayed really close for a year, and then they just drifted apart," said Doug Hannah. "It might have been the first time that anybody told George, 'No.' There is not a long list of people who have walked away from George Bush. Cathy was one of them."[21]

Hannah was worried about his usually upbeat friend. "That came as close to undoing him as anything that ever happened to him. She was spectacular, and they would have been a very good pair."[22] Bush had known, once the wedding was postponed, that there probably would never be a wedding at all. The couple had talked about preparing and printing wedding invitations, but Bush also knew that once he left for basic training, it would probably spell the end of marriage plans. After Wolfman graduated from Rice, she went to work in Washington, D.C., and met a Harvard MBA graduate named Roderick Young. They were married in May 1969. From friends in Houston, he heard that she had met someone, maybe in Washington, whom she was growing close to. Bush has rarely spoken publicly about the breakup, but in a 1998 interview with the *Fort Worth Star-Telegram*, he said that things had basically ended with the wedding postponement: "I went to basic training, and that's really the last time I spent any time with her. She met some other guy and she went off and got married."[23]

Hannah and several of their Houston friends continued to gravitate toward Lacey Neuhaus, who seemed to know everyone in town, who knew about the stock market, who knew famous people. She would become a Ford Agency model, an art gallery owner, and an actress. She would also move to Washington, D.C., when she was hired by economist Arthur Laffer to "work on a film series explaining the Republican economic philosophy to voters."[24] From 1981 on, references to her would abound in *The*

Washington Post—she reportedly dated Canadian Prime Minister Pierre Trudeau, Senator John Warner, and Senator Ted Kennedy and was "pal to the likes of . . . Andy Warhol, Barbara Walters and heaven-knows who-all."[25] There were, as well, news items indicating that she and Kennedy considered marrying. Neuhaus would also serve, for a while, in the Bush administration as the director of a State Department program that involved placing prominent works of American art in several U.S. embassies.

In the summers, Christina "Tina" Cassini also came to visit Houston and her old friends, including Neuhaus, Hannah, and George W. Bush. She was the daughter of actress Gene Tierney and international fashion designer Oleg Cassini. Tierney, semiretired and living in Houston, had appeared in thirty-three films and three Broadway plays and starred opposite Clark Gable, Spencer Tracy, Henry Fonda, Tyrone Power, and Humphrey Bogart. She had once been courted by the roving playboy Prince Aly Khan, Howard Hughes, and the young John F. Kennedy. Then, in the mid-1950s, she had been beset by mental health problems. For years she had drifted in and out of clinics and hospitals. She had been given shock treatment and "cold-packed," wrapped tightly in wet sheets. She had finally spent a year in the Menninger Foundation sanitarium in Kansas and, after her release, had married a larger-than-life, free-spending Texas millionaire and oil wildcatter named W. Howard Lee in the summer of 1960. Lee had once been married to another superstar actress, Hedy Lamarr, and his brother-in-law had been the model for the character Jett Rink in the quintessential Texas novel and movie *Giant*.[26] In starstruck Houston, W. Howard Lee was an oversized Texan with the penchant for Hollywood legends—and Gene Tierney was, really, a form of royalty. The couple were invited to every important function, fete, ball, and political fund-raiser in the city, as was Tina Cassini when she was in town and staying with her mother.

"This will piss Lacey off, I'll go after her [Cassini], check this out," Hannah heard George W. say one night. Hannah watched his friend: "There was that kind of thrill there. She was a real show pony, and George latched on to her. They paraded for a summer. Tina was spectacular. It was a real salvation for George to have a woman that everyone wanted to be with. We got to hang around with Gene Tierney. [Tina] was younger than we were, and she had to go back to school. It was a good fling."

Hannah believed that Bush's parents had pushed his friend toward someone who had as impressive a family pedigree as Cassini. "Mr. Bush knew exactly what he was doing. He would set up guys and girls that he thought belonged together. He even set up his own brother Jonathan with the daughter of a stockbroker, tried his damnedest to get that working. Mr. Bush would set up people, get them dates, give them money to go out and have a good time, and just revel in his abilities to put those things together."[27] Daugherty, one of George W.'s friends in the National Guard, had also once dated Cassini: "She was a real sweet, pretty girl, and when she was in town, we were all rushing to take her out. She was here a lot during the holidays for debutante parties."[28]

By November 1968, after basic training in San Antonio and a brief stint as a "gofer" for Edward Gurney's Florida senate campaign, Bush was shipped out for a year of National Guard flight training. Cassini would marry, become Christina Granata-Belmont, have four children, and live in Paris.[29] In the fall of 1968, Bush packed his blue Triumph convertible and drove east on the interstate toward Moody Air Force Base in Valdosta, Georgia. There were seventy other airmen, many destined for Vietnam after their year-long flight training. They came from various military branches; he was the only Guardsman.[30] Back at Yale, things were continuing to unravel. The DKE house was on the verge of being shut down. Bobby Seale and the Black Panthers would bring New Haven to its knees. Tanks would roll down Elm Street.

AT MOODY, Bush trained on F-102 Interceptors, nimble but increasingly obsolete jets that had been used for weather reconnaissance, checking target areas, and as defense-minded companions to bombers. Pilots called it a sports car because of its light wing load and its ability to quickly climb to 40,000 feet, but in the early 1970s the plane was considered a dinosaur and not an integral part of the armed forces. The F-102s that were used in Vietnam were assigned to fly alongside B-52s during combat air patrols, armed with Falcon missiles. In 1974, the 147th would be one of the last National Guard outfits to retire the plane. Military historians have said that there was a shortage of F-102 pilots in the late 1960s and early 1970s because the plane was considered obsolete—and because the U.S. military considered it a much higher priority to have pilots trained for other, more important aircraft.[31]

At Moody, the fledgling pilots arrived from around the country. They were briefed by the airmen who already knew the lay of the land. They said Valdosta was corrupt and racist—and worse, it was practically dry. Said Bernard Reynolds, one of the trainees, "There was one bar and one whorehouse in town and both were 'owned' by the sheriff—at least that's what the rumor was. You have no idea how far back in history this place was. The civil rights laws were on the books, yet there was a big sign in the store window that said 'No Niggers.' It was a very backwards town."[32]

The pilots learned about the F-102, a plane they called "The Deuce," during flight simulation sessions. Some of the pilots kept an initially skeptical eye on George W. Bush. He was a rapidly promoted Guardsman from Texas, and he already had his assignment. He knew where he was going, back to Texas when they were all through, and in a way he had no real incentive to do anything other than survive training at 600 to 650 miles per hour. There were courses in aerodynamics, the Morse code, and physiology. On Friday and Saturday nights, there wasn't much else to do but spend time in the officers' club, trying to hustle moments with the women who came in from Valdosta and the smaller rural Georgia towns. The place was jammed, a band called the Bulls was playing in the corner, and some people couldn't wait for them to finish so they could plug quarters in the jukebox. There was beer. More beer. And enough women that the joke was that they were being bused in from all over the state. "There were the aviation groupies that would come to the club a lot. Some were very nice girls, and some you just knew what they were there for. It wasn't a bad place to spend a Friday night," said Roger Dahlberg, a down-home trainee from Memphis who became friends with Bush.[33]

The pilots who were committed to the Air Force and likely tours in Vietnam eventually cut the lone energetic Guardsman some slack. Some said they respected the way he handled a plane when he and Joe Chaney, an airman from Montgomery, Alabama, took off together in a tight formation. "Everybody knew who he was and who his father was," said Norman Dotti, who was in Bush's's training section. "They knew he was there from the Texas Air National Guard. If anybody felt negative about that, nobody said anything. He was certainly competent. He didn't put on airs."[34]

And for Bush, it was really just like being back at the fraternity, back in the tomb of Skull & Bones. Bush dished out nicknames to everybody. Jeff Kenyon was . . . *Fly!* . . . and Ralph Anderson . . . he was . . . *Road!* . . . and Terry McCollom . . . he was . . . *Chubby!* "We worked hard and played hard, throwing dice and talking about flying and drinking. We went to the bar, played bar games, swapped lies. He was extremely intelligent, very witty and humorous," said Chaney.[35] And there would always be a crowd around Bush and he was doing that thing—again—just like in Houston, over the summers: *"Can anybody tell me all—all—of Willie Mays' batting averages?"*

Sometimes on weekends they'd play softball, or members of his training sector would venture past the pine trees and into downtown Valdosta,
the pilots from the North on the verge of barfing from their first taste of
grits, and they would marvel at the way the short-order cook was sub-
merging the bacon in the deep-fat fryer. To clear their minds, Bush and
Dahlberg took one weekend trip to Panama City, Florida, and then returned to Florida when everyone got a day off because Eisenhower had
died. During training, one of the junior pilots was talking about his marital troubles. Bush pulled him aside and lightened him up. He was organizing the card game—moving, cursing, yelling nonstop even when he
knew they were laughing about the way he was alone in the cockpit during flight simulation sessions, going over the checklists and animatedly
jabbering to himself. "He was talking so much about what he was doing
while he was doing it. I guess it's a politician's nature. I guess he was practicing for it," said Jeff Kenyon, another flyboy at Moody.[36]

THERE WAS another buzz about Bush that was beginning to hum through
Moody. Midway through the year-long training program, word spread
that a government plane was scheduled to arrive from Andrews Air Force
Base in Washington to pick up the Guardsman, George W. Bush. President Richard Nixon's daughter Tricia needed a dinner date, and Nixon
had ordered that a plane be sent to Georgia to fetch the son of the forty-
five-year-old Houston congressman—the climbing congressman Nixon
had ardently, dutifully campaigned for on two different occasions in Texas.
In Washington, it was no secret that Representative Bush wanted to prove
to Nixon that he could finally win a Senate seat in Texas. Prescott Bush
had once advised his son against running for the Senate, but his other children knew what George Herbert Walker Bush was aiming for. Jonathan,
for one, believed that his older brother simply wanted to leave the House
because the Senate might be a better launching pad toward a run for the
presidency.[37] Besides, Congressman Bush had heard what he needed to
hear when LBJ stared into his face one day down at his ranch in Texas:
    *"Son . . . I've served in the House. And I've been privileged to serve in the
Senate, too . . . and they're both good places to serve. So I wouldn't begin to advise
you what to do, except to say this: that the difference between being a member of
the Senate and a member of the House is the difference between chicken salad and
chicken shit. . . . Do I make my point?"*[38]
    Nixon was wholeheartedly in support of the Bush for Senate cam-
paign. Nixon was also interested in pushing along the Republicanization

of Texas. He had named Mexican Americans to positions as head of the Small Business Administration and as U.S. attorney for the Southern District of Texas.[39] Nixon and Vice President Spiro Agnew jetted down to Texas, along with five cabinet officers, to repeatedly stump for the Bush for Senate campaign. Meanwhile, Nixon's longtime political backers had allegedly been affiliated with a scheme to contribute money to a secret fund, called the Townhouse Operation, destined for favored GOP candidates. Bush wound up receiving $106,000.[40]

With Nixon, Agnew, and Senator John Tower, the head of the Republican Senate Campaign Committee, all contributing heavily to the elder Bush, it was a prudent time for the first son to get on a government plane and fly to Washington for a date with Tricia Nixon. As if there were need for another reason, there was also the undeniable, ever-threatening presence of former Texas Governor John Connally, the self-made millionaire who had survived the gunfire that had killed President Kennedy in Dallas and the one man who could thwart any plans that the elder George Bush might have had to move closer to Nixon and beyond a congressional seat from Texas. Nixon had openly targeted Connally as a possible key Texas ally and convert to the GOP, someone with the hard, conservative credentials that could deliver the state to the Republicans.

In Washington, there was already high-level speculation that Nixon had looked at a long-range scenario that would involve Connally joining his Cabinet. With Connally and the elder George Bush jockeying for Nixon's affections, it was, really, a good time for the younger George Bush to be on his way to Washington to meet the president's daughter.

As word got out that someone was actually going to leave the base—and that he was being picked up on an official government transport to date the Finch College graduate, one of the pilot trainees asked him, "Are you sure you just don't want to bring her down here?"

The date wasn't a memorable one, though the Moody AFB pilots wouldn't let him forget it when he returned from his two-day trip. He would never divulge the details, and the Vietnam-bound pilots wouldn't ease up about his devotion to duty—his devotion to his father's aspirations for the Senate and beyond. Of course, word even went all the way back to Houston. His friends there knew that he had hated the entire episode, hated being forced to endure that long plane ride to Washington. "We went to dinner. It wasn't a very long date," was all Bush would ever say.[41]

What was memorable was the fact that anyone, even the son of a congressman from Texas, could get the hell out of that deep-fat-fried outpost, out of the mind-numbing boredom. Now, said some flyboys, *that* was impressive. Misery loved company that summer in Georgia—from the total immersion in the grinding reality of life at Moody, the gnawing possibilities of something going wrong in the air, suffering through another bad cover tune by the Bulls . . . and the other pilots' prevalent thought that they could be sent to Southeast Asia. There really wasn't time or room for any sort of a pecking order to develop. But now somebody had the *juice* to get way off campus, and that was way off the usual charts and checklists. "He did have the opportunity to leave south Georgia when the rest of us couldn't. If you're not from that environment, it's interesting to observe the things they do that none of us had ever known about. He was already mixed up in higher politics," said Dahlberg.[42]

Romance with President Nixon's daughter never blossomed. Back at Moody, Bush led his training section's basketball team to a second place finish. In the fall, he started seeing a young woman from Valdosta, picking her up in his sports car on Friday nights and bringing her back to the officers' club. Everyone knew her simply as Judy, a striking woman who seemed dedicated to George W. The relationship lasted a few months, ending close to the time he was set to rotate out of Georgia permanently.[43]

He was awarded his National Guard wings in December 1969 and started on his way back, in the blue Triumph, to Houston and an assignment flying night maneuvers at Ellington Air Force Base.

AFTER GEORGE W. Bush returned, his father officially declared for the Senate in early January 1970, and the old crew quickly began reassembling to help out with time and money—all those friends from the private schools, the country clubs, and the National Guard, many of whom had helped his father run in the past.

The Bush-Walker fund-raising network, the one that had grown in efficiency as Prescott Bush's political career advanced, was still in place, but by now it was slowly being cushioned in energy and sheer dollars by the dozens of prominent oilmen, including the Liedtkes and Mosbacher, who had thrown themselves into GOP politics in Texas. Some of his father's wealthy supporters from the oil sector, running in a line from Midland to Dallas to Houston, had been searching, in the late 1960s and early 1970s, for an entirely new set of extravagant challenges, and it was a pattern of support that would be repeated over the next two decades in Texas for both father and son.

In Houston, he agreed to share an apartment with another National Guardsman, a Jaguar-driving future airline pilot named Dean Roome, just down the road from the NASA facility outside Houston. His roommate, close to five months ahead of him in the pilot training class at Moody, knew the young Bush was worried about the way people viewed someone with a famous name. "If you have a famous father, it was harder than easier. You had to be a role model in your own right. It was at least as hard or harder," said Roome.[44] But there were benefits, too: "He was a good-looking first lieutenant–bachelor–fighter pilot. Just think of the environment."[45]

Then, in March, a press release was delivered from the National Guard to the editors at *The Houston Post* and the *Houston Chronicle*—amid all the press releases about Senate candidate George Bush:

ELLINGTON AFB, Tex., March 24, 1970—George Walker Bush is one member of the younger generation who doesn't get his kicks from pot or hashish or speed. Oh, he gets high, all right, but not from narcotics.

Bush is a second lieutenant attached to the 111th Combat Crew Training Squadron, 147th Combat Crew Training Group, Texas Air National Guard at Houston. . . . After his solo, a milestone in the career of any fighter pilot, Lt. Bush couldn't find enough words to adequately express the feeling of solo flight.

"It was really neat. It was fun, and very exciting," he said. "I felt really serene up there. It's exciting to be alone in such a big aircraft and it's a real challenge to fly such a powerful airplane by yourself."

Fighter planes are Lt. Bush's "thing." He says he has no ambition to fly any other type of aircraft.

"Fighters are it. I've always wanted to be a fighter pilot and I wouldn't want to fly anything else," he said. "You have such speed, such power in a fighter, that it's just fantastic."

Despite the fact that he's flown the F-102 solo for the first time, Lt. Bush isn't letting it go to his head.

"I've got a hell of a lot more to learn," he said. "I've got to learn to respect the aircraft and its capabilities, as well as my own abilities."

Lt. Bush is the son of U.S. Representative George Bush, who is a candidate for the U.S. Senate seat of Senator Ralph Yarborough. The elder Bush was a Navy fighter pilot. Lt. Bush said his father was just as excited and enthusiastic about his solo flight as he was.

Lt. Bush, who is 23, is due to complete his pilot training June 23. He will then be released from active duty and assume reserve status in the Air National Guard. He plans to fly as much as possible with the Air Guard and work in his father's campaign. Beyond that, he hasn't any plans.

As far as kicks are concerned, Lt. Bush gets his from the roaring afterburner of the F-102.

"Flying, the whole thing, is kicks," he said. "But afterburner is a real kick."[46]

HE WAS STILL on full-time active duty, aiming to complete the final stages of pilot training by midsummer. He arranged to take an early-April trip to Washington to be a member of the wedding party for the son of Pennzoil president Baine Kerr and the daughter of newsman and LBJ confidant William S. White. He also began talking to some old friends from the DKE house about going to law school. He had narrowed his decision down to the University of Texas, the school he had told Houston friends in 1964 he was dead set on attending until he was finally notified of his acceptance to Yale. His decision to explore law school, especially at the University of Texas, was something he had talked about in detail with Donald Ensenat. His DKE brother had been one of the rare politically focused people in his circle at Yale; Ensenat came from an old Southern Democrat family, and after college he had gone to work for Hale Boggs, the House whip from Louisiana and ardent supporter, along with Representative Bush, of protecting oil interests and the oil depletion allowance. Boggs and the elder Bush were on the Ways and Means Committee, and when George W. would travel to Washington to visit his parents at their two-story brick town house, he would run into Ensenat around the city. The elder Bush gave his son's fraternity brother the name of the Bush for Senate personnel director and told him to call. Ensenat landed a campaign job, moved to Houston, spent time living with George W., and eventually became one of the elder Bush's principal aides.[47]

After six months with Roome, Bush moved into an apartment complex on Beverly Hills Street called the Chateaux Dijon, one of the sprawling singles-oriented, garden-style compounds that were springing up in the middle of the growth-spurt zones of Houston and Dallas. The Chateaux, completed in 1963, had 353 town homes and flats fanning out around six swimming pools in the Uptown-Galleria area. Every weekend there were coed volleyball games, impromptu water polo matches, and beer-blast parties with Rice University students, ex–military men who had gone to work at NASA, and small-town Texas women who had moved to Houston to take jobs as secretaries for downtown oil companies. Bush's one-bedroom apartment, Apartment 29A, looked like his fraternity room, clothes piled in clumps on the floor, crumpled cans, softball gloves. When Sandi Martin moved into the apartment next door to Bush's, the manager let her know that her neighbor was "the Congressman's son."[48]

Owing to National Guard officer training, weekend duties, and remaining on call, Bush found it difficult to devote his exclusive attention to his father's campaign. There were occasional, one-day blitzkrieg trips, sitting on board his father's six-seat King Air campaign plane, the twenty-four-year-old Bush noticeably dressed in his National Guard flight jacket and looking thin and leathery to friends. Sometimes George W. would step to the microphone, those ubiquitous Bush Bluebonnet Belles behind him again, and say a few words. It was 1970, and the Bush for Senate campaign was targeting small, conservative cities around the state. The congressman's son was also taking his first few extensive turns serving as his father's surrogate candidate. "The funniest part of the whole thing was watching George try to be his father—and talk like him, and picking up the mannerisms. He ultimately did it perfectly. I don't know if it was conscious or not," said Doug Hannah, who sometimes traveled with the family.[49]

"HEY, RUBBERS!" was what Ways and Means Committee Chairman Wilbur Mills would yell when he saw Congressman George Bush—a nickname he had selected because of Bush's fixation with family planning. The elder George Bush knew he was finally going to move to the Senate, the launching pad for a ride to the White House. He was more than "just" a moderate conservative, he believed Texans supported having soldiers in Vietnam and he had an expanding GOP power base running from the oil patch to the big-city suburbs. Nixon took *Air Force One* to campaign in East Texas and Dallas, all the while convinced that the elder George Bush had ignored the advice of Nixon's top aides to be more aggressive, to do more in Texas to finally erase those Rye-Greenwich perceptions. Almost as if to counterbalance Nixon's more predatory political tendencies, the somber Prescott Bush and Dorothy Walker Bush also came to Texas to campaign on behalf of their son. But their plans, what seemed like an even more perfect political opportunity, were shredded when millionaire Houston insurance executive and cattle baron Lloyd Bentsen upset the liberal Ralph Yarborough in the Democratic primary.[50] By the fall, Bentsen's surging momentum beat the elder Bush with 53.4 percent of the vote.

Bentsen, who had also won a Distinguished Flying Cross in the Army Air Corps and then attended the University of Texas law school, beat the elder George Bush the same way Yarborough had six years earlier. There were still lingering suggestions about the elder Bush being a latter-day northeasterner dispatched to Texas by the family; it was all there, said some people who watched him, in the way he carried himself, in his inability to convince Texans that he was more than a "plucky lad," as one Texas writer would later describe him, in his inability to consistently behave in a grittier, homespun, Lone Star way. Nixon believed that the elder Bush detested the grip-and-grin of "retail politics" and he would say: "Bush despises campaigning. You can see it all over him. It's not that he doesn't like people; it's just that he's not very comfortable out there on the stump trying to connect with them. He tries too hard to be one of them, eating pork rinds and the rest, but he is not one of them, and it comes across."[51]

As she had after previous private and public losses, Barbara spent the next day playing tennis and breaking down into tears. George W.'s father was, essentially, unemployed. But within weeks after the defeat, his despondent father had flown to a closed-door White House meeting to petition Nixon for the ambassadorship to the United Nations. Connally had already outmaneuvered the elder George Bush for the position both men wanted, secretary of the Treasury, and now the elder Bush was essentially selling himself to Nixon. Washington insiders were talking about Connally's vice presidential and presidential possibilities—about the way he and not the elder George Bush would probably be the significant presidential contender to emerge from Texas.

In the White House, Bush's argument to Nixon for the UN post solely revolved around his belief that he had the right style, the right ability to mingle, the proper comportment, to serve as the U.S. representative. For years, Nixon was known to frequently shout out "Ivy League bastards!," even in front of Bush, whenever he thought someone who had attended Yale or Harvard was too weak-willed, too clubby, too conspiratorial, or too preppy. Now Nixon apparently understood that Bush might not have been efficient at "retail politics" but he could probably carry the country's banner in the social whirl at the United Nations. The Bush-Nixon discussion remained remarkably clear of foreign affairs; to compound it all, Bush later also heard from his old Skull & Bones loyalist Lud Ashley, "George, what the fuck do you know about foreign affairs?"[52] Bush was sworn in late in February, the family moved into the five-bedroom Apartment A on the forty-second floor of the elegant Waldorf Towers in Manhattan, and Barbara Bush borrowed paintings from the Metropolitan Museum of Art, including ones by Mary Cassatt and John Singer Sargent. The building's occupants included Mrs. Douglas MacArthur, actress Carol Channing, and former U.S. Senator Bill Benton. From Houston, George W. made trips to New York to visit his parents and the other members of the Bush-Walker family who were in New York.

Once, Ambassador Bush rented a theater, invited a hundred guests, and had a private showing of *The Godfather,* which had just been released and was sold out all over New York City. Uncle Herbert Walker, the financial angel who had helped fund the multimillion-dollar Bush family oil ventures in Midland, was a part owner of the New York Mets, and the family had a standing invitation to see as many games as they would like. On one visit to New York with George W., Doug Hannah reached out for a piece of Steuben glass, making a joke about stuffing it in his pocket. He looked up and saw Barbara Bush staring at him. "Neither you nor I can afford to get caught," she said.[53]

Finally, George W.'s parents embarked on a worldwide trip so the new ambassador could introduce himself abroad and when they left, the first son's friends saw a change in the younger Bush. In Houston he was drinking, hanging out late, and, as one class-conscious friend said, keeping the company of people who weren't "his equals." It had, said Doug Hannah, everything to do with the fact that his father had lost the race that was a prelude to the presidency. Hannah added, "He was so lost and floating that he had several places to go and never really was at any of them. He was getting fairly aloof, and part of it was the embarrassment of his father losing in the Senate race. It was the first time that he had kind of lost his anchor. He wasn't doing anything."[54]

IN HOUSTON, other friends wondered when, not if, Bush was going to follow his father into either politics or oil. They assumed that since he had followed his father so closely before, he would do it again. But the oil industry, "the oil bidness," as his Uncle Jonathan Bush liked to call it,[55] was still mired in uncertain times. The slump had run hard through Midland in the 1960s. In 1959, $36 million worth of building permits were issued in Midland; in 1970, only $5 million. Worse, people were leaving the city; the population declined by 4,500 from 1964 to 1970. Downtown stores were closing; seemingly every week a new one shut down. The Urban Land Institute suggested razing an eighteen-square-block downtown area and starting all over.[56] George W. wasn't going to Midland while people were leaving. Instead, friends said he spent time at the Milieu, a nightclub favored by people near the Chateaux Dijon. The lower Westheimer district, with bars and restaurants, was another inner-city area where people from the Chateaux congregated. And when he drank too hard, he told people that he always felt that all his energy was being used up. Sometimes his competitive, combative tendencies would surface—he would rock on his heels, bobbing, looking for a place to throw a dig, even at his father. His closest friends would say that when he drank too much he would try to be funny; he would think he was wickedly funny, but everything he said was distinctly unfunny. His friends knew the story about the time at the society party, with the guests turned out in elegant attire, when he might have tossed back one too many. He wobbled his way through the fete, spied an older woman who was a close friend of his parents, and blurted, "So—what's sex like after fifty, anyway?"[57]

After talking it over with his friend Don Ensenat, he had also finally assembled his Yale transcripts and sought admission to the state university law school in Austin. His application was rejected. "After his dad lost, we both applied to the University of Texas law school, and we both got turned down. He got turned down because he was just George W. Bush from Houston, Texas, applying and he didn't pull one string. And nobody else did," said Ensenat.[58]

That year he was firmly entrenched as a weekend warrior for the National Guard. His Guard buddies knew he never lacked a date. At the Thursday-night parties at the Ellington officers' club, at the pool parties at Chateaux Dijon, he was always with someone. He spent, he said, "enormous amounts of time and energy courting women."[59] He also enjoyed reporting back to the Ellington air base; it was always a reunion, seeing the familiar faces from the Kinkaid–St. John's network. And one weekend, it was as if the political Olympians of Texas had assembled their National Guard sons on the swampy outskirts of Houston, out where the city begins to give way to the murky hem of the Gulf of Mexico. First Lieutenant George Bush was there with First Lieutenant Lloyd Bentsen III and Captain John Connally III at Ellington Air Force Base.

Bentsen's father and Connally's father had both beaten George W.'s father. But if there was any lingering animosity from young Bush over the way Bentsen's father had won the Senate race or the way Connally's father had been rewarded by Nixon with a Cabinet post, it wasn't apparent. Each of the three still had powerful parents, among the most politically influential in the state: Bush's father was the ambassador to the United Nations; Bentsen's father was a U.S. senator; Connally's father was secretary of the Treasury and former governor of Texas. Each of their fathers had already been subject to speculation about future presidential prospects. And each of them happened to have sons in the Texas National Guard at the same time.

"You must be a little closer to the powers that be because you got promoted ahead of us," young Bentsen said, laughing, when he saw young Connally.

It had really been an impromptu but not entirely surprising gathering. Connally's family was also solidly entrenched inside the tight-knit oil, politics, and business corridors of Houston, and it wasn't unusual for him to seek out Bush and Bentsen at Ellington. Young Bentsen, for one, could feel it: It was unspoken but plainly there: their fathers were, with LBJ abdicating and seeking solace in the Texas Hill Country, jockeying for political control of Texas and ultimately aiming for even bigger, more important things. As usual, George W. took control of the situation.

"Let's go out to the alert shack," he suggested.

The trio headed to the base area where the F-102 Interceptors were kept on twenty-four-hour alert. The "shack" was a good place to hang out, and base officials had set up a little area where personnel could play Ping-Pong, read magazines, listen to music, watch TV, and play cards. Officers from the 147th drifted in and out.

The three men decided to pass the time by playing darts. They put their names up on the blackboard: Bentsen, Bush, Connally. They played for twenty minutes, thirty minutes, forty minutes. Finally, it was time to report back to their respective stations. As they were walking out of the alert area shack, they turned to check the final blackboard tally: Bentsen, 148; Bush, 256; Connally, 220.

"Holy———, you know what that looks like? That looks like an electoral vote tally. If someone walked in here, they'd think we were taking over the whole United States!" Bentsen heard one of his two friends shout. Bush, Bentsen, and Connally scurried to find a rag. Then they soaked it in water and hurriedly erased the figures from the blackboard.[60]

8

Primogenitor

Robert Gow was a physically large man, a true believer in the art form of the elegant entrepreneurial adventure, and he was George W. Bush's first boss in a year-round job. He had roomed at Yale with the elder George Bush's cousin Ray Walker. He had gone through all that Skull & Bones business, that Tin Tin–meets–Tom Jones–meets–Dink Stover business. Gow had managed the Yale football team, and every time there was a home game, he and Ray would be picked up for a big dinner with Ray's father, Herbert Walker, a loyal old Bonesman and the biggest investor in Zapata. Herbert Walker liked his son Ray's focused roommate, the way he was good with numbers and new ideas. And yes, there was a job for him in Texas as the vice president of Zapata Offshore. Gow was a sweater-over-the-shoulders guy, always carrying that sweater, no matter how hot it was, and he was practically oozing potential, always flying coach instead of first class, because the business was what really mattered.[1]

When Gow had stepped off the airplane in Houston in 1962 and the climate felt as if it had been transported straight from the Ganges River Valley, he had had his moments of doubt. In Houston, George Herbert Walker Bush was his immediate boss, right up until Bush left for Washington, D.C., in the winter of 1966 and Gow was named president of Zapata. Working for the elder George Bush for those four years, Gow learned something: the elder Bush wasn't one of those guys with a long-range business plan: "I guess you'd call it the 'vision thing,' " Gow would later say.[2]

In 1969, Gow left the comfort of Zapata and started a new agricultural-and-ranching conglomerate named Stratford, after the Texas Panhandle town; it was later changed to Stratford of Texas to avoid legal problems with a pesky wig company that had been using the same name. Looking for partners, Gow met his Texas match in the large, imposing O. S. "Todd" Simpson, Jr., a rancher and businessman with interests in the Texas-Mexico border town of Del Rio and in Houston, who had made good money turning rice hulls into cattle feed. Simpson's Delta Industries was merged into Stratford; the whole thing went public and immediately attracted a large, far-flung ensemble of investors: lawyers, chicken breeders, and eager Texas oilmen.

Stratford was voracious. It ran large-scale chicken-processing plants in East Texas, west Louisiana, and Mérida, Mexico. It had what was reputed to be the largest hog ranch in the United States, located outside Houston. It had an egg-separating facility near Kansas City—a plant that at least one Stratford vice president was convinced had once been quietly owned by the Kansas City wing of the Mafia, men who weren't averse to suggesting that they'd do more than break eggs if anybody from Texas started acting up with them. Stratford also had multiacre nurseries and greenhouses in central Florida, Jamaica, and Costa Rica—and a forest in Guatemala that harvested teakwood. Finally, there were massive cattle feedlots in the Panhandle and West Texas.[3] The Stratford theory was that if you put more and more cattle—up to 550,000 head—on a regulated feeding program each month, you could ignore the business cycle and minor fluctuations in the price of beef.

In the heart of this new adventure away from the oil business, Bob Gow had a vision. He also had 100,000 shares of Stratford and at least one easy answer. He knew why George W. Bush was sitting across from him in his office in the Tenneco Building in downtown Houston that day in 1971. Gow had been brought to Texas by the Bush family, and, as he told people, it was "turnabout that George came and worked for me."[4]

BUSH WAS given the use of a small office, told to wear a coat and tie to work, and informed that he would be an all-purpose assistant trainee for any of the executives who needed help. He worked under the wing of Peter Knudtzon, who was researching and negotiating the purchase of jumbo horticultural operations in the United States and Central America. Like most people in their part of the Tenneco Building, Knudtzon was well aware of Bush's pedigree. He knew how the affable George W. had gotten the job. "You could say it was a favor in a way. I mean, in that respect, George was viewed by some people with suspicion," said Knudtzon.[5] The two traveled to Orlando to check on a nursery and took at least one excursion to Guatemala. With Simpson, the company cofounder, Bush also found himself on a three-day trip to Pennsylvania, exploring the purchase of a mushroom farm. Simpson liked Bush, and he was relieved that Bush was a hard worker who hadn't pulled rank, even though Bush's old man had gotten him the job.[6] Bush sat in a small office preparing reports and attending meetings on how the company's various farms might do, what the upside might be for mushrooms, eggs, and houseplants, and sometimes planning for the next trip to places such as Toledo, Ohio—to meet with another wary farmer who was expecting the deeply financed Texans who said they were interested in cutting him a really good deal.

For a while, Gene Biddle, a plainspoken poultry operator from the piney woods of deep East Texas, was the largest shareholder in Stratford. Biddle came from the same chicken-laden part of the state as chicken mogul Bo Pilgrim, an ardent political supporter of the Bush family who would later hold fund-raisers at Chateau Pilgrim, what the locals would label "Cluckingham Palace." Biddle had 400,000 shares of Stratford, but he never liked coming into Houston; he preferred to keep as much distance as possible between himself and the city. After spending thirty years cobbling his business together up in Tenaha, Texas, he was intrigued by Stratford's dynamics, by all the wacky guys—as he called them—that the company had brought together. When he joined, he was instantly made a director. From where he lived, he was vaguely aware that there was now a Bush on board. "It was a name deal entirely," he said.[7]

After a while, George W. began talking to people at Stratford about the exact value of the family name, about how it was an asset. He tolerated being called Junior but usually only by close friends, family, people he trusted. His cousins still called him Little George; his aunts and uncles sometimes continued to use Georgie. And, in Texas, many people had simply reduced it to "W"... *Dubya.* In 1971, he talked to Gow about what the Bush name might mean to him practically speaking, especially as a way to escape Stratford. He was bored, and he was sure that he was not ready for this brand of corporate life. When people asked what Stratford was all about, he just said, "A stupid coat-and-tie job."[8]

The twenty-five-year-old Bush liked the people at Stratford—he played tennis with Knudtzon and once dated his sister. But the work was tedious, compared to the thankful interruptions when he went off to National Guard duty. The work, really, paled alongside that one heady week when, according to Guard historians, he and four other pilots were shipped to an air base in the Florida Panhandle and given the chance to fire one live missile each at a drone. Flying planes across the United States was still fun; trudging into the Tenneco Building every morning was sometimes not. He went to Gow, the Stratford president, the old family friend . . . a *Good Man*. It wasn't the first time Bush had pulled Gow aside. There had been other, shorter chats about where the younger Bush was headed. This time, though, Gow could tell that Bush was especially serious when he came to his office. He told Gow he was unsure what he wanted to do, unsure whether he wanted to stay in the business. He said he was thinking of running for a seat in the Texas legislature.

As Gow listened, a thought instantly ran through his head. He had been through this before, when the elder Bush had decided to run for office while still working for Zapata. The elder Bush had always been very clear with Gow, even when Gow had been frustrated that the elder Bush wouldn't, couldn't look at long-range plans for Zapata: *"I want to be a U.S. senator."*

It had been confusing then, thought Gow, and if the younger Bush decided to emulate his father, it would be confusing again. The younger Bush had never held a job for more than a few months, he hadn't been widely known to express public opinions on issues affecting Texas, his exposure to politics had been on the mechanical side—working on his father's campaigns—and now, at the age of twenty-five, he was abruptly thinking of running for office. Gow would later say that he knew that Bush wanted to get ahead, "to prosper." It was what all the Bushes and Walkers wanted, but the younger Bush was unclear on exactly how to do it—and now he was suddenly thinking of running for office. "If you're going to run, then you should leave the company," Gow told him.

Bush said he would talk to other people. And another thought occurred to Gow: if he had been young Bush, he would probably have looked hard at his only asset: "The one thing that he had was his name."[9]

Gow believed that George W. was certainly expendable as an employee. He had a vivacious personality and seemed bright enough, and he did have obvious political connections. But he was just a trainee who was obviously unhappy. Gow remembered when he had been starting out, when the elder George Bush had been starting out, when all the Bushes had been starting out—and what all the Bonesmen, the Yalies, had been looking for: "You know, we were always taught to do things that would make us prosper in life. With the Bushes, certainly with George, with Prescott, with George Senior, we were all focused on getting ahead and figuring out how to get there. It was what we did. George Junior had the same thinking. He was the same way. But the thing was, he was unclear on how to do it."

Like Bush's friends in Houston, Gow wondered whether his father's heading to the United Nations had caused all the uncertainty. Gow was familiar with the family's pressures and expectations, which were something he had talked to other members of the extended family about. Several people in the family had told Gow that the younger Bush would "be [made] unhappy by doing what his father had done." Now Gow saw a son following his father every step of the way: "to be a fighter pilot, to go to Yale, to go into Skull & Bones—whose pattern did he follow?"[10]

Gow knew that George W. was leaving. Gow assumed George W. would probably continue to follow his father for a long time. "I wish you luck," was all Gow told him.

THERE WAS a new seat opening up in the Texas State Senate. District 15 was a complex zone that ran from the affluent Memorial and River Oaks neighborhoods toward less exclusive African-American communities redlined and effectively cut in half by massive highway projects that had consumed churches, homes, schools, and even some forgotten cemeteries for freed slaves. And a few days before Halloween, Bush's friends were buzzing over the short item that had been given to *The Houston Post*: "Legislative Race Eyed by Bush Jr." The paper had gotten his name wrong in a headline, in the first story ever published about his own political aspirations—he wasn't a Junior.

Bush said he was considering running for the Texas House or Senate in 1972, probably in District 15. He said he would make up his mind in the next two to three weeks.[11] But by the end of the year, after talking it over with his father, he decided to abandon a try for the bumpy, fractious Texas legislature. It was too early. The district was a tricky one with its polarities of race, extreme wealth, and extreme poverty. Houston's political structure was changing, and new, young, powerful black politicians—Mickey Leland, Craig Washington, and Anthony Hall—were ready to bring their well-honed opinions to state government. George W.'s father had a better suggestion. It was something that would expose George W. to the inner workings of a campaign on a full-time basis. It would be a way for him to learn what it means to craft a campaign in the polarized Deep South—and to again study politics with a trusted family ally, someone whom George W. would feel comfortable with from a completely West Texas point of view.

AS ONE of the members of the Bush inner circle said, "Before there was a James A. Baker III, there was Jimmy Allison."[12] The family called the Midland newspaper publisher simply "The Aide." Allison was a native of

Lincoln, Nebraska, and a self-taught operative, someone who had risen through the insider ranks of the GOP with the elder George Bush every step of the way. The soft-spoken, square-faced Allison had been brought onto the 1964 Bush for Senate campaign by Midland attorney Martin All-day and then had decided to stay on as Bush's principal adviser and political operative. When Bush eventually went to Congress, Allison served as deputy chairman of the Republican National Committee. Even though Bush needed him in Texas for his second try at the Senate in 1970, Allison remained in Washington and helped oversee GOP efforts to seal a Senate majority for Nixon. Allison was always burdened by the belief that he had been responsible for letting Bush lose the 1970 Senate race. It was something that drove him to tears as he sat in a dark room at the RNC headquarters and realized that his friend in Texas was failing. Now, in the early 1970s, he had formed a political consulting firm with RNC Communications Director Harry Treleaven, the media master who had helped orchestrate the elder Bush's congressional victory.

In 1972, Allison was going to work as one of the Senate campaign managers for Winton M. "Red" Blount, a close friend of Nixon Treasury Secretary Connally and, without question, one of the most powerful Republicans in the Deep South.[13] Blount, a Montgomery, Alabama–based construction magnate, had managed the 1960 Nixon presidential campaign in eight southeastern states. A ferocious conservative, he would remain a lifelong supporter of Nixon in private, in print, in speeches.

In May 1968, he was elected president of the U.S. Chamber of Commerce. That year, he was worried that he would have a hard time adhering to the chamber's suggested code of bipartisanship—and to avoid temptation during the infamous Democratic National Convention in Chicago that summer, he rented William F. Buckley Jr.'s schooner and sailed the New England coast, trying to keep distance between himself and anyone who would ask his opinions. In 1969, he accepted a Nixon appointment as postmaster general. In 1970, George Wallace was running for Alabama governor, and he took populist potshots at Blount, suggesting that Blount was a gilded symbol of what needed to be changed in Alabama and in the country. It drove Blount crazy, and he wrote about it in his autobiography:

> Wallace would bring a bedsheet up to the dais and peek under it, saying 'Who do I see under there? I see the postmaster general.' He called me a rich war contractor up in Washington telling Alabamans how to vote. And he claimed my house in Montgomery had 26 bathrooms and lavish stables. (Our house has six bathrooms.

While that may seem like a lot to some people, it's a big house—and six is a far cry from 26).[14]

After the elder Bush and Blount met in Washington, they realized they had things in common. The Alabaman had served as a pilot, and, almost better, he had developed a written code of behavior with a heavy emphasis on personal responsibility as the key to milking capitalism's full potential—a philosophy that appealed to the Bushes, who had gone to desolate West Texas in 1948. The Alabama construction king simply called it "The Blount Philosophy," and it was outlined for employees in his book *Doing It My Way:* "We brook no adherence to any other way of life."[15] Blount retired in 1971 after three years as postmaster general. He really had wanted to be governor, but there wasn't a gubernatorial race in 1972. Instead, National Republican leaders suggested a Senate race. Nixon, whom Blount had unflaggingly served for a decade, was still driven by a desire to dent the Southern Democratic stronghold. The Senate race in Alabama was considered a possible domino in the South, something that could knock other seats toward the Republicans. According to Blount's son, Winton Blount III, Jimmy Allison, who had orchestrated Bush's southern congressional victory in 1966, was dispatched from Washington to help run the race. And George W. was sent from Houston to live and campaign in a state with a larger-scale version of the glaring and painful socioeconomic disparity that he would have faced if he had run for the District 15 seat back in Houston.

By May, he applied for and was given special permission from the National Guard to put in his weekend warrior duties with the 187th Tactical Reconnaissance Group in Montgomery, Alabama.[16]

BUSH CANVASSED the state as the campaign's paid political director, doing advance work, setting up rallies, pushing the candidate's literature at barbecues—*"Red Blount—he can do it!"*—and meeting the isolated grassroots GOP workers in the Alabama outback. He was ready, if necessary, to make runs in the direction of Birmingham or Mobile in order to pitch the Blount Philosophy. And meanwhile, it appeared that he and Allison were reprising some themes from the Team Bush races in Texas—there were always some cheerleading Blount Belles hanging off to the side of the stages, decked out in straw Blount Boaters and swirling around the awkward-looking construction magnate. Sometimes Bush surprised the GOP campaign workers in the Deep South with his Yankee affectations, his alien, preppy way of wearing penny loafers without any socks.[17] He was also on a steep learning curve in a tricky, shifting political environment in a state that hadn't gone Republican. As Blount's son, Winton, got to know him better, Bush struck him as hard-nosed, intense. "He was politically astute," said Winton. The Senate candidate's son also quickly realized that Bush was a bachelor crisscrossing Alabama: "He was unmarried. I've been there."[18]

Blount was facing John Sparkman, the Democratic incumbent, and Sparkman leveled some of the same charges against him that George Wallace had used, among them that Blount was a walking symbol of fat-cat excess. Sparkman's radio spots attacked the wealthy Blount, including a repeat of the twenty-six bathrooms theme. And Bush and the other Blount staffers learned a hard lesson when Nixon, realizing the race wouldn't be won after all, made a public display of sending a government plane to fetch Sparkman for a less-than-important Senate vote. Bush's political education, which he had been undergoing since watching his father organize in Midland—and watching his grandfather's Senate races, his father's two runs for the Senate, his father's run for Congress—was something he rarely talked about with his National Guard friends. But it was something they thought was inescapable—as inevitable, said friends and even some family members, as his following his elders into Andover, Yale, and some sort of military service. Even if he weren't an intellectual or an ideologue, they said, he was faithfully doing what Bushes were supposed to do.

THAT SUMMER, Bush took a break from the campaign and joined his father in Miami for the GOP National Convention. After his law school rejection, he had begun thinking about business school, maybe Harvard, and about the fact that he would need to do something once his National Guard duties were completed. His experience at Stratford had been uninspiring, but he told Houston friends that it hadn't steered him away from the concept of making money. There was still that big-cash dream he had shared with his friends in Houston, the one about being the next big-time Bush-Walker stockbroker.

The Watergate break-in had occurred on June 17, the Vietnam War persisted, racial tensions remained high. At the Doral Hotel in Miami, Robert Reisner spotted Bush and said hello. Reisner, Bush's brother from the DKE house, had recently graduated from the Harvard B School and had gone to work for the Nixon reelection campaign. He was, like many, a true believer, someone who seemed energetically dedicated to the cause. The two fraternity brothers struck up a conversation in the campaign headquarters' hotel. They decided to have a beer. Bush was concerned:

"Bobby, what's going on here?" he asked, making reference to the way the Watergate break-in story wouldn't go away, how it seemed to have more legs than the usual political story.

"I don't know, but it sure is getting out of control," replied Reisner.

"Well, if there isn't something going on, it sure looks like it, because nobody acts innocent," Bush blurted.[19]

Reisner studied the twenty-six-year-old who had once been the head of their beer-bash fraternity at Yale and decided he wasn't being sanctimonious, just spontaneously reacting to all the Nixonian uncertainties—ones that were coming closer to home, to his family's role in the GOP and at Nixon's side. After the convention, Bush returned to his immersion in hardball politics as a member of the Blount Senate campaign in Alabama. And he resumed his weekend warrior stints with the Montgomery branch of the National Guard.

Two months later, on October 8, Prescott Bush, who had been befriended by Presidents Eisenhower and Nixon, died at the age of seventy-seven following a bout with runaway lung cancer. During the annual August trip to the family compound, Dorothy Walker and the caretakers first began noticing Prescott's lingering cough. As the family had done with three-year-old Robin, he was taken to Memorial Sloan-Kettering hospital in New York and treated for three weeks, but the cancer had already spread. Without question, George W. had seen his grandfather as a living treasure, a living legacy, the symbolic core around whom the family revolved, someone whom everyone deferred to. And, of course, he had seen the things that defined Prescott Bush—his ties to Eisenhower and Nixon, his symbolic presence at the helm of Yale—directly and indirectly assailed over the last decade.

Prescott Bush, like the headmasters at the two private preparatory schools that George W. had attended, was an unyielding proponent of unambiguous comportment. Prescott's sons said that, even up to the end, he remained a foreboding and commanding presence. Now George W.'s grandmother Dorothy Walker, competitive and feisty even then, had instructed everyone attending the service in Greenwich's Episcopal Christ Church, where the family had been members for years, to go against tradition and dress colorfully. Walker had also decided that she was going to sit in the pews with the next generation, the grandsons, the political heirs in the Bush-Walker house—including Jeb, the nineteen-year-old who had followed his older brother to Andover and who was now a promising University of Texas student. Jeb, the family thought, always behaved in a more reserved, constrained, fashion than his older brother. Prescott Bush's widow insisted that the grandchildren, the boys, serve as Prescott Bush's pallbearers. Prescott was buried in historic Putnam Cemetery alongside a small piece of white marble commemorating the memory of his grand-daughter Robin.

IN RIGIDLY old-school Democratic Alabama, the GOP Senate candidate was being, in his own words, "swamped" and "trounced." From the outset, Blount's wealthy campaign had been doomed. It had never sparked or ig-nited inside the Dixie Democrat stronghold, and now Bush was facing a re-turn to Houston and unemployment. The Alabama experience had been useful, in the sense that it had served as a daily exposure to the importance of personal politics, to the roots of the decades-old southern resistance to Republicans, to the innate reluctance of some rural southern voters to swal-low anything resembling the patrician politics of his father and grandfather.

Campaigning in deep Alabama had also been a study of the pervasive nature of the anti-Washington bias. It was an eye-opening insight into a demanding, special world of hard-core Christian conservative values, the way a big moral umbrella was held over a resistance to big government, big regulation, and big taxes. George W. Bush had learned politics, in part, by watching his father's first close political adviser, Jimmy Allison— the Midland publisher who seemed to privately and publicly embody the notion of "personal responsibility" as the only true path to financial, emo-tional, and familial security.

After the fall elections, his father was summoned by Nixon to the presidential retreat at Camp David, Maryland, and asked to take over the chairmanship of the Republican National Committee—something Bar-bara Bush was initially vehemently opposed to, assuming that her husband would eventually be blamed for the never-ending GOP and Watergate de-bacles. In December, though, the Bushes agreed and moved from their Waldorf Towers suite to a house in Washington, D.C. During the ex-tended Christmas holiday, as at all the holidays, the family members duti-fully assembled wherever the parents were. Coming home was something the Bushes required, whether at holidays or in the summertime at Kenne-bunkport. It was assumed, unspoken, like so many other things.

"One reason we came home was the atmosphere was comfortable and warm," said George W. "Another reason we came home is the way we were raised. I've never heard George and Barbara Bush utter a harsh or ugly word to each other, never heard either of them characterize each other in an ugly way. They set the tone. The final reason we came home was unconditional love. Mother and Dad always had a home of love. They loved each other and there was no question they loved us children."[20]

Neil was always Mr. Perfect—that's what George W. called him. He had an impish grin, he was the one other people oohed and aahed over. The family had watched over him as he worked his way through his dyslexia; he seemed to lack the smart-ass sarcasm his oldest brother had perfected. Jeb could suddenly turn serious when he needed to; he had ready answers, and he was the first one who had grown up in River Oaks, in Houston circles, instead of in the free-ranging spaces of West Texas. Some family friends had a hard time placing Marvin; he was unflaggingly polite, maybe not as opinionated or as politically oriented as his two oldest brothers. Dorothy simply deferred to her brothers, especially in public settings, and some suggested that she would have to work harder to overcome her innate shyness. But George W. was the family lightning rod, the one the teenagers flocked to when he walked through the door, the one they liked having around to absorb their parents' bad moods.

"In our house, you could count on George to liven things up" was how Marvin, who was sometimes surprisingly droll, liked to put it.[21] George was the loudest rainmaker, sneaking outside for a Newport he had lifted from his mother, dispensing nicknames . . . *Mr. Perfect* . . . and demanding that someone, anyone, beat him in a race across the grounds at Kennebunkport or in naming all the baseball players on the hundreds of cards in his shoebox. People who knew the family well said that he was like a tightwire, testosterone version of Dorothy Walker, the way he wanted to compete all the time, throwing down challenges, telling his brothers to suck it up as he passed them out on the jogging track. At the dinner table, he was blustery, nonstop, sharp-elbowed, always digging—the one who, when his mother looked away, would make a face. His cousin John Ellis was always amazed. The Bushes always woke up at 75 miles per hour, he thought. But George W. was in another zone entirely. "Primogenitor, baby!" Ellis would yell.

IN WASHINGTON that holiday, twenty-six-year-old George W. asked his fifteen-year-old brother, Marvin, to keep him company on a car trip to a friend's house in the Washington area. At the friend's house the brothers tossed back some alcohol, too much of it, and finally tried to aim for the furnished home that Barbara Bush had hastily found, the one that was convenient to Marvin's and Dorothy's private schools. Drunk and driving erratically, George W. barreled the car into a neighbor's garbage can, and the thing affixed itself to the car wheel. He drove down the street with the metal garbage can noisily banging and slapping on the pavement right up until he made the turn and finally started rolling up and onto the driveway of his parents' home in the pleasant, family-oriented neighbor-hood they had just moved into.

Marvin stepped inside, his words sloshing around as he offered an ex-aggerated greeting . . . *"Helloooo"* . . . and then his father, who had been reading, wanted to see George W. in the den—immediately. Angry and flushed from the liquor, George W. barged in. His younger brothers, the ones who couldn't wait for him to come home from Andover, Yale, Geor-gia, Alabama, were there. It had been only a few weeks since Prescott Bush had been buried.

"I hear you're looking for me," said George W. "You wanna go mano a mano right here?"[22]

Jeb watched the edgy scene unfolding and decided to intercede, to shift the focus by offering up some news that no one else in the family knew: George W., said Jeb, had recently been accepted to the Harvard Business School. He hadn't decided whether to go or not. The family was stunned. Their father had some advice: "You should think about that, son."

George W. knew his parents were happy. But he had something else to tell them: "Oh, I'm not going . . . I just wanted to let you know I could get into it."[23]

MARVIN IDOLIZED his oldest brother and thought, as did all the children in the family, that George W. was always the funniest, the quickest, the most combustible—in both the good sense and the bad sense—the one most apt to energize something or start a fire. He also knew that George W. was the one most prone to his father's knack for draining people emo-tionally, for dropping mountains of disappointment on their shoulders. He knew that George W. could easily be made to feel as if he were an out-law, as if he and he alone had broken all the rules. "He would be made to feel that he had committed the worst crime in history," Marvin said about the way his oldest brother reacted to their father.[24]

That Christmas, the family recognized that George W. was making some sort of symbolic decision. As he had told his parents, applying to Harvard was a way of sending a message. His friends recognized it, and some of them even said it was really all about competition, not about a burning desire to map out a strict career path and study macroeconomics in the Northeast. Doug Hannah had applied to Harvard and hadn't got-ten in. He always thought that sometimes George W. Bush was competi-tive to a fault. Hannah wondered if someone had said to George W., "Hey, you can't do that either." Hannah could hear George W. saying, "So here, I'll give it a shot."[25]

THE POSSIBLE move to Harvard was at least nine months away. George W. was out of work again, but his father had another solution, something that would begin to flesh out his son's otherwise slender civic résumé in case he ever wanted to run for District 15 in Houston. The elder Bush had served as honorary chairman of an inner-city Houston program that tried to hook up famous basketball, baseball, and football players with children and teenagers. Bush was going to work at 1711 McGowen Street in the heart of Houston's Third Ward. The Professional United Leadership League (PULL), headquartered in the same building as a probation office, was the invention and mission of two prominent professional football players, John White and Ernie "Big Cat" Ladd.

White, a former star at Houston's Texas Southern University, had become one of the first African-American players on the Houston Oilers. Ladd, a student at Grambling, had met White when their schools would play their traditional annual football game and then gone on to become a superstar for the Kansas City Chiefs, the San Diego Chargers, and the Houston Oilers. White, a streetwise visionary, had asked Ladd what he thought about a program that could bring stars such as baseball players Joe Morgan and Jimmy Wynn, or basketball legend Elvin Hayes, into contact with kids in the beleaguered Third, Fourth, and Fifth Wards of Houston. Ladd liked the idea—he thought it was important for athletes to return something to the community—and they sought to establish a politically neutral program that could lure all manner of supporters from in and around Houston. They contacted school administrators, business leaders, and the most prominent black physician-and-blues-nightclub entrepreneur in Texas, Dr. John B. Coleman, asking for advice, time, money. Members of the Houston Astros, the Houston Oilers, and the Harlem Globetrotters, even Muhammad Ali and George Foreman, were also asked to come to the PULL facility at the edge of the skyscrapers. The unrelenting John White began calling up anybody he thought was connected to the political power circles in Houston, including the former Congressman Bush, and wondering if he could use his name, if he would like to sit on the board of directors or be an honorary chairman. Through White, the elder Bush arranged a position at PULL for his son.

Houston was gripped in a wary dance between the police and the minority communities; economic progress, the kind of unbridled Texas capitalism that had drawn George Bush to Midland and then Houston, had completely bypassed the black and Hispanic neighborhoods that ringed the downtown area. And in glaring instances, giant portions of those old neighborhoods had been steamrolled to make way for new offices and wider, oil-truck-friendly highways. Houston's infamous Fourth Ward remained an insistent reminder of the wretched economic disparity, with its yawning collection of ramshackle shotgun shacks—small enough to fire a shotgun from outside the front door and not hit a wall as the bullet flew out the back. As Houston grew, parts of the old freedmen's villages, where freed slaves had been allowed to settle, had been condemned, mysteriously burned, or destroyed. Miraculously, some churches had been allowed to stand, even though an interstate now separated the buildings from congregation members whose houses hadn't been taken away. Sometimes on Sundays, there would be a small, earnest parade of people walking from their homes, under the highways, and toward their old church, now isolated in the middle of some towering office buildings.

The inner city of Houston, especially the African-American neighborhoods, was left to rot. And the Third, Fourth, and Fifth Wards—the last one dubbed "The Bloody Nickel" by weary residents—had been the scenes of all manner of police brutality and confrontations. Tensions at the predominantly African-American Texas Southern University, a few blocks away from PULL headquarters, were still especially high. A few years earlier, students had barricaded Wheeler Street near the university and lit a bonfire. Shots had been exchanged between the police and demonstrators. When the confrontation had ended, one policeman was dead, two wounded; one student had been wounded and 462 others arrested. The aftershocks of that incident, unparalleled in Houston history, were still lingering when Bush reported to work a few blocks away. "His dad and John White brought him right to the black belt. Any white guy that showed up on McGowen was gonna get caught in some tough situations. You better be able to handle yourself," said Ladd.[26]

By 1973, the center was furnished with Ping-Pong and pool tables; it provided rap sessions, chess and checkers, tutoring sessions for kids who had been booted out of school, motivational programs, and free snacks. From the makeshift PULL office, staffers and volunteers drove to schools, gave speeches, and held fund-raisers. Wary PULL workers and administrators such as Edgar Arnold studied the new employee. Arnold was a college tennis star who in 1973 had been brought in to supervise most of PULL's daily programs. He saw the deferential way people were reacting around the guy in blue jeans and T-shirt and with a lop-sided grin. "I concluded that he was somebody because of the way people acted around him. He was instrumental in connecting a lot of the upper-class and well-to-do people with the program," said Arnold. That fact hit home when Arnold asked Bush to accompany him on fund-raising trips to River Oaks, Tanglewood, and Memorial on the other side of town from the Third Ward. "You look just like your dad," people would say to the younger Bush on almost every visit with Arnold. When they did, Arnold made a mental note: "This is somebody I need to know."

For several months, the two worked closely together on raising PULL's profile in Houston, and Arnold decided that Bush was an expert at giving his little spiel in rich people's homes and offices. He and others watched as Bush also grew close to an unruly, tough Third Ward kindergartner who somehow managed to show up at PULL every day. The two were inseparable, and when Jimmy would arrive shirtless and shoeless, Bush would take him out for new clothes. Watching Jimmy hanging on his leg, grabbing at his arm, tugging him out the door, people said that there was a genuine bond between them—one that would linger with Bush for years after he had left the Third Ward. David Anderson was another PULL employee, two years older than Bush, and he especially liked the fact that Bush had made arrangements to take some of the PULL kids such as Jimmy up for their first airplane ride. The day of the ride, Bush asked his sixteen-year-old brother, Marvin, to come along. One of the PULL kids started popping off, making noise, once they were up in the air. Bush stalled the engine for a second, and the passengers, scared to death, grew quiet.[27]

After work, Edgar Arnold would run to catch up with Bush as Bush steered his late-model Oldsmobile out of the parking lot. "Edgar, c'mon, they got Nickel Beer Night," yelled Bush. Arnold would clear mounds of chewing gum and garbage off the front seat, and the two would head to an Astros game and cheap drinks. He and Bush would talk baseball for hours, and Arnold was surprised if Bush didn't go to every game. The only time they talked about politics, they talked about politicians.

"Most of the people up in Washington, up on the Hill, are disorganized," offered Arnold as they drove one night.

"My father is very organized. But you're right, most politicians are very, very unorganized. They don't know what the right hand is doing from the left," Arnold heard Bush say.[28]

IN HOUSTON, the contrast between oil-inspired wealth and grinding poverty was more pronounced than in any other city Bush had ever lived in. That summer of 1973, George W. made up his mind to quit after nine months in the Third Ward, one of the poorest neighborhoods in Texas, and move to Cambridge, Massachusetts, to start the fall semester at the Harvard Business School. Years later, writers and broadcasters would fall in line to ask him about his immediate years after college, leading up to his departure for Harvard, his postcollegiate "nomadic" years spent moving among Houston, Georgia, and Alabama. Sometimes, in unguarded moments with a writer, he and his brother Jeb would chuckle at it—at the way the mythology of his postcollege years had taken root and been rehashed.

After Yale, he was committed to a defined period of time in the National Guard, his father had found three jobs for him, he applied to the most powerful business school in the world, he worked on three Senate campaigns, and he earnestly planned his own run for political office in the overheated, rambunctious Texas Legislature. His friends in Houston—the ones who had stared into a room in the Bush house one summer and seen how the family had already zealously wrapped their Christmas presents, who had marveled at the fact that the organized family had thought to put a fire escape on their home—saw too many Bush-Walker checkpoints, too many gatekeepers in his father's Rolodex, too many times when his attendance was required at Kennebunkport, in Florida, in Washington. His life and his family's life were too political, he was too involved in other people's campaigns or thinking about his own to be anywhere near as nomadic as some others who had graduated from college in 1968. He didn't, as he would tell someone years later, go to Woodstock. He didn't go to Canada to dodge the draft because, as one of his best friends and closest fraternity brothers would suggest, he was worried about destroying his father's plans for the Senate and beyond.

Years later, Jeb Bush acknowledged that he and his brother were reaching the same conclusion about the late 1960s and early 1970s: they were witnessing the birth of what they believed was a confessional era. It would lead, Jeb said, to a "therapeutic age" alien to the extraordinarily influential political environments their great-grandfathers, grandfather and father had emerged from in the Midwest, New York, and Connecticut. From the first whiff of those intellectual self-doubters at Andover, up through Yale and into the 1970s, George W. repeatedly told people he was not prone to self-analysis. His friends agreed that he was decidedly less than introspective. And when his father began aggressively, repeatedly positioning himself for the White House, he was leery about the way his father's principal political advisers wanted to reinvent the elder Bush, to make him "more real." But as much as he loathed the suggestions, the younger Bush would eventually begin to weigh the expediency of putting a ginger, carefully measured foot into the therapeutic age—of reinventing others' perceptions of him. This process was intuitive at first, then apparently deliberate, and some of his father's highest-level advisers would say that it would make the first son a far better politician than his father.

THAT FALL, George W. wrote a letter to his commanding officers: "I respectfully request my discharge from the Texas Air National Guard. . . . I am moving to Boston, Massachusetts, to attend Harvard Business School as a full-time student."[29]

His military service obligation was scheduled to end on May 26, 1974, but he was granted an expedited release. His military files said: "Lt. Bush's major strength is his ability to work with others. Lt. Bush is very active in civic affairs in the community and manifests a deep interest in the operation of our government."[30]

Two decades later, officials with the National Guard helped coordinate efforts to clean up one of the F-102s that Bush had flown when he had been a member of the 147th. The plane had been sitting idle for fourteen years. It was rotted and rusted. Funds were raised to clean it up, and it was painted, mounted, and put on display. As a final touch, his name was painted on the canopy. By mistake, the wrong name, "Lieutenant George Bush, Jr.," was put on the plane.

9

Despair and Capital Sins

When Nat Butler was a cheerleader at Exeter, he enjoyed attending the annual dinner that preceded the big football game against Andover. It was always a convivial scene, and the cheerleaders would introduce themselves to one another, mingle, chat, and maybe break bread together before lining up the next day on opposite sidelines, along with the other members of their pep squads. It was, of course, natural that Butler would meet Andover's head cheerleader. The pair shook hands and, then, over the next several years, would occasionally bump into each other. Butler had friends at Yale, and sometimes on campus he would see his old rival cheerleader and relive school times. And now they were starting Harvard Business School together as part of the eight-hundred-member first-year class. Butler chatted with Bush about what he wanted to do, what he expected his education at HBS would lead to after graduation. Butler quickly discerned that Bush hadn't yet nailed down what he wanted to achieve with his Harvard MBA. "Some people at that school wanted to be head of Citicorp," said Butler, who would go to work in state government in Massachusetts, "but he didn't have a specific focus like that."[1]

As Bush was launching his Harvard career, he and several Bush-Walker family members had already talked about the way both the school and lifelong Republican families were sometimes viewed on campus; he was back in what was, for him, an increasingly unpleasant part of the Northeast. Fewer than 4,000 of Cambridge's 50,000 registered voters were Republican. Spiro Agnew would resign as vice president in October. Early that year, the Harvard Republican Club made a public plea to bring back the canceled Reserve Officers Training Corps (ROTC) program, but no students responded to the plea. A feminist group staged a "pee-in" to protest the lack of women's bathrooms at Harvard; students cross-dressed and wore swastikas at a "male chauvinist pig dinner." An angry Harvard professor was accused of shoving slow-moving members of the Students for a Democratic Society out the door of his classroom.

Meanwhile, almost one out of every ten of the Fortune 500 companies were under the direction of HBS graduates. Harvard was simply the most powerful business school in the world, an institution that, like Andover and Yale, relied to an extraordinary degree on the ever-multiplying layers and networks created by each new graduating class. In 1973, as in many other years, HBS was not necessarily looking for the most brilliant emerging economist; it did, however, take note of the pedigree potential of each of its applicants. "The Harvard Business School was not looking for the brightest academic stars in the firmament," said Butler. "They were looking to enhance the Harvard Business School, and one of the ways to enhance Harvard Business School is to accept people who look like they are going to make their mark on the world once they graduate. Being the son of George Herbert Walker Bush, right there, that is helpful."[2]

Butler and Bush immersed themselves in the rigid program of case studies; Butler had heard someone say once that the school was a place where students did a lot of push-ups, learning an approach, a technique, rather than a theoretical body of knowledge. He, Bush, and some other students sometimes had to study three cases a night, making extended inquiries into problems real companies were having with infrastructure, hiring, wages, price controls, and tax burdens. Butler was convinced that the case study system was a methodology perfectly suited to George W. Bush. It was practical more than big-picture; it was about fixing and revving existing machinery rather than building an entirely new model.

Bush could tell that, on the surface, Harvard had bent a little with the times: there were fewer coats and ties at the B School. But in the end its focus was the same: Course work was painstakingly analytical and detailed, with a priority on probing into minute institutional dysfunctions followed by rapidly developing point-by-point countermeasures. Students were required to write a 1,500-word paper once a week and attend several management classes involving teamwork, study groups, and cooperative problem solving. J. P. Goldsmith, who had gone to Yale with Bush, said that the Harvard Business School approach was best summed up by one word: "militaristic." George W.'s uncle Jonathan Bush who had an extensive background as a New York money manager, saw it the same way: "You work until midnight, one o'clock in the morning. It's just a fantastic basic training for business. It's the same thing as Parris Island for the Marines."[3]

Jonathan and other older members of the Bush-Walker clan who were watching George W.'s progress, and possible preparation for Wall Street, had come to the same conclusion: the Harvard Business School would drive discipline into the twenty-seven-year-old. His flirtation with Texas politics two years earlier, the fact that he was thinking of running for office without having held a job for longer than a year, was in marked contrast to the way his grandfather and father had set their political careers into motion once they had become millionaires. Prescott had been fifty-five before he had run for the Senate; his father had been almost forty before he had run for the Senate.

Most faculty members and students knew who George W. Bush's family was, and several knew of his grandfather's and father's relationship with the increasingly haunted president of the United States. Butler had thought Harvard was "a place where people are very aware of power and who has it and how everybody is related to it."[4] Still, George W. believed that HBS might be a good outpost, a buffer against change, especially for someone who had just finished more than four years of National Guard duty. He hoped that Harvard wouldn't be infected by the same perceived "heaviness"—the guilt, the arrogance—that had been welling up just before he left Yale. Said one classmate, "There was a sense that the Harvard Business School is a somewhat insulated kind of place, that people who choose to go there, the courses that people took, the instructors, and so forth are pretty much concerned with management issues rather than societal issues. It's not like you are concerned with what was going on in the undergraduate level. These are straight-ahead, serious people who want to make money, entrepreneurial types, and I would say that George Bush was in that direction."[5]

THE ENTERING CLASS was divided into ten subsets, sections of eighty students each, and Peter Gebhard was a member of Bush's pod for the two-year duration of the MBA program. The first thing that jumped out at Gebhard, who sat next or behind Bush for much of the program, was his flight jacket. Frequently, Bush would be seen purposefully striding across the Harvard campus, aiming for the B School's glass-and-brick buildings, toward Kresge Hall, and he would be the only person wearing an old Texas Air National Guard flight jacket. There were campus protests against a visit by Vice President Ford. Activists in sympathy with Cesar Chavez and the California grape workers rallied against Gallo winery officials coming to the B School to recruit students for its upper-management openings. There was a series of protests aimed against the CIA presence on campus. And an angular-faced Bush would arrive for class, still refusing to take off his weathered National Guard flight jacket. He was, remembered Gebhard, very proud of it.[6]

The two worked together in a class called Human Organization and Behavior, sometimes simply called HOB. It was a class Bush loved said classmates; it was one of the B School classes that truly sparked a deep, committed interest in him. As usual, case studies, anywhere from one to one hundred pages long, were handed out to the class. The object was to analyze each case study and pinpoint its key areas for debate and discussion in the class. Each case study was meant to impart some real-life lesson on marketing, production, financing. But in HOB, Bush was almost single-mindedly interested in the way companies were organized, their structural dynamics, their pecking order, the food chain, the way management was structured. "He was pretty concerned about how organizations worked and how people worked in those organizations," said Gebhard.[7]

There was something else, too. He was telling a cousin that already he was seeing the same intellectual insolence he had seen in the Yale faculty— the protesters, the students, who he was convinced were scrambling away from the privileges of the finest schools in the world. It was not just having to read one hundred to three hundred pages a day and sitting in classes for five to six hours with eighty other students staring at you, knowing full well, as Gebhard put it, that so many of them were obviously smarter than you were. Too many people at Harvard, Bush told a favorite aunt, were mired in the by now fully realized feelings he had seen taking shape toward the end of his career at Yale—too many people desperately blaming themselves, anybody, for the guilty consequences of privilege. The word for his experience at Harvard, the word he used to describe Yale, the word he returned to over and over again was "claustrophobic": "claustrophobic, intellectually and physically" he would say.[8]

The more outside political events intruded on campus—especially each new and stunning revelation about Republican corruption and Watergate—the more Bush deliberately withdrew and sought solace from his cousins, aunts, and other nearby members of the Bush-Walker family. In November 1973, after a brutal two-hour debate, the Harvard Republican Club voted to ask Nixon to resign; it sent a letter to Nixon, with copies to Ford, the national media, and Republican leaders. But as at Yale, Bush aggressively avoided becoming involved in the political infrastructure, the journalistic opportunities, the campus civic organizations in which some young Republican stalwarts were defending Nixon to the end. Instead, he spent weekends visiting Bush-Walker relatives in New York, Maine, and Connecticut, and he played softball and basketball on intramural teams. He did what he had done in the dying days of DKE: He developed quick, lasting friendships with other apolitical B Schoolers, he spent time at Boston nightclubs. He invited trustworthy students to the family homes. And one cousin could tell he had turned inward. He was telling people that he was "withdrawing, just staying focused on the task at hand."[9]

It wasn't that he had gone grim, but there was obviously something grating, grinding on him when he was with family members at their homes in Boston or at the family reunions. Any changes in the first son, of course, were obvious—anything less than a rollercoaster load of energy was going to be apparent. Jeb, his sometimes disaffected brother, was experiencing his own low-level form of early-1970s self-doubt, but people in the family didn't worry about Jeb so much—he could appear indifferent, or he could give the impression that he was weighing cerebral matters. With George W., more than anyone else in the extended younger generation of the Bush-Walker clan, if his histrionic brand of self-confidence was even fractionally dented, it would be dissected. His outspoken aunt Nancy Ellis was living in Boston at the time, and he frequently sought refuge with her and other family members passing through the area. He and his aunt were especially close; he could talk to her, and she knew what a "rotten time" it was for her nephew, the usually irrepressible, ebullient one who was saddled with more expectations than almost anyone else in the next generation of Bush children: "You know Harvard Square and how they felt about Nixon," said Ellis. "But here was Georgie, his father head of the Republican National Committee. So he came out a lot with us just to get out of there."[10]

He also gratefully looked forward to the times when one of his favorite cousins, Elsie Walker, would visit for a weekend. Walker cared deeply for George W., and she was almost painfully aware of the Bush family's self-appointed station in life and how it isolated him. "The whole time was just very, very, very confusing—painful," she felt. She saw some sort of self-imposed discipline setting in. "He was working hard. He was eating carrots and drinking carrot juice. He was on a health kick and running a lot," she said. "This is not an easy family to grow up in. All of us had to come to grips with the fact that there are enormously successful people in it and a lot of pressure to be a big deal. And all of us have had various, varying success with coming to grips with those pressures. And everybody has to make their own peace, and find their own peace with to what degree they want to be successful and how to have a really happy, balanced life."[11] As always, according to several members of the extended family, it was all unspoken but clear. His parents didn't, as George W. said, sit down and have "the talk" with him: "We had others in my family who wanted their boys to be on the baseball team, to do this or that," his father would later say to reporters. "But Barbara and I never tried to put any pressure on our five kids to be something they didn't want to be. I was blessed with a father who treated me that way. And I would hope we've tried to say to George, 'look, be what you want to be, and don't let them fit you into a mold where everybody's got to be exactly alike.' "

His uncle Jonathan Bush knew what was happening to the first son, the unbridled one who always moved faster than any of the other children. "If your family has kind of carved out a path in a certain area, it isn't too hard for you to imagine yourself in the same thing—and it's not hard for other people to imagine you in the same area," he said.[12] For years—forever, it seemed—the parallels had been there but were never mentioned or analyzed by the father and the first son. But Bush's brother Jeb, the one who pondered at least some of the same societal paroxysms in the late 1960s, had a personal theory about his eldest brother, the one who seemed to look more like his father every year: The irreverent part, the close-to-brazen way of dealing with strangers and friends alike—that was still easy to ascribe to their mother. The art of pushing and skewering, the spontaneous warm embraces and thunderclaps of anger, eyes unforgiving, unrelenting, and locked on their target—that side of his older brother could easily be traced to his mother. It was what people in the family liked to say, and it was what George W. liked to say, almost as if he were straining to convince people that he was more like his mother than his father, the man he was a dead ringer for. It was a definition he would latch onto years later and then rehearse, something that he would use for full effect whenever he needed to speak on behalf of his own political career. It would always draw a laugh, and he knew it as he said it over and over again: *"I've got my daddy's eyes and my mother's mouth."*

"He has my mom's irreverence—he has a lot less of it than he used to," said Jeb one day. "But I think he has a lot of my dad in him. I think he has a lot more than he might realize."[13]

HE GREW CLOSE to Tom Riley and Ron Spogli, two business school classmates who would later serve as bridges between the Bush family and wealthy Californians interested in rising GOP stars. Riley was destined for

Silicon Valley. Spogli, who roomed with Bush for a time during their time at Harvard, would later become a partner in a billion-dollar Los Angeles investment firm, Freeman Spogli & Company, that poured money into national supermarket and restaurant chains. On weekends, Bush was sometimes in Boston with Gebhard or other classmates. "We all had a steady girlfriend, all defined as one week at a time," said Gebhard. "Drinking and womanizing—what else is there to do in your spare time? George was no different than anyone else. They're going to ask him whether he drank, he's probably going to say, 'Yes.' People are going to ask him whether he went out and womanized, and he would probably say, 'Yes.' And they'll probably ask him if he's taken drugs. I don't know how he'd answer that, but I have no personal knowledge of it. Most of us guys that went to the Harvard Business School were pretty serious folks, we didn't have time to do drugs."[14]

Old friends from Andover and Yale who were now at Harvard would also call on Bush, and they said he would insist that the group head to one of the only places in the mid-1970s in Boston where you might hear a George Jones record: the Hillbilly Ranch. Still in his flight jacket, he talked constantly about Texas and chewed tobacco. Sometimes he would see cousins and John Axelrod, an animated Harvard Law School student and ex–Andover classmate . . . *Ax . . . Rod . . . Roddy!* Stretching back to Andover, Axelrod had always felt that Bush "wasn't a jock per se, he was a gentleman jock; you know the difference between being a farmer and a gentleman farmer?" He also wasn't surprised that Bush dragged everyone to the Hillbilly Ranch. "He liked to party, but I never saw him overwhelmingly party. He was certainly not one of these people who never touched a drop, but I never saw him go to an extreme," said Axelrod, whose family owned the Sheraton Rolling Green in Andover.[15]

And when he was out on the town, he still avoided politics, even through the welling, discordant Watergate revelations and Nixon's ultimate abdication in the summer of 1974, everyone at the B School watching TV and with the elder Bush standing right there on the South Lawn of the White House at that famous moment when Nixon stepped toward the helicopter and disappeared inside. His father's name had cropped up in campus debates over who was best suited to serve Gerald Ford as vice president: Nelson Rockefeller or George Herbert Walker Bush. But the president of the Harvard Republican Club that year couldn't recall any encounters with George W. Bush.[16] And things stayed that way as his last year at Harvard unfolded and his father met with Ford in September and was finally named chief of the U.S. Liaison Office to China, the de facto ambassador, a post that some Washington insiders were saying would serve to keep the elder George Bush as far away as possible from the still unfolding Watergate scandal.

George W. had withdrawn on a campus that was openly debating a legally mandated affirmative action program, where the administration was extending invitations to Muhammad Ali and Dick Gregory to address students, where activists had been demanding the impeachment of the man who had given his father his last two jobs. And in February 1975, he learned where the previous year's B School graduates were finding work and money: HBS released figures that showed that the highest-paying jobs were in the petroleum and research industries; minimum starting salaries were pegged at $30,000 and expected to quickly go much higher. The energy sector salaries were, in fact, projected to be two to three times higher than what some Harvard Law School graduates and Harvard Ph.D.s were making. The newest oil boom was on in Texas; the suddenly ubiquitous Organization of Petroleum Exporting Countries was driving prices skyward and forcing the words "per barrel" into common parlance on American street corners. Life in Midland and West Texas was good again, and the oil train was careening forward as the rest of the country worried and took a place in the gas pump queue. Emergency rationing plans were released, the lines got longer, consumers were lectured about fossil fuels, and somewhere in Texas, someone was getting the idea to market a bumper sticker that Texans gleefully affixed to their pickup trucks: DRIVE 95, FREEZE A YANKEE.

Calling home from Harvard, Bush told his relatives and friends that it was time for him to leave the Northeast; Harvard had been stultifying, to the point that he felt physically constrained. In March, he took a spring break vacation to visit a friend in Arizona. Members of the Greenway family, the friends of his father who had served in the Senate and Congress, who had hosted the Roosevelts, and who owned the ranch he had been sent to as a teenager, also owned the Arizona Inn in Tucson. On his way to Tucson, he decided to stop in Midland to see Jimmy Allison, his mentor and the man who had crafted his father's first political campaigns. Allison told him the oil boom was real, and Bush could sense it very clearly: "I could smell something happening." It was abrupt, and it was in front of him: "All of a sudden it dawned on me that this is entrepreneurial heaven. This is one of the few places in the country where you can go without portfolio and train yourself and become competitive. The barriers to entry were very low in the oil sector. I can't tell you how obvious it was."[17]

He decided to skip the corporate opportunities in New York, even though almost 65 percent of the Harvard Business School graduates were headed to large corporations. His father, with the full financial backing of the Bush-Walker house, Neil Mallon, and many of the other friends from Yale, had gone to West Texas and then left opportunities for his children to follow him. It had been only little more than a decade since his father's Zapata Off-Shore Petroleum had merged with the Liedtke brothers' Pennzoil Corporation. Now waiting for the younger George Bush in West Texas were dozens of FOBs—*Friends of the Bushes*—including Jimmy Allison and Martin Allday, the two Texans who had been the most instrumental in managing his father's entrance into Lone Star politics.

IN JUNE 1975, Muhammad Ali spoke on campus as part of Class Day ceremonies, and his thoughts, offered to 1,100 people at Burden Auditorium, made the front page of *The Harvard Crimson:* "The greatness of a man depends on his heart, not on his education or his wealth."[18] Dick Gregory had also accepted an invitation to join the roster of speakers, including economics professor John Kenneth Galbraith, who would address 2,000 students and faculty at different Class Day exercises. Gregory said that young whites in the mid-1970s were being manipulated by the power elite and that they were "America's new niggers."[19]

Bush loaded his jogging clothes and his tennis shoes into his blue 1970 Oldsmobile Cutlass. He took something else, too: $20,000 from a Bush-Walker fund that was being unleashed as seed money for his trip to Texas. His yearbook photo from the Harvard Business School Class of 1975 showed a hawk-faced, seemingly well tanned young man in a rumpled, unbuttoned polo shirt. All of the other MBA students had donned suit jackets, pressed shirts, foulard ties, even bow ties. Later that summer, he planned to drive to and settle in the Midland-Odessa region, the same way his father had driven there in a brand-new Studebaker in 1948. The barriers to entry, as he told people, might be low in the oil sector, but they would be even lower for someone with seed money and the Bush name. And the barriers to entry into politics would be even lower. Allison and Allday, the two West Texans who had overseen the efforts to sell the Connecticut Yankees to Lone Star voters, knew he was coming.

Over the years, he had preferred to see and describe his father's original trip from the Northeast to Texas in a trailblazing, dusty-saddle kind of way—as a bit of his father's Manifest Destiny and a clean break from the family and its arching expectations: "Moving to Texas was one of the greatest things my Dad has ever done, because he shunned the path that everyone expected him to take."[20] Now he weighed his own well-funded trip to Texas, his haste to leave the Northeast and get to Midland, in almost the same way. His wicked distaste for the way recent history seemed to have conspired against what he had envisioned life to be in the Ivy League was obvious: "Cambridge, Mass. is a very heavy environment compared to Midland. People there don't realize that horizons can be broadened. There is no growth potential there. West Texas is a doer environment. People can do things."[21]

BEFORE HE SETTLED into Midland, there was a summertime excursion to China with three of his siblings; Jeb, who had just gotten married to Columba Garnica, a woman he had met during a senior year work-study trip to Mexico, would not make the trip. China was, of course, still a largely closed society for Americans, and, according to his mother's memoirs, in late June, Marvin, George W., Neil, and Dorothy took the long way to Beijing, stopping for a visit to Hawaii. Their parents met the plane after it touched down on a dusty runway, and almost immediately George W. contracted a lingering cough. He spent weeks touring, jogging in the segregated areas forbidden to the Chinese, and playing Frisbee at a seaside resort called Beidaihe, a nineteenth-century outpost maintained for use by foreign dignitaries. He returned to Beijing to help his father decorate the Liaison Office with red, white, and blue bunting for the Fourth of July party.

In the middle of China, the elder Bush insisted on a Midland-style cookout, complete with hot dogs and hamburgers. The children got up early in the morning to hand out food, and later they cleaned up in the withering heat.[22] The next day the children embarked on a tour of other cities, including Shanghai, Wuxi, and Nanking. That summer, George W.'s father, the former church deacon in Midland, insisted on doing something else, something even more openly symbolic than the red, white, and blue Fourth of July party: he wanted to have sixteen-year-old Dorothy baptized in a nondenominational Beijing church. There would be no Chinese in attendance, only other liaison officials and ambassadors from foreign countries. With someone playing at an ancient organ, the Bush children and the other attendees resolutely sang "Onward, Christian Soldiers."

FROM AFAR, several of the older members of the Bush-Walker house were anxious to see what George W. would do once he finally returned to Midland. His uncle Bucky always thought that the thing that really began knocking the errant, adolescent cockiness out of his nephew was graduating from the Harvard Business School. "That kind of swagger was replaced by a much more intelligent approach to things. And I'm not sure what it was there, it may have been the peer pressure—that 'Jesus, they're a lotta smart guys in the world and if I'm gonna compete against 'em I can't bluff it, I've really gotta know my stuff.' It gave him a hell of a lot of confidence."[23]

In Midland, he moved into a back-alley guest cottage on a street named after the school he had just graduated from. His two-room brick place at 2006 Harvard was on the grounds of a house owned by the Rutter family, friends of his father, in a west Midland neighborhood amid the houses of other millionaire oilmen who had made fortunes in Texas, Oklahoma, and even overseas. The Bush name had grown in stature among those older oil barons who had first settled in the desert in the 1950s. Many of them had made enough money to weather the 1960s downturn, and many of them were perfectly situated to capitalize on the awesome rebound that began in the early 1970s—and many of them were still tilting mightily toward the GOP, toward the antitax movement, toward anyone who could understand the importance of protecting big-oil interests. In Midland, the people who had stayed the course loved to talk about their old oil friend George Bush in Washington, at the United Nations, at the RNC, and now in China. The Bush family's Texas oil ties, running from Midland to Houston, were extraordinarily consistent due to the elder Bush's diligence; no matter where he and Barbara were, they were beyond proficient in maintaining ties to Pennzoil's Liedtke brothers, to Robert Mosbacher, to dozens of the most important Lone Star energy czars.

His father was also a measure, for the entrenched Midlanders, of success beyond the oil patch. The way he had used his West Texas and Houston ties to prime the Republican Party coffers, the way he had parlayed his business connections into political muscle, were things that were tracked and admired almost as closely as the price per barrel. Inside the narrow but wealthy social confines of West Texas, throwing some money toward his father and his campaigns was a way to gamble at a whole new, higher level. The elder Bush was the one who had moved beyond the meetings at the YMCA and the handshake deals in the Scharbauer Hotel's coffee shop. In Midland, people returned his son's phone calls as a matter of both loyalty and obligation. "He could get into doors with his name that you and I couldn't—with oil people. His Dad had friends, and he didn't mind calling on them," said surgeon Charlie Younger, one of George W.'s best friends and one of the members of the gaggle of kids from the 1950s who had grown up, moved away, and then returned in 1975.[24]

THERE WAS a tangible energy coursing through the city—as well as in Odessa, San Angelo, Abilene, Fort Worth, and Dallas. People were dropping out of their steady jobs from one end of West Texas to the other, signing up for geology classes, moving into the handful of available Midland apartments, and trying to chase the oil bonanza straight up the ladder. Charlie Younger saw it: "A shoe clerk could become a land man overnight just because the demand was there."[25] There was also a reunion of old childhood friends, all of them returning to booming Midland almost simultaneously. There was Joe O'Neill III . . . *Spider* . . . Bush's elementary school bike-riding friend, the drawling oilman whose ex-FBI father had brought the O'Neills to Midland and wound up making millions. O'Neill had spent four years in a seminary, traveled, married, and was now back in West Texas from San Francisco to help run his family's oil holdings. He was garrulous to a fault, a self-admitted hard drinker, and he and Bush instantly linked up again. O'Neill and the rest of the reassembling crew who had grown up in Midland in the 1950s had come up with nicknames for Bush: *The Bombastic One, The Bombastic Bushkin.* The names fit that rogue preppy just perfectly, some people thought.

O'Neill quickly came to a conclusion about what was motivating George W. Bush now that he was feeling comfortable, now that he was back in the thick of the Permian Basin, where people were judged primarily on whether they could make oil come out of the ground: "He was focused to prove himself to his dad." O'Neill knew something else—that the newly arrived Bush was focused on proving himself beyond the oil patch. "Right away he started talking about running for Congress."[26]

ASIDE FROM ALLISON, the first two people his parents told him to visit were old family friends, Good Men . . . FOBs . . . *Friends of the Bushes.* The first was Martin Allday, the loyal attorney who had run his father's first Senate campaign. The second was Walter Holton, a Connecticut man and Colgate graduate whose uncle had played golf with Prescott Bush in Greenwich in the 1950s. He was one of the northeastern converts, someone who had opted against an offer to work for the FBI and headed for the easy money and the unpretentious layers in West Texas. He had also been one of the regulars at the Old Man's Martini Bowl in the 1950s. Holton, who had gone to work for Magnolia Petroleum, knew that the younger Bush had probably absorbed the lingo of the oil patch but that he still had a lot to learn. He agreed to be Bush's oil tutor. He had simple advice: make some day money—$50, $75, $100 a day—by visiting the immovable Rosenelle Cherry at the courthouse and checking deeds and mineral rights records for other oilmen. If the cards were right, the job could evolve into work as a land man, the middleman who hustled deals, found out who was drilling on what piece of land, and then ran like hell to make an offer to farmers and ranchers who owned any adjacent piece of land. Bush was going to be like all those caffeinated, competitive, never-standing-still land men he had seen pouncing on any news, any rumor, outside the Midland courthouse when he was young—all those smiling, honey-tongued salesmen who could put a quick deal together and who knew how to bring those tobacco-chewing ranchers together with Wall Street types and convince them all, sweet Jesus, that this mixed marriage was for a greater good. It was the right move for a stickball commissioner–cheerleader–fraternity president accustomed to coordinating and orchestrating disparate bits of walking testosterone; it was also the "low-overhead move," the relatively independent move, he thought: "I wasn't about to do something that I didn't want to do. I was single. My overhead was extremely low. I knew I didn't want to work for anybody for a while," he told *The Dallas Morning News.*[27]

FROM MIDLAND, George W. was also fast developing a lasting bond with a twenty-three-year-old political operative he had heard about and met through his father the year before he had gone to China, someone who was part of a wave of unapologetic politicos such as Lee Atwater who were redefining what it meant to play hardball in the 1970s. During the elder Bush's tenure as head of the RNC, a *Washington Post* reporter had called in August 1973 and said he was investigating reports that a paid GOP official named Karl C. Rove had taught political espionage and "dirty tricks" during seminars for college Republicans—before and after the Watergate break-in.[28] The elder Bush, who was struggling to distance himself and the RNC from the Watergate debacle, was now faced with the fallout from another lengthy *Washington Post* story: "GOP Probes Official as Teacher of 'Tricks.'" When the story ran, of course it was placed directly adjacent to yet another *Post* investigation into the Watergate matter.

The Denver native Rove, who told people that he had been a Republican since the age of nine, had emerged, with Lee Atwater's help, as the executive director of the College Republican National Committee. And now the *Post* was exploring allegations that Rove—who would attend several colleges but never graduate—was using false names, falsifying campaign documents on opponents' stationery, and releasing false invitations to political events. The *Post* said it was pointing out reports that the elder Bush and the RNC already had. Chairman Bush told the *Post* he would organize a GOP investigating committee "to get to the bottom" of the allegations against Rove. Months later, after the story disappeared from the headlines, Chairman Bush hired Rove as his special assistant at the RNC.

During a 1974 trip to Washington to visit his parents before his father's departure for China, George W. was introduced to Rove, and they saw each other when George W. traveled to D.C. to escape Harvard. Rove knew what his job was whenever his boss's son was scheduled to arrive: "I was supposed to give him the car keys whenever he came to town."[29] Rove would evolve into George W.'s closest political adviser, image shaper, and strategist, and would be lauded as a "political wizard" by the Texas media and singled out in headlines: "Top Bush Aide Brings Aggressive Style to Effort."[30] Rove had to have a nickname—"Turd Blossom," as a high-ranking Texas elected official, a mutual friend, would grin and say. The name was perfect, people said, because whenever Rove was around, something was sure to pop up. For years after Rove moved to Texas, he and Bush would talk for hours on the phone or in person, sometimes about the way they had seen so many people wasting their time, their energies, their lives in the 1960s. Rove's home in Austin was an oasis where Bush could go to clear his head, where he could reconfirm his harsh feelings toward the 1960s, and where, some said, the self-educated Rove would recommend that Bush read works by David Horowitz and especially Myron Magnet, writers who had come to view the 1960s as "the destructive generation." Bush felt comfortable around Rove in a way he never had around many of the young people he had encountered at Yale or Harvard. The apparent fact that Bush had developed a streak of anti-intellectualism suggested that Rove's résumé, his lack of a college degree, placed him in a trustworthy light. He could be viewed as a thinking man's anti-intellectual, someone who perhaps professed a similar disdain for the ivory-tower excesses of the 1960s—the way people such as Coffin, Timothy Leary, and the students at Columbia University had stood Ivy League educations and traditions on their heads.

Years later, Bush would scrawl a note: *Dear Karl—Thanks so much for the wonderful dinner—good eats, good friendship. There are few places I can relax. Yours is one. . . . Best Regards, G.*[31]

• • •

"HARVARD, at first, was a hindrance," remembered Ed Thompson, the former director of the Permian Basin Petroleum Association.[32] Following established ritual and at the invitation of Holton or other old Bush family allies, George W. began going for black coffee and drinks in the Wildcatter's Room at the private Petroleum Club. He would sit with friends outside the inner circle of the serious rainmakers and heavy hitters who were polite but still suspicious of newcomers, Harvard types, again flooding into Midland—shades of some of those oil-chasing Yankees who had come in the 1950s and vanished as soon as the wells went dry and the prices skidded. "He did a lot more listening than talking," said Thompson. "He was pretty cagey. He didn't force himself. He played his hand close to the vest. He got involved in civic things. He began to fit into the group. Eventually he was invited to sit in."[33]

The price of oil had been soaring from $2 to $12 to $36 a barrel, and when he first arrived at the Midland Country Club, some of the tobacco chewers in their expensive Lucchese boots slowly looked down at the flimsy black Chinese slippers he had brought back from his trip to the Forbidden Country. For the usual smattering of civic functions at the United Way, First Presbyterian, and the YMCA, he wore the hand-me-down sharkskin shoes Uncle Jonathan Bush had given him. The floor of his guest cottage looked like the one in his college dormitory, strewn with empty cans, dirty laundry, and yellowed newspapers. His bed frame was broken, and he lashed it together with neckties. O'Neill gave him his old shirts, and he wore them for years. The first day that Walter Holton took him to the Midland County Courthouse, his first day learning how to check deeds and mineral rights records, Holton looked down and noticed that Bush was wearing one blue sock and one green one. He Scotch taped the tassels onto his loafers. His Cutlass needed a paint job. As a goof, one of his 1950s friends went to "nigger town," as his friend called it, bought a ratty, used sweater in a thrift shop, and gave it to the Bombastic One.[34] He wore it for months. And if he was out for drinks, dating a woman who was working as a "land man" for ARCO, he would let the check linger on the table. "The buffalo would squeal when it left his hand," Younger liked to say.[35]

One of the members of the Bush crew, a young bank president, had an idea at Christmas: he took old Christmas cards from an oil field service company, crossed out the company names in an obvious way—and then forged Bush's signature on the cards. People all over Midland started receiving crudely recycled oilfield company Christmas cards that appeared to be from George W. Bush. A tight quartet was forming: O'Neill, Bush, Younger, and oilman Don Evans. The group was often inseparable, always somewhere in the good seats at the minor-league Midland Angels double-headers, and Bush's friends all knew that coming to the Saudi Arabia of the Southwest had more implications for their high-spirited friend than for them. O'Neill called it "a two-edged sword" that could open doors but also involved ceaseless obligations to assume the politically expedient role of su-percitizen his father had played twenty years before. It wasn't just that Bush was required to volunteer to run the United Way, which he did; he was also "expected to be in church every Sunday when other people were not."[36]

In the afternoons, Bush jogged hard at the high school track with Younger and Evans, then showered in Younger's medical office, dressed, and headed a few blocks toward downtown. He stretched his seed money, still not making any real returns from oil, not drilling anything, until an attorney in town introduced him to Fletcher Mills . . . *Buzz!* . . . and Ralph Way, two oilmen who had about a decade on him in age and also had the wrinkled, weathered, impossible-to-surprise countenance bred by too many up-and-down years in the oil patch. They had seen the bottom and lived through it, they had perfected the drop-dead art of oil patch black humor, and now they were entranced by the rambunctious, fast-talking newcomer who was still shaking off his preppy accouterments—the tasseled loafers and the Chinese slippers. Way instantly called him "Little George"; Buzz Mills preferred "Bush Boy." Bush Boy was incorri-gible, a foul-mouthed cutup who was trying hard to be one of the natives. When they took him out to the Midland Country Club for the first time, his golf shoes were falling apart, they looked like clown shoes, and they immediately bought him a new pair.

By the end of his first year in Midland, he had enough leads to think about forming a one-man show called Bush Oil. Mills and Way let him move into a furnitureless water-cooler room in their offices at the old Mid-land National Bank Building—the bank the elder George Bush had helped to found. The deal was that Bush would have to give Way and Mills first crack at any leads he was developing; in exchange, they would offer him a "participatory interest" in their wells. At the airport one day, he ran into another old pal from the seventh grade. Bob McCleskey . . . *Chief* . . . had become an accountant, and Bush needed one as he began figuring out how to structure partnerships with possibly far-flung investors, including ones being brought to him by Jonathan Bush and various members of the Bush-Walker family on Wall Street. McCleskey, whose office was dotted with trophy animal heads from hunting trips, visited Bush's tiny water-cooler operation, saw the Coke-bottle crates he was using for chairs, and told him he was the only accountant Bush could afford. Joe O'Neill III told people in Midland that being a land man was not "rocket science" but more like being a quarterback who knew how to send people off in different directions to accomplish different tasks—and he told people that it was the right place for Bush. McCleskey also thought the land-man avenue was the right way for Bush to enter the business. "You get a lot of exposure without putting up a lot of money,"[37] said McCleskey, who would serve as Bush's accountant for the next two decades.

The elder Bush had known that business in small Texas towns was spurred and massaged on the weekends. The younger Bush played touch football, went to every Midland Angels AA game, signed up to teach Sunday classes at First Presbyterian, the same church where his father had taught Sunday school. The gravel-voiced warriors, the older bourbon-sipping oil czars, began brightening when they saw him at the country club, at the Petroleum Club; they appreciated the fact that good-humored Bush chewed tobacco, told jokes, drank, and cursed harder than a grease-stained roustabout. At night Bush was on the town, headed toward the 19th Hole, the bar at the country club, eating at La Bodega or driving twenty minutes west to the still wide open Odessa and its loud, sweaty honky-tonks. "Wherever he went, he would have a date, and she would be a pretty good-looking one, too," said Holton with admiration.[38] Sometimes, even though he never needed another name or phone number, even when he wasn't looking for dates, one of the other west Texas friends of the family, including the Alldays, would fix him up with someone.

Out at the high school track one day, Bush was sprinting by old G. W. Brock, a grizzled oilman; he yanked Old Brock's running shorts down around his ankles and zoomed right by. Another time, friends said, Charlie Younger and Bush rented the VFW Hall and flew in five hundred pounds of crawfish and a Cajun band from Louisiana—for no reason other than a party.[39] Younger's father, another wily old-school oilman, knew a little about patience and caution in the Permian Basin. He told his own son to ease off the beer and focus on his fledgling medical practice. Later, Younger's father found out that Bush's father had also been cautioning his unreserved first son, at the exact same time, to lay off the drinking and take care of his fledgling career.[40]

Some people in Midland knew about the night Charlie and Dubya went to Odessa—"you raised hell in Odessa and you raised your family in Midland" was the old slogan—to hear Willie Nelson, the only musician in the history of Texas who had pulled off the neat trick of being equally appealing to stoned, pan-fried hippies in Austin and scotch-sipping, buttoned-down conservatives in north Dallas. That night they were almost invisible, bulletproof, maybe in the way that too much of something can sometimes make you feel. Somehow they scrambled onstage, uninvited, and began warbling behind the great prairie visionary Willie Nelson.[41] All over Midland, people said that George W. Bush, now that he was back in Texas, seemed very content.

10

Someone Really Political

In 1976, Donald Ensenat, Bush's dependable fraternity brother from New Orleans and personal assistant to Bush's father, asked Bush to be one of the groomsmen at a wedding deep in the heart of the Mississippi Delta. After he and Bush had been rejected by the University of Texas, Ensenat had decided he would try law school later on; years later, in partial recognition of his unrelenting loyalty, the family attorney, Don Ensenat, would be appointed ambassador to Brunei. In the Delta, in Greenville, Mississippi, with the big river close by, the extravagant wedding was a reunion of old Yale drinking buddies and a gathering of powerful southern clans, including publisher Hodding Carter's family. Everyone in that florid ensemble deep in the bittersweet and usually impoverished Delta, where Robert Johnson, Muddy Waters, and others had invented American blues music, knew who brash George W. was, especially the women. "That wedding was wild. All the ladies were going crazy over him," remembered Julia Reed, who became a writer for *Vogue*.[1]

With the levees and sharecropper shacks not far away and various political stalwarts from Mississippi and Louisiana on hand, the drinks flowed. People were lit—"We all were," said Reed—and she remembered Bush arriving dressed in cream-colored linen trousers, a flowered tie, Gucci loafers, and a navy blazer and drawing on an expensive cigar. People knew his family, and it added to his cocky aura, something she liked to call the "preppy scoundrel" demeanor. "When coupled with young George's bad-boy good looks, the total package was enough to send the many eligible twenty-somethings into a collective swoon."[2]

Now, weighed against the family standards, against what his grandfather and father had already accomplished at the same stage in their careers—military heroes in world wars, Yale standouts, parents, millionaires immersed in successful careers—George W. Bush was turning thirty in 1976, and he viewed portions of his own life as something of a wastrel's guidebook. He would say, simply, that he was "drinking and carousing and fumbling around."[3]

BACK IN MIDLAND in the summer of 1976, another ally from DKE came to see him. Bob Reisner was working for the Federal Energy Administration, and he had flown to West Texas to lecture—gingerly—the bellicose, surly wildcatters about the much-loathed federal price regulations. In the closed, small world of Midland, Bush heard that Reisner was coming to town and made a point of scheduling an appointment. Right away Reisner could tell how the Yale- and Harvard-educated Bush was enormously entertained by the Midland good old boys who were awash in cash, behaving like superheated Kentucky moonshiners around tax revenuers.

In an isolated environment such as Midland, in a state that had once been a country, it wasn't hard to find hundreds of oilmen who hated Washington and all the regulators they presumed were dead set on putting shackles on their ankles, maybe even killing off the last vestiges of what insiders liked to call the ABC Plan of oil royalties—a splendid loophole set up between investors and their banks that saved everyone involved from having to pay income taxes.

Reisner and the other federal energy officials rented a movie theater to present their proposals to the millionaires—but the theater owner only agreed to rent his place if the feds would indemnify him against the damage to the screen that would surely take place when one of the roaring oilmen whipped out his gun and started firing. Reisner and his colleagues, who were escorted to the theater meeting by the FBI, survived their potentially volatile West Texas encounter. Reisner, of course, eventually chatted with Bush, who wanted to explain to his fraternity brother exactly how the oil game was played.

"Let me tell you, Bobby," Bush began, "how you do quantitative analysis. You do all your analysis, you do all your statistics, and then you punch a hole in the ground. And if there's no oil there, you just lost five million bucks."[4]

It was obvious to Reisner that there was still a frontier mentality in Midland and that Bush, even with his obvious family ties, was subscribing to it; Reisner didn't need any reminders that millions of dollars were just beginning to flow in West Texas in proportions that were almost ungodly. It was, as more than one oilman said, the New Gold Rush. It was as breath-taking as the 1950s, and people were going to be paying bags of cash for Jaguars in Dallas and driving them back across that pancake-flat landscape; the status symbol of choice was going to be the private jet; the new Lone Star sheiks were about to buy up the condominiums in New Mexico resort towns and the best seats at the million-dollar quarterhorse races in Ruidoso. Writers, documentarians, and even the occasional tourist who wanted to witness the latest, crackling incarnation of the New Oil Age, left the city in awe of the fact that the nouveau oil barons had created a thriving Midland Polo Club in the middle of the arid expanse—and that it had become an un-likely way station, a desert fixture, for George W. Bush and the sons and daughters of the first- and second-generation oil pioneers.

It was, really, like turning the clock back twenty years, when Midland had had one of the highest incomes per capita in the world—when Mid-land had been a startling, bauble-laden Emerald City where instant, some-times defensive, millionaires juggled their conspicuous consumption with their orderly, entrenched commitment to small-town civic-mindedness. It was, as Bush's childhood friend Randall Roden had once said about the place they had lived in during the 1950s, as unreal as winning the lottery. But now it was also an even more immoderate time in a slightly bigger city, when young oilmen, who hadn't ever had to endure giant losses in the oil patch, had neither the time nor the patience to wait things out.

At the Midland Country Club, more than a few younger oilmen were embittered by the obvious fact that the "handshake" era of their fathers was clearly on the wane—the fabled, uncomplicated days that they had seen and heard about from their wildcatting fathers was withering away, strangled by the regulations, the accusations by environmentalists, the spreading sense that a small group of 1970s Texas oilmen was holding the rest of the country hostage. That heady, unbureaucratic method of making money the way George W.'s father had in the 1950s, when few questions had been asked beyond a man's creditworthiness, was almost completely gone.

From Connecticut and Wall Street, the Bush-Walker network had once sprung, almost reflexively, to his father's side with unprecedented amounts of money at every critical juncture of his father's foray into the Texas oil patch, even in 1965, when Hurricane Betsy sucked Zapata's hundred-yard-long oil rigs to the floor of the Gulf of Mexico. It was, accord-ing to George W.'s uncles, always a given that the elder George Bush was going to have easy access to the deep-rooted family network. But the New Oil Age was something else entirely; now George W. was going to inherit his family's connections, and some of its investment money, but it would always be bitterly obvious to him that he was toiling in a more complicated oil era. Texas now had something else to contend with, something that his father and his friends' fathers had never truly encountered in the 1950s in Midland and Houston: the knocks against oil profits and loud calls for environmental protections and price controls. The perceptions, the society and class distinctions that had sometimes worked against him in the Northeast and that had also blocked his father's ambitions for the Senate and thus the White House, hadn't really ended when George W. left Andover, Yale, and Harvard. In the West Texas Permian Basin, they simply took on a different, nagging form in a place where people insisted they were average even though their investment portfolios suggested otherwise. Back in Texas for less than a year, George W. Bush was bantering—moving running around—out late. And the more Reisner studied the man he had first gotten to know at Yale, the more he thought it was simply a way of life in West Texas, simply a way of dealing with the uneasy but addictive nature of the big-stakes oil game, "part of a way of dealing with the enormous risks."[5]

NOT LONG AFTER Reisner's delicate trip to Midland, Bush banged on the door of Susie and Don Evans on an otherwise placid Sunday afternoon and suggested to Don that they head out to the airport and spend a few bucks for a spin over the desiccated Permian Basin in a single-engine Cessna. Susie Evans, who had gone to elementary school with Bush, was a longtime Midland presence, and when she had been dating her future husband in Houston, she had frequently stayed at the Bush house. She had moved back to Midland, and after she had heard that Bush was back in town, she and her husband had frequently invited him over.

Her husband Don Evans . . . *Willard* . . . was a short, fastidious, narrow-faced oilman in his early thirties who was poised to assume control of the Tom Brown Company, one of the legendary older names in the West Texas patch. Bush had begun spending more time at the Evanses' apartment in the Windsor Courts, drinking cocktails with them and leaving his laundry for Susie to do. Bush liked Evans's politics, he liked that they were about the same age and that both of them had recent MBAs. He liked the fact that Evans's old man had landed on the beach at Normandy during World War II.

Evans said he'd love to go flying. At the airport he watched Bush stare at the controls, at the panel, and he realized that Bush—though not admitting it—had no idea how to fly the thing properly. After finally figuring out how to launch the plane, Bush pushed the Cessna hard down the runway. Evans screamed, "Give it some gas!" The Cessna's warning system was blinking and crackling. Bush tried to lift his craft fast, almost as if he were piloting a jet back in the Texas Air National Guard. The plane wobbled into the air, and the unsubtle maneuvering threatened to shove it into a stall. Now the rented plane was rattling in the sky over Midland. The endless petrochemical complexes, all the aluminum and steel and smoke stacks that pockmark the Permian Basin, were spiking up just below the aircraft. Bush nervously turned to Evans, put his hand on his knee and blurted in his self-mocking West Texas way, "Okay, Evvie, I've got it under control."

After more seemingly endless moments, he somehow got control of the plane again. He aimed the aircraft down, and the landing was as shaky and brutal as the takeoff. The plane careened off the runway and onto the desert. Evans sighed in relief. Then an unbelieving Evans braced himself as Bush suddenly and unexpectedly spun the plane and bounced back along the runway. Evans stared at Bush. He could see the fear and panic flooding his face. Bush pressed on. Evans had no idea why Bush wanted to go again. The plane wobbled uncertainly back into the West Texas skies, and Bush turned to Evans.

"Hey," said Bush airily, as if he had just had an original, amusing idea, "let's fly around Midland."

The men began cracking up. Bush brought the Cessna back to the airport. It was the last time he flew a plane. Evans would be one of the three people at Bush's side in almost every public venture for the next twenty-three years.[6]

By 1977, Mills and Way had let him in on a few holes. He was a small player, someone who was there to learn, Way told people. When Mills and Way decided to drill in Sutton County, they let Bush have his first piece, for a few thousand dollars, in a "participatory interest." Of course, the hole was bone dry. That jarred him: "I'll never forget the feeling, kind of, 'oops, this is not quite as easy as we all thought it was going to be,'" Bush told a Dallas writer. It was a wake-up call, and people saw the way he reacted. Mills and Way moved the rig and drilled in another four spots. Bush was worried—he called himself "Mr. Frugal"—and Way could see it. Then the wells began to hit, trickling with a little oil. There wasn't much, just enough to recoup the losses and put a few thousand back in the bank. After a while, Bush got the idea: you just keep moving until something happens. You call more people, raise more money, drill more holes.

Bush also liked the fact that, like some of the other oilmen in Midland in the mid-1970s, Mills, Way, and Evans weren't knee-jerk opponents of the Republican Party. In the sixteen years since Bush had lived there, the Southern Democratic base had clearly eroded, and more Republicans were moving in from out of state. And now the biggest political news in West Texas was the fact that Democratic Representative George Mahon, who had been the only West Texas Congressman in the forty-four years since the Nineteenth Congressional District had been created, might finally be abdicating. It was, decided Evans and Bush, probably the most perfect political opportunity to present itself in a long time. "You've got to find the right spot and the right time," said Evans. They talked assets and liabilities, what it would mean if someone born in Connecticut and named George Walker Bush was on the ballot in places as isolated and fiercely Texan as the Permian Basin, the Texas Panhandle, and the cotton fields of Lubbock and Plainview. Along with O'Neill and Younger, they talked about whether or not George W. Bush had been in town long enough and whether he would be able to abruptly launch a campaign for Congress. When the thought was introduced in the small but growing GOP committee meetings, local party members promised full support even though Bush had only been living in Texas for less than two years— and many of them openly mentioned the pragmatic possibilities of inheriting the entire Prescott Bush and elder George Bush campaign networks. But Evans, already a cautionary sounding board for Bush, said that it would be unwise to underestimate the Democratic strongholds in West Texas. "We'll take them on," Bush told Evans.

When George W. talked to his father, the elder Bush was pleased that his first son was finally going to follow his and Prescott Bush's legacy. When Gerald Ford had taken office in 1974, the elder Bush and Nelson Rockefeller had been the two most prominent vice presidential names being debated by the new administration and any of the old Nixon loyalists who were still in the White House. In the end, and in good measure because of the Bush family's close ties to Nixon, Ford had decided that Rockefeller would be the safer choice. The elder George Bush's own political thirsts were further complicated when Ford insisted that he segue from his post in China to a position as the director of the CIA, and in Washington, many GOP operatives had instantly assumed that the appointment was also Ford's way of crushing Bush's obvious interest in the presidency.

The elder Bush quietly weighed whether Ford was out to "bury" him at the CIA, but he finally accepted the position in 1976, knowing full well that it would be a short-term appointment if the Democrats took back the White House later that year. The family's political advisers had suggested that it could actually serve as an important prelude to a presidential run; it could be a post that would serve twin expediencies: ratcheting down the still festering doubts about the elder Bush's firm-gripped commitment to conservative principles and immersing him in the sophisticated, upper-level Beltway corridors that he might have missed when he had been rejected twice for the Senate.

When Jimmy Carter was elected and the elder Bush's tenure at the CIA was effectively ended, Bush received a special Texas guest at Walker's Point. Future billionaire Ross Perot, whose Dallas-based computer company had monopolized the distribution of federal Medicare payments, had flown to Maine and said the elder Bush had a standing offer to run one of Perot's other ventures, some oil interests in Houston. Bush had said no, and it was something that reportedly angered the volatile Perot for years.[7] Now, after being bypassed for the vice presidency and stepping down from the CIA, it was one of the few times in the last twenty-five years that there were no members of the Bush-Walker family in a high-profile national office.

In Houston, the elder Bush was, as he said, pleased that his son was simply competing. And as he reflected on it with a historian, he thought that his son was really doing exactly what the Bushes were supposed to do: "passing on of tradition, passing on legacy."[8] His first son's decision to run for Congress was, he told that historian several years later, all about the encompassing concept of competition that had been inculcated in each of the children and grandchildren by Prescott Bush and Dorothy Walker during almost every day on Grove Lane in Greenwich or each August at Kennebunkport: "You can't win unless you run."[9]

When the seventy-seven-year-old Mahon announced in the summer of 1977 that he was retiring after twenty-two terms, national GOP officials openly dubbed the race one of their national priorities. Like the races his father had run in Texas, it was a possible domino, a seat that could turn the tide in a crucial state. And Bush was already telling people at the Petroleum Club that Jimmy Carter was not their friend: the damned way he was trying to control natural gas prices made it seem as if he were hell bent on turning America into France or Italy or some other socialism-friendly system that would squelch the soul of the Texas wildcatter. He began telling people that something should be done. He tried out an idea on the unsuspecting oilmen: What if I run for Mahon's seat? What if we sent a Friend of Oil to Congress for the only time in the last four decades? "They were a little confused about why I was doing this, but at that time,

Jimmy Carter was president and he was trying to control natural gas prices, and I felt that the United States was headed toward European-style socialism."[10]

Karl Rove, who was working for Bush's father in Houston, came on board as a personal adviser.[11] After the allegations against him had disappeared and he had gone to work for the elder George Bush, Rove had become the finance director for Gerald Ford's 1976 Virginia campaign. Then he had moved to Texas to work with James A. Baker III on the elder Bush's prepresidential political action committee. Meanwhile, Joe O'Neill promised that if Bush ran he would never need to worry about raising money; he would serve as treasurer and raise cash from his father's friends in the oil patch. Don Evans said he would do the same, and he offered to essentially comanage the campaign. Jimmy Allison and Martin Allday, the Midland attorney who had served as Bush's father's campaign chairman during the first Senate race, had all of their connections. Robert McCleskey . . . *Chief!* . . . would be the comptroller.

There would be no shortage of money, and dozens of contributions could be expected from influential donors around the country. Finally, twenty-three-year-old Neil Bush would be dispatched from Houston to West Texas. The ongoing political education of the children was a given in the family, and Neil seemed to have struck some balance between the hard-charging demeanor of his eldest brother and the dogmatic, preachy tendencies of Jeb. Neil was, they said, the one who could possibly be the perfect politician to emerge from the next generation of the Bush-Walker clan and someone who could best serve his father's ongoing presidential aspirations. Beyond the direct exposure to gloves-off political power in a West Texas congressional race, sending Neil to that part of the state would also serve as a good exposure to the petroleum gods. The third son had just graduated from Tulane, and the family decided he would move into Lubbock, the Democratic soul of the congressional district, and be given the title of co–campaign manager for his oldest brother.

THE ALMOST INFAMOUS Midland bachelor had already made July announcements that he was running for the Nineteenth Congressional District. One Tuesday, he had made speeches, in Midland and in Lubbock. The district was dominated by three cities—Midland, Odessa and Lubbock—and Lubbock was the largest and most crucial. Unlike Midland-Odessa, Lubbock revolved around farming and ranching markets; it had been Mahon's stronghold, and it was a city that lived and died by federal agricultural legislation. "I'm not an expert now on agriculture but I plan to be one," Bush said in Lubbock. And without any prompting, he suddenly decided to address the obvious question of his political lineage by saying he would "keep reminding people that I will be campaigning on me," not his father. He was cocky, speaking in bursts and rocking back and forth as he outlined the fact that he had a lengthy but quiet history in political campaigns: "The opposition will not be of any concern to me. I'm accustomed to tough campaigns."[12]

There were few policy or ideological specifics in his short press conference, other than that he called himself a conservative, he wanted the energy industry deregulated, and he was going to battle "the bureaucratic spread of federal government that is encroaching more and more on our lives." He also said that it was wrong that a farmer earned only four to five cents on a fifty-five-cent loaf of bread. Democrats were already openly speculating about how to take advantage of his admitted lack of knowledge about agricultural concerns and how to capitalize on the contention that he was running for office without any substantive civic record or platform. Meanwhile, after listening to him in Lubbock, several long-suffering members of the GOP thought he represented the best chance they had had in decades. Ruth Schiermeyer, an insurance agent and veteran GOP activist in Lubbock, was one of them.

She had stayed the course during some troubling times for the Republican Party in deep West Texas, and she liked Bush's energy. She thought he had an uncanny ability to shift from being wickedly intense, from never letting his eyes drift away from yours, to suddenly becoming folksy, down-home, laid-back. And of course she didn't mind when he met her and wondered if his brother Neil could come and live at her house. Neil was, some friends concluded, the only one in the family who could get away with calling his mother "The Enforcer." When he arrived in West Texas, Neil moved into Schiermeyer's house in Lubbock, the largest city in the congressional district—and the one where the Bush family would have the most trouble playing down its haunting carpetbagging image.

Some of the other Bush campaign workers were not impressed with Neil. One said Neil tried too hard to impress people, eventually doing annoying things at serious moments—to the point of blowing up campaign balloons and letting the air out fast so the balloon would make a disturbing sound. "George had a lot of friends who were country-club types," said one Bush campaign staffer, who added that "they put up" with Neil because he was George's brother.[13] Schiermeyer was glad to have the son of the director of the Central Intelligence Agency living in her house.

George W. Bush's grandfather Prescott Bush—family patriarch and Connecticut senator. Prescott's father, a steel and railroad magnate, personally advised President Herbert Hoover.

GEORGE BUSH PRESIDENTIAL LIBRARY

George W. Bush's grandmother and family matriarch Dorothy Walker Bush. Her father founded a powerful Wall Street investment house and was a personal adviser to Franklin Delano Roosevelt.

GEORGE BUSH PRESIDENTIAL LIBRARY

Nine-month-old George W. Bush, born in New Haven, Connecticut, with his father in 1947.

GEORGE BUSH PRESIDENTIAL LIBRARY

Four-year-old George W. Bush with his mother, Barbara, his father, George Bush, and his grandparents Dorothy Walker Bush and Prescott Bush, at the airport in Midland, Texas, 1950.
GEORGE BUSH PRESIDENTIAL LIBRARY

Robin Bush, 1953.
GEORGE BUSH PRESIDENTIAL LIBRARY

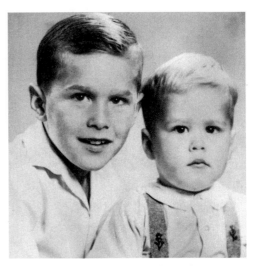

George W. Bush and his brother Jeb in 1955.
GEORGE BUSH PRESIDENTIAL LIBRARY

George W. Bush and his parents in Rye, New York, 1955. From the late nineteenth century forward, the extended Bush-Walker family frequently spent time at family estates or residences in Rye, Long Island, Manhattan, Maine, South Carolina, or Florida.

George W. Bush with his father at a 1956 ceremony to launch a multi-million-dollar offshore oil rig in the Gulf of Mexico.

Senator Prescott Bush and Dorothy Walker Bush, center, with their children, grandchildren, and in-laws in 1956. Grandson George Walker Bush is standing, far left, next to his mother and father. GEORGE BUSH PRESIDENTIAL LIBRARY

(*Above*) Head cheerleader George Walker Bush at Phillips Academy in Andover, Massachusetts.

(*Left*) Head cheerleader George Walker Bush, in the black jacket, with his squad from Phillips Academy.

George W. Bush followed his father, uncles, grandfather, and several other members of the Bush-Walker clan to Yale and to the same Yale "secret" society.
GEORGE BUSH PRESIDENTIAL LIBRARY

Former fraternity president George Walker Bush being sworn into the Texas Air National Guard in Houston in 1968.

The father and his four sons, left to right: Neil, George Bush, Jeb, George W., and Marvin, 1970. GEORGE BUSH PRESIDENTIAL LIBRARY

Newlyweds George W. Bush and Laura Welch Bush on the campaign trail in the doomed congressional race of 1978. GEORGE BUSH PRESIDENTIAL LIBRARY

George Herbert Walker Bush with sons George Walker Bush and Jeb fishing off the coast of the Walker's Point compound, built by the family at the turn of the century in Kennebunkport, Maine. GEORGE BUSH PRESIDENTIAL LIBRARY

George W. Bush with his wife, Laura, watching, as he announces his candidacy for the governor's office in Texas, 1993. David Woo/Sygma

Texas governor Ann Richards with her opponent George W. Bush at a Texas Rangers baseball game.
Bob Daemmrich/Sygma

Gubernatorial candidate George W. Bush standing on a diving board in Houston and campaigning in 1994. BOB DAEMMRICH/SYGMA

Lieutenant Governor Bob Bullock, the most powerful and unpredictable Democrat in Texas, applauds as George W. Bush is sworn in as governor, 1995. F. Carter-Smith/Sygma

Barbara Bush watches as her son campaigns in San Antonio just before the 1994 election.
BOB DAEMMRICH/SYGMA

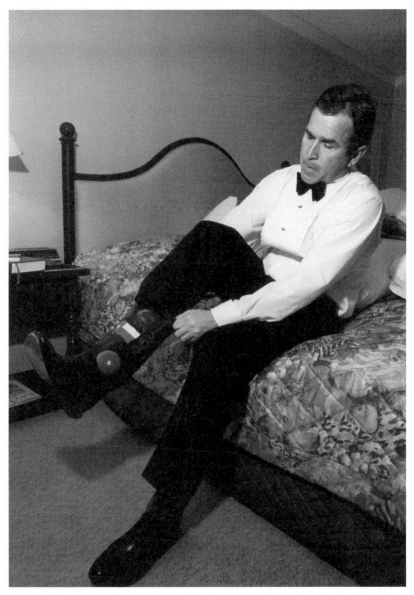

George W. Bush pulling on his eelskin boots, emblazoned with the Texas flag and insignia, before inauguration parties in 1995. DAVID WOO/SYGMA

Newly sworn-in Texas governor George W. Bush, 1995.

Portrait in power: Lieutenant Governor Bob Bullock, the most influential back-room Democrat in Texas, whispers some words to newly sworn-in Texas governor George W. Bush in 1995. ALAN POGUE

Barbara Bush, George Bush, and Jenna Bush listen as George W. Bush is sworn in as Texas governor in 1995. ALAN POGUE

She knew people were going to question the value of the Bush name; even lonely Republicans looking for some sort of opening were going to question if newcomer George W. and his brother were just piggybacking on their father's lingering reputation in Midland and Odessa. "You don't think I'd be running for this if my name was Smith, do you?" she was told Bush had said one day.[14]

As BUSH's campaign moved forward, O'Neill and his wife, Jan, tried the same thing they had been trying to do for the last several months: introducing Bush to the reserved, well-grounded Laura Welch, a thirty-year-old elementary school librarian and the daughter of Harold and Jenna Welch. She was an only child, and her father was a well-known developer and home builder in Midland; her mother, Jenna Hawkins Welch, was an active presence in the civic clubs who helped to keep her husband's books. Her father was born in 1912 in Ada, Oklahoma, but raised in Lubbock, where he had attended Texas Tech University. He served four years during World War II, including a sixteen-month stint in Europe with the 555th Anti-Aircraft Battalion. He and Jenna Hawkins were married in 1944, and after the war they settled in Midland. He had become a credit officer and had formed a profitable construction company with fellow developer Lloyd Waynick. Spurred on by the postwar explosion in Midland, Welch had been instrumental in creating five subdivisions around the mushrooming city—ones that had catered to the steady influx of outsiders relocating to West Texas in the 1950s and the 1960s.

Laura Welch was born on November 4, 1946. By the time she was in second grade, she told her parents that she had decided on a career as a teacher, and for years she reiterated that goal. She attended the First Methodist Church, and she was always a bit more orderly and disciplined than other Midland children; she lined up her dolls in neat rows, and she would pretend, in play sessions, that she was a teacher orchestrating another day at school. As an only child with only two first cousins, she spent time with her wing of the roving Midland gang who lived on the well-off west side of the city in the 1950s. Throughout her high school years in the 1960s, she struck friends as being more grown-up and reserved than most. She was an A student who spent hours reading, who hung out at Agnes's Drive-In, and who learned to smoke with Regan Gammon, her best friend since third grade, by her side in a car and taking turns hopping over the backseat, crawling onto the floor, and sneaking a smoke while the driver looked for spots where they wouldn't be caught puffing away.[15]

After high school, she left Midland to become an education major at

Southern Methodist University, a virtually all-white school located in one of the two most exclusive communities in Texas. In a way, it was a safer alternative than Rice for some upper-income families in Texas. Not as rigorous as Rice but as prestigious in its own way, SMU was in University Park, a wealthy, closely guarded municipality within the Dallas city limits. SMU was building a reputation for athletic prowess completely out of proportion to the size of its student body that would eventually lead to one of the most widespread investigations into alumni payoffs and student graft in the history of college sports. SMU was intentionally—and effectively—isolated from the rest of Dallas, from the growing racial tensions in the southern side of the city. In a sense, it was not unlike Midland; it was a world unto itself, with clear boundaries. At SMU, Welch was a popular presence on campus; she always had a boyfriend, and she was known to spend hours leafing through and reading magazines, newspapers, and books. Her friends noticed that she had a polished reserve, a way of easily letting others lead the conversation. Laura Welch was content, they said, to listen—and listen attentively, a fact that would reveal itself when she would mention something someone else had said months before.

She received favorable grades at SMU, especially in English courses, and toward the end of her college career made inquiries about elementary school teaching positions in Texas. At times, she would bring home to Midland someone she had met at SMU, a guy she wanted her parents to meet. After graduating from SMU, she traveled through Europe and then moved to Houston, where she had been offered a job as a second-grade teacher at John F. Kennedy Elementary School. She lived in the Chateaux Dijon apartment complex; Midland friends had recommended it to her as the place where young singles lived in Houston.

At the Chateaux she was never a regular at the raucous water polo games and beer blasts; she lived on what she always told people was the "sedate" side of the singles complex, the opposite end from where George W. Bush was living at the same time. At Kennedy Elementary, near the predominantly African-American Independence Heights neighborhood north of downtown, she asked to teach the same children when they moved to the third grade. By her mid-twenties, she knew she had probably settled into her life's work. And she had a strained conversation with her parents revolving around her feeling that they had paid for a college career that had culminated in her becoming a teacher, a role considered a safe alternative for women—but that they hadn't offered to pay for an education as a lawyer, maybe because it was considered a profession for men. Her stunned father offered to send her to law school. She laughed and declined. By her twenties, she had developed a clear understanding of something: "I've always done what really traditional women do, and I've been very, very satisfied," Welch said.[16]

She wasn't especially keen on teaching math, thinking that she wasn't really good at it. What she did enjoy was reading to her second- and third-graders. This led to a decision to enroll at the University of Texas and study library science. She relocated to Austin, commuted frequently to Midland to see her parents and friends, and graduated in 1972 with a master's degree. The next year, she moved back to Houston to work as the children's librarian in the McCrane–Kashmere Gardens Library, a division of the mammoth Houston public library system. Then, in 1974, she returned to Austin to work as the librarian at mostly Hispanic Dawson Elementary School on the south side of the city. At the time, Austin was the only real liberal oasis in the state of Texas, a place that could appeal to journalists such as Ronnie Dugger and Molly Ivins, progressive musicians such as Willie Nelson, and even the flamboyant atheist Madalyn Murray O'Hair. It was home to the largest state university in Texas, it had a burgeoning music community, and by the mid-1970s, it was the center of what passed as the white counterculture in Texas—a not entirely politically confrontational counterculture, but a Texas subset looking for a lifestyle oasis.

People fleeing from more conservative areas of Dallas and Houston, and in Willie Nelson's case from Nashville, moved to Austin and the nearby Hill Country to grow their hair long, escape traffic, and avoid urban, often racial, tensions. Friends and family said that Laura Welch did not move to Austin, like thousands of others in the 1970s, because it represented an escape. She was there because she had found the job she had always wanted, the perfect bridge from her own goals as a child to what she had studied in college. Friends would say that the open, experimental tendencies of the late 1960s and early 1970s had passed Laura Welch by, even when she was in the one place in Texas where those tendencies were sometimes aggressively encouraged. Her father was a thirty-second-degree Mason and a stalwart of Midland, someone the oilmen went to when they wanted a new home or advice on spreading their oil money around by getting into real estate transactions. Harold Welch's daughter was, one friend said, rarely apt to do anything foolish or wildly impulsive.

A few years earlier, Jan O'Neill and Laura Welch had lived together in Houston at the Chateaux Dijon. O'Neill had married in 1972, and most of her friends were already married or thinking about it. Now, O'Neill worked to get her old high school friend from Midland a date with Bush. She and her husband saw them as different but complementary, bookends, the way he was so extroverted, the way she was reserved and calm and accustomed to corralling energy in a classroom—someone who had gone into a line of work where silence didn't necessarily mean a virtueless void. The first time the O'Neills suggested a meeting with Bush, she declined. She knew who he was, she knew the family's role in Midland and the world. There was a reason, she told people, why she wouldn't agree to see the younger Bush: "I was so uninterested in politics. . . . I thought he was someone real political, and I wasn't interested."

Then, in August 1977, knowing she would be coming from Austin to Midland to visit her parents, Jan O'Neill asked her again to meet Bush at a backyard barbecue. She finally agreed, in part because she was slightly lonely, in part because she was beginning to think that there weren't too many unmarried people left in Midland. She had thought about having children, though not to the point of obsession; she had always assumed she would get married, but she certainly wasn't melancholy. At the get-together, Bush talked nonstop, and Laura Welch seemed to listen to every word. She told her mother, "The thing I like about him was that he made me laugh."

ONLY DAYS AFTER meeting Laura Welch, Bush was in Kennebunkport for the annual Bush conclave at the family compound. He told his parents that he had met someone in Midland. "I found her to be a very thoughtful, smart, interested person—one of the great listeners. And since I'm one of the big talkers, it was a great fit," he said later. While in Maine, he was on the phone, calling repeatedly back to her apartment in Austin. Then he told his mother that he was leaving Kennebunkport early; he was trying to reach Laura Welch, but she would rarely answer the phone, and when she did, she would say that she was very busy and would try to call him back. Barbara Bush knew her son was serious when he flew back to Texas in midvacation and then continued to make repeated weekend trips from Midland to see Laura in Austin. Jenna Welch was worried about the pace of things. She thought they were being pushed too fast by the suddenly eager bachelor who was running for Congress. "I was afraid George was going to ruin the whole thing because he was rushing it. In the past, when Laura brought home these nice young men from SMU, that had turned her off," said Jenna Welch.[17]

The two made plans for a wedding in early November, only three months away. In October, on the day after his parents returned from China to their house on Briar Drive in Houston, Bush and Laura traveled to Houston for her first meeting with the family. His brothers were there, as was his uncle Bucky, who was passing through Texas on business. The family could tell that Laura was nervous when she and George W. walked through the front door. Jeb, who had never met Laura before, walked up to her and went down on one knee. It looked to their uncle as if Jeb were imitating Al Jolson.

"Did you pop the question to her, George, old boy?" demanded Jeb. His brother turned red. She replied for him, "Yes, as a matter of fact he has, and I accepted."[18]

In the family and outside, several people would say that she was similar to the public Barbara Bush in two regards: she was content to talk about her role as a "traditional" wife and glad to profess her interest in reading. The day she was introduced to the family and everyone was informed that the couple were going to be married the next month, Bush's brothers and sister erupted in cheers. His brothers had already known they were getting engaged; his parents were surprised. "We didn't even know he wanted to get married until he showed up at the door with this beautiful creature, Laura, and announced that she was going to be his wife," said his mother.[19]

Welch was eventually introduced to the steel-willed, competitive matriarch of the Bush family, Dorothy Walker Bush.

"What do you do?" demanded Walker.

"I read," replied Welch.

Bush told Laura that there would be no time for a honeymoon. They returned to Midland and were married a month later on November 5, 1977, the day after her birthday, at the First United Methodist Church, in front of seventy people. They spent the next few days making a series of campaign visits in West Texas. If there was any temptation by the hardball-slinging West Texas Democrats to portray George W. Bush as the ultimate carpetbagging Ivy League playboy, it was all effectively muted by his marriage to the shy Methodist librarian from Midland. "It seems whirlwind. But George was running for Congress and we lived in two different towns. It wasn't like other couples who might let a relationship drag out because they had time to. If we were going to be together, we needed to get married and I needed to move to Midland," Welch said.[20]

She knew that if the man she had met only three months earlier, the one who had just announced that he was running for Congress, was good at anything, it was timing: "George sort of did leap into it, but even back then he was smart enough to know that a lot of politics was simply timing. You know, there are a lot of would-be governors of Texas sitting around today who never took the opportunity to get into a race when the time was right. If George is good at anything, it's timing," she said.[21] He and Laura had "discussed what the first year of marriage was going to be like."[22] She told people that she was still worried; it had been only twelve weeks since she had expressed her aversion to politics and even politicians. "I worried about the stress of the political campaign combined with the stress of being newlyweds."[23]

He promised she wouldn't have to give speeches when he wasn't there; she agreed, as an exchange, to take up jogging. Three months after they were married, she was on the courthouse steps in Muleshoe giving her first campaign speech after he told her he had a scheduling conflict and that she would have to take his place. It was an unpleasant experience, especially when she ran out of words.

On a night later during the campaign, they were driving home from Lubbock to Midland. Bush had just given what he thought was a convincing speech. "Tell me the truth, how was my speech?" he asked as they pulled into the driveway of their new home, a brick town house on Golf Course Road. "Don't criticize his speeches," her mother-in-law had advised her just after their marriage.

"Well, your speech wasn't very good," Laura said. As he listened to her, he drove straight into the garage wall.

AFTER A DOZEN possible contenders for the GOP nomination dropped out, the two remaining candidates were Bush and Jim Reese, a former sportscaster and ex-mayor of Odessa who had become a stockbroker. Reese was a veteran campaigner who had gotten 45 percent of the vote against Mahon in 1976. Reese was also a card-carrying Reagan Republican who had worked on Reagan's campaigns deep in the heart of West Texas. Reagan had always remembered Reese and decided to endorse him in the Republican runoff in June 1978. The Texas GOP chairman, Ray Barnhart, declared the race "one of the most highly targeted in the country." In Washington, George Bush placed a call to Charlie Black, the political director of the Republican National Committee who was helping to craft some of the new hardball political tendencies along with Lee Atwater.

"You know, my son's running out here in Midland, and he's got a primary, but I'd want the RNC to help him after the primary and all that," Black heard Bush say.

"Of course, Mr. Bush, you know the party'll be neutral in the primary, but I hope he'll come to Washington and visit after he wins that," replied Black.[24]

In the spring of 1978, Reese began mass-mailing Reagan's endorsement letter. Reagan and the elder George Bush were jockeying for the 1980 GOP presidential nomination. And Reagan told Bush that he wasn't going to be endorsing his son. He said that he had endorsed Reese in 1976 and would remain loyal. Meanwhile, another staunch Reaganite, newly elected Utah Senator Orrin Hatch, also wrote a widely distributed endorsement for Reese—and then called the elder George Bush and apologized. Reagan's political operative Lyn Nofziger also donated money to Reese through the pro-Reagan Citizens for the Republic political action committee. And finally, other supporters, including the Oklahoma GOP national committeeman, a major force in Reagan's 1976 run for the presidency, flew into Midland for a press conference endorsing Reese.[25]

"I'm not interested in getting into an argument with Reagan. But I am surprised about what he is doing here, in my state. . . . They are making a real effort to defeat George," the elder Bush testily told reporters.[26]

Privately, said friends, George W., his father, and the entire Bush-Walker family were seething at the way GOP leaders such as Reagan had exercised political muscle in a part of Texas that the Bushes had presumed belonged to them:

"To me it's still the most amazing insight into that family that Ronald Reagan came to campaign against that family," said Doug Hannah, the longtime family acquaintance from Houston. "Three years later, here's his father touting how great a man this guy is—and this guy had campaigned against his son. I know for a fact that if George Bush could have killed Ronald Reagan, he would have done it. He couldn't stand the man. And three years later, he is ready to run on the ticket with him."[27]

REESE, energized by the apparent national GOP abandonment of Bush, stepped up his attacks just before the June runoff. Reese supporters charged that the elder Bush was simply orchestrating the entire campaign from Houston. In his campaign literature, Reese claimed that George W. had claimed to be born in Texas. He also mailed out letters saying, "I am very disappointed that he has Rockefeller-type Republicans such as Karl Rove to help him run his campaign." Bush countered by saying that Rove "has had nothing to do with my campaign"[28]—even though Rove would later testify that he volunteered on the campaign. As the runoff approached, George W. raced through smaller towns outside his oil-center power zones in Midland-Odessa: Muleshoe, Friona, Bovina, Farwell, and Littlefield.

The lessons from his father's two Senate losses in Texas, including one just seven years earlier, were readily apparent. In the months leading to the heated, nationally chronicled runoff, Bush urged his father to not make any campaign appearances. He also began pulling out his birth certificate at speeches to prove that his middle name was different from his father's.[29] Reese kept attacking, challenging whether Bush was actually chairman of a company called Field Services Inc.—Reese said he had never heard of the company and it wasn't in the phone book.

On election night, June 3, Bush campaign workers set up a sign that read DRINK ME FIRST on a beer keg in the hallway past the front door of the George Bush for Congress headquarters. All night, campaign workers drained the keg and watched the election results. By 10:30, Bush was way ahead and the Midland police were ordered to patrol the area because of the beer and because "things are getting rowdy."[30]

Bush won 6,787 to 5,350. Reese was philosophical about the loss; he had said he had been beaten by the family's friends, money, and connections. "Yeah, the name ID, and the fact of the associations that his father had out here—all those were a factor," he said.[31]

Some of the gilded perceptions that Reese was just beginning to explore would be thoroughly heated up by Bush's aggressive Democratic opponent, State Senator Kent Hance. The drawling, combative thirty-five-year-old Hance was a graduate of Dimmitt High School, Texas Technological University in Lubbock, and the University of Texas Law School. He taught business law at Texas Tech and mingled easily with the farmers in his part of Texas—he talked their language. And he knew that he stood in marked contrast to Bush: he had served as a state lawmaker, had attended public schools, had lived in the area virtually his entire life. Bush promptly announced that he and Laura would find an apartment in Lubbock, so as to attack Hance in his stronghold. But Hance felt secure; he knew that Bush had paid a courtesy call to national Democratic political kingmaker Bob Strauss and that Strauss had told Bush, "You can't beat Hance. There are other things you can run for, but you can't beat Kent Hance."[32]

Hance felt even better, more in tune with Tip O'Neill's observation that all politics is local, when he saw the first Bush ads. They showed the young GOP candidate out jogging under a broad West Texas sky. "You know," said Hance to a Dallas writer, laughing and stretching the words out, "that was a mighty nice ad—but it wasn't West Texas."[33] Hance's pollsters were sent out to ask rural voters what they might like about George Bush, if anything, and the answers would invariably begin, "Well, he's been doing a great job in China." As the increasingly raw campaign got under way, one of Hance's advisers, a Lubbock businessman named C. R.

Hutcheson, asked him how he thought Bush would do. Hance replied, "Well, I don't think he's ever been in the back of a pool hall in Dimmitt, Texas."[34]

THAT THEME—that George W. Bush was just a modern carpetbagger, an effete outsider, parading into West Texas with nothing more than his father's name and his family's platinum connections, someone whom sensitive souls in Lubbock heard mispronounce their city's name as "Lubbick"—screeched louder and louder. In March, suspicions that he had accumulated a small fortune without having worked full-time in the oil patch were inflamed when he told the Lubbock newspaper that he was worth "over half a million dollars."[35] Attention to his financial health reached a pitch when his campaign contribution records were filed with state officials and his opponents instantly pointed to the exotic—by West Texas standards—names and companies on the list.

Bush had easily raised $406,000, with contributions coming from Scott Pierce of Rye, New York, George W.'s uncle and an executive with E. F. Hutton; James McDonnell, president of McDonnell Corporation; Baine Kerr, president of Pennzoil and neighbors of the Bushes in Houston; Hugh Liedtke, chairman of Pennzoil and the elder Bush's old business partner in Zapata; John Loeb, partner in the investment firm Loeb, Rhoades; Winton "Red" Blount, Nixon's postmaster general, whom Bush worked for in the doomed Alabama Senate campaign; Lowell Thomas, the journalist who had been a special guest of the Bushes a year earlier in China; Commissioner of Baseball Bowie Kuhn; Los Angeles Dodgers owner Peter O'Malley; legendary college football coach Bud Wilkinson; John S. Greenway, the Andover friend of his father who owned the ranch where George W. had been sent one summer; entertainment executive Jerry Weintraub; Mrs. Douglas MacArthur, who lived in the Waldorf Towers in Manhattan with the Bush family; William Ford, vice chairman of Ford Motor Company; John Macomber, president of the Celanese Corporation; family friend and oilman Robert Mosbacher; Herman Lay of Frito-Lay; family friend and oilman Earle Craig; radio executive Gordon McClendon; former U.S. Ambassador to England Anne Armstrong; former Secretary of Defense Donald Rumsfeld; former CBS President Frank Shakespeare.

The Democratic operatives took note of the fact that his father had held four fund-raisers for him, in Washington, Dallas, Houston, and Midland. Half of his money was coming from oil and gas interests; a third of it was flooding in from outside West Texas. And really, money was never an object. Bush flew to Washington, along with other candidates from across the country, for a GOP "campaign school" conducted by the Republican National Committee. And when the dozens of candidates were asked to raise their hands if their campaigns were in debt, only George W. Bush kept his down.

In October, Hance used the ballooning outside contributions as a launching pad for several stinging head-on confrontations. At a Jaycees debate in Odessa, Hance swaggered up to the microphone: "My daddy and granddaddy were farmers. They didn't have anything to do with the mess we're in right now, and Bush's father has been in politics all his life. . . . George Bush hasn't earned the living he enjoys. I'm on my own two feet and I can make my own living." Bush took his turn: "I'm proud of what my father has accomplished and I'm proud of my education, but I have spent half my life in West Texas and this is my home."[36]

Sensitive to the blaring carpetbagging indictments, he announced that he had had offers of support from ex-president Gerald Ford but had told him not to come to Texas. He said he was still an uncompromising, hard conservative. He said he remained opposed to sanctions against South Africa. He was also opposed to the Equal Rights Amendment and national health insurance. He added that Andrew Young's appointment as ambassador to the United Nations had been "a mistake."

Late in the campaign, a Bush staffer placed an ad in the Texas Tech newspaper promising free beer at a "Bush Bash." Hance's people picked up on the possibilities right away; it was no secret in Midland that Bush enjoyed drinking, that he had once gotten up onstage with Willie Nelson. A Hance staffer sent letters about the Bush Bash to four thousand avowedly antialcohol Church of Christ members: "Mr. Bush used some of his vast sums of money in an attempt, evidently, to persuade young college students to vote for and support him by offering free alcohol to them."[37]

Hance jumped on the minidebacle and said that the "Bush Bash" may "point out probably a big difference in our backgrounds. Maybe it's a cool thing to do at Harvard or Yale." The last week of October, Hance and Bush met again at the Branding Iron Restaurant in Odessa for a noon debate. Local radio talk-show host Mel Turner was there again as the moderator. He decided to pose a quirky, paranoid question that was repeatedly being fired at Bush by suspicious, government-fearing West Texans who were wondering about someone whose father was tied so heavily to Wall Street, to the Northeast, to the Skull & Bones Society, to all those things that seemed so foreign. Turner, speaking for a good chunk of West Texas, wanted to know if the young Bush was a tool of some shadow government; it was the same thing people had confronted his father with when they had called him a "tool of the eastern kingmakers":

"Are you involved in, or do you know anybody involved in, one-world government or the Trilateral Commission?"

Bush, who had been telling people he was tired of being hammered for having "connections" through his father to the eastern establishment, was fuming. "I won't be persuaded by anyone, including my father," he said, with a biting tone in his voice.

On the way out of the restaurant, Bush was still livid. He refused to shake hands with Turner. "You asshole," Turner heard him hiss as he walked by.[38] Turner had been leaning toward voting for Bush but had changed his mind: "Hance was much better at talking to the average workingman. Bush never worked a day in his life. Bush was born with a silver boot up his ass. Everything was handed to him."[39]

THE SAME WEEK, Hance called Bush an "outsider as far as understanding our problems." Hance knew that, policywise, there were few distinctions between the two conservative candidates; in good measure, the race was boiling down to perceptions. Hance had the police report from Bush's arrest in Connecticut in hand, but he chose not to release it—he was unsure what the political fallout would be. Instead, he quietly laughed when, right up until election day, gaggles of farmers were still quizzing the unsuspecting Bush about the Trilateral Commission, about limousine Republicans and their swanky Rockefeller-style soirees, about how the Bush-Walkers no doubt figured into certain global socialist conspiracies.

Through the campaign, Hance also kept hoping that the elder Bush would show up and campaign for his son. It could only help the portrait Hance was painting of an East Coast establishment elitist who spent every August at Walker's Point instead of the oil-stained Texas Gulf Coast with its murky waters.

Hance wasn't adverse to dumping a special brand of irritating, home-spun West Texas humor in his opponent's face at the different debates and forums in the congressional district. One day, with an anguished Bush sitting nearby, Hance began drawling: "There was this farmer, sittin' on his fence one day when this big, fancy limousine comes rolling up the dirt road and stops right in front of him. The windows roll down and the fella inside says, 'You know the way to get to Lubbock?'

"The farmer, he chews on the straw for a couple of seconds and points up the dirt road and he says to the chauffeur, 'Go on up the road a couple of miles till ya' see the cattle guard, then go left and pretty soon you'll be in town.'

"Well, a while goes by and the farmer sees the big fancy limousine coming back down the dirt road. The window rolls down and the chauffeur says, 'Forgot to ask, what color uniform is that cattle guard wearing?'"

By then, Hance had his audience of West Texas farmers snorting with laughter. In Lubbock and other remote parts of the state, Hance was well known for his timing, his ability to deliver the most deadpan punchlines— an almost brutal brand of Will Rogers humor. And of course, he was ready for his footnote to his joke about the farmer and the rich man's chauffeur. Hance turned to look at George W. Bush and said:

"You see, that limousine wasn't from around these parts. I think it had one of them Connecticut licenses. That where you from, George?"[40]

Hance's campaign released radio ads pointing out the fact that when he had graduated from Dimmitt High School in the Nineteenth Congressional District, Bush had been attending a private preparatory school for boys. Bush was part of a hungry American dynasty, and that wouldn't, couldn't, play well in Texas, Hance told the Lubbock Press Club: "There's somewhat of a tendency in George's campaign to ride the coattails, I think, of his father, because you do not see a distinction in the ads between George Bush and George Bush."

During the same press club function, Bush listened and oozed frustration: "Would you like me to run as Sam Smith?" he demanded. "The problem is, I can't abandon my background."[41]

ON ELECTION DAY, Bush's college roommate Clay Johnson was in Midland. "Why are you doing this?" he whispered to his friend. Bush didn't answer.

That night, Bush and Don Evans were sitting in Bush's bedroom, listening to the radio reports; at first they were energized by the early returns. Bush had outspent Hance by 25 percent, and the early Midland votes—he was tallying 14,159 votes to Hance's 9,285 in Midland—had given him a boost. But as the night went on, it was clear that Lubbock was swinging hard against him. Even though he was ahead by 8,000 votes according to the broadcast returns, Bush called Hance up and conceded: "You got me."

Bush lost fourteen out of the seventeen counties; Hance won 53,917 to 47,497, with more than 53 percent of the vote. The next day, Bush donned a suit and was in tears at his postmortem press conference. He said there was a word to describe why the "outsider" tag had worked so well and why so many farmers and rural voters had rejected him: "provincialism." Standing on a folding chair, he thanked his supporters. As he walked out to a thunder of applause, he saw Johnson leaning in a doorway, watching him carefully. "That," said Bush as he walked by and his crew of oil buddies were still clapping, "is why I'm doing this."

During the campaign, he repeatedly said he had only one regret—that he hadn't been born in Texas. It was important, he had joked before the election, to stay with his mother after he was born, and "she happened to be in New Haven, Connecticut." Years later, he would think about how his father had first started and how he had also lost his race in Texas—because he also had been perceived as an outsider, a career politician whose family had studied Texas and simply decided to make it their own. Now, in Texas, GOP leaders openly speculated whether Bush had lost his first race in Texas because people were voting against him or because they were voting against his legacy. The entire race, the way it had been played out against him—the way the very first suggestions of a voracious Bush dynasty had been shot like warning flares over the skies of West Texas—it was a powerful lesson.

"Frankly," said Bush later, "getting whipped was probably a pretty good thing for me."[42]

11

The Big Elephant Field

The Midland crew had been utterly convinced that the 1978 election was the perfect piece of timing; they knew Bush had shaken the big money tree harder than anybody else had ever done for a congressional race in Texas—but the Panhandle farmers still hadn't seen him as anything other than a fortunate son with silky Yankee tentacles. Joe O'Neill always thought that Bush would have won had he not missed out on the Reagan Revolution by a year or two; it just wasn't the right time, and next time he could make better speeches: "He didn't make any Nixon or MacArthur statements, nothing you could carve in stone."[1]

Bush warned his friends that he wasn't interested in being elected the way Hance or Reese had, he wasn't interested in starting out and working his way up from the mayor's office or as a state senator. If he was going to run again, it would be for high office, either congressman, senator, or governor. Timing really was everything—he had even lectured Laura about it—and he was convinced that Republican oil-drilling contractor Bill Clements's shocking upset win as Texas governor would create other political opportunities for the GOP, as well as give him time to correct the nagging personal perceptions.

Karl Rove had helped mastermind Clements's watershed victory, allowing the gruff, blunt Dallasite to become only the second Republican governor in state history, and Democratic archenemies and even some members of the Texas media were beginning to both fear Rove and accuse him of having tendencies toward the new edges of political campaigning. Rove and Bush continued to talk regularly about the first son's future in the state, and after the election, Bush also made a point of quickly meeting with O'Neill, Evans, and the young oilmen who had bankrolled a good portion of his plump campaign—all those second- and third-generation oil millionaires at the Midland Polo Club, the Midland Country Club, and the Petroleum Club. At dinner one night he told them that next time he would spend more time outside the Texas cities where the GOP had made so many obvious inroads among conservative, affluent suburbanites and transplants. Midland had already turned Republican, and Dallas and Houston were headed that way. Next time, Bush told his friends, he would spend more time and more money in the hundreds of hard outposts of Texas, the places where only a land man would have the nerve to show up and start shaking hands. Remember, he told O'Neill, his father had lost his first race for office in Texas—and then won his second.

After the election, he also had news for Mills, Way, and his accountant McCleskey: just like his father, he was forming his own oil company, and, also just like his father, he was going to give it a Spanish title. Instead of Zapata, his company would be called Arbusto, the Spanish word for "bush" or "shrub." "Kind of a weird name," he said. "Off the cuff."[2] Of course, it was a time-bomb joke waiting to explode among the die-hard wildcatters, and Buzz Mills, the epitome of the droll, slow-talking, crew-cut-wearing West Texas well puncher, almost couldn't stand it. It was only a matter of time before Arbusto started drilling dry holes, started losing money—started busting—and it would be only a matter of time before Mills and the rest of the Midland crew started breaking his balls and chanting "*Ar-BUST-oh!!*" when Bush walked down Texas Street and into the Petroleum Building.

FOUR MONTHS after Bush glumly watched Hance take office, he flew to Washington when his father announced to the National Press Club that he was running for president. Immediately after Carter's election in 1976 and after his father's short tenure at the CIA had ended, the family and its still expanding network of Texas oil allies had begun mapping out a strategy to finally position a Bush for a dedicated run for the presidency. George and Barbara Bush had moved back to Houston from Washington and embarked on a flurry of profile-raising and money-raising endeavors across the United States and abroad. The elder Bush joined the boards of Baylor University, Trinity University, and Andover; he orchestrated Yale's 1978 fund-raising campaign; he served as a director, partner, or consultant to Gulf, Eli Lilly, First International Bankshares of Dallas, and several other lesser-known but highly capitalized companies with ties to the Liedtkes, the Mosbachers, and dozens of family friends in Texas; he also immersed himself in the Trilateral Commission, that often-criticized entity that brought together farflung international investors and diplomats. And, to underscore the perception that he was a president in waiting, the Bushes hosted both Nelson Rockefeller and Jordan's King Hussein in their home in May 1977.

The early presidential strategies were aimed at contrasting Bush's experience in international affairs—his resumé at the United Nations, the CIA and in China—to Ronald Reagan's background as an actor and governor. The family also agreed that after his own failed campaign, young Bush would assist his father's White House bid only in a limited capacity. The other children were a different story. The 1980 campaign was the first time all of the other children were appointed to key, visible political positions. They were dispatched in different directions to do various full-time jobs: Marvin took time off from the University of Virginia and went to Iowa; Dorothy had taken a nine-month secretarial course and was given a job in the Boston campaign headquarters. The elder Bush knew that Jeb could speak Spanish, and he asked him to give up his branch bank manager job in Venezuela and work exclusively on the campaign, especially signing up anti-Castro, pro-Bush delegates in Florida; Mr. Perfect— Neil—flew to New Hampshire to get the campaign under way.

George W. was a surrogate, occasionally arriving in trouble spots to reinforce his younger brothers and sister. He went to Iowa and joined Marvin for a brief foray, campaigning during the caucuses out of a Chevy Blazer and preaching to wary pro-gasohol farmers about the necessity of protecting crude-oil interests. In Midland, he continued to make spot campaign appearances for his father in the city, nailing down the fat West Texas financial support. He worked the phones, making fifty, sixty, seventy calls a day, hammering his oil investors around the country, asking them to pony up dollars for his father—"The Man," as he sometimes called him.

He took time off to attend his brother Neil's wedding at the St. Ann Church in Kennebunkport, the same church that Prescott Bush and Dorothy Walker had been married in almost six decades earlier. But by the end of May, he was watching the political mood swings, the way his father's campaign was foundering. There was no passion in the race; even his father seemed to slow down. And Reagan, the "Western" man, as George W. would call him, was riding a wave of support by harder-edged conservatives and evangelicals, the same voters who had once turned against George W. in West Texas. The elder Bush was being cast as a moderate who lacked the clear vision and the will to be an effective conservative. It was Reagan's time, and the elder Bush called Midland and talked about the possibilities with his son, especially about the fact that the timing was all wrong. George W. wanted his father to consider taking a possible vice presidential bid from Reagan. His father didn't want to talk about it, and he didn't want to talk about 1984 or 1988. His father said he had sent Reagan a telegram congratulating him on his campaign.

At the Republican National Convention in Detroit, the elder Bush was informed that Reagan was holding on a phone line into the Bush suite at the Hotel Pontchartrain. In the weeks leading up to the convention, there was speculation that Gerald Ford, Howard Baker, and Jack Kemp were the vice presidential front-runners. The suite was crowded as always, but it was subdued that July. Surrounded by his family, including his especially glum son Jeb, a surprised Bush gleefully accepted Reagan's offer to be his vice presidential running mate. The more demanding disciples of the Reagan Revolution were instantly displeased with the choice; it was, really, the same burden of perceptions that had stretched back to Prescott Bush and Walker's Point. For the more insistent, unyielding conservatives and the emerging evangelicals, the selection of Bush as vice president was a clear nod to the entrenched northeastern, royal layer of the GOP and the Bush-Walker ties to the presidency since the early twentieth century. The final weeks of the Reagan-Bush campaign were almost anticlimactic for the younger Bush; he had told friends that he had been utterly convinced that his father, through sheer willpower, all his Walker's Point brio, all the debts owed him by the GOP, was going to earn the presidential nomination. His father had paid his dues, had carried Nixon's baggage during Watergate, had accepted whatever long-distance assignments he had been given. His father, thought George W., was loyal, and he should have been served better by all the other damned party loyalists.

When the Reagan-Bush team won the 1980 election, the Bushes sold their house in Houston for $843,273 and rented a suite at the Houstonian Hotel to maintain as their legal residence; the elder Bush spent another $250,000 to buy his share of the Kennebunkport estate. And George W. returned to Midland, to his own one-story $200,000 brick house with a circular driveway on Golf Course Road.

BUSH WAS IMPRESSED with Reagan, he said over lunch one day in mid-February 1981 in Midland, and the thing he liked most about him was that he was the crafty epitome of the outside-the-Beltway campaigner; he was not an East Coast politician, he was clear-headed; he was "easy-going in the Western sense," someone who had already succeeded by not letting "the trappings of the presidency overwhelm him." That afternoon at lunch, he excitedly told people he especially liked the way Reagan hadn't hesitated to fire his campaign manager immediately after winning the New Hampshire primary. It was, marveled Bush, "brilliant . . . and there was no hesitancy in it. Reagan is a man of decisive action."[3] In Midland, it was an open secret that running for office was still squarely on Bush's mind. He told O'Neill and Evans that he was worried that if he ran again soon, voters and the media would say what they had been saying since the day he had arrived in the city: George W. Bush is riding on his family's back again. He saw how his father had been swallowed alive by timing and perceptions. It was Reagan's time, not his father's.

"1980 just wasn't the time," George W. had said a few months earlier.[4]

DURING THE CAMPAIGN and for years afterward, when George W. would make the occasional speech before the Lions Club, the United Way, or the West Texas Press Association, some people would turn away and bury their grinning faces in a handkerchief when the eager Bush would start rushing fast, mashing all his syllables together—or when he frequently would reach for a particular word but pluck an entirely different one. "It was just inebriating what Midland was all about then" is how he described the heady life in the oil patch[5]—and people heard him say that he was "totally inebriated with hitting the big one."[6]

He worked later and longer, and on weekends he was the first one in the Midland crew to be up at 7:15 in the morning, nagging Evans to hurry his ass so they wouldn't be late for eighteen holes at the Midland Country Club—and nagging his ass again when they headed straight from the last green to the high school for a three-mile jog. He had no campaign debts, but the oil boom was still on and there was still money just below the surface. He scheduled a meeting in New York with Uncle Jonathan Bush, the trusted Wall Street stockbroker–money manager. His uncle told him he could help set up a limited partnership catering to big investors around the country looking for entry points into the energy sector. Arbusto, Bush's private partnership fund, was hawked to his uncle's East Coast clients as a low-risk, low-return way of playing in the oil patch.

Bush, his accountant Robert McCleskey, and oilman James C. Brown were named to the board of directors. Bush incorporated Arbusto in June 1977, but it didn't begin active operations until March 1979. It could possibly be sweet, it could be big, taking Arbusto from a one-man operation and turning it into a muscular operating company, a contender, an energy outfit that could afford to invest the millions of dollars needed to drill nationally, globally, maybe as his father had done with Zapata Offshore.

His first hire was twenty-six-year-old secretary Kim Dyches, a Midland native; his second was Mark Owen, a soft-spoken and respected geologist who had gotten his master's degree from Baylor University.

Uncle Jonathan had steered him right, and Arbusto was ready. In his first year as president and director, he was working with $565,000 in investments from twenty-eight limited partners; in 1980, another $1.24 million came in from thirty-six investors; in 1981, an additional $1.72 million came in from thirty-four investors. Part of the plan was to avoid having Arbusto drill all its own wells, by piggybacking on surefire winners owned by other companies and picking up an investment piece here and there. Oil analysts said Arbusto, like other small-scale start-ups, was a possible win-win company; even if no oil gurgled up, it could always take big tax write-offs. Again, the family had set him in motion.

"I introduced him to clients," said his uncle. "I marketed his firm. I think I was probably pretty helpful. It didn't hurt him in the fact that his father had been in the oil business, so he knew a lot of the players. At the time there were big tax advantages in drilling oil wells. In those days, it behooved you to drill. You didn't have to do terribly well in order to do well because you got so many write-offs. So it was an attractive way to invest money and save taxes."[7]

Venture capitalist William H. Draper was good for $172,550. So was John Macomber, the CEO of the Celanese Corporation and a contributor to George W. Bush's congressional candidacy in 1978. And under the Reagan and Bush presidencies, Macomber and Draper would take turns as the president of the U.S. Export-Import Bank. His grandmother Dorothy, always ready for a risk, put up $25,000; Fitzgerald Bemiss, Marvin Bush's godfather and his father's childhood friend, invested $80,000; George L. Ball, CEO of Prudential-Bache Securities, invested $300,000. There was also Jim Bath, a National Guardsman from Houston who had served with Bush back in the 1960s and who now pumped $50,000 into the Arbusto pot. Throughout the 1990s, Bath would be described in various news accounts as an influential Texas aircraft broker for wealthy clients from the Middle East.

Bush was still pushing hard, leaving Midland, connecting through Dallas, and traveling to New York and the Northeast to raise capital. His secretary, Dyches, was frightened by the way Bush was cursing like a sailor; she worried what his unfettered language would mean to business prospects. She knew he wasn't an oil expert, that he was learning as he was going, and that he mostly enjoyed hustling up investment dollars: "My suspicion was that he enjoyed raising money more. I'm sure he was somewhat charismatic, and name recognition and all of the ties made it easier for him. I think that the company was marginally successful. I really don't recall us ever drilling a well and making anything all that great."[8]

The company's three-room office was cramped and filled with rolled-up oil-field maps and some file folders Bush had excitedly salvaged from the Henry Petroleum Company's trash bin down the hall. He borrowed cigarettes from Dyches every day and nicknamed her Red; she liked the fact that he and Laura both smoked; she also liked the fact that she would run into Laura at a Junior League function and there she would be in the corner, by herself, puffing away. He offered Dyches $100 if she would name her newborn son George, but she declined; she was surprised that a Republican didn't mind that she brought her infant to work sometimes.

On the day in March 1981 when Ronald Reagan was shot, Bush told her to hold all calls. He was anxious to keep the lines clear; he didn't want to miss his father's call. He seemed shaky—and he never really had seemed shaky before.

THE COMPANY tried "corner shoots"—punching a hole as close as possible to somebody else's well and hoping for the best. There was a time near Abilene when, by accident, the drill team missed the sand zone it was aiming for and actually slopped into some oil. They found two fairly good gas wells in Young County, and Arbusto drilled an average of ten wells a year, spending $250,000 to $500,000 for each well and coming up with a fifty-fifty ratio of dry holes to winners. By comparison to hundreds of other oil ventures at that heady time in Texas, the company was never even remotely one of the leading independent oil outfits. Its expenditures always outweighed revenues, but the tax write-offs smoothed out most of the wrinkles.

Mark Owen continued to be amazed at the way Bush never gave up, how he constantly talked about running for office again, how he was always out making contacts, cackling, running through the door in khakis and button-down shirts as rumpled as a shar-pei's face. He was speaking at the YMCA, coaching Little League, teaching Sunday School—and his coteacher, Becky Ferguson, was shocked to see those same preppy loafers with the tassels still Scotch-taped to them.[9]

"Running again came up a lot. After '78, he consciously decided to concentrate on his business and family, but he was always a politician. When his dad was vice president, he didn't want to get in on that because the 'dad's coattails' thing would come up. He was waiting for the right time. It's in his blood," said Mark Owen.[10]

He saw that Bush's talents were as an intermediary, a go-between who was proficient at schmoozing, hustling leases from ranchers, and then racing to New York for backing. But Bush wanted what some Permian Basin diehards called the "Elephant Field" and Bush called "The Liberator," the big mother lode. Bush spent time trying to convince the trustees of one of the fabled ranches in Texas, the 500,000-acre Waggoner Ranch near Wichita Falls, to let his two-man operation explore for oil there. But the project was too big in scope for the company, the leases ran into tens of millions of dollars, and Bush passed the project off to bigger explorers headquartered in Dallas. That was the one he was waiting for, and it would have been too perfect to have a strike on the iconic Waggoner Ranch in the middle of a sky-wide section of Texas mythology.

But the project was simply too large for him, and it was like putting a steel cap on a dream. Owen knew that it was too big and Bush was "extremely" disappointed at losing the "big company maker, a home run," the chance to be deeply, independently capitalized without having to rely on his uncle's investors.[11]

"We had never found the huge liberator," is what Bush once said to a Dallas writer.[12]

IN THE SUMMER of 1981, Laura was pregnant with twins. Word had filtered up to the northeastern wings of the Bush and Walker families that she had been having trouble conceiving. She and Bush had always been anxious to have children. Bush was thirty-five, Laura thirty-three. Several of the other wealthy young couples in their part of Midland were having trouble with their pregnancies or, like Evans, Younger, and O'Neill, would adopt children through a Fort Worth–based foster home. Now, on occasion, it was clear that she was struggling with her pregnancy. Doctors informed them that she was in the early stages of toxemia, also known as preeclampsia, a third-trimester malady that can lead to blurred vision, dangerously high blood pressure, and edema. In some cases it can erupt into life-threatening seizures and require either induced labor or a cesarean delivery.

The children had been expected close to Christmas, but in the fall the toxemia grew more severe. In early November, the family made a decision to move Laura from Midland to Dallas's Baylor Hospital. She was admitted seven weeks before her due date, put under close monitoring, and ordered to stay in bed. Five weeks before her due date, with the toxemia cresting, the doctors scheduled a cesarean section. Baylor officials called Bush in Midland and told him he would have to be in Dallas by the next morning: "Your children will be born tomorrow, or your wife's kidneys will fail."[13]

Close to 10 A.M. on November 25, 1981, the two children were born. Jenna Welch, named for Laura's mother, weighed four pounds, twelve ounces; Barbara Pierce, named for Bush's mother, weighed five pounds, four ounces. Photographers and reporters were on hand to see the vice president's fourth and fifth grandchildren and to talk to his first son. "I witnessed it all. It was beautiful," said George W.[14] Six weeks later, the vice president and Barbara Bush took a trip to Midland to see their new grandchildren and check on Laura's health. She was recovering quickly. "She loves our daughters more than anything, she would lay her life down for them and nearly did at birth," George W. once said.[15]

AFTER LAURA'S dangerous pregnancy, and now with children in the house, Bush made another decision. He wanted—needed—to be taken more seriously if he was going to run for office again. In the small, tight-knit Midland oil fraternity, there were endless cracks about "Ar-bust-oh," and Bush confided to Evans that he was thinking of changing the name to the more serious-sounding, harder-to-mock Bush Exploration. For years, he insisted that he hadn't changed the name to capitalize on his father's position as vice president of the United States. Nor had he done it, he told reporters, to erase any doubts about his abilities as a businessman or as a prospective political candidate.

He remained, almost, a *character* in Midland. At the Midland Country Club, they started up the George W. Bush award for the worst-dressed golfer, and when he walked through the door of the Spot, the definitive greasy-spoon diner, people would crack up as he prowled the place, slapping old Tom Fowler on the back, jawing with Buzz and Brock, leaning over to aim a wad of chewing tobacco into a paper cup. And driving by in their Cadillacs and new, tricked-out pickup trucks, the older, guffawing oilmen could see him—*Dubya!*—out jogging every day in the goddamned heat, his face shiny as he coasted by everybody else on the track. Around the office, he couldn't sit still, he would twist pieces of his face up as if they were gobs of Play-Doh, wiggle his ears without moving any other part of his body, crack up a lease broker's kids.

In December 1981, he was allowed to acquire "working interests" on property owned by Pennzoil, the mega–oil firm run by the Liedtkes, the brothers who had formed Zapata with his father and were fiercely loyal Bush campaign contributors. By January, he was excited; the newly named Bush Exploration Company got its biggest investor to date in Phillip

Uzielli, a friend and Princeton classmate of James A. Baker III, who had managed his father's presidential campaign and was now serving as Reagan's chief of staff. Uzielli, who co-owned an investment firm in Panama, pumped $1 million into the Arbusto–Bush Exploration coffers in exchange for 10 percent of the company.

As the year marched on, Bush decided to try to raise another $6 million by taking his drilling fund public and selling $5,000 blocks of the company. Some analysts were predicting that oil was zooming to $100 a barrel; it was the outer limit of the energy-sector craze. But close to his birthday, there was bad news: Penn Square Bank in Oklahoma City had gone belly-up, and economists were saying that the ripple effects from it and other bank collapses would eventually shake the world markets. Over the next few years, the price of oil would hastily cower, dozens of exploration firms would close, the major oil companies would begin wholesale white-collar layoffs, and finally, once-muscular banking institutions across Texas would choke as a result of their dangerously bloated energy and real estate portfolios—all debilitating events that would trigger other financial collapses around the country. This time, even Bush's family and friends were wary. He got only $1.2 million of the $6 million he wanted to raise—and timing was everything. "Going public was a mistake," he glumly admitted to a reporter years later. "We weren't prepared for it. We didn't raise any money, we weren't able to get enough exposure for our partners as a result. . . . I made a bad mistake."[16]

THAT YEAR, Prescott Bush Jr., the insurance executive from Greenwich and the oldest son of Prescott Bush, had raised almost $1 million and was deep into a run for his father's old Senate seat in Connecticut. His opponent was two-term liberal incumbent Lowell Weicker, who only two years earlier had infuriated the Connecticut wing of the family by refusing to endorse George Bush for vice president. With the full support of Dorothy Walker Bush and the other relatives who would assemble at the "family conclaves," as Prescott Jr. called them, the campaign rolled efficiently forward.

Steady updates were being delivered to Prescott Jr.'s brother at the White House or the vice president's mansion. But at the end of July, five weeks before the Republican primary, the fifty-nine-year-old Prescott Jr. stunned his supporters by abruptly dropping out of the race "in the interest of the unity of the Republican Party." Accusations had been slowly building that he was too much like his father, in the sense that he hadn't had a lengthy interest in public service but simply seemed to have seized a political opening now that he was in the financial position to mount a well-funded campaign. It was, of course, the same nettlesome criticism leveled against his brother and his nephew in Texas—that the Bushes were running because it was what the Bushes did, that the Bushes were craving public office not because they were driven by a burning ideology but because it was their station in life. Dissecting Prescott Bush Jr.'s surprising decision to abandon the race, Washington insiders also wondered whether White House messages were being sent to him to avoid riding on his younger brother's coattails—and whether he had been told that another member of the Bush-Walker family would simply never be elected in Connecticut because it could amplify the perceptions that the vice president was from a family of monied, career politicians.[17]

In Texas, by the end of that dismal year, George W. had been joined on the oil firm's board of directors by others: Uzielli, Don Evans, Midland accountant Mike Conaway, and Walter Marting, who had been at the Harvard Business School with Bush and who would talk to Bush about investing in his own star-crossed company with the sadly evocative name Lucky Chance Mining Company. Suitors around the country who received the Bush Exploration prospectus learned that Bush still had big plans to drill down to 7,000 feet on leases spread across Ward, Stephens, Fisher, and Howard Counties. But by the end of 1983, Bush Exploration ranked 993rd in terms of oil production in Texas. During the ride, Uzielli lost most of his $1 million investment. "It was disastrous, through no fault of George's. The good Lord just didn't put any oil out there," he said.[18]

That same year, a friend of Martin Allday named Paul Rea set up a meeting between Bush and two Cincinnati investors. Rea had once worked for Bill DeWitt Sr., a roving baseball executive and ultimately the owner of the Cincinnati Reds. Rea switched to geology, moved to Midland, stayed in touch with DeWitt, and helped the baseball baron invest in the oil business. In the early 1980s, DeWitt's son asked Rea to be the exploration manager for a new oil-investing fund called Spectrum 7; several of the fund's directors, including DeWitt Jr., were graduates of Yale or Harvard.

In late 1983, DeWitt Jr. told Rea that he was diversifying his holdings and wanted to come to Midland to find someone to handle the fund from Texas. Rea arranged a lunch meeting with Vice President Bush's son. Rea thought it would be a good match: DeWitt Jr. and Bush had attended the same schools; they were about the same age; they could both sling the baseball statistics; both their families had deep roots in the rarefied fraternity of baseball owners (the elder Bush's Uncle Herbert had been one of the backers behind the creation of the New York Mets). The pair hit it off, and two months later, DeWitt Jr. called Rea and asked him if the vice president's son could learn the business end of Spectrum 7.

On February 29, 1984, after weeks of negotiation, the badly foundering Bush Exploration merged with the successful Spectrum 7. Bush was named chairman, overseeing the fund's fifteen employees. He was paid $75,000 a year and given 1.1 million shares. Almost as soon as the deal was cinched, he and Rea booked flights to the Northeast, trying to sell partnerships, spreading the risk, trying to fund Spectrum's 180 wells, including some of the old, slow, low-production "stripper wells" that dotted the desert of West Texas. Bush was happy; it was good to be in the sales game again, making sunrise flights out of the little airpark in between Midland and Odessa, and meeting the investors his uncle Jonathan had lined up from his office in New York.

At five one morning, Bush scrambled outside and into the dawn light, aiming for his station wagon, racing to meet Rea at the airport. It had poured all night, and the streets were flooded with sandy brown water. Zipping down the sewerless streets, Bush smacked his car into a deep patch of floodwater. The engine died. In the front seat, he quickly stripped off his clothes down to his underwear and hopped out into the muck and rain. Clutching his pants over his head, he sprinted through the water and back to his house with the circular driveway. The neighbors watched as the vice president's son scurried past their windows. His friends joked that neighbors probably thought somebody's husband had just caught him in the act and he was fleeing for his life. Bush called a cab, put his suit back on, and made it to the airport just before takeoff.

REA AND OTHERS in Midland knew that Bush was still immersed in politics, even though the family was never seriously worried about the Reagan-Bush 1984 reelection bid. George W. went to the 1984 convention in August and stared out across the hideously ugly, blocky convention center that oppressively hot day in Dallas—a day so hot that some members of a local Boy Scout troop outside the Convention Center keeled over from dehydration. The thing that registered on him most was all the signs pushing candidates for 1988 . . . *the Old Man didn't have any of those signs.*

In September, Bush flew to Nashville to begin a seven-city blitz with GOP Senate nominee Victor Ashe, a friend from Yale who was running against Al Gore. George W. told an audience he hoped his father would run in 1988, especially after seeing the signs bobbing in Dallas. "We're all competitors and love sports and things like that, and our competitive juices began to flow. So I hope he does, as a selfish son, but also as a selfish American. But believe me, he has got no plans or plots or future strategy right now."[19]

Immediately after the reelection, the family began planning for the 1988 race. In April 1985, Bush flew to the East Coast and a Camp David family conclave for the first pre-presidential-race sales call—by Lee Atwater, the emerging prince of the smash-mouth New Politics. The Bushes were wary of the mercurial South Carolinian. He was too prone to embarrass her husband, thought Barbara Bush. The whole clan was there: the five children, the three uncles, and one aunt. Atwater gave a bravura performance, ad-libbing, sermonizing, and pontificating with southern-fried homilies and hints at the new rules, the way the new, confrontational, hardball politics were going to be played on behalf of the Bush-Walker family.

George W. studied the forceful thirty-four-year-old Atwater. He was only four years older than Atwater. Bush wasn't suspicious about the stories he had heard—about Atwater being a ferocious womanizer or a party animal with a surprising, non-Bushian tendency toward hanging out on Beale Street in Memphis with soul man Rufus "Funky Chicken" Thomas or B. B. King and other blues guitar players. He was more worried about whether Atwater would be fanatically loyal to the family or not—whether he would be a soldier, a warrior . . . a Good Man . . . an FOB. George W. wasn't alone; Jeb was worried too. "I had real trouble understanding how loyalties would work. Who would he be loyal to?" George W. asked his brother.

They knew that Atwater's high-octane political consulting firm was openly seeking business from other presidential candidates, including Jack Kemp. George W. lectured Atwater: "If there's a hand grenade rolling around George Bush, we want you diving on it first."

Atwater replied, "Are you guys really worried about my loyalty?"

The brothers said yes.

"If you're so worried about my loyalties," said Atwater, "then why don't one of you come in the office and watch me, and the first time I'm disloyal, see to it that I get run off?"

Atwater knew George W. would take him up on the offer, and he would have to deal with having the vice president's son hanging around, monitoring the loyalty levels inside the Team Bush campaign headquarters in Washington. Atwater liked running the show, and he also suspected that George W., on their first encounter, had viewed him as a necessary evil. But he knew he could charm Bush; he knew people just like him; he had grown up with in-your-face people in the South. And, like Bush, Atwater lost a sibling at a young age; when Atwater was six, his three-year-old brother died after being scalded by hot oil in a household accident.

"I'd rather have him [George W.] inside the tent pissing out than outside the tent pissing in," Atwater told people, stealing a line from LBJ, one of the ghosts he most admired.[20]

GEORGE W. flew back to Midland, and for the next few months he and Rea arranged more dog and pony presentations in the Northeast and Chicago, often to other Yale and Harvard graduates. Rea would let Bush work the room; then he'd come on with the academic stuff, the dry stuff, the impressive-sounding geology. But by the end of 1985, the world oil markets were collapsing; the price eventually plummeted to $10 a barrel in April 1986. The partnership evaporated almost instantly. Worse off than Arbusto and Bush Exploration, Spectrum 7 was dying, facing a widespread shutdown. Oil insiders said it was only a matter of time. In six months, the company had lost close to $400,000, and "the banks hadn't foreclosed, but that was in the wind."[21] Bush called the investors and told them he had begun arrangements for Spectrum 7 to be bought by Harken Energy, a Texas oil company openly expressing its interest in picking up struggling energy outfits. Bush pushed hard for some guarantees for Spectrum's employees. Six of them landed work with Harken.

Harken was owned in large part by global billionaire investor George Soros, Saudi investor Abdullah Taha Baksh, and the Harvard Management Corporation, the investing division of Harvard University. Harken offered to trade stock worth $2.25 million for a company whose net asset value was close to $1.8 million. With Spectrum 7 and the vestiges of Bush Exploration fading away, the vice president's son was given $600,000 in Harken shares; he was also told he could stay on as a director and he would be paid from $50,000 to $120,000 a year as a consultant for "investor relations."

Watching it all unfold was Phil Kendrick, the slow-talking, seasoned wildcatter from Abilene who had formed Harken in 1973 in a place that once had been a funeral home and looked that way for years. For a time, Kendrick had had to chase florists with funeral wreaths out of the lobby and tell mourners that there were no more goddamned bodies to view in open caskets—this was a Texas oil company, not a bereavement palace.

Kendrick had eventually sold almost all of his stake in Harken, and he watched as it become a bottom feeder, bailing out sagging oil companies. He noticed that Harken rarely retained executives from the firms it snapped up. But he wasn't surprised to see George W. Bush kept on board for several years. "It's obvious why they kept George Bush. Just the fact that he's there gives them instant credibility. He's worth $120,000 a year to them just for that," Kendrick once said.[22] "It helps," he later drawled, "to be the son of a president."[23]

It was a good time to flee the oil business. Thousands of people were being laid off, banks were imploding, construction projects all over Texas slammed shut. Even the invincibles such as ARCO were contemplating the largest white-collar layoffs in Texas history. No one, not even a Bush-Walker investor, was anxious to throw mad money into bleeding West Texas. In Midland, Rea wondered when young George was going to get out of oil and follow his father back into politics. He wondered if he had ever thought about running for governor of Texas—a state where the governor's office is a constitutionally weak one, where the governor frequently concedes to the might wielded by the speaker of the House and the lieutenant governor. In Texas, Rea told people, being governor was really like being the head cheerleader or the public relations person. He didn't have to say it, but it was also like being the land man, the door-to-door salesman who patches together deals.

"Well, I don't know of any other state where the governor has less authority than the lieutenant governor. The governor's office is more of a cheerleader and a p.r. person . . . veto power and making appointments, that's about their duty," he'd say years later to a Dallas writer.[24]

HARKEN WAS headquartered in a Dallas suburb, and Bush had to travel to Big D to nail down bits and pieces of the demise of Spectrum 7. While he did, he would also make time to visit GOP and family friends. One afternoon at a Mexican restaurant in Dallas, he spied Al Hunt, *The Wall Street Journal*'s Washington bureau chief. Hunt and his family, including his four-year-old son, had just settled into their seats. It was early April. In Washington, the latest issue of *The Washingtonian* was making the rounds, and it featured a short series of crystal-ball predictions from top political pundits: Sam Donaldson, John McLaughlin, Rowland Evans, Fred Barnes, Judy Woodruff, and Hunt. The campaign watchers had all agreed to name the candidates they were predicting to be on the ballot for the 1988 presidential race. The only mention of Hunt read, "Al Hunt, *Wall Street Journal:* Kemp and Indiana Senator Richard Lugar against Hart and Robb."[25]

Now Hunt spotted the thirty-nine-year-old George W. Bush winding over to his table.

"You no good fucking sonofabitch, I will never fucking forget what you wrote!" he heard the vice president's son sputtering as he stepped up to Hunt and his family.

Hunt stared at him, nonplussed. He didn't know Bush very well, had hardly seen him around the campaigns or at the White House. Lingering for thirty seconds by Hunt's table, Bush mentioned *The Washingtonian*. Hunt was confused. He hadn't thrown any darts, let alone any hatchets, at Bush's father. He also assumed that Bush had been drinking heavily, that "he was quite clearly lubricated." And after Bush left Hunt and his family alone, a thought blinked in Hunt's head: "This is a guy who's got problems."[26]

IN MAY 1986, during the early negotiations with Harken, unassuming Marvin was diagnosed with colitis. He eventually lost forty-five pounds and spent several weeks in a Washington-area hospital. George W. talked with Marvin about their families. Marvin and his wife were in the final stages of adopting a child from the same Texas foster home where several of George W.'s Midland friends had gotten children. Bush returned to Texas to tie up loose ends on the Harken deal and to celebrate the upcoming fact that he, Laura, and several of their friends were about to turn forty or were on their way into their forties. He didn't hesitate when the O'Neills suggested a getaway weekend at one of Bush's favorite spots, a place close to where Neil had moved in order to start his own oil ventures. The Broadmoor Hotel in Colorado Springs had been built in 1891 as a casino but in 1918 had been turned into a lavish hotel by Spencer Penrose, a Philadelphia investor who had made a fortune in gold and copper mining. Set on three thousand stunning acres close to Pikes Peak, the facility included three golf courses, including one designed by Arnold Palmer. Presidents Hoover, Roosevelt, Nixon, Eisenhower, and Reagan had stayed there, as had Nelson Rockefeller, Henry Kissinger, Adlai Stevenson, Barry Goldwater, the king of Siam, and Jordan's King Hussein.

The three inseparable Midland power couples—the Bushes, Joe and Jan O'Neill, Don and Susie Evans—were going. George W. talked to Neil, who said he would make the hour's drive down from Denver and join them for supper. There was a tentative plan to wake up Sunday morning and go to the nearby Air Force Academy's Cadet Chapel, one of the largest tourist attractions in the state. That night, the group assembled and drinks flowed. Laura watched her husband . . . "Laura's quiet, but she accomplishes a lot with that quietness," Barbara Bush had once said. Laura had seen this before, almost since they were married, the way that after a few drinks he'd think he was funnier than he really was. A thought would occur to her: "Isn't that what every drunk thinks?"

She had always felt that her husband was good at impulse and not introspection; he wasn't going to spend time trying to find out if he had a clinical problem with alcohol. She had said it was "necessary" to stop. It was almost a bad joke: *choose me or Jim Beam.* Some people in West Texas clucked and said she was tired of waiting at home when he was out, and when they heard that his all-time favorite musician was George Jones, "Old Possum," it was almost too perfect—Jones was the archetype of the boozy country singer single-mindedly insisting on fraying his syllables and his liver.

That evening the group split up, and Bush wound his way back to his room. The next morning, it was as bad as ever. Bush woke up with a pounding, churning hangover but somehow managed to go for a run. If there were plans to go to the places the Midlanders normally liked to visit, maybe the Air Force Academy Chapel, they didn't seem appealing anymore after a night of drinking. He told Laura that he wasn't ever going to drink again. Later, he pulled O'Neill aside and confided the same thing to him. His longtime drinking buddy wasn't surprised, even though he had always felt he could go longer and harder than Bush. O'Neill had never thought that Bush had a "quote-unquote drinking problem"—"if anyone had a problem it was me," he said, and in time O'Neill would openly talk about checking himself into the Betty Ford Clinic. O'Neill realized that there was something else in the abrupt decision Bush made that day at the spectacular, plush Broadmoor—one that Laura had been suggesting for years but that Bush had ignored until that crucial summer as the family prepared for the launch of his father's presidential campaign.

"He looked in the mirror and said, 'Someday, I might embarrass my father. It might get my dad in trouble.' And boy, that was it. That's how high a priority it was," O'Neill said. "And he never took another drink."[27]

THAT SAME month, the pecking order inside the campaign was becoming clear. Lee Atwater and the elder Bush agreed that George W. would become a senior adviser to his father and have the highest profile of the children in the Bush campaign. His tasks were narrowed down, and a decision was reached to have him serve as a loyalty monitor for his father and also to become instrumental in bridging the gaps to the unpredictable but gathering political power bloc that his father feared the most and understood the least: the far Right of the Republican Party, especially the Christian Right. As Jerry Falwell and Pat Robertson were cresting in visibility and apparent influence, the Christian conservative movement was also demanding increased access to the White House and issuing less-than-vague threats about how it would use its collective political might. True or not, who could really tell? Political analysts were suggesting that there were 22 million once-slumbering evangelical voters ready to reclaim the country. There was immediate, open jockeying among all the presidential aspirants for the time, attention, and affections of Falwell, Jimmy Swaggart, Oral Roberts, and even the popular gospel-rock singer Amy Grant.

By the summer, Vice President and Barbara Bush met Jim and Tammy Faye Bakker at the vice president's mansion and told them they enjoyed watching the Praise The Lord (PTL) Club on TV. The elder George Bush reminded right-wing Christians—and West Texas farmers—that he had resigned from the Trilateral Commission, the all-purpose bogeyman institution that still frightened the Christian Right's conspiracy theorists. The elder Bush also appeared at Jerry Falwell's Liberty University and made a video talking about his versions of a Christian conversion experience—"life-changing experiences"—that he shared with evangelical leaders in private screenings at the Christian Bookseller's Convention in Washington.[28]

Worried about the elder Bush's reputation as the weak link in the Reagan Revolution, his campaign strategists were scrambling to retain their Reagan credentials with the harder conservatives, while also quickly identifying and cultivating the most potent faces in that imprecise evangelical realm. He needed help, and he needed someone who could bluntly serve as both a convincing salesman to the evangelicals and reassuring emissary to the skeptical Right and the wave of uncompromising New Right linchpins such as Paul Weyrich, the founder of the Free Congress Foundation. Weyrich was a former congressional aide who had assailed Ronald Reagan for not being conservative enough—"so tough he gets hate mail from Mother Teresa" was what some joked about Weyrich in Washington. Weyrich disliked Reagan's choice of Bush as his vice president, and he had once ominously promised that "there will be a fight" if a moderate Republican such as George Bush ever ran for president. More than one Washington insider assumed that Weyrich had been talking about Vice President Bush when he had told *The Washington Post* in 1983, "The problem with Republicans is that most of them in leadership positions never had to work for a living. Those people in the White House who have clout are from the upper crust. If you wear a certain kind of mink fur, if you are a Hollywood star, or David Rockefeller, or one of the biggies from California, you're welcome. But if you're the average guy, who've you got speaking for you?"[29]

BY ORCHESTRATING the sale of Spectrum 7 to Harken, a company anxious to have the son of the vice president and maybe the future president on its board, George W. would be able to move to Washington. The sale was a high priority; it would give him a giant swath of stock, and it would allow him to "consult" without having to be in Texas. That summer, turning forty, he also decided to go sober, openly becoming the redeemed angel, the Prodigal Son who had returned home. It was a fortuitous decision—especially if he was going to help court the obvious beyond-the-Beltway leaders of that ill-defined "Christian populist movement," as well as the other lesser-known but possibly influential Christian conservatives who were still suspicious of his father. During his congressional race, George W. had faced the exact same charges in the Texas Bible Belt—carpetbagger, limousine Republican—in the unforgiving Christian quarters of West Texas.

He and the Bush-Walker family had been cast as elitist—"that might be cool at Harvard and Yale" Kent Hance had once said—probably out of touch with true conservative, true Christian political values. The same month that George W. gave up drinking and freed himself from his day-to-day business ties to Texas, a flattering profile of the vice president orchestrated by the Bush campaign appeared in an influential evangelical magazine called *Christian Herald.* The article had been cobbled together by Doug Wead, who had been assigned to be George W.'s aide.

Wead was a short, wiry Assembly of God evangelist who was also a frequent associate of Jim and Tammy Faye Bakker and who had spent twenty years as a high-ranking member of the politically conservative Amway products network. In 1980, Wead and his brother Bill had published a Christian-oriented "quickie" book about Ronald Reagan that had been timed for release at the GOP National Convention; the book had featured a passage about Wead's introducing Reagan to an Amway convention in Charlotte, North Carolina. (Amway's two founders, Richard DeVos and Jay Van Andel, would become members of President Bush's Team 100, the 249 people who had donated at least $100,000 each to his campaign.) Over the next several years, Wead entered into a close, long-term partnership with conservative entertainer Pat Boone; he cowrote another book with ex–Interior Secretary James Watt, who had resigned from the Reagan-Bush administration in the wake of making offensive remarks about Jews, blacks, women, and Native Americans; he later began marketing motivational tapes called *God, Money & You*. Wead had sometimes stayed at the Bakkers' house and vacationed with the Bakkers in France; he had reportedly appeared on Bakker's television show sixty-seven times and served as a guest host five times.[30]

In June 1985, Wead had offered Bush staffers something they desperately needed: a fifty-eight-page analysis of George Bush and the evangelical movement. A wickedly fast writer, he followed it up with an avalanche of briefing papers and memos to Lee Atwater on the same topic. Finally, he was offered a ride on *Air Force 2* and invited to join the vice president and Barbara Bush for dinner up front. In December 1985, he wrote one more valuable thirty-five-page operations manual entitled "The Vice President and the Evangelicals: A Strategy."[31] Wead suggested that Pat Robertson was going to be a serious contender for the presidency, but several members of the Bush inner circle were keeping an eye on Wead, worrying that he hadn't risen up through the traditional GOP-Bush ranks, that he was carrying too much weird baggage. After reading his memos, the elder Bush and George W. saw him as the campaign's best chance of deciphering and connecting to the threatening, elusive bloc of hard-right Christian conservative voters, the ones who might harbor deep concerns about whether the Bushes were iron-willed enough to do the right thing.

"Signal early," Wead had recommended to the vice president and his advisers, "do whatever . . . for evangelicals early, so that it would not appear hypocritical."[32]

By 1986, Wead met with Vice President Bush's longtime personal aide David Bates, who had grown up with Jeb in Houston. Bates told Wead that he was going to be given the heady job of arranging private meetings between Christian Right leaders and the vice president's people.[33] Wead was given a new title—Liaison for Coalitions to the George Bush Committee—and told that he would be reporting directly to George W. Bush instead of campaign adviser Ron Kaufman.

When Wead went to see the first son, George W. told him, "You're mine. You report to me."

For the next fourteen years, Wead would be one of George W. Bush's closest friends, advisers, and mentors on Christian politics. He traveled the country with George W., introduced him to the most powerful evangelicals, wrote reports ordered by the first son, and worked as a bridge to national journalists—to the point of heading out to the airport to fetch writers for weekly newsmagazines who wanted to meet the first son. One of Wead's first, most serious orders of business was meeting with the first son and other advisers and deciding how to get the elder George Bush on the cover of a magazine that would solidify the elder Bush's Christian credentials. In March, Wead had shipped, via Federal Express, a draft of the article to Kaufman, head of Bush's political action committee. Kaufman quickly fired off a memo to Craig Fuller, the vice president's chief of staff, saying that he would examine and share the draft copy of the interview with Team Bush leaders over the weekend. When the article appeared in June 1986, the same month George W. gave up drinking, the article featured a prominent thought from Kaufman.

Vice President George Bush, he said, was best summarized in two words: "compassionate conservative."[34]

Years later that exact title would be resurrected by the first son as his own favorite national campaign slogan. He would carefully choose those same two words to describe himself as he began following his father and making the same run for the presidency of the United States. They were ultimately controversial words, summoning up ceaseless criticism from harder-edged conservatives who said that the Bushes and Walkers were still, always, imprecise and tied to their family's anemic, gilded tendencies. The first son and his handlers would choose his father's slogan over and over again as they tried to distinguish George W. Bush from every other politician in America.

12

Behavior Modification

*E*squire magazine profiled Lee Atwater—"Why Is
Lee Atwater So Hungry?"—and he was dressed
in his underwear and his socks, stepping into the
bathroom and talking while taking a leak, and then he was going on an un-
Christian-like road trip and peeking into massage parlors in Austin while
revealing the secrets of the Bush campaign: "I'm telling you, this here's a
young man's game. This is stress, high motherfuckin' stress. When you're
working with the front-runner, you're gonna get shot no matter what you
do."[1] Atwater looked and sounded like a man whose boundaries might
stretch way beyond loyalty and, in fact, there would be a second unsettling
appearance by Atwater in the magazine that would outrage Barbara Bush
all over again. In the Bush-Walker camp, some friends quietly laughed at
Atwater's brazen self-promotion, his nonstop schoolboy-intellectual shtick,
and his barbecue-stained language.

But Barbara Bush was livid; it wasn't just that it was undignified, it
was a stupid error made by someone they were paying $120,000 a year and
at a critical time when she was as interested as anyone else in drawing
closer to the Christian Right. She talked to George W. and ordered him
to keep a closer eye on Atwater. Her role in the campaign was amplified at
the moments when Atwater, Craig Fuller, or others were singled out for a
stinging rebuke. In the weeks after the article appeared, George W.
arranged a histrionic, showy act of contrition, convincing Atwater to write
a letter apologizing to his mother. Atwater sometimes saw Barbara Bush
the same way her son did—as the no-bullshit disciplinarian, the one with
the real message discipline, the unlikely looking one who was always the
precise political animal of the family.[2]

Atwater was learning, and George W. was helping him understand something few people outside the Bush inner circle adequately understood: Barbara Bush's political role was never to be underestimated or ignored—never to be confused with her easygoing public persona. For a portion of the campaign, George W. would be the one summoned by his mother to convey her displeasure with Atwater, Fuller, and anyone else she wanted dressed down for making her husband seem intellectually bankrupt by "siphoning" his ideas and claiming them as their own—or, in Fuller's case, simply not relaying phone messages to her fast enough. "There were times that people did some things that I think upset my mother," the younger Bush told Washington writer Ann Grimes. "Leaks, and staff siphoning credit for ideas originating with the candidate, especially infuriated her. I would then go talk to that person and inform them that they needed to amend their ways—and explain to them that if they weren't careful, the wrath of the Silver Fox would fall upon them. Who knows what would happen? It may not happen immediately, it may happen as time would go on."

His mother, he told people, would vent through him. On his way to see a worried, guilty party in the back of the airplane or the campaign bus, George W. often knew something about his role in the campaign and the family and its relationship with his father ("The Man"): "When you have a family member start talking to 'The Man' about how terrible someone is, the tendency is for the confidence of 'The Man' to be eroded in that person," he said to Grimes. "A lot of those people lived in fear of my mother. . . . People needed to be aware of her presence. No one wanted to irritate her."

For George W., the shield was sometimes lowered and replaced by what he called behavioral modification; "I shielded people from Mother. If she was upset about something I would help vent it. She could vent to me. . . . You know, I was the enforcer when I thought things were going wrong. Because of the access I had to George Bush, I had the ability—and I think I used it judiciously—I had the ability to go and lay down some behavioral modification. So as a result I had the confidence of . . . most of the people in the campaign."[3]

During the 1988 campaign, he quietly told reporters that his role in the Bush presidential campaign was really the same role that Robert F. Kennedy had served for his brother—that he was an aggressive general charting many of the campaign's boldest moves. Behind his back, one veteran Washington reporter at a newsmagazine derided his comparison as "egotistical" and inflated. RFK had generally been considered the lead, sophisticated strategist in the Kennedy campaign; George W., for many people directly familiar with the campaign's hierarchy, was more of a quick-tempered, fast-talking loyalty thermometer than anything else.[4]

LOYALTY WAS all that mattered, and, despite the media lapses, George W. was rapidly becoming convinced that Atwater really would throw himself on the grenade—even if he couldn't relate to Atwater's voracious appetite for seemingly paradoxical bits of culture. Atwater was equally prone to quote from Robert Caro's works on LBJ, Otis Redding's songs, or Alvin Toffler's prophecies. Unlike any other political adviser George W. had seen, Atwater had, at the very least, extraordinarily catholic passions, ones that, from a generational perspective, were completely different from what Bush had been exposed to through Jimmy Allison or the other older, staid pols his father had set him up with over the years.

As the campaign rambled on and George W. worked out of an office next door to Atwater at the Washington headquarters, it became obvious in strategy sessions that Atwater was moving on two fronts: balancing Team Bush between moderate conservatives, even plain old moderates, and the hard-right commanders such as Weyrich, Falwell, and Bakker, and wanting to wrench some semblance of passion from his candidate, to imbue him with easily definable ideas, with the "vision thing," with un-derstandable ideals and passions, to make him, well, more like ordinary Americans. In one later instance, he even shoved an electric guitar into the elder Bush's awkward hands. Atwater did it all, including reminding peo-ple that the elder Bush ate pork rinds and could drive a bulldozer. No one had ever done it before, no one had ever suggested it needed to be done as blatantly as Atwater did. George W. would grow to love Lee Atwater like a brother. Atwater was a revelation—someone who argued that the elder Bush's real and perceived personas were out of step with what Jeb Bush would later call the media-driven, "therapeutic" times.

Atwater desperately wanted George W.'s father to move well beyond the sense of nineteenth-century noblesse oblige that George W.'s great-grandparents had first inculcated in the family, the conceit of the prosper-ous but civic-minded leader who served the people not because he was possessed by righteous anger or ideals but because it was his duty and be-cause no one else really had the time or money to do it. Even Atwater's le-gions of enemies—all the critics who were repelled by Atwater, insisting that he was the prince of dark campaign tricks, a womanizer who was dragging politics even lower, if that was possible, by baiting gays and blacks and scaring the holy hell out of nervous white voters—even those people agreed that Atwater was right in wanting the elder Bush to inch a little closer to living in the same ordinary moment as most Americans.

Atwater's strategy was to try to convey the impression that his candidate was more than a predictable, rich guardian of the status quo, more than just another Prescott Bush or Dorothy Walker. And by the middle of the campaign, insiders could tell that George W. was coming closer to Atwater's vision of generational politics and that the master of new politics had evolved from a necessary evil into an intimate mentor to the first son—"Junior!" Atwater would yodel when he crash-landed in George W.'s office. It was a name George W. didn't like hearing from many other people than the ballsy Atwater. Their close relationship was underscored by Atwater also describing George W. as his "alter ego" in the campaign.[5]

Atwater was loyal to a blunt, outspoken fault, but loyalty was all that mattered as the Bush campaign began jockeying for position against Bob Dole and Pat Robertson: "Both Georges were always big on the loyalty-is-not-a-character-flaw idea" was how Jim Pinkerton, who was doing opposition research into Michael Dukakis, liked to put it.

Like everyone else in the campaign, Pinkerton was eager to get on George W.'s good side whenever the first son arrived from Texas. Pinkerton was an unfettered true believer; no one ever doubted his conservative tendencies in the tug-of-war between the hard-assed Nixon-Reagan conservatives and the Bush moderates. And Pinkerton always breathed a little more easily than the others. He felt that his long history with the Reagan campaigns had given him a favorable edge with the first son. George W. believed that the hard-core Reaganites such as Pinkerton might actually have a better finger on the GOP pulse than all the other blindly loyal, moderate "Bushies."[6]

George W., friends said, remained a ferocious admirer of Ronald Reagan and his ability to seem natural and self-confident in his conservatism. Unlike the elder Bush, caught between generations and seeming now and then to be uncertain about how to handle the changes, Reagan had remained blithely optimistic about his politics. "He [George W.] thought Reagan had accomplished a lot" was what Fred Malek, Nixon's ex-aide who had become a top Bush adviser, said.[7] And sometimes his own father, said George W., was too frozen by his upbringing, too thoughtful for his own political good. One of Dorothy Walker Bush's unbreakable edicts had been that her children must never cease competing but must also never possess anything remotely resembling braggadocio; Barbara Bush said that Dorothy Walker Bush had "had ten times" more influence on her five sons than Prescott Bush did. "Dad's instinct is always for the thoughtful thing, and that's probably to his detriment in the world of cutthroat politics," George W. told the *Chicago Tribune*.[8]

Pinkerton, so trusted by George W., felt something else: if somehow familial loyalties hadn't been a factor, the first son would have felt much more comfortable working for a man like Ronald Reagan. Watching the younger Bush, seeing him in the campaign, a thought occurred to Pinkerton: "Had he not been his father's son, I think that George W. would've been a Reaganite."[9]

IN THE FACE OF painful poll numbers, George W. flew to Des Moines and opened his father's campaign office. This was what he was good at and getting better at, being the highest-ranking GOP emissary sent straight from Washington and into the heart of what George W. liked to call "retail politics": the small-town rallies, the church meetings, the staged street-corner speeches. In Iowa, even in Dallas or Houston, there was always one person who emerged from the back of a room with a camera and barked out his disappointment: "You're not the real George Bush." The reporters could see the quickly erased but worn look on his face before he moved on to shake more hands. It made what his close first cousin John Ellis said about George W. and his father resonate even more: the key to understanding George W. was his relationship to his father. His mother? That was still easy—they jabbed each other until they both collapsed in laughter. His mother knew how it was: "[W]e fight all the time, we're so alike in that way. He does things to needle me, always."[10]

He plowed through receiving lines, acting as his father's surrogate at swings through the southern states; glad-handing evangelicals at the Washington campaign headquarters and being the family spokesman in the intense and often uncomfortable mating ritual between Team Bush and the Christian Right; posing for pictures with businessmen in Chicago; chewing out supporters who had made the public relations mistake of picking up key members of the Bush team in foreign-made automobiles instead of American-made cars. Throughout the spring and into the late summer, he was conferring with Wead about how to seal Team Bush ties to Weyrich and the unflinching Christian right wing—how to do it the way that Reagan had done it—and they were also talking about the book he was helping oversee with Doug Wead that would serve as one of the "authorized" Bush campaign publications. Aimed at evangelicals and right-leaning conservatives, it would be entitled *Man of Integrity*, and the eager-to-please Wead was working closely with the first son. Shaped as a series of questions and answers with the elder Bush, his wife, George W., and the other children, the book highlighted, for the first time in print, George W.'s relationship with Billy Graham, whom the first son said had led him back to Bible study, to exploring the concept of whether only Christians can go to heaven. The campaign publication included a chapter with a direct nod to the Bush-Walker dictums, "Prosperity with Purpose," and it catalogued the Bush family's relationships with several other religious leaders, especially "dear friend" Jerry Falwell.[11]

When he returned to Midland from Washington, George W. told Laura that they would have to move the family to the East Coast as soon as possible. Friends weren't surprised at the abrupt departure from West Texas, a place that he had repeatedly said he vastly preferred over the Northeast. The oil crash had devastated good chunks of Texas, banks were closing or changing hands seemingly every few days, and the fallout from crooked loans and sour deals would last for a decade. Some said it was an inevitability, only a matter of time before he would leave and push the Bush-Walker political legacy in Washington, and some people in Midland pointed out that George W. Bush was leaving Midland after almost a dozen years—really, the same number of years his father had spent in West Texas. He told his West Texas oil friends that he needed to be in the campaign headquarters in the run-down Woodward Building on Fifteenth Street full-time. In April the family had packed and moved to an apartment at the northwest end of Massachusetts Avenue in Washington. He took an office between Atwater's and campaign cochairman Bob Teeter's. He nailed a few Texas knickknacks to the wall and immediately planned trips to Illinois and Pennsylvania to introduce himself to the local GOP leaders running his father's state campaigns.

At the end of June, as the Iowa campaign staggered with bad numbers and open defections, George W. and Atwater hastily conferred about some extraordinary damage control. Rumors were moving fast in *Newsweek* and *U.S. News and World Report* that his father was having an affair, maybe with one of his longtime aides. It was plutonium, something that could certainly give a boost to Pat Robertson's chances in Iowa—or anywhere else there was an evangelical voter. The campaign headquarters groaned under the weight of fifty calls a day from the national media. (The breaking point came years later when a CNN reporter stunned the elder Bush by shouting out a question about the allegations.) His father's holier-than-thou anger at the question didn't satisfy anyone, and the fire continued to spread. At campaign headquarters dread was in the air, and, except for Atwater, people tended to steer clear of George W. "We gotta do something about this because we're not answering—no one's saying anything!" Atwater had yelled.

Finally, Atwater and George W. decided that the first son would deliver the official family disclaimer. Atwater would reportedly ask *Newsweek*'s Howard Fineman to meet him for an off-the-record lunch and offer up something that Junior had said about the adultery allegations. *Newsweek* eventually ran a short story indicating that George W. had asked his father about the allegations, his father had denied them, and Junior had one thing to say about the whole matter: "The answer to the Big A question is N.O."[12] The snappy one-liner got picked up rapidly by other publications, and in a few weeks the matter had basically disappeared.

Atwater's philosophy had always been to "pierce the boil" and let the poison run out; skewer the problem, don't let it linger, keep moving. George W. was impressed. He had worked his way through two crises with Atwater, and by the end of his first year in Washington, two of the top-ranking White House reporters said that he was still watching Atwater—except that now it was to learn how to deal with the media and even how to control his anger, to let the poison out. "We're beginning to get a relationship where I tell him things and he tells me things," Atwater told one of the Bush campaign's leading advisers.

The Washington reporters had come to a conclusion in the months that George W. had been in the incestuous Beltway loop of aides, staffers, and spin doctors: he had started in Washington with a cockiness that boiled over into hot-tempered arrogance and a special contempt reserved for members of the media who presumed to probe his father's character. He had, said one veteran White House reporter, a lot to learn about the fine art of cultivating friendships in the press, parceling out information, even acting polite—especially after word made the rounds that the vice president's son had gone on a little too long in a shouting match with a network cameraman.

His role in the national campaign's inner circles was relatively freeform but always powerful: he was the loyalty monitor, he was the stand-in for his father at fund-raisers and fetes, and with Doug Wead's help he was the quick-talking bridge to Weyrich and the Christian Right. He was also the one who yelled at lower-rung staffers that they had screwed up by ordering alcohol for a political banquet aimed at teetotaling evangelicals.

George W.'s relationship with the Washington media was less precisely defined. It was a work in progress, something he was learning at the highest level alongside Atwater, the man who had no peer in the fine art of media seduction. George W. had, White House reporters said, a long way to go before he could even begin to approach Atwater's Machiavellian edict of keeping your friends close and your enemies closer. One other thing was clear: he initially didn't feel completely comfortable with the clubby, collegial way his father and Prescott Bush had chosen to deal with the Washington press corps. His grandfather and father were accustomed to knocking back drinks with selected members of the media, pitching horseshoes with writers such as George Plimpton, inviting writers on trips to China, to dinner, on tours of Kennebunkport. And those who covered the elder Bush said that he was almost stunned by the evolution of the new media, the way the old-school, confidential relationship that Prescott Bush had enjoyed was fading and reporters hounded him about inconsistencies and "gotchas." The elder Bush had wanted to work hard to do what he and Prescott Bush had always done, pulling people into their confidence. Eventually he went so far as to tell his spokesman Marlin Fitzwater to gather together the photos of the thousand members of the Washington press corps so he could memorize all their names; the Bush men were always startlingly better than anyone else at memorizing names.[13]

Atwater was more in tune with the new way of doing things. He was adroit at disarming potentially problematic reporters, toning down the confrontational process by feeding reporters snippets of the Bush campaign strategy or doling out an occasional insider anecdote. He also knew the value of establishing an intimacy with a reporter. He would talk unabashedly about getting laid, getting drunk, taking a shit, or anything else he thought he could mention that would throw the reporter off the hunt. It was an old southern political trick that had been perfected by LBJ and other career politicians in Texas, including one of George W.'s future confidants, Texas Lieutenant Governor Bob Bullock. Initially, the drawn-out, behind-the-scenes dance with the national media was anathema to George W.—for him it was catering to the cynics, wasting energy on people who didn't deserve it.

And to one distinguished White House reporter, he was an edgy, ominous presence from Texas, rocking on his boot heels, or standing off to the side of his father and glaring with a half-cocked grin at someone pressing his father on the adultery question, the wimp question, the gilded-upbringing question. To others he was just a no-bullshit samurai, but still someone who fundamentally didn't like many of the national journalists. "He was known as temperamental. He was widely regarded as a sort of family enforcer, the guy who would not hesitate to set things straight, to cut through the BS. He disliked journalists, and I felt he was suspicious. I never felt that he wanted to talk or give an interview," said David Hoffman, who covered the presidency for *The Washington Post*—and was among the reporters the elder Bush liked the least.[14]

Margaret Warner, the *Newsweek* writer, felt George W. served a particular purpose: "I am sure in any campaign where someone like George W. is the son of the candidate, he would be in touch with the Texas money people, with friends of the father and all that. That is the care and feeding of the big donors, you know, the old family friends. It's an important role, they all felt that they could get someone they could call in the campaign."[15]

Sometimes he would mutter "No comment, asshole" and "look at you like you had just crawled up out of a hole in the ground, just for asking a question," said another veteran White House reporter for a national news outlet.

WITH THE ADULTERY allegations under control, George W. flew to Alabama and then to Texas to campaign. In Austin, he told writer Sam Attlesey what his campaign title was: "Senior Adviser they call me, but when your name is George Bush, you don't need a title in the George Bush campaign."[16] He confided that he had other duties, including determining whether "we are talking to the press too much" and handling the "complaint department" for loyalists who were grumbling about who got the most access to his father.

In Washington, Robert Mosbacher, the finance chairman who had an office down the hall at campaign headquarters, saw the way George W. handled those loyalists, especially Atwater. Atwater and George W. were growing closer, and some staffers presumed it had to do with their southern ties, but especially with Atwater's plan to push George W. even closer to Weyrich and the religious Right—to make George W. the single most important Bush family liaison with the right wing and the Christian conservatives. In George W.'s ten-by-fifteen-foot cubicle, high-ranking campaign staffers suddenly saw people the Bush camp had rarely regularly dealt with in person: "The first time I ever met Dr. Jim Dobson, it was in George W.'s office in the '88 campaign. George W. was meeting with a lot of the evangelical groups and other conservative groups. Jerry Falwell had his group in and, y'know, other kinds of conservative groups, everybody from the American Conservative Union to the right-to-lifers to the anti-gun-control groups," said political consultant Charles Black.[17]

In the inner-circle staff meetings with Atwater, Kaufman, media man Roger Ailes, pollster Bob Teeter, and Mosbacher, the first son's role was obvious: to tell everyone how "his father would react or his family would react."[18] Atwater, Kaufman, and the others would defer to George W. when he sat at the table. "Well, he was certainly welcomed by me because clearly the [father] thought a great deal of him. He was around a lot," said Ailes, the ex-Nixon aide who was handling public relations, television packaging, and advertising.[19] "George W. was always a good one to say, 'I can tell you right now that my dad would never say that' or 'My dad would never do that,' " said David Bates, his father's longtime political assistant who had grown up with the younger Bush brothers in Texas.[20]

On the Monday in October 1987 when the family gathered to stand alongside the elder Bush as he formally announced his candidacy, *Newsweek* ran a devastating cover story entitled "Fighting the Wimp Factor." The primary photo showed Bush gripping the wheel of his motorboat, and the story explored whether his stiff-backed, privileged upbringing would ever translate to working Americans—and especially whether his father had determinedly sailed through public life avoiding confrontations. In the Bush camp, it was difficult to tell who was more angry, the Old Man or the first son. It was the timing, it was the questioning of character and the use of the neutering word "wimp"—the "W-word," as the two called it, that made them seethe. It was, George W. said when he called back to Midland and spoke to the members of his old oil patch network, the essence of what he hated about the cynics in the northeastern media, all those guilt-laden intellectuals who had everything in common with the arrogant, suffocating products of Yale and Harvard. In the Bush camp there was vague macho muttering . . . *We'd like to take them out on the boat* . . . about *Newsweek* and about Margaret Warner, who had written the piece. George W. later insisted that he was so furious that he called Warner, "let her have it," questioned her "journalistic integrity," and suggested that she quit. Warner, in turn, later told people around the country who inquired about the episode that she had no vivid memory of him ever delivering a tongue-lashing.[21]

Then, in what seemed like a freelance attack and a disavowal of Atwater's dictums about disarming the media, George W. dialed one of his favorites, *Newsweek's* White House correspondent, Thomas DeFrank. *Newsweek* had been planning an exhaustive, staff-written book chronicling the inner workings of the 1988 campaign, and it was going to rely on

high-level access to the candidates and their staffs as the elections unfolded. When DeFrank answered, George W. was curt: "Tommy, I've got
bad news. *Newsweek*'s been cut off. You're out of business."[22]

The three or four reporters who persisted in talking to George W.
about the war against Dole and Robertson had been accustomed to finding him in his office, on the right as you walked in, munching fistfuls of
popcorn, shooting the shit, and talking in a Texas twang while calling the
oil patch and Evans, O'Neill, and Younger—while pointing to an empty
chair and commanding the visitor to sit down. Several reporters said they
knew they were being carefully measured by George W. to see if and how
they used what he said—and whether they passed the loyalty test. After
word snaked through the press corps about his alleged blowup with De-
Frank, some reporters speculated that the whole episode had actually been
a carefully contrived act -that, as in the adultery allegation episode,
George W. had been tabbed to be the mouthpiece for the family's righteous indignation. That theory was reinforced when Atwater and other
Bush staffers called reporters and said that they shouldn't worry, nobody
was being "cut off."

As the story grew, his reputation in Washington, the way he was defined on Capitol Hill, also grew. One writer would paint him as the
"Roman candle" in the Bush camp—sparkling and riveting but sometimes
too hot to touch. But another writer said he was more like Sonny Cor-
leone out doing some manly defense to retain respect for his father. Other
members of the media who were planning books similar to the *Newsweek*
effort also had to meet with the first son. In 1986, magazine writer
Richard Ben Cramer had started turning the wheels on his own exhaustive
examination of the 1988 presidential race. According to John Ellis,
George W.'s cousin and confidant and one of the most politically attuned
members of the Bush clan, George W. was one of the gatekeepers who
arranged for Cramer to enjoy unusual access to his father and the other
Bushes; to confirm the accuracy of information, Cramer would read every
section of and any quotes in the book to the candidate, a family member,
or a close aide.[23]

Among the pool of national reporters who trailed the campaign or
the family in the late 1980s and into the next decade, White House veterans said that Cramer, DeFrank, Fineman, Kenneth Walsh from *U.S. News
& World Report*, ABC's Brit Hume, and John Mashek of *The Boston Globe*
were among the very few George W. would work with, spend time with.
Some, like Mashek, had been favorites of the elder Bush, and Mashek
knew enough to occasionally call the younger Bush for help with some in-

sights into the inner workings of the White House and the Oval Office: "If there was a crisis going on, you would try to reach him to see if he could help you out with any information," said Mashek.[24] But except for Cramer, the first son adamantly refused to allow deep access to any reporter he suspected was interested in capturing something in his father's soul. For years, for example, he continued to scoff at Gail Sheehy and the other writers who wanted to delve too deeply into his father's interior being, his character.

"You're not going to write some goddamned *psychobabble*, are you?" he once demanded, his black cowboy boots propped up on his cluttered desk, his hands behind his head, and his eyes boring into a veteran Texas writer who had said he was working on a longer-range project touching on what really stirred him and his father.

TO GET AWAY from it all, there were regularly scheduled Sunday lunches at the vice president's estate, and there was always attorney Collister "Terry" Johnson, his New Jersey–born college roommate for three straight years. Bush had been an usher at Johnson's wedding, and he was godfather to Johnson's daughter; when Bush ran for Congress in 1978, Johnson had tried to raise money. Sometimes he would just jet down to Midland to pal around, play golf, and relive the DKE days. Johnson, who lived in McLean, Virginia, would also meet Bush in the Washington area, and they would sometimes play eighteen holes of golf at Chevy Chase or Burning Tree, the latter being the course Prescott Bush had preferred to play on when Nixon or Eisenhower had challenged him to a game.

On one of their visits, Bush surprised Johnson with some news: "You know, I'm going to give up smoking." Johnson looked at his old fraternity president and replied, "Gee, that's great, cause it's not really good for you." On their next golf date at Chevy Chase, George W. had more news: "Guess what, I gave up smoking." Johnson asked when. "This morning," answered Bush. Johnson wanted to know if he was kidding, but Bush assured him otherwise. "I told Laura that I'm not going to smoke anymore," said Bush.

The pair teed off and wound their way around the stunning golf course. By the ninth hole, Bush was actually starting to shudder and shake, apparently going through nicotine withdrawal. Johnson, watching him twitch, finally decided to speak up. "C'mon, let's stop," insisted Johnson, hoping that they could head back to the clubhouse.

"No, no, we're going to keep going, we're going to keep playing," said Bush, still twitching. Johnson stared at Bush and thought about the awkward, personal moment, "I've never seen this and I'll probably never see it again in my life."[25]

IN JANUARY, George W. was in Oklahoma City, still pushing hard to cultivate his father's marriage with the reluctant Christian Right. George W.'s adviser on the right wing, Doug Wead, had been ordered to play Pat Robertson in practice debates with the vice president, and at campaign stops, George W. made digs at Robertson, the surprisingly resilient candidate who was mucking things up in Iowa.

The first son's and the family's strategy to prove the elder Bush's mettle to the evangelicals—by engineering an appearance on the cover of a Christian magazine, by working with Wead to cultivate relations with the uncommitted evangelical leaders, by publicly disclosing meetings with Billy Graham, and, arguably, by giving up drinking and smoking—didn't seem to be enough. At one point in Iowa, an exasperated George W. announced at a rally, "There is more than one God-fearing man running for president of the United States." And a month later, with Wead, he launched one of his most important, ground-level bits of political legwork on behalf of his father.

In Iowa, Wead began charting ways to directly shred the threatening, unpredictable Robertson network. Bush campaign staffers were still undecided about Wead's motivations and his background with Amway and in the Assemblies of God denomination. Wead, in turn, believed that the upper-level strategists advising the family were incredibly confused. According to him, Janet Mullins, one of the campaign's top political advisers, had pulled Wead aside and suggested that they could counter Bob Dole if they could figure out some way to get Elizabeth Dole on the cover of a hard-core Christian magazine. Wead, who called Mullins "Darth Vader," had of course already crafted the cover story on presidential candidate George Bush for the cover of *Christian Herald*. Now Wead told people that Mullins's attempt to "discredit" the Doles by putting them on the cover of a Christian publication was indicative of the massive confusion in the Bush campaign about how to handle what he liked to ominously call "the movement"—the still unpredictable, uncountable Christian evangelical voting bloc.

Wead told people that he believed that only the father and George W. adequately understood the importance of currying favor with the evangelicals. And in the last precaucus weekend in Des Moines, Wead said that he and the first son decided to head directly into what Wead called "enemy territory"—to, as Wead put it, "neutralize" the entire Robertson campaign at its "home base." Wead arranged a private visit and prayer session with the leaders of the First Assembly of God Church, a congregation that had evolved into the beachhead of Robertson's crucial campaign in Iowa. After the meeting, Wead was satisfied that he had helped the Bushes "neutralize" Robertson's headquarters and that they could steal Robertson's thunder if the Bush campaign attacked the evangelist at the ground level.[26] Of course, Iowa proved to be the nadir of the campaign; Dole finished first, and Robertson finished ahead of Bush. Wead complained that they had started too late, that if Kaufman and Atwater had listened to him more often, they wouldn't have been divided on how to deal with the evangelicals. The disgusted elder Bush left Iowa early, and it was up to the first son to explain to the media and increasingly skeptical members of the hard Right why his father wasn't the true, clear-eyed equal of Ronald Reagan—why Bush wasn't able to attract the evangelical vote in America's heartland. George W., Neil, and Doro, as everyone called Dorothy, were the ones staying behind, and George W. did the talking: "What happened in Iowa is we got whipped," he reluctantly announced.[27]

Thankfully, after Iowa, he learned that the paean to the evangelicals that the family and Wead were working on was finally back from the printer. The campaign needed something, some direction; too many things were slipping in too many directions. That June in Knoxville, he seemed exasperated as he talked to local GOP leaders about the fact that somehow people thought that Michael Dukakis was as conservative as his father. The next month, the media were informed that George W. and his aide Doug Wead would be introducing and talking about the new book, *George Bush: Man of Integrity*, at the July 1988 Christian Bookseller's Association Convention in Dallas.[28]

IN AN ALMOST salaciously humid New Orleans in August, George W. was named the spokesperson for the Texas delegation at the GOP convention. Atwater and James A. Baker III also told him that they liked the idea of the first son announcing the Lone Star votes. After midnight in the Big Easy, Atwater, who had essentially conceded control of the campaign to Baker, was prowling by himself down Bourbon Street, lingering to listen to R-and-B music pouring out of a dark club. George W. was still working the phones back at the hotel suite.[29] Three weeks earlier, he, Baker, and GOP convention coordinator and Harvard B School graduate Fred Malek had been pitching horseshoes with his father at the vice president's home on the grounds of the U.S. Naval Observatory in Washington. George W. had kept trying to guess the name of his father's vice presidential running mate. He had tossed out name after name. His father had simply shaken his head. Nobody had mentioned Dan Quayle. Now, in New Orleans, George W. knew before anyone else. He was right there in the room when his father, reclining in a bedroom at the vice president's mansion, finally reached for the phone and placed the call to Quayle.[30]

In New Orleans, people could see the first son bouncing with energy. What most FOBs didn't know or wouldn't talk about was that he was surprising one or two people at the convention by publicly admitting something that he had never admitted before, that he was wrestling with ways to rein in his sputtering rage. He called it "feisting out"—"having to curb his usual hot temper when people start bad-mouthing his Old Man."[31] It was, some people in Texas later said, an odd way of putting it—"*feisting out*"—something you might hear in the South when someone was talking about feisting curs, small mongrel dogs that could corner wild boars or snarl for hours at a squirrel they had sent up a tree.[32]

He was everywhere at once: overseeing the Texas delegation, grabbing maximum exposure in the media-packed hotel lobbies, telling Malek how to package the presentation of his father—"*It's simple, you portray him as George Bush. You ought to not present him as some regal being sitting on a throne, you ought to present him as a real man with concerns about people*"[33]—reviewing his father's acceptance speech, arranging his own postconvention showcase appearance alongside Pat Robertson, which would obviously, publicly, link Team Bush with the Christian Right.

George W. was pumped up about the obvious outcome, about the fact that he would say the words that would put his father over the top—and still angry with the way the then relatively obscure Texas state treasurer, Ann Richards, had spiked the entire family with her lingering Lone Star line at the Democratic Convention. She had begun her keynote address by reminding her audience, already mesmerized by her appearance, that they should listen closely because they could hear "what a real Texas accent sounds like." To reprise that still-resonating image of the Bushes and Walkers as carpetbaggers with the thinnest ties to native Texans, she added, "Poor George, he can't help it . . . he was born with a silver foot in his mouth." That, knew George W., had actually made his mother physically ill as she watched Richards on TV during the summer retreat at Kennebunkport.

During the convention, he had told family members that once it was over, he would return to Texas; most friends and some cousins assumed that meant Midland and joining his friends and the struggling survivors in the capricious Lone Star oil patch. But, he had already decided to move to Dallas: it would put him closer to the Harken boardroom, but, more important, it would put him closer to the biggest muscled-up GOP fund-raisers in the state. Dallas, more than any other city in the state, had become the uncompromising Republican stronghold, fueled by a conservative media, the still-swelling suburbs in the northern quarters, and a steady wave of major corporations relocating from the Northeast. Dallas's GOP credentials, forged four years earlier when the city had spent millions reinventing itself on behalf of the Republican National Convention, would eventually be enough to attract several high-ranking Bush campaign and administration officials—from Fred Malek to Reagan-Bush legislative lobbyist Fred McClure. In New Orleans, with the convention's outcome a foregone conclusion, the younger Bush had also arranged to meet with a reporter from the largest paper in Texas. The interview was a convenient forum to introduce his thoughts on his personal political ambitions: "I want to make it clear that I'm not running for anything right now, but if I do decide to in the future, I'd have to work hard at establishing my own identity."[34]

After a bit he mentioned something else, his belief that he'd actually be more successful if his father lost. It sounded odd as soon as he said it, and he knew it. "That is a strange thing to say, isn't it? But if I were to think about running for office and he was president, it would be more difficult to establish my own identity. It probably would help me out more if he lost. He'd be out of politics and be a private citizen. And, you know, people have certain expectations from the son of a president, particularly the oldest one."[35]

AFTER HE ANNOUNCED the 111 Texas votes in New Orleans—for Texas's "favorite son and the world's best father"—he began a September barnstorming tour in the Lone Star State, appearing in twenty-two cities in the first week. Then he flew to California. "I recognize most undecided voters don't really care about the Bush junior varsity. My typical audience is our own base," he said to some supporters in Newport Beach.

At the Team Bush headquarters, co–campaign chairman Bob Teeter had always understood the best way to utilize the first son: dispatch him. It was, really, the same thing that applied to the Silver Fox: "He was far and away our best surrogate candidate. Obviously it helps your effectiveness if your name is George Bush, the same as the candidate's, and you're his son, his eldest son. This is not to minimize anything else, but his greatest potential was as a surrogate candidate. I mean, he and his mother were the two people, other than the president, that you could really send to any place—successfully."[36]

A month before the election, George W. heard from Bill DeWitt Jr., a Cincinnati oil investor whose father had been a top-ranking baseball executive for years. DeWitt had learned that the Texas Rangers, owned by aging Fort Worth oil baron Eddie Chiles, was up for sale. And he had learned that Baseball Commissioner Peter Ueberroth was vehemently opposed to anyone who did not have local connections buying the team; baseball had a bad enough image problem without inviting outside ownership. Chiles had made his fortune in the Permian Basin oil patch alongside the Bush-Walker clan in the 1950s; their families had been close, to the point that Chiles had made his personal plane available when Robin Bush was dying and needed transportation to leukemia specialists in New York. DeWitt Jr. wondered if George W. was interested in entering into negotiations with family friend Chiles and owning a small piece of the Texas team.[37] They agreed to talk after the election.

For months George W. had endured inquiries into the fact that he and Dan Quayle had both been members of the same national fraternity and had both gained admission to the National Guard. Campaign observers also began hearing relentless, creeping suggestions that, aside from being about the same age, the pair were remarkably similar in their upbringings and personalities: handsome descendants of the old money captains of industry, less-than-stellar university students, deemed extraordinarily charismatic and charming by their old college mates, big-time golfers. George W. concentrated on deflecting the National Guard comparisons and told reporters he had wanted to fly and hadn't been sure he would get to do that in the Air Force or anywhere else.[38] He said that he and Quayle—even though neither enlisted and served in Vietnam—should be lauded for not going to Canada: "The thing that's important is he didn't go to Canada. Remember, Canada was an option. He didn't go. Let's keep it in generational perspective," George W. said.[39]

A week before the election, George W. agreed to attend a quiet, unpublicized lunch in an exclusive Washington club. He met with the conservative leader Paul Weyrich, along with Coors Brewery executive Robert Walker. George W. and Weyrich had been speaking during the campaign; when Weyrich or other supporters of the Heritage Foundation wanted to get a message to the White House, they got in touch with the younger Bush or his aide Doug Wead. Weyrich had already told George W. that he and other right-wing bombardiers were disappointed about the apparent lack of a clean conservative battle plan inside the Bush camp, and especially the fact that rumors were flying that Dan Quayle was going to be exiled from the ticket because he had warped into a one-man punching bag. After he conveyed his feelings to George W., Weyrich was satisfied that the son would perform his appointed task—passing on protestations and demands from the brash Right—and that he would immediately go to his father with Weyrich's message.[40] Now, a week before the election, George W. wanted to make sure that the most conservative power brokers in the country weren't still worried about his father's spine: "George Bush to the conservatives will be like Richard Nixon in China. You'll be astounded at how conservatively he will govern," the first son insisted to Weyrich.[41]

George W. returned to Houston, knowing his father would win and satisfied that he had done his job crisscrossing the country, playing hardball and salesman with hundreds of evangelicals, paving the way for the Christian Right and the ultraconservatives. He knew that his aide Doug Wead would have a very visible job as a special assistant in the Bush administration and that Wead . . . *Weadie* . . . would be there to mend fences with Falwell, Weyrich, Robertson, the pro-lifers, and the dozens of forums and foundations that mixed conservative politics with Christianity.

THE DAY AFTER the election, George W. decided to lead the family prayer at the private 7:45 A.M. service at St. Martin's Episcopalian Church, a favored house of worship for the family in Houston: "Many of us will begin a new challenge. Please give us strength to endure and the knowledge necessary to place our fellow man over self . . . please guide us and guard us on our journey, particularly watch over Dad and Mother."

The first son, Laura, the twins, his father, and Barbara flew to Washington immediately after the church service. On the plane, the seven-year-old twins were delirious, and they kept ramming wads of paper into the toilet—and Barbara Bush would write in her memoirs that she had to reach in with her hands to yank it out. While they were on the way to Washington, negotiations were being closed on George W.'s new house on Northwood Road in Dallas.[42]

IN WASHINGTON, George W. was immediately named head of the Scrub Team, a secret, internal Bush team that would decide which people deserved to take jobs in the White House, which people were truly loyal or were still under suspicion. Bush chaired the group, which included Atwater, David Bates, former press secretary Pete Teeley, campaign deputy Margaret

Tutwiler, and White House personnel director Chase Untermeyer. There was no uncertainty about who was in charge: "He was in charge, to make sure folks that had worked for Bush loyally for a long time and would be good in government wouldn't be overlooked," said Bates.[43] The group quietly met on six occasions through early December, arguing over who should be rewarded—or at least extended an invitation to take a position that he or she would probably never accept.

George W. told aide Doug Wead that he was appointed to the Transition Team. Then Wead was later named special assistant to the president and assigned to work out of the Office of the Public Liaison; he would continue to be a pipeline directly to the first son. Wead's job was to be the aggressive dancer on one side of a thorny tango: while the White House moderates made overtures to AIDS groups, gays, and minorities, Wead's mission was to reassure suspicious Weyrich, Falwell, and the others that Team Bush was still working in the best interests of the hard Christian Right. Wead's job was an extension of a delicate, insider, hotly debated balancing act that the GOP, both in Washington and in Texas, had had to deal with from the late 1970s and would continue to have to deal with throughout the next two decades. Wead was in because he was George W.'s man. Others weren't so lucky.

At a Scrub Team meeting, George W. suggested someone he knew from Texas: wealthy Dallasite Roger Horchow, publisher of the Horchow catalogs and an associate of George W.'s college roommate Clay Johnson. What about Horchow as head of the National Endowment for the Arts? The other Scrub Team members were confused about the selection, about who the nominee was and why the Old Man's son was pushing him so hard. Maybe it was a Texas thing. Somebody asked George W. how he had come to decide that Horchow should be the next chairman of the NEA.

"Because he gave money to my father," replied George W.

A check of the campaign contributions list revealed that Horchow had also donated to Dukakis. "That's it," said George W., erasing Horchow's name from consideration.[44]

GEORGE W. closed on his low-slung north Dallas home three days after his father was elected president. By the middle of December, the Bekins moving truck had loaded everything and was on its way to the affluent, tree-lined Preston Hollow neighborhood, close to the homes, churches, or gathering spots of the city's leading figures: Tom Landry, Ross Perot, Stanley Marcus, and Dallas Mayor Annette Strauss, sister-in-law of

Democratic kingmaker Bob Strauss. The night before his father's inauguration, he talked about the growing speculation that he was interested in running for something in Texas. The word "dynasty," emerged, of course. "Dynasty connotes inheritance," he said to a writer. "Nothing is inherited in Texas politics."[45]

Even though the Scrub Team was no longer regularly meeting and had changed its name to the Silent Committee, Bush retained the unofficial rank of senior adviser to the president of the United States. From Dallas, he regularly conferred with Atwater, Wead, and Bates and he began sending notes to presidential counsel C. Boyden Gray and other high-ranking staffers on a variety of matters: serving as honorary chairman of the Bush-Quayle Golf Tournament at the Shannon Green Golf Course in Fredericksburg, Virginia; getting the Old Man's autograph on a photograph for an auction at a deep-pocketed GOP fund-raiser in Dallas; agreeing to serve, with Laura, as surrogates for his mother and father at international events. On one occasion, he dispatched a note suggesting that Don Ensenat's nomination of someone for a judgeship be considered seriously. Ensenat was his Houston roommate and old running buddy from the Delta Kappa Epsilon house: "Don Ensenat is a very good man and good friend of all Bushes—please give Joy any consideration you can."[46] He wrote a similar letter to Gray about Mississippi attorney Rhesa Barksdale: "Boyden, this guy up for federal judgeship. He is a very good man . . . any help would be appreciated."[47]

Sometimes there were even harsh reminders that he was serving as the out-of-sight but never out-of-mind loyalty monitor for his father. When he read that Representative Chris Shays of Connecticut was consistently voting against Bush administration policies, he quickly called up his cousin Dorothy Stapleton one afternoon and insisted that something needed to be done. Stapleton was Shays's finance director, and when she got his angry call, she dashed off a handwritten note to his father: "Junior phoned me this afternoon and I reassured him that I had already taken up the 'gauntlet.' "[48]

There was one other important issue to address now that his father was settling in—and now that George W. was beginning to weigh his own political prospects. He quietly conferred with Doug Wead and instructed him to produce what would become a forty-four-page, eleven-chapter publication that would be called "All the President's Children," a confidential document that explored how the children of presidents were perceived by voters and the media. The report by the Bush adviser and White House staffer was a laundry list of the foibles, failures, public perceptions, and pressures ascribed to several generations of presidential children, including the Reagan clan. But the George W. Bush–ordered report was also a telling insight into the way American political dynasties are shaped, the way they are sometimes viewed, and the strategies necessary when a president's child begins his or her own political campaign. The report was kept quiet for months and then fortuitously released to a single reporter about the same time wholesale allegations and investigations into the business dealings of the Bush children were making the front pages:

> Being related to a president may bring more problems than opportunity. Almost any enterprise is criticized. If successful, it's assumed that it is because of the relationship. If not, the public assumes the son or daughter is lazy or incompetent . . . the presidential child in business faces the pressures of enormous scrutiny. Two things the media and the public won't allow? Success or failure. Keep the business mediocre, maintain a personal low profile and you will be left alone.[49]

IN WASHINGTON, Barbara Bush's close friends asked her if her eldest son was going to run for office in Texas. She said she didn't know but that Neil—Mr. Perfect—"was dying" to be elected to something. Two days before the end of 1988, columnists Rowland Evans and Robert Novak ran a column calling George W. "the increasingly likely Republican candidate for governor . . . engaging and articulate, more conservative than the president-elect and the family member with the purest Texas accent." In Texas, suspicious Democrats chortled, suspecting that they saw Karl Rove's handiwork churning forward with the same columnists that George W.'s mentor Lee Atwater had allegedly enjoyed planting stories with. Now that the first son had been back in Texas for two weeks, they thought, his political adviser must surely have begun the national media packaging of candidate George W. Bush.[50]

A veteran political insider in Washington says that Bush called an old friend in Texas, a woman who had served as a high-ranking GOP operative and pollster. Bush had the Wead report, and now he needed some real reports from the ground in Texas. He needed to see how the name George Walker Bush would play as a possible candidate for Texas governor: "You know who our friends are, talk to our friends, talk to them, talk to people I don't even know and find out whether I should run," he said to her.

The Texas GOP operative did George W.'s bidding and quietly ran his name by possible big-money GOP party members, people who were card-carrying FOBs, and allegedly independent voters. When she called back from her reconnaissance mission, she had bad news: "George, everybody likes you, but you haven't done anything. You need to go out in the world and do something, the way that your father did when he left Connecticut and the protection of his family. You just haven't done shit. You're a Bush and that's all."[51]

TWO MONTHS AFTER George W. settled in north Dallas, he scheduled a round-the-state circuit of profile-raising appearances. In mid-February, he was in Angleton, an oil town on the Gulf coast, unwinding and waving a cigar in his hotel suite while talking to a Texas reporter. He was still flushed and heady from his father's recent inauguration. He had a droopy Bush-for-President tie around his neck. He had just given a Lincoln's Birthday banquet address and some interviews about his political future. He was experimenting with an answer to the same old question: What makes him different from his father? After one answer got some laughs, he began to use it over and over again: "He went to Greenwich Country Day School, and I went to San Jacinto Junior High."

He tried it in Angleton and other places, and it was a surefire hit in what some people said was the most xenophobic state in the country, certainly the only state that regularly advertised itself as a "whole 'nuther country" and where the Battle of San Jacinto, the fight for the Republic of Texas, was still taught in almost every school. It was good to mention that he had gone to *San Jacinto* Junior High. He liked—*loved*—the way the line was playing. In his hotel suite he had no doubt at all: "If I run, I'll be the most electable. Absolutely. No question in my mind. In a big media state like Texas, name identification is important. I've got it."

He was vague on what his platform might be: "I want to affect the lives of people. I want to make life better." He talked, for a minute, about political dynasties and the Kennedys. It was something people were bringing up more often now that his father was president, now that people assumed that he or Jeb would run for high political office. Dynasty "implies you inherit something . . . the concept of dynasty just doesn't exist. If you mean political tradition, then yes."[52]

There was always the specter of the Kennedys, the family that was increasingly mentioned in the same breath as the Bushes. The Kennedys were always too close to the things he had hated at Cambridge, and he was dismissive: "They never had to work. They never had to have a job," he said. But he saw the way people wanted to draw parallels, and, now, instead of directly comparing himself to Bobby Kennedy—as one news-magazine reporter had heard him do—he suggested that it was something other people were saying about him: "Those who liked me said I was the eyes and ears of the campaign. Those who didn't said I was the campaign's Bobby Kennedy."[53]

His home in north Dallas, at 6029 Northwood, was a wide-open, ranch-style structure with a limestone facade, a circular drive, wooden floors, a cream-colored living room couch, an office that he had decorated with a half-dozen western paintings, a swimming pool, and towering oaks at the sides. His daughters were enrolled in the area public school system and then later in the $8,000-a-year Hockaday school, often considered the finest preparatory institution for girls in Texas. Laura was immediately absorbed into Dallas's network of fund-raising and charity balls—guided through the almost byzantine layers by Nancy Brinker, whose husband ran restaurant chains and who had contributed money to George W. in the 1978 congressional race. At home, on the phone constantly, he massaged the Texas Rangers baseball deal. He told people in Midland that it was just like the oil game all over again: you work the phones, you sell the investors on investing in the package.

His great-uncle Herbert Walker had helped fund the New York Mets, and Baseball Commissioner Peter Ueberroth was an easy ally for the president's son. It would be good for slumping baseball to have the Bushes affiliated with a team, it would be a double bonus, a Texas connection to the most prominent college baseball player to ever be elected president of the United States. But Ueberroth still wasn't comfortable with the lack of Texas investors. George W. was going to put up only $606,000 and would thus have only an 1.8 percent interest in the investment group. The only other big investor was garrulous Roland Betts . . . *Rollie* . . . a fourth-generation Yalie and hockey player from Bush's days at Delta Kappa Epsilon. Betts had formed a film investment firm called Silver Screen that had sunk $1 billion into various productions, including *The Little Mermaid, Beauty and the Beast, Pretty Woman, Gandhi*, and *The Killing Fields*. George W. had called Betts three weeks after the presidential election, and Betts ultimately agreed to invest $3.6 million; Tom Bernstein, Betts's partner in Silver Screen, said he would put up $2.4 million.

At first Betts talked about owning the team with only one other partner, maybe selling shares of the team through Silver Screen. The complex plan fell through, and meanwhile Ueberroth was still demanding more local investment. George W. was on the phone: "Join us, we're going to have a lot of fun, we're not going to lose any money," he said. Ueberroth and Rangers owner and oilman Eddie Chiles were still heavily leaning toward the Bush connection; Chiles and the elder Bush had known each other from the 1950s in Midland, and the president's son certainly looked like somebody's vision of a garrulous Texan, twirling an unlit cigar, cursing to beat the band, and ordering $2,500 black eel-skin boots from legendary Houston bootmaker Rocky Carroll. But in February Ueberroth told Bush he still wanted more Texas investors—any Texas investors aside from the president's son and his $606,000.[54]

George W. decided to do exactly what he used to do in West Texas, when he would look up Yale alumni or step out of his car, unannounced, and knock on some rancher's door. He cold-called the quiet billionaire Richard Rainwater, who had made a fortune handling investments for the legendary Bass family from Fort Worth. The Bass family had contributed heavily to his father's campaign, and they had an interest in Harken's operations in Bahrain. Rainwater would take his call.

But Rainwater turned Bush down. He had been offered the Rangers years before, and he hadn't wanted them then. Ueberroth decided to take charge; he flew to Texas and was able to coerce Rainwater into investing; Rainwater, in turn, called a handful of other wealthy Texans, including Edward "Rusty" Rose III, a Harvard B School graduate from Dallas who had been nicknamed "The Mortician" for making $70 million to $100 million by short-selling overvalued stock in companies that would soon wither away.[55] Rainwater and Rose loathed publicity. "I can't figure out any reason why I would want my name in the paper,"[56] Rose once said. For a fabled Lone Star clan like the Basses, baseball was a higher-profile game than short-selling or even investing mammoth sums of money. Rainwater and Rose told Ueberroth they weren't sold on the deal, mainly because they didn't want to deal with the media. Ueberroth knew that the younger Bush was willing to absorb the glare. Bush wasn't worried about dealing with the media; he had learned how to do it with Atwater in Washington, at the highest, most intense level. He was working at it, *"feisting out,"* controlling it. "I know how to handle the press," he told Rose and Rainwater.[57]

THAT SPRING, the group began to cohere, with George W. readily agreeing to be the public spokesman for the far-flung investment group. He had contacted Fred Malek in Washington, with his lengthy connections to Nixon and Team Bush; Malek had proved a durable figure,[58] having survived his controversial admission that he had once searched the Bureau of Labor Statistics, under direct orders from a paranoid Richard Nixon, to determine how many of its ranking officials were part of what Nixon called a "Jewish cabal." Malek agreed to put up $653,938. George W. had also called loyal Bush cousin and real estate investor Craig Stapleton in Greenwich, Connecticut, who had also agreed to invest $1.06 million. Rainwater and Rose brought more friends to the table. Megafinancier Rainwater eventually told reporters, in a rare interview, that he was the one who had pulled the deal together from his office in Fort Worth. "I put the entire financing together. I structured everything. I put in place the management team," said Rainwater to a Texas writer. Fred Malek didn't think so; it was George W. who had called him, and he always felt that it was George W. who had cobbled the investment group together: "I can't imagine who would say that somebody else was driving the train," said Malek.[59]

At every meeting, George W. assured each of the much larger investors that if they put up the money, he could handle any problems the media presented.

WITH THE APPROVAL of the other investors, he and Rusty Rose were named the two general partners; he and Rose would have to vote unanimously on every decision that crossed their desks. Bush further agreed to be the public face, the "managing" general partner, and was given a $200,000 salary. He warned reporters in Dallas that he was ready for any criticism about whether he had the skills to speak for the investment group: "I've seen this before. I'm a guy whose father was called a 'wimp' on the cover of *Newsweek* the day he declared his race for the presidency. If it gets too bad, I'll let you know. I damn sure will let *Newsweek* know."[60]

On Saturday, March 17, he made good on his promise to serve as the willing media liaison. He announced that the sale was secured, and some people who heard him that day said he sounded like someone who was running for office rather than someone who owned 1.8 percent of a franchise. The sale was a "business investment with a civic dividend," said Bush at the press conference. "I just want people when they say 'Texas Rangers' that they think here's a group of people trying to improve somebody's life . . . it's not called motherhood, apple pie and baseball for nothing . . . it's not called motherhood, apple pie and track."[61]

In Washington, his mother, who was having lunch with reporters, was asked if her son was really positioning himself for a run for office in

Texas. "I'm rather hoping he won't because everything that happens bad with the administration is going to be young George's fault," she said.[62]

At the ballpark in Arlington, midway between Dallas and Fort Worth, George W. handed out baseball cards he had printed up with his picture on them. Sometimes he met with Karl Rove, who would fly up from Austin, where he was directing his successful business in direct-mail campaigning for GOP leaders across the country. Rove, who was in love with the visibility factor, frequently told Texas reporters that Bush was the "owner" of the team: "As owner of the Rangers, he is anchored in the minds of Texans as a Texas businessman. It gives him instant exposure and identification."[63] And now he and other GOP leaders loved the fact that George W. was in his box seat by the Rangers dugout, sitting next to Dallas Cowboys immortal Roger Staubach . . . *Captain America* . . . or handsome golfer Ben Crenshaw . . . *the new Ben Hogan.* Bush told writers he liked being in the box seats, he liked "peeing in the same urinals" as the average fan, instead of being sequestered in a hidden owner's box. Sometimes people would lean over and ask for an autograph from "the first son" instead of from Staubach or Crenshaw. It was odd, he would admit to a member of the media, hearing somebody say "the first son"—and then he would start grinning, bobbing in his seat, shoving a George W. Bush baseball card at the autograph seeker. Sitting in one of those seats one day, a thought washed over him: get Barbara or his father to throw out the first pitch.

Almost instantly, from opening day really, he was walking through the aisles, slapping backs in the locker room, peppering his vocabulary with curse words, shooting the shit behind the batting cage with Nolan Ryan and hiking up his pants legs to show off the Texas flags stitched onto his cowboy boots. When he was growing up, he would wait by the mailbox to see if any big-league players had actually mailed back the baseball cards he had asked them to autograph. He had grown up spouting earned-run averages and slugging percentages at society parties in Houston, in his high school dormitory, at the DKE house, at the National Guard Officers' Club, and on his father's campaign planes, telling reporters that, unlike his father, he didn't harbor any longtime ambitions for the presidency: "I grew up wanting to be Willie Mays, but I couldn't hit the curveball." He had also grown up knowing that his great-uncle was the second largest shareholder of the New York Mets, and at Yale he had had to contend with that inescapable picture of the Old Man, the one with Babe Ruth. Now he had the best seats in the house, the ultimate stage pass in Texas.

"It solved my biggest political problem in Texas. There's no question about it, and I knew it all along," he told a reporter. "My problem was 'What's the boy ever done?' I have to make a fairly big splash in the pool in order for people to recognize me. My pool has been expanded so much because of who my Dad is. The advantage is that everybody knows who I am. The disadvantage is that no matter how great my accomplishments may be, no one is going to give me credit for them."[64]

13

Amazing Grace

George W. had agreed to a March 1989 closed-door meeting with former Congressman Kent Hance, the man who had successfully attacked him as an effete northeasterner and a carpetbagger and had beat him in the 1978 congressional race. Since he had gone to Washington, Hance had undergone a political conversion experience not unlike that of other high-ranking, once-sworn Texas Democrats, including John Connally and Phil Gramm: he had moved to the Republican Party, and now he was desperately looking for a way into the governor's office. The GOP's growth in Texas, aided by the elder Bush's efforts in the 1960s, had continued. Hance wanted some information and reassurances from the president's son. Hance was still in office but as Texas railroad commissioner, a position that, for the most part, helps oversee Big-Oil concerns in the state.

In the Anatole Hotel in Dallas, a secure place preferred by both Ronald Reagan and Michael Jackson on their visits to the city, Hance told Bush in his thick Texas Panhandle accent that he was determined to run for governor in 1990. Anyone in politics knew that razor-tongued Ann Richards was rising as one of the Democratic nominees—and Hance knew how Bush felt about her after she had savaged his father in the 1988 campaign. But Hance also knew that the president's son was trying to raise his profile with the Texas Rangers. Hance had a hunch that the timing wasn't right—that it was too early for Bush to seek revenge on the whip-cracking Ann Richards. But Hance needed to know for sure that the president's first son, the one who hadn't declared he was running but was already showing such strong poll numbers in Texas, would get out of the way.

"I owe you one. If you want to run for governor, I will support you. But if you are not going to run, I want to run," Hance insisted.

"Well, I'm not in a position to tell you right now," Bush replied. Then he added, "But let's stay in touch."[1]

IN JUNE, a Dallas sports promoter had a bright idea: line up Texas sports owners and players and convince sports nut David Letterman to come to town and do his show. "Who is this guy, Letterman?" remarked Bush when he was told that he was one of the possible Texas people being lined up.[2] The next month, as he was preparing for the annual trip to Kennebunkport, a Mason-Dixon Poll showed that he was the leading gubernatorial choice of likely GOP voters. From the moment he had returned to Dallas, he had been meeting with the most influential state senators and representatives, leading Republicans who could open up avenues into the political power base that he really wanted: the affluent suburbs in Austin, Dallas, San Antonio, and Houston that were bursting with disenchanted white-collar families and California or East Coast transplants, voters who might nominally have been Democratic but could be swayed over to Republican family values. His mother had publicly gone on record as being opposed to his running. The net effect, of course, was that the Silver Fox became the foil—and how could the first son publicly disobey his mother, America's mother? She had publicly proclaimed that it was too soon, that George W. would be drowned by any reflected misery flowing downhill from the White House to Texas.

Bush's Texas advisers were still telling him that a perception of him as a Texas businessman, not just the son of a famous father, hadn't even remotely taken root. "I knew that any political future I might have would be very difficult as long as my father was president," Bush later said.[3] He needed real distance from his father in Texas—unlike Jeb in Florida, to which Jeb had moved and where he told people it had been a deliberate, conscious escape from his father's "shadow." In Florida, the Bush-Walker roots still ran deep, though not in overt involvement in state politics. Dorothy Walker Bush and other family members, including her two brothers, still spent part of the year on exclusive Jupiter Island, north of Palm Beach. In time, powerful businessmen such as IBM's CEO, Louis Gerstner, and Mobil's CEO, Rawleigh Warner, would come to the island enclave. Dorothy Walker Bush's home was set on the par-four, 355-yard fairway of the first hole at the Jupiter Island Club golf course; a church, Christ Memorial Chapel, sits on the seventh hole of the same golf course. In the 1990s, a study of housing prices in the United States showed that

Jupiter Island had the highest median housing price in the nation at $1.7 million.[4]

Meanwhile, there was Laura, who was still learning to tamp down the knots in her stomach when she was approached for a comment by the media or asked to speak to a civic group. She was still finding her way in Dallas and, the family knew, was an unproved asset. The ex-librarian was perfectly pleasant, certainly more controlled than George W., and she was completely in tune with the issues the first lady had made her own: reading and literacy. But could Laura campaign hard and efficiently, as determinedly as her mother-in-law, especially against a prairie heavyweight like Ann Richards? Laura's first political baby steps, her public appearances out in deep West Texas in 1978, were underwhelming. Back then no one was buzzing at the Petroleum Club about the stunning speech Laura had uncorked at the campaign appearance in Lubbock, Odessa, or Midland. She couldn't ad-lib as well as Barbara Bush, and if she was pressed to give a talk she was frequently worried about not having the speech in her hands. In a way, she too would be measured against her husband's parents and even family matriarch Dorothy Walker Bush.

George W. told the family he was going to clear up any messy mixed messages before he left the state for the annual Bush-Walker gathering at the Kennebunkport compound. On August 2, he gave a short, pointed speech before a lawyers' association in Dallas. Many of the lawyers had expected to hear him talk about the Texas Rangers and, hopefully, to share some Nolan Ryan stories. It was, in a way, the essence of the perception problem: to them he was just the new spokesman for the local baseball team and not a fully fledged political option among the hardened ultra-Texan candidates like Hance, Richards, or cowboy-hatted Midland oil millionaire Clayton Williams. That Tuesday night, August 1, he told the surprised lawyers, "I've decided at this time that I would not run for governor of Texas in 1990. For now, I want to focus on my job as the managing general partner of the Texas Rangers and more importantly as a good father and good husband."[5]

TWO WEEKS LATER, he was weighing his tee shot at the first hole at the Cape Arundel Golf Club near Kennebunkport. He was watching his dad's backswing. He and his father were squaring off in one of their hypercompetitive rounds of speeded-up golf where the two would sprint from their carts to the greens, trying to finish eighteen holes in under two hours. His father liked to call it "aerobic golf." George W. told the Old Man they were actually playing "polo golf." The two of them had a lot to talk about:

the poll numbers in Texas, the fact that Jeb was anxious to move beyond his job as secretary of commerce in Florida, what it all meant for the extended family. Plans were already under way to dispatch several Bush-Walker relatives abroad on official presidential delegations. In the first year and a half of the Bush administration, Bushes and Walkers helped lead fifteen of the forty-one presidential delegations that flew, usually on official U.S. Air Force jets, to special international ceremonies.

Nancy Bush Ellis would lead the U.S. delegation to Athens in honor of 2,500 years of democracy in Greece, and she represented her brother on a visit to the leaders of Western Samoa; Jonathan Bush represented his brother and the United States in the Ukraine during a ceremony marking attacks against Soviet Jews, and he also attended the 1989 presidential inauguration in Argentina; William "Bucky" Bush represented the United States during Malta's independence celebrations, and then traveled to Turkey to honor the patriarch of the Eastern Orthodox Church; Neil and his wife, along with a family nephew, were sent to Benin for presidential inauguration fetes; Prescott Bush Jr. flew to ceremonies in Bolivia; George W.'s sister, Dorothy, was going to Paraguay and Morocco.

Various cousins and nephews of the extended Bush-Walker family would also be sent around the globe: the president's nephew James L. Bush was sent to the swearing-in ceremony for the president of Guatemala; Suzanne Robinson, a Bush cousin, was sent to a ceremony dedicating a new hospital wing in Poland, an event that included Pope John Paul II and Polish President Lech Wałęsa. George W. and Laura were scheduled to travel to Gambia in the next few months, as head of the U.S. presidential delegation celebrating the twenty-fifth anniversary of that country's independence.[6]

"For a guy your age, you hit it pretty good," he told his father at the golf course. The Old Man mulled over George W.'s reference to his age. "For a guy my age," he repeated.

Two days later, with the five children and eleven grandchildren finally all assembled on Walker's Point, his father took the family boat back out with George W. and the twins. The speedboat's existence on the devastating cover of *Newsweek*, the one that suggested his father had been a "wimp," was still a sore point—a symbol of the perceptions of the Bushes and Walkers as anemic career politicians. Junior bet his father eleven dollars he wouldn't jump into the icy water. Without hesitating, his father stripped down to his bare chest and dived into the sixty-degree water. When he popped back out, he made sure to collect the money from the eight-year-old twins. Watching a network cameraman bobbing off in the distance on a chase boat, George W. had an idea. He turned and stared in the direction of the faraway boat with its high-power microphones and telephoto lenses guided by gyroscopes that defeated the rocking motion of the water.[7]

"I just want to make sure you can hear me," he said.

THE NEXT MONTH, Jack Anderson broke a story saying that hit men from Colombian drug cartels were roaming the United States and had targeted the president. Stories leaked by Washington intelligence officers said that the Bush children were now under extra Secret Service protection because they had been targeted for kidnapping. In Texas, George W. began arriving at the ballpark knowing that the guys in sunglasses and sport shirts, the ones without beers, the ones sprinkled incognito in various seats behind the Rangers' dugout, were all Secret Service detail. And at the occasional board meetings for Harken Energy, he'd fly into the room, grabbing hands, gulping coffee, and wagging a thumb over his shoulder to explain who the men in dark suits following him were.

Early in the new year, the investigation into Neil Bush and his role in the 1988 Silverado scandal, the collapse of one of Denver's largest savings and loan associations, was worse than a lingering distraction. George W., as always, spoke defiantly for the family. He shifted between anger and incredulity: Neil was "getting hosed" because his father happened to be president of the United States. "He's probably got the biggest heart in the family, and there's not a devious bone in his body," said George W.[8]

The April that the Silverado scandal was mushrooming, George W. flew to Midland to serve as his father's stand-in during the induction ceremonies into the Petroleum Hall of Fame. While he was in West Texas, a surprising announcement in obscure petroleum industry publications caught the attention of battered investors still trying to crawl out of the energy-sector swamp: Harken Energy had finalized a deal for its first international drilling operation off the island nation of Bahrain, fifty miles east of Saudi Arabia's famed Ghawar field, the largest oil reserve on the planet. Bush owned 345,000 shares of Harken, he was still on its board of directors, and he also sat on Harken's exploration advisory board. Oil analysts were stunned that bottom-feeding Harken, headquartered in a Dallas suburb, could hook such a meaty international contract over industry giant Amoco, which had been openly negotiating with Bahrain's oil ministers: not only hadn't Harken drilled overseas, it had never drilled in water.

Speculation immediately surged that it was because Bahrain wanted to do business with the son of the U.S. president. As the allegations unfolded, George W. became furious; he told people that he had predicted this would happen, that there would be "bad political fallout" if Harken drilled in the Middle East: "I expressed concern at the board meeting that the company not participate in a project overseas. I had absolutely nothing to do with the Bahrain deal."[9]

Oil insiders simply chalked it up to the salesmanship skills of Alan Quasha, another Harvard B School alumnus and Harken's chairman, who had previously lured in international billionaire investor George Soros. Since 1984, Quasha had steered Harken into trading commodities, making offers on oil refineries and buying a gas station chain that was alleged to have caused widespread groundwater and soil contamination. "There's been so much promotion, manipulation and inside dealmaking. It's been a fast-numbers game," said a bewildered Phil Kendrick, the wildcatter who had founded Harken in a tiny Texas funeral home years before and was now watching it try to drill in the Middle East.[10]

On June 22, 1990, Bush decided to dump two-thirds of his stake in Harken—212,140 shares at $4 a share for a total of $848,560 and two and a half times the original value of the stock. He told friends he needed the money to pay off the loans he had taken out to fund his 1.8 percent stake in the Texas Rangers. Six weeks after his trade, Iraq invaded Kuwait. Harken's share price nose-dived on concerns that the megadeal with Bahrain would be frozen by the tensions in the Middle East. Then, another two weeks later, Harken announced disastrous numbers in its quarterly report: losses heading to $21.8 million. The stock slumped lower, to $2.38. The company, some observers said, was hemorrhaging. Allegations would eventually emerge about the timing of Bush's sale, about whether he had had advance knowledge of Harken's significant drop in value, and the accusations would linger for at least the next nine years.

A week after his trade, Bush traveled to Fort Worth for the state GOP convention, stood to the side of the main stage in the Convention Center Arena, and was listening to a Texas Rangers–Boston Red Sox game over a small transistor radio held up to his ear. GOP gubernatorial nominee Clayton Williams, the wildly twanging millionaire oilman from Midland, was preparing to give his speech. Williams, running against Ann Richards, preferred wearing white cowboy hats, and he had unleashed TV ads in Texas in which he had promised to introduce drug dealers "to the joys of bustin' rocks" when he took office. Williams was already spending close to $12 million on his campaign and was leading by double digits in several polls. And now he was yodeling out his appreciation to staunch Texas GOP luminaries—"the great men who have transformed Texas into a Republican stronghold"—especially two people who had benefited from Karl Rove's handiwork: oilman turned governor Bill Clements and Democrat turned Republican senator Phil Gramm. As Williams stepped down from the stage, Bush put his transistor radio aside, approached the GOP gubernatorial candidate, and demanded to know why Williams hadn't thanked his father. The forty-four-year-old Bush "cussed Claytie out royally" said one of Williams' handlers.[11]

Immediately after the encounter at the side of the stage, GOP convention attendees suddenly saw and heard Williams stepping back to the microphone to announce that he had mistakenly left out one important thank-you.[12]

WEEKS LATER, and with the nation's attention focused on the tense events in the Middle East, only a few Washington politicos and powerful right-wing and Christian conservatives took note of the fact that the first son's "man" in the White House had unwillingly left his post as special assistant to President Bush after he was ordered out under orders from Chief of Staff John Sununu. In August, Deputy Chief of Staff Andy Card summoned Doug Wead and told him that he should leave—"sooner than later."[13]

His political demise had been set in motion three months earlier, when Wead had written an apologetic letter to conservative leaders on White House stationery after gay activists were invited to the White House signing ceremony for the "Hate Crimes" bill: "Quite frankly, the President's staff did not serve him well," Wead wrote. When word spread, there was a lingering negative reaction to the letter outside the White House. Wead had been increasingly monitored by vigilant Democrats, moderates, and liberals since he had set foot in the Bush administration and as he had evolved into the increasingly visible White House link to the hard right. Among the moderate, image-conscious White House staffers, Wead was already suspected of being an undisciplined opportunist, someone who had too much access to and influence on George W. and thus the president. A source in Sununu's office quietly told Wead that he would be "blamed" for the offensive letter, adding that somebody would have to take a fall, undergo a public execution.[14]

Wead, who had spent twenty years as an Assembly of God minister, had always felt that Sununu was trying to make the hard-edged conservative wing his own, that he resented Wead's influence on George W. and the president. Afraid for his political life, Wead called the only senior adviser to the president that he could trust: he talked to George W. "every day," and he had spent months, years even, instructing the first son on how to cultivate relationships with Weyrich, the Christian Right, Pat Robertson, Jerry Falwell, and Jim and Tammy Faye Bakker. During his tenure in the White House, he had continued the same extensive outreach work to the Christian right that he and George W. had begun on behalf of Team Bush in the mid-1980s. He had sent out dozens of reassuring letters from the White House to Falwell, Robertson, Gary Bauer, and almost every other important hard-edged conservative or Christian leader in the country. In one letter to Falwell, Wead had alluded to the early signs of an ideological power struggle in the Bush White House, the battle between the Reagan revolutionaries and the moderates:

> THE WHITE HOUSE . . . June 30, 1989 . . . Dear Jerry, The workload here is tremendous. The displays of personal ambition at the President's expense are sometimes very discouraging. What helps me is the knowledge that the President cares very deeply about you and others who did so much to help him. If I'm needed here it's to make sure you and others are looked after and heard from. . . . Thanks for everything . . . please, give me a call when you have a chance. . . . Doug Wead.[15]

Now, after he reached George W. in Dallas, Wead said that Sununu's office would try to call George W. on the Friday before they did the firing; people in the upper ranks of the White House obviously knew that Wead was George W.'s "man," and they would want to give the first son advance warning. George W. said he would fly to Washington immediately.

"If they call me Friday, they will get me at Camp David, and I will be with the president and he is not going to be pleased," Wead heard George W. say. "You want me to fire somebody? What do you want?"[16]

The evangelist and Amway representative who had slavishly worked for Team Bush for years, acting as a guide, translator, and missionary demurred. He knew the forty-four-year-old Bush was really hoping he wouldn't call in a favor. Wead agreed to leave his $55,000-a-year post as special assistant to the president relatively quietly—and after he did he composed a fruitless memo asking Craig Fuller whether there might be a chance of an ambassadorship for an old, loyal Christian soldier on Team Bush—maybe to one of the tiny countries?—maybe to Barbados?—maybe to Lesotho? Wead, who had been handpicked by the first son, had once arranged for Falwell, Robertson, Paul Crouch, and dozens of other insistent, suspicious evangelicals to gather in the White House for a closed-door briefing in late 1989, complete with appearances by the president, the vice president, and Chief of Staff John Sununu. In the upper echelons of the Christian Right, people talked for months about that day, about how George W.'s aide Doug Wead had established a first-time-ever beachhead in the Oval Office. And when Wead was banished, Gary Bauer, Richard Viguerie, James Dobson, and other influential conservative gurus dutifully made note of his departure, some of them suggesting that the Bush administration was finally showing its spinelessness.

When Wead packed up and moved out of his office, he was sure he would be openly discredited by one of Sununu's aides. But he heard that George W. had warned Sununu's office, "Leave Wead alone. Don't touch him."[17]

Wead liked to think that because of his firing some small part of the younger Bush would always be inclined to dislike John Sununu—that maybe, in some small way, George W. would exact revenge on Sununu. For years after he was banished from Washington, Wead would continue to regularly advise, call, and fax the first son. George W. had awarded him the highest Bush compliment: *Wead was a Good Man.*

"Sometimes in White House circles, people have knives out for you. I think Doug got caught up in that. I always thought Doug Wead was an ally for my Dad. He was a good man to have around," said George W.[18]

LOYALTY, thought the new commissioner of baseball, was hard to come by. Fay Vincent, the old family friend who had roughnecked in Midland while living at the Bush house with George W., had taken over as commissioner after Yalie Bart Giamatti died. Vincent was almost immediately at odds for endless, slippery reasons with warring factions of ego-bloated owners. Many of the owners began avoiding and finally derided Vincent, but George W. was the first and sometimes the only one to defend Vincent at league meetings.

Vincent, beleaguered and isolated, was grateful. By the summer of 1990, it was all about loyalty: Vincent, after all, was an FOB, someone they had let live in their damned house in Midland.[19] The commissioner liked being around Bush in his seats behind the dugout; Bush had still deliberately decided to be where everyone could see him, and it remained an ongoing publicity miracle. The cameras were constantly whirling in his direction, and every night he forked over dozens more of the cards he had made up with his name and picture on them—almost as if he were up on stage again with the Bush Bluebonnet Belles, the Blount Belles, and handing out campaign literature to anybody who came walking by. Nor did he seem to mind when one of his oil friends from Midland settled back into his seat and gleefully reported that the men's-room floor was littered with Bush baseball cards.

The day-to-day baseball operations of the Texas Rangers were being handled by general manager Tom Grieve and ultimately by Tom Schieffer, a former state representative who had joined the investment group. By design, Bush's principal work was as a roving goodwill ambassador, a highly connected public relations person, a promoter for a new baseball stadium and a loyalty monitor—many of the same functions he had fulfilled in Washington. Longtime Texas observers of the family said that, in effect, the role was the same one that his father had fulfilled at the United Nations: mingling, relaying messages from the management group, keeping a convivial dialogue open. Vincent thought it was invaluable to a struggling franchise, a perpetually inept team completely overshadowed by the presence of America's Team, the Dallas Cowboys.

Bush would make the batboy run off to get him some more sunflower seeds or bubble gum and demand, in the Spanish he had picked up at Andover, that the Hispanic ballplayers give him a hit. And with the commissioner of baseball next to him, he would yell at Rafael Palmeiro: "Hey, Raffy, the commissioner is tired! Why don't you hit a home run?" Of course, Raffy would uncork a home run and coolly tip his cap when he jogged past first base. Bush was an omnipresent figure in the locker room and at the batting cage, gravitating, like most people in the stadium, toward Nolan Ryan, the lanky, lionized strikeout king from tiny Alvin, Texas, the one bona fide Hall of Famer on the team and arguably the best-known athlete in the state. It was openly speculated that Ryan harbored his own political aspirations in Texas, that he might just win whatever he ran for, and Bush studied him: "There is a brilliance in his simplicity . . . it accentuates why Texans see him as such a hero."[20]

IN APRIL 1991, the Securities and Exchange Commission announced that Bush had reported his sale of Harken stock eight months after the official federal deadline for filing notice of an insider trade. According to SEC regulations, he had been required to report the trade by July 10, 1990. Bush said that he had filed the papers but that they had been misplaced by the SEC; the SEC, in turn, said it couldn't find any missing paperwork. The alleged violation of SEC laws rippled through several publications, and his entire relationship with Harken was thoroughly reexamined, including the other allegations that he must have known that Harken's stock was going to crash because he was a valued member of the board of directors who had recently been asked to weigh the restructuring of the firm.

"I'm not a wealthy man. When I need money, I sell assets," he said.[21] "I'm not a punk kid. I've lived in the fishbowl a long time and have lawyers who review everything I do before I do it."[22]

As the SEC investigation into the stock trade slogged on, his father had decided to set the first son on his most important White House mission. At the end of October, the elder Bush composed a discreet letter and sent it to his eight closest, most trusted political advisers: Mosbacher, Baker, Malek, and the others he was convinced were utterly loyal. He had suspicions about Sununu, the ambitious chief of staff and the man some staffers suggested was dead set on exercising maximum control over the White House. There had been rumors and bits of evidence that he was too independent, a distraction, no longer blindly faithful. The outside criticism about a conflicted, internally troubled White House was now beginning to ooze inside the Oval Office. The elder Bush was beginning to gear up for reelection, but his numbers were slipping. The media was piling on, poking, prodding at Quayle, at Neil, at George W.

There was a gnawing sense that President Bush was distracted, marching in place, still trying to live down everything from the "wimp factor" to his infamous promise to read his lips when he had said "No new taxes." When his letter was delivered to his trusted advisers on the last day of the month, it must have read like a disquieting plea for reassurance—and it was hard to miss the name of the man he had appointed to serve as the king's listening post: "I have asked son George to very quietly make some soundings for me on 1992. I'd appreciate it if you'd visit with him on your innermost thoughts about how to best structure the campaign," the letter said. "My plan is still to wait—defer final campaign structural decisions until after the first of the year at least; but there seems to be a fair amount of churning around out there."[23]

Even after Doug Wead had been ordered out of the White House, George W. had remained publicly unswerving in his support of Sununu. With Wead gone, Sununu represented the best opportunity to keep the ties open to the evangelicals, the Christian Right, the hard conservatives. But by November, half the Cabinet was refusing to speak to Sununu and White House staffers were muttering about Sununu's snap decisions to cancel presidential appearances. Even Sununu's own political advisers, including Charlie Black, had pulled him aside and told him to slow down, to make peace with the Cabinet. By November, Sununu knew he was in trouble. One of his friends talked to him and walked away knowing that he understood he would have to resign but was procrastinating.

In his office building in north Dallas, forty-five-year-old George W. was hearing all about the erosion of confidence. Then, in November, he received a call from a staffer relaying the fact that Sununu had just been on TV suggesting that the president had "ad-libbed" during a speech. The elder Bush had said that banks should lower credit card interest rates, and almost immediately, the financial markets had swooned. Sununu hadn't defended the Old Man. He hadn't jumped on the grenade. "We have a saying in our family. If a grenade is rolling by The Man, you dive on it first. The guy violated the cardinal rule,"[24] George W. told the staffer who delivered the update on the latest breach of loyalty. Sununu was already drowning in embarrassing allegations that he had developed a royalty complex, that he was bending the White House guidelines on the personal use of government-owned jets and limousines. Sununu would have to go. George W. flew to Washington, armed with the responses to his father's letter. Republican National Chairman Rich Bond hadn't held back when he communicated with George W.: "I told him what an idiot I thought John Sununu was."[25] Only Malek had voted to keep Sununu on Team Bush. But Malek knew what would happen, and he knew why George W. would be the one to handle things when he arrived in Washington: "George W. knew in his heart that his dad's desire would be that John would step down."[26]

Sitting in Sununu's office in the West Wing of the White House, George W. was blunt. "I'm not speaking for my father. I'm not a messenger. But the way things are going, it might be in everybody's interest if you would step aside," he said, according to one of Sununu's close friends. Then George W. suggested that Sununu go see his father.

George W. flew back to Texas to prepare for his father's reelection campaign. Sununu resigned on December 3 and George W. had achieved what his father had wanted in his heart but couldn't bring himself to do directly by firing Sununu. George W. had gotten the White House chief of staff to do what a Good Man—an FOB—would do. "He knew what his father wanted without being asked," said Malek.[27]

BACK IN DALLAS, George W. was staring out his ninth-floor office window in the spring of 1992. Pat Buchanan had put the fear of God in the campaign by squeezing out 37 percent of the vote in the New Hampshire primary. After New Hampshire, trying to find out what the hell had happened, the elder Bush had called two people: George W. and conservative sounding board William Bennett. They had told the president the same thing: the right wing was being stolen, the president was in danger of having the hard-core bedrock ripped out from under him.

The son had wondered what it would take to get his father's campaign up to speed. It was a pleasant time of year, really the only pleasant time of year in Dallas, just weeks away from the smothering blanket of 100-degree days. Across the street, he could see people bustling into and out of another office. They were weighed down with signs, boxes of bumper stickers, and posters for Ross Perot and his nagging, hard-to-define army of volunteers springing up in suburban zones and rural outposts of California, Colorado, and Texas. Bush stared harder. People were pulling up, running inside to pick up stickers, and slapping them on their cars. The parking lot was jammed. As he told a friend in Dallas, he reached for the phone, called his father at the White House, and said, "I want to tell you what's going on outside my window. We've got a problem here. The lot is like ten cars deep with people stopping to get bumper stickers. You can't write this guy off."[28]

Driving home, he found it hard to miss the Perot petition-signing booth just a few blocks from the house. Finally at home, he stood on the curb with Lawson Pedigo, a federal prosecutor who lived three houses down. Pedigo was trying to make small talk, steering toward neutral chitchat about the military and the Gulf War. Without warning, without segue, and almost as a non sequitur, Bush began blurting out praise of his father—"the best commander in chief since World War II"—and Pedigo was knocked off guard, not sure why Bush had been so abrupt.[29]

Not long after, a busload of laughing Perot volunteers decided, hell, why not go to the Texas Rangers' ballpark and sign up some Perot backers right in front of President Bush's son? The Perot "movement" was, in Dallas, seemingly omnipresent on the streets and in the media. The Perot Army volunteers gathered a thousand signatures before security guards arrived and they were ordered off the property.

IN DALLAS, George W. tried hard to immerse himself in the correct profile-raising things in between the constant tugs of going on Dutiful First Son missions and making appearances in Washington. In May, he listened to his mother tell Queen Elizabeth II—his father's thirteenth cousin—over lunch that she had deliberately seated her first son and Laura at the end of the table and ordered him not to address the royalty. "Are you the black sheep in the family?" asked Queen Elizabeth.

"I guess that might be true," he said.

"Well, I guess all families have one," replied the queen. When the queen asked Barbara what made him the black sheep, his mother said that he always said what he felt and wore what he wanted, including cowboy boots with TEXAS or GOD BLESS AMERICA on them. When the queen asked him which ones he was going to wear at that night's lavish state dinner, he quickly answered, "Neither. Tonight's pair will say GOD SAVE THE QUEEN."[30]

Back in Dallas, George W. and the family were fixtures at the Highland Park United Methodist Church, one of the most powerful, best-endowed congregations in the country. He joined the Ambassadors Forum, a group of CEOs and politicians who promoted Dallas as an "international" city and whose ranks included oilman Ray Hunt, investor Harold Simmons, Texas Instruments executive Jerry Junkins, and Dallas Cowboys owner Jerry Jones. He lent his name to the Wesley-Rankin Center, a nonprofit group that offered extensive child care, tutoring, and other services to Mexican-American residents on the city's struggling west side. He also quickly agreed to join the board of Paul Quinn College, a historically black college on the forgotten far south side of the segregated city and whose buildings were crumbling and whose finances were in shambles. As usual, Bush was asked to make some calls, raise some cash. He and Laura organized their first black-tie fund-raiser at the symphony hall in Dallas, one of the cornerstones of the patrician, almost old-South way of power broking in the city, and it featured Dionne Warwick and Danny Glover. But the school kept fading, to the point that the IRS warned the institution that it would be held liable for not paying payroll taxes. The Southern Association of Colleges placed Paul Quinn on probation, federal funding was drying up, and by 1992 the school was worse off than it had ever been. The place almost looked abandoned; its walls were falling down and the weeds were forehead high. One fellow board member, an accountant brought in to help the situation, said that the formerly ubiquitous, helpful Bush was no longer as visible.

"He backed out and quit helping. He disappeared. He got very nervous because his father was in the middle of a campaign. I think he was a little concerned that if it didn't work out, he didn't want to have his name in the newspaper associated with an institution that wasn't paying federal payroll taxes," said Jette Campbell, a partner at the KPMG Peat Marwick accounting firm who assisted Paul Quinn for another year, flying back every three weeks or so from London, where he was employed. In early 1992, after less than a year on the board, Bush resigned.[31]

AT THE SAME TIME George W. quit Paul Quinn College, two other board members and friends of George W. also resigned: Comer Cottrell, head of the Pro-Line Corporation and the most influential black businessman in Texas, and Alphonso Jackson, the head of the Dallas Housing Authority. The two men were the first son's strongest links to the African-American community in Texas, and Bush had asked Cottrell to invest in a percentage of the Texas Rangers. The ownership group was exactly like all the others in baseball, dominated by older white men, and it would be good to have some visible diversity in the face of emerging, national accusations over the lack of minority management.

Cottrell agreed to invest a half-million dollars. He knew about visibility and perceptions, he knew that Bush had been made the managing general partner "because of his high profile."[32] As soon as he joined, he was anxious to see how Bush would handle the increasing allegations from minority leaders in the Dallas–Fort Worth area that the upper management of the Rangers was playing racist politics when it came to offering jobs and contracts to minorities—especially as Bush took on a role that almost every other single investor assiduously avoided: promoting $135 million in controversial tax and bond proposals that could help fund a new stadium. For years, the impossibly interwoven plans to build a ballpark at Arlington turned into a shrill debate. Accusations were coursing through North Texas that land was being condemned unfairly, that the Rangers were sucking up sweetheart tax subsidies and "corporate welfare," that they had conducted unfair bidding practices aimed at excluding minority participation.

Bush, still the public face of the publicity-shy management group, went to the largest black church near the proposed new stadium and gave a spirited speech about why people should support a half-cent sales tax to fund construction. At Mount Olive Baptist, the head of the local NAACP branch was instantly wary about why the president's son was pushing so hard. He wanted to see serious proof that minorities would be offered construction contracts. "I resented him coming into a church," said Harry Gugder.[33] He called Cottrell, who promised to see what he could do to convince Bush and the ownership group to make contracts available. Cottrell asked the first son to come to his office for a meeting. "It's important that we show we are making an effort," Cottrell said.[34]

Bush agreed to follow Cottrell's suggestion that they hire an African-American vice president of community affairs to aid in the bidding process, but the move barely silenced the rumblings; the leaders of two other Texas NAACP chapters and the League of United Latin American Citizens also demanded more contracts. Gugder increasingly became more furious and told people that he was laying the blame with the president's son: "They had very few minority contractors. So small, I don't think that I could name them. People of color are getting tired of hearing a lot of lip service and not seeing any action."[35]

Cottrell thought that Bush had handled the confrontation as best he could. "What happened is, in my evaluation, people didn't really know the process of how to bid," he said. "I know a lot of people, because he is a Republican, tend to think he might be a racist. He's anything but that."[36] The bond issue passed by a two-to-one margin and plans were announced to have the stadium open in time for the 1994 season.

BY THE SUMMER OF 1992, Bush had finally joined the ranks of high-ranking GOP advisers who were talking to the president about the politically risky move of dumping Dan Quayle and finding somebody else to be his running mate: Colin Powell, Bob Dole, or Dick Cheney, perhaps. By the summer, he had also seen the latest numbers showing that 40 percent of voters were clearly against his father. And outside his window in north Dallas, he could still hear, right in front of him, the insistent drumbeats from Ross Perot—stealing away hearts, minds, and money right in the Dallas bastion of the GOP. George W. didn't like the way any of the unpredictable business with Perot was going—why people in the White House, in Washington, hadn't seen this third-party juggernaut coming. He also didn't like the way people were drawing lines between the SEC investigation into Harken and his father; in June, he resigned as director and consultant for Harken. Now, late in the campaign, he began working almost exclusively on the reelection effort. Some Washington observers said it was already too late, and they wondered if his own political ambition, nurturing his public image through his fractional ownership of the Texas Rangers, had kept him away at the exact time his father needed him most.

George W. had reportedly harbored some misgivings about Bob Teeter, who was helping orchestrate the reelection effort against Bill Clinton. The first son could tell there were confusion and too many missing links in the upper echelon. It was nothing at all, he thought, like the smooth-running, post-Reagan, loyal group who had put his father into the White House in 1988. George W. told his father he would have been better served by somebody with managerial skills, somebody like ex–Secretary of Transportation Sam Skinner, who had taken Sununu's place as White House chief of staff. His father ignored the advice.[37]

George W. began commuting regularly from Dallas . . . the buzz was loud when the campaign staff heard from schedulers that he was coming to "shake things up." It was clear what he wanted when he settled at the table for high-level strategy sessions with Skinner, Teeter, Malek, Bush spokesman Marlin Fitzwater, campaign political director Mary Matalin, pollster Fred Steeper, and Budget Director Dick Darman.

"He has his father's agenda in mind at all times, and he pursues it relentlessly" was how Craig Fuller once analyzed it. George W. boiled it down for a reporter wondering what he could possibly do to help his father: he would be the discriminating messenger, the last chance to get a memo or plan to the president. He knew that his role had taken on a strange life of its own; people who heard him talking about even a mundane topic were trying to read into it and fearing the worst: "Access is power in Washington. Okay? And I had more access than anybody to George Bush."[38]

When the Team Bush 1992 inner circle gathered in Room 180 of the drab, standard-issue Old Executive Office Building, Marlin Fitzwater could feel the strained mood, as if no one wanted to be there, as if none of the people in the room respected one another. Fitzwater, maybe more than anyone else, had come to the belief that the Bush campaign hadn't lost focus—how could it? It had never had a focus to begin with. As Steeper glumly kept arriving with the latest polls showing that Bill Clinton's and Ross Perot's numbers were bobbing forward, the president had ordered the team to give him a detailed progress report every Thursday afternoon.

By the fourth roundtable session with the president, Fitzwater was almost dizzy, seesawing between anger and hopelessness. He jotted down a note and handed it to George W., knowing full well that going through George W. was the best backdoor way to get a direct answer from the president. George W. looked at the scribbled message from the increasingly discontented Fitzwater: "When do we get a campaign plan?"

The first son waited until midway through the meeting to demand an answer to the question. The reply was a not entirely convincing one: "Soon."[39]

IN JUNE, *The Washington Post* released its poll showing President Bush finishing third behind Clinton and Perot. As the numbers continued to slip, the campaign's fractious power brokers paid more attention to internal allegiances. George W. talked to his father about the people who had to go, about the people who either weren't throwing themselves on the grenade or were simply dragging his father down. He told his father that the overly intellectual Richard Darman, the man many people were fingering for President Bush's devastating invitation for people to "read my lips" about new taxes, would have to be dumped. There was a growing consensus that Darman had become a liability, and almost everyone that George W. had worked so hard to cultivate for the Bush White House, all the steely conservatives and evangelicals, were clamoring for some heads. With the campaign skittering out of control, Teeter, Quayle, and George W. had all come to the same conclusion. "We're supposed to be the pros. But so far, we can't get it right," George W. complained to a staffer.

He knew what the solution was, but he wouldn't want to broach it even with his father. What his father needed, almost more than anyone else, was Jim Baker—the quintessential loyalist, the unflappable presence from Texas, an outside force whose sheer magnitude could lend stability and gravity to the campaign. Teeter talked to the first son, the backdoor man, pleading with him to talk to his father—to argue that his father *needed* to call Baker, to bring him back into the White House. George W. agreed that Baker would be welcome cavalry, but even though he had openly confronted his father about all the other high-level changes, he wasn't going to touch this one. He also wasn't going to rush to his father's defense by taking over the campaign himself. The relationship between Baker and the entire Bush-Walker family was richer and more complex than anyone in the White House or Washington could know; it traversed decades of politics, religion, and big money in Houston and the Northeast, and it was bound up with the very formation of the modern Republican Party in Texas.

George W. told Teeter he wouldn't lobby the president about James Baker—Darman, maybe, but not Baker: "I don't have the brass to tell my Old Man how to run his White House," said George W.[40]

MARY MATALIN, a consummate political survivor who had one of the better handles on what loyalty meant in the Bush family and who had assumed Atwater's role as the campaign's media seducer, knew it was a good idea to gravitate toward George W.'s corner as the race slipped into Bill Clinton's hands. In a foggy, backstabbing political environment, it was smart to be aligned with the king's son, his senior adviser. Like Matalin, George W. was blunt. He had told her once that the women in the White

House didn't want her being promoted so high in the campaign—that they thought she didn't have the Bush decorum, the White House code of comportment. But they'd gotten over it, and Matalin, like Atwater, was sometimes allowed to call him "Junior." He told people that she had "the best political antennae on our side."[41]

Matalin had met Junior in 1981, after she had moved to Washington. In the 1988 campaign, along with everyone else, she had deferred to him: "first among equals—he wasn't the campaign manager, but he definitely could trump anybody else on the campaign," she said. Matalin could tell that the person the president trusted most was his first son, and by 1992, even though George W. wasn't in Washington as much as in 1988, Matalin talked about him as a wickedly confident authority figure, bold about both internal and external strategy, a true, fully formed "political campaign terrorist" who wasn't afraid to take prisoners when he flew in from Dallas. "He is not as ham-handed as the typical terrorist," said Matalin. "He's much more of a stiletto as opposed to an ax murderer. He comes into a room, you know he's there."[42]

It was clear that the campaign was also suffering from Lee Atwater's absence. Atwater had succumbed to cancer on Good Friday 1991, and at his funeral on April Fool's Day, soul man James Brown had mingled with Dan Quayle and others. Even in death, Atwater seemed unabashedly unafraid of merging seemingly disparate pieces of the new political puzzle. The death of George W.'s political mentor, more than one staffer lamented, had stripped the reelection effort of the only strategist who would have known how to respond to the obvious anti-Washington, anti-Bush sentiments that were keeping Clinton and Perot aloft. Matalin, for one, had decided that the younger Bush had learned his lessons well from Atwater; she considered him and Atwater to be political equals. "They were equally skilled strategists," she said.[43]

In mid-July 1992, George Walker Bush took a fund-raising trip to Missouri, not to stump for his father George Herbert Walker Bush but to campaign for George Herbert Walker III. The president's first cousin and the chief executive of the Stifel, Nicolaus & Co. brokerage house in St. Louis was yet another family member involved in a political race: running for the GOP nomination in the Second Congressional District. In the caretaker, noblesse oblige spirit of the family patriarchs, Walker had announced that voters would be best served by a "citizen-legislator" such as himself. In St. Louis, people who watched Walker said that he sounded remarkably like his famous cousin; and his GOP rivals, taking note of George W.'s arrival in Missouri, instantly dubbed Walker a complete insider with ties to the "Washington establishment." Walker responded that he wasn't a Bush "clone" and that he had tried to avoid the burden of the Bush-Walker name by asking that his name appear as Bert Walker on the ballot.[44]

UNLIKE IN 1988, George W. didn't have a full-time office presence in Washington, but he could walk into any meeting anytime he felt like it. Malek secretly wished that George W. had moved to Washington instead of being in Texas so much; he wanted him around the same way the first son wanted James Baker around. Having the first son would remind the disparate forces what the real mission was. Some people were still wondering what had kept George W. in Texas so long. Having the first son there all the time in the high-stakes game would have been good—at least you knew your message would go where you hoped it would. "If you needed to get a particular message to his father or if you felt that you had a selling job to do, he was always there," said Malek.[45]

By July, the younger Bush told his father that they would need to skip the annual vacation to Kennebunkport—and that Team Bush needed to remember the Right, the conservatives, the people who had put Republicans in the White House in 1980. He was still trying to fend off the Ross Perot tide, the gathering movement emanating from Dallas, of all places, and moving outside the normal political boundaries. It was as imprecise and hard to define as the evangelical movement, and the younger Bush was annoyed at the strident accusations emanating from somewhere inside the Perot camp that the president's first son was using below-the-belt dirty tricks to derail the Dallas billionaire. George W. made sure that everyone knew he had named his golf cart "Perot": *you could just never tell if it was going to run or not.* And he made sure that Tom Luce, the powerful Dallas attorney and Perot's onetime campaign manager, enjoyed a visit to the White House—in Texas, some people were saying that the buttoned-down Luce was seriously thinking of running for governor.

By the time of the 1992 GOP convention in Houston, some of the highest-level members of Team Bush were already viewing it as a sun-baked pause on a meandering march to the inevitability of Bill Clinton beating George Bush—and reducing him to the one-term-president level of Jimmy Carter. Seventy-one members of the Bush-Walker family arrived in Houston, most of them checking in at the lavish Warwick Hotel or the Houstonian Hotel, where President Bush had maintained his Texas residency by renting an apartment. George W. and his brothers worked the convention hard, coordinating events and appearances for several others in the family; dozens of Bush-Walker family members served as delegates or surrogates at GOP functions spread across the city—"working like dogs," said Aunt Nancy Bush Ellis. In strategy sessions, a decision was made to have at least twenty-five members of the Bush-Walker clan step onto the Astrodome stage during "Family Values Night." Even with the sniping rising in the campaign, with the complaints that the candidate was unfocused and that the high-level staff changes had frozen strategists into indecision, it was, at least, a useful big-time coming-out party for future gubernatorial candidates Jeb and George—sitting with Arnold Schwarzenegger and Maria Shriver, being hustled by a scheduler to one of the dozens of back-to-back interviews.

The conflicted relationship between Team Bush and the media was accented by the omnipresent T-shirts and buttons on the convention floor advising people to "Annoy the Media, Vote for Bush." When George W. sat with Larry King, he said that he loathed the media cynics, he wanted them to apologize, the ones like Maureen Dowd from *The New York Times* who were getting it all wrong, or Strobe Talbott at *Time*, who had graduated from Yale the same year as George W.

When George W. did his dance with Dan Rather, whom the president had once blown up at when he thought Rather was baiting him, the interview began like a rooster's arcing barnyard strut. "It's a pleasure to be with such a star," said a grinning George W. when Rather approached him at the base of the presidential box in the Houston Astrodome.

"That was going to be my line to you," replied Rather instantly.

"*The New York Times* and all these East Coast press who say that George Bush isn't ready to fight are wrong," said George W. He told Rather that he wanted the paper to apologize to his father for its "outrageous" coverage and that Rather, "being a good Texas boy that you are" had to agree.

"Of course, it's not my job to agree or disagree, outrage or otherwise," said Rather.

"Well, excuse me," said George W. He added that "we've got people in the Clinton camp who are saying unkind things about my dad. A few of them are saying unkind things about a nice fellow like me."

At the end of the interview, George W. beamed at Rather. "You're not as bad a guy as they say you are, you know that?"

"I'm glad you think so. Do me a favor," said Rather. "Tell your mother hello for me."[46]

Later, at a scheduled stop with Brian Mullahy from KSL-TV in Salt Lake City there was a different encounter—maybe not enough *feisting out.*

Bush suddenly ripped the microphone off his coat—"That's it, buddy!"—and stormed away from the cameras before they had even really gotten started. Mullahy was gingerly trying to open the door to questions about the way reporters were treating the Republicans, the way the Republicans felt reporters were chasing after rumors about the president. "Listen—you know, if you want to try to do this to me then I'm not going to talk to you," said George W., stabbing his finger at Mullahy. Mullahy chased after him and tried to apologize, but Mullahy and the other reporters from his station were instantly cut out of the Team Bush loop. The station's scheduled interview with Barbara Bush was canceled, as was every other interview with any big name in the campaign.[47]

BY SEPTEMBER, George W. told Malek that he was worried, that his father had started the campaign too late. Even after the testosterone-enhancing public relations bounce from Desert Storm, his father and the family couldn't shake that same old image baggage, the sense that the Bushes and Walkers were still too preppy, too wimpy, too rich, too out of touch with real, working Americans. His father tried to cheer him up: "I'm gonna win this election. Make no mistake about it. I'm gonna win."[48]

The first week of October, George W. bleakly sat at a bipartisan banquet and listened to people howling with laughter as Texas Governor Ann Richards craftily told a slowly building joke about how hunters sometimes dress up as a "bush" or "harem rejects" or "the Chicago Bears in really bad drag" when they want to lure a turkey: "A bird in the hand may be worth two in the bush, but a bush in disguise is worth watching."[49]

The last four weeks before the election, tempers ran high in the entire inside circle. Loyalties were openly questioned. And when George W. went to a Washington law office to rally a campaign team dubbed the "Bush-Quayle Lawyers" people were surprised to hear him suddenly attack GOP Senator Alfonse D'Amato, saying he'd like to "wring his neck" for not being more loyal to his father.[50]

On the last day of the campaign, he stood rocking back and forth, flushed with anger, out on a tarmac in New Jersey. A wary Mary Matalin and a perplexed John Harwood from *The Wall Street Journal* were right there, and George W. was muttering to Harwood, this time about a story about the Bush children and their business dealings that had run in *The Wall Street Journal*. Matalin didn't know where it was all headed. Nor did Harwood. He hadn't written the story, and he had never met George W. Bush before.[51]

On *Air Force One*, George W. settled into his seat. The rest of the family was there. George W. was miserable with the media: as far back as the "W" cover, the "wimp" cover, they had never understood how moral his father could be—and, worse, they had said he was a loser, that this campaign was over before it had started. Clinton, they were saying, had aced his father at generational politics, at all those hip, New Politics things that Atwater had seen coming, all that Atwater business of effectively selling a human persona to baby boomers. George W. knew that his father felt it had been simply the worst year of his long political life.

Just days earlier, in the middle of the withering campaign, in the middle of the crumbling, disorderly kingdom, his father had come across a black-and-white photograph of Prescott Bush in his files; shot from a low angle, Prescott looked like a huge, stern-faced statue with a brilliant white handkerchief elegantly emerging out of the breast pocket of his imposing suit. "Golf's Leader for 1935," it said underneath, as if Prescott had been the only one. The Old Man liked this orderly photograph from when Prescott Bush was head of the United States Golf Association and thought that maybe George W. would like to have it.

He had ordered it sent to Dallas from the White House right away: *Dear George: Someone gave me this shot of Dad that I thought you might like to have for your scrapbook. . . . Devotedly, Dad.*[52]

Now, on *Air Force One*, people could hear the slow, throaty sound of the Oak Ridge Boys. They had been traveling with the family, stumping for a campaign that was giving ground to Bill Clinton, and now they were harmonizing, slipping into one sonorous gospel song after another. And when they started singing the ultimate going-to-the-hereafter anthem, "Amazing Grace," George W. and his father began to sing along. The two were in tears, and his father said the song had made him think about his father—about Prescott Bush.

14

A Dog with a Bone

In the fall of 1992, Bush began to meet every six weeks
with Alphonso Jackson at an Italian restaurant near
Northwest Highway in Dallas. Jackson, the head of
the Dallas Housing Authority, was godfather to Supreme Court Justice
Clarence Thomas's only son and a leading black GOP leader in Texas.
Jackson could serve as a behind-the-scenes adviser for candidates wanting
to put a dent in Governor Ann Richards's enormous popularity among minorities—Texas blacks and Hispanics had never had the access to state
power they now had under the Richards administration. Since he had
moved to Dallas in 1988, Bush was simply doing what his father had done
in the 1950s in Midland, but on a statewide scale. With Karl Rove's help,
he targeted key state lawmakers and public officials such as Jackson, and he
embarked upon what was essentially a quiet but whirlwind courtship. Jackson, who had served with Bush on the board of Paul Quinn College, could
be an ally. Bush needed help in the minority community, and not just with
raising votes. Jesse Jackson was coming to Dallas, ready to hold a press
conference to announce that he was serious about starting a boycott of
major-league baseball if the teams didn't improve their minority hiring.

Alphonso Jackson was never guarded around Bush; "George, I know
you ran for Congress—have you ever thought about running for governor? The best time to run against somebody is when they're at their best,"
said Jackson.

"I looked at it last time," said Bush, "but no."[1]

IN THE DAYS after Clinton's election, George W. had been maybe the
worst some people had ever seen him; the seam-bursting energy, what

people on the receiving end called arrogance, wasn't there. He thought about running the Dallas marathon around White Rock Lake but skipped it because he had a head cold. Then, on Thursday, November 19, shortly after 5 P.M., ninety-one-year-old Dorothy Walker Bush died at the family house in Greenwich, Connecticut. She had outlived Prescott Bush by twenty years. A few years earlier, her son, then the vice president, had written a Mother's Day article for the *Greenwich Times:* "Every mother has her own style. My mother's was a little like an Army drill sergeant's. . . . I can hear her now: 'You can do it. You'll get it. You'll get it.' . . . She also tamed our arrogance. I'll never forget years ago, saying rather innocently, I thought, 'I was off my game.' Mother jumped all over me. 'You are just learning. You don't have a game.' "[2]

More than a hundred mourners assembled for the private funeral service in Greenwich at the Christ Episcopal Church, where the Walkers had been members for more than four decades. For the last twenty years, since Prescott Bush had died, Dorothy Walker Bush had had a carefully regulated schedule: She traveled from the family estate in Greenwich, Connecticut, to the enclave on Jupiter Island in Florida every November; then, after spending the winter at the Florida home, she would return to Greenwich in May; then she would move to the family compound in Kennebunkport from July through August. Her children, especially daughter Nancy, said that the ferociously competitive Dorothy Walker Bush had never been the same since Prescott Bush had died.[3]

Now, under sunny skies, President Bush and his security detail arrived by motorcade from Westchester County Airport and stepped to the front rows for the forty-five-minute service. White House Chief of Staff James A. Baker III, old family friend and Treasury Secretary Nicholas Brady, and Vice President Dan Quayle were there, along with dozens of Bush-Walker relatives. Prescott Bush Jr. read a letter his mother had written about the importance of her spiritual beliefs; two organists played; three clergymen, including the primate of the Episcopal Church of the United States, presided over the prayers. After a luncheon at the Bush-Walker home, George W. and the rest of the family departed to Putnam Cemetery for the burial services. Her ashes were placed alongside the markers for her husband, Prescott, and George W.'s sister Robin.

NOT LONG after the funeral, George W. decided he would start training for the Houston-Tenneco marathon. Maybe that would help erase the memories of what had happened in the last two years: the media's love affair with Clinton, all the questions that had spilled over onto him from his father's campaign, even the ones that had to do with his *brothers* but that he had been forced to explain: the SEC inquiry, lingering suggestions that he had masterminded a political dirty-tricks siege against Ross Perot, the minority contracts at the baseball stadium, the National Guard, Neil's mess at Silverado. Worse, there were the open suggestions in almost every political corner of the state that the younger Bush would never win in Texas, against native Ann Richards, against his father's reputation as a one-term president unceremoniously ousted from office.

Every day, his neighbors on the wide, meandering streets of Preston Hollow, the closest thing to Connecticut lanes in Dallas, saw him headed to the Dallas Aerobic Center or sprinting down the road in a sweat-stained jogging outfit. In January, he and Laura went to see his father and Barbara in the small house that the ex-president had rented on West Post Oak in Houston.[4] He wanted to carboload, for the Houston marathon, and his mother cooked up what she thought was cardboard-tasting maca-roni; the next day, the family lined up to watch him finish the race in three hours and forty-four minutes. When he came back to Dallas, people who saw him said he seemed more focused than he had in weeks.

By February, he and Jackson were meeting again, but this time in Bush's ninth-floor office. Reporters had been calling, asking about rumors that the ex-president's son, or maybe the ex-president, might be pursuing the high-profile job as commissioner of baseball now that Bush had been unable to save family friend Fay Vincent from being deposed, but baseball insiders were saying that interim commissioner Bud Selig hadn't been en-couraging and that George W. would never be seriously considered.[5] They were also calling about a Justice Department probe into the fact that George W. Bush had hired U.S. Archivist Don Wilson to run his father's presidential library in College Station, Texas; the Justice Department wanted to know why Wilson had given his father exclusive control over five thousand White House computer tapes the day before the president had left the White House.

Suddenly Bush blurted out, "Hey, A.J., what do you think of a run for governor?"

Jackson almost couldn't contain himself. This was good.

"Let's kick her ass!" he shouted.

"You think we can do it?" asked Bush.

"Hell, yeah, let's go," Jackson reassured him.[6]

Now Jackson knew what even Bush's next-door neighbors had fig-ured out when he had stopped to talk to them during one of his almost ob-sessive daily runs. "Running for governor is a marathon. It's a stamina race," Bush had said one day to Mark Langdale, a hotel investor and friend who lived down the street.[7]

WITHIN WEEKS, the newest Team Bush began assembling, some of its members jetting from Midland and Austin for five-to-six-hour, closed-door strategy sessions at the office on Berkshire Lane. "I think I can win this," Bush told all the old friends of the family, all the old friends of his father, from whom he began soliciting advice: Bobby Holt, his father's moneyman from Midland, would help raise the millions of dollars that would be required to make a serious run at Richards; Austin-based spin-meister Karl Rove, who had been building his entire career toward this very point; Insider–adviser–public relations man Jim Francis, who was the same age as Bush and had worked for his father as his deputy scheduler; Fred Meyer, another Harvard B School grad, a marathon runner who lived one block from Bush, state Republican Party chairman, senior ad-viser to Senator Phil Gramm, and the man who had convinced Vice Pres-ident Bush to bring the 1984 GOP National Convention to Dallas; Fred McClure, who had served both Reagan and his father as the White House's Senate lobbyist and who had moved to north Dallas so his kids could attend the same schools as the Bush twins. McClure, especially, wasn't afraid to say what others were thinking, that there was a "genera-tional difference" between the first son and his father when it came to po-litical skills: George W. had "better skills when it comes to the political side"[8] and he was "no doubt the biggest political animal in the family—and clearly more competitive than his father."[9]

There were plenty of other allies who weren't in on the early strategy sessions or offering up private advice on how to attack Richards but who could be counted on for other incalculably important services, such as Nancy and Norman Brinker, who ran national restaurant chains and were king and queen of the Dallas museum-symphony-fund-raising circuit. They could continue to provide a valuable entrée for the candidate's still-unknown wife, who had been resisting immersion in another political bat-tle. Neighbors on their lane in north Dallas understood that Laura was still faltering at the thought of being sucked full-time into a life in the Bush-Walker Bubble—and that he was wrestling with her indecision about becoming a career politician's wife. He later said she was "throwing cold water on it." Worse, he believed that she was concerned about his motivations, whether he was just interested in extending the Bush political legacy: "She wanted to make sure that this was something I really wanted to do and that I wasn't being drug in as a result of friends, or, well, 'you're supposed to do it in order to prove yourself vis-à-vis your father.' " She said she didn't want him embarrassed. That was a thing she hated—that and the possibility that he might not really have a chance to beat Ann Richards.[10]

Alphonso Jackson, who attended one of the power strategy meetings in Bush's office, thought that really there was a different problem, The Problem as far as Bush was concerned, the one that had everything to do with the images of his father, the sense of a powerful dynasty continuing to unfold: "The one he thought about most was that no one would perceive him as a real person," said Jackson.[11]

THAT WAS the least of Ann Richards's problems. She was perceived as very real, almost too real, and at the strategy sessions they talked about how to combat her cult of personality, how she had risen from the dirt-poor core of Texas and emerged as a frothy political figure strapped to the back of a bucking yahoo Lone Star bull, kicking it in the ribs and launching herself into orbit as that rarest of elected officials: the politician as celebrity. During her tenure, the state was clawing out of its groveling mode for being the national whipping post for all those bad 1980s loans, all those cratered banks and crooked real estate deals that had rippled out of Dallas and Houston and made the markets groan, with all those bumper stickers affixed to the sides of Wall Street computers that read *Don't mess with Texas*. In the mid-1980s, the two most popular tourist attractions in Dallas encapsulated Texas's nasty image problems—the Kennedy assassination site and the faux-elegant monstrosity at Southfork where *Dallas* had been filmed—and served up self-fulfilling prophecies about what people suspected was really going on in Texas. In no small measure, the state needed some smart, splashy PR person who could finally lay to rest the notion that Texas was still the violent, dangerous place that had killed JFK and the place that had celebrated the birth of J. R. Ewing by cashing in on big oil, bad loans, and bloated defense contracts.

Richards ran a populist campaign that was rendered almost prairie pure when her opponent, Clayton Williams, the GOP's Midland oilman, had refused to shake her hand, called her a liar, and unleashed an undisciplined string of troubling, sexist comments that had forced even conservative Republican women to flee his camp. Williams, a relative unknown, had told a joke comparing inclement weather with rape: "If it's inevitable, just relax and enjoy it." Williams, who would eventually spend almost $22 million on his campaign, also talked about being a young man getting "serviced" by Mexican prostitutes. When Richards announced that she was celebrating her tenth year of abstention from alcohol, Williams said, "I hope she didn't go back to drinking again."[12]

And when she took office in 1991, having won by less than 100,000 votes out of the 3.8 million total, her slogan proclaimed a cocky zeitgeist: "The New Texas." In one of the most self-congratulatory states in the nation, people were tired of being ashamed, and she had promised to realign Texas's stars, unabashedly wallowing in the mythology, her mythology— reminding people that her family's roots were in down-home places called Bugtussle and Hogjaw. She staged a symbolic retaking of power with a "People's March to the Capitol" that moved north on Congress Avenue in Austin and straight through the towering wooden doors: *Today we march to reclaim our Capitol and our future . . . the people are back.* Kris Kristofferson and Willie Nelson were ready to play anthems, and there were feminists, gay activists, and more minorities on the grounds than anyone had ever seen in the history of the State Capitol. There was a palpable sense of righteous victory among Richards's supporters that satisfied the aching yearnings of the bedrock of Austin-based liberals and progressives and that began to attract more writers, actors, and artists to the governor's side than ever before in the state's history. GOP members were aghast at what they thought was some form of encroaching socialism. The reaction ran from the new wave of younger, white-collar Republicans such as Bush and McClure, who were crowding into north Dallas or the Houston suburbs, to the old wave of deep-money oilmen, financiers, and CEOs such as Robert Mosbacher and James A. Baker III, who had been in the delivery room when the modern Republican Party in Texas was born.

Richards was a grandmother who had come to politics late in life and whose Texas mentor was Barbara Jordan, the first black woman elected to Congress from the South. She was also the most famous governor in America, an organic force with high, steely Republican-style hair, a Texas-to-the-highest-power sense of what was truly droll, and huge approval ratings. Her election and her rising profile also had a salubrious impact on other women running for offices across the country. Richards was often impossible to corner with any political precision; she could dance with a self-effacing grin and on the edge of a Texas caricature and then slip into an all-business mode from her days as state treasurer. During Richards's administration the color and gender of the state's gubernatorial appointees began to diversify—and, owing in part to her saleswoman's skills, the economy also began to diversify, attracting a broader range of entertainment and Silicon Valley investors interested in Texas's absence of income taxes and organized labor. To friends, during the 1992 presidential campaign, Bush used to say that one of the things that Clinton could do was "talk Texas." But nobody could talk Texas like Ann Richards; her Texasisms would eventually be collected in a book, and the Republicans' ire grew in direct proportion to her national profile. There was a palpable angst in GOP circles, a coalescence against her "cult of personality" that reached a peak midway through her term. Richards was undeniably attracting famous supporters, and when her friends decided to hold an "Ann-at-Sixty Birthday Celebration" in September at the Austin Coliseum, the fund-raiser was hosted by actress Alfre Woodard and featured music and appearances by Don Henley, Lyle Lovett, Willie Nelson, Liz Smith, and Molly Ivins.

KNOWING THAT a race against Richards was really a race against a national political figure, George W.'s strategists made a decision to test the waters by having him travel on behalf of Republican Senate candidate Kay Bailey Hutchison. His segue from Texas baseball "owner" to Texas gubernatorial candidate could thus be easily gauged, and Rove would be able to see how George W. Bush the Possible Candidate was perceived during the 1990s version of the barnstorming tours the elder Bush had taken thirty years before as he built the GOP in Texas. At every stop, when Hutchison's handlers glumly watched reporters scurrying after Bush instead of their candidate, he was invariably asked about his future. "Put me down as interested" was his stock reply.

When Hutchison raked in the largest GOP margin in the history of statewide elections, Rove and the others knew that the timing was chugging toward perfection. Hutchison's election to the Senate could be construed as a rejection of Richards; maybe there were Republican women organizing in the still-growing suburbs who simply didn't like Ann Richards. And when Terry Johnson said he would be visiting Dallas from Washington, Bush quietly decided to bounce the idea off his old Yale roommate and DKE brother. They took a weekend off and traveled to an isolated bass-fishing vacation home Bush had purchased on Rainbo Lake in Athens, a place surrounded by dense groves of maples and dogwoods heading into the thicker pine woods of East Texas. Bush hadn't said a word about running for governor. Then, during the car ride back to Dallas, he suddenly told his college roommate, "I'm really thinking of running for governor."

Johnson asked, "How do you answer that Teddy Kennedy question: 'Why do you want to be president?' "

Bush paused and then launched into a laundry list: education, tort reform, business climate—he already had a complete series of checkpoints and campaign buzzwords laid out.[13]

Meanwhile, in Austin, Rove . . . *Turd Blossom* . . . was busy spinning gold out of poll numbers that showed that Ann Richards had a 58 percent approval rating. "They like her hair, but they're not strongly anchored to her," he insisted.[14] Other polls said that 20 percent of voters thought pollsters were bringing up George W.'s father when asked if they would consider casting a ballot for someone named George W. Bush. Still, Rove and most members of the inner ring of the GOP leadership in Texas believed that Ann Richards hadn't really won the governor's race but that Clayton Williams had lost it by lacking the discipline to control himself, the media, and his message. Richards, they said, would never have been governor if Clayton Williams had learned to shut up. At strategy sessions, a decision was also made to begin leaking some preannouncement announcements, some publicity-building teasers offered up the first week of August by selected members of the strategy team and friendly state lawmakers. Everyone agreed that an official announcement would come sometime after Labor Day and that the interim period would give Bush some more time to travel and make sure that the GOP field was completely shaken out. Wealthy downtown Dallas attorney Tom Luce, the even wealthier Rob Mosbacher (son of the old Bush family friend, adviser, and Secretary of Commerce Robert Mosbacher), and State Representative Tom Craddick from Midland were all considered likely opponents.

As they let the early drumbeats sound out, Bush left Texas and flew to the American Club resort in Kohler, Wisconsin, to try to broker a deal among baseball club owners warring over an ill-defined revenue-sharing plan. Bush was worried that a baseball strike might affect the grand opening of the new Texas Rangers' stadium in 1994. Serving as a visible intermediary between big-market owners such as George Steinbrenner and small-market teams such as Florida and Colorado would also be a good way of proving his consensus-building skills, his ability to work on a bipartisan plane. Bush was peripatetic at the meetings, but no breakthrough was announced. After the stalled meetings, he flew to Kennebunkport for the family's annual summer conclave. His father had been out of the Oval Office for only seven months, but now he was the political adviser to his two oldest sons, including Jeb, who had decided to move beyond his position as Florida's secretary of commerce and run for governor. Said George W.: "For the first time in our family, Dad knew he was not going to be the center of attention. He knew it was another generation's time."[15]

The interwoven Bush-Walker advisers in Florida and Texas had decided that there would be an excruciatingly fine line between familiarity and distance—between public allegiances to the family and publicly distancing George W.'s Texas campaign and Jeb's Florida campaign from the things that had caused their father to lose the presidency. On rare occasions, Prescott Bush Jr. and a few others had talked with historians and friends about the ultimate impact of the long family history. It wasn't so much that the distant roots to European royalty were part of the "perception problem." If there were politically prohibitive perceptions, they were tied to the many things that had evolved after family members had arrived in seventeenth century America and later helped to found important Wall Street investment banking firms or sat on the boards of the most influential institutions of the last two centuries. With the Bushes and Walkers firmly entrenched for decades in the seats and sites of power—from the 10,000-acre family plantation in South Carolina, to the seaside compound in Maine, to the enclave on Jupiter Island in Florida, to the homes in Greenwich and Rye—the perceptions were something the family would always struggle against.

George W. gingerly told writers that his father's message had been "obscured" in 1992: "the messenger was unable to carry the message." That, he had decided, was something he knew better than to let happen to him in Texas. Perhaps timing, not Bill Clinton, had actually beaten his father, in the sense that the new, psychological media had dwelled too much on his father's image, his upbringing, his interior, and not enough on his message. It wasn't hard to argue that his father had been a casualty of conventional politics, that he was an outmoded link to what Dorothy Walker and Prescott Bush had personified: the carefully burnished comportment, the evanescent thing that John Kemper had talked about on graduation day at Andover—style—as the ultimate barometer of a Good Man, maybe even a good politician. The Bush campaign in Texas had very clear theories on how not to let the message become obscure, how the messenger should carry the message.

WHEN GEORGE W. flew back to Texas, he went to Houston and met with oilman Rob Mosbacher for ninety minutes at his downtown oil business headquarters. Their families went back a few decades in Texas, and Mosbacher's father was joined at the hip with George W.'s father. Bush's advisers were worried that somebody with Mosbacher's endless resources would steal their thunder by pushing himself as the candidate with the most "business experience"—one strategy that the Bush inner circle had weighed as a way of attacking Ann Richards. But Mosbacher told Bush he wasn't interested in spending up to $15 million and going to war with the entire Bush family and then Richards. After the meeting, Bush pushed past reporters without saying a word.[16] A few hours later, in Dallas, the other shoe fell when Tom Luce abruptly announced that he was out of the race; Luce was carrying excess baggage from his allegiances as Ross Perot's old campaign manager, and people suspected that he knew the Bush network in Texas would never forgive him for it. Even though he had jumped off the Perot ship, some measure of flesh would probably be extracted for the way Perot, operating literally underneath the first son's office window, had savaged the Old Man and the children during the 1992 campaign. State Representative Craddick was out as well, and now the path was perfectly clear.

The wholesale capitulation to George W. Bush had happened with almost perfect precision. It was, old Lone Star pols said admiringly, the only one-day gubernatorial primary in Texas's history.

IN SEPTEMBER, George W. added several more names familiar to the national Bush political network to his campaign. As his campaign manager he named Brian Berry, who had run Hutchison's race and had been the southwest regional political director for his father. Former U.S. Assistant Attorney General Carol Dinkins was his campaign treasurer. Dinkins, who had earned the ire of activists by representing large corporations in environmental disputes, was also someone people had been betting would make U.S. attorney general under his father. Fred Steeper, his father's trusty pollster, was also hired and started coming to Texas for meetings. Bush flew to Midland to speak at a businessmen's luncheon. He told his friends that he had filed election papers but was going to hold off on an official announcement until after the baseball season.

Back in Dallas, at the last game of the season, Bush's eyes were watery; Nolan Ryan, the uncomplicated Ronald Reagan of baseball, was retiring. George W. was cheered by the presence of Rush Limbaugh; he had invited the conservative talk-show host to be his guest at the final game. Limbaugh had been at George W.'s side before, even clutching the first son's hand at the New Jersey rallies the day before the Old Man had been voted out of office. Limbaugh was an open opponent of Ann Richards, and he couldn't help but be fascinated by the process unfolding that fall. Two Bushes were running for governor, and already they were echoing each other and using their children to distance themselves from their father: "I'm not running because I'm George Bush's son. I'm running because I'm Barbara and Jenna's dad," the first son was telling people in

Texas. In Tampa, Jeb was using almost the exact same words, simply substituting his own children's names for those of the twins.[17]

They were on parallel tracks, but Jeb was still admittedly in awe of his older brother, especially his energy. He was equally impressed by what he called his brother's "new self-constrained persona." Jeb felt that he knew his older brother maybe better than anyone else did, and Jeb was one of the few people in the family who even mentioned the obvious pressures, the legacy between a son and a father who shared the same name: "If you have lived it and breathed it and seen it, you are not fearful of it—the fears and trepidations. Most people that haven't experienced it as intensely as our family has—the politics, the public life—shy away from it. I mean, it looks foreign, it looks very weird. George had the advantage—none of those barriers existed. I can't emphasize that enough."[18]

GEORGE W. handed out a schedule and waited for reactions. They would stop in twenty-seven cities in five days, starting with the kickoff announcement in Houston: fifteen-minute news conferences, a short rally, on to the airport. Houston, San Antonio, Austin, Dallas, Wichita Falls, Amarillo, Lubbock, Abilene, San Angelo, Midland, El Paso, Nacogdoches, Tyler, Longview, Marshall, Texarkana, Sherman-Denison, Fort Worth, Waco, Temple, Bryan–College Station, Beaumont–Port Arthur, Corpus Christi, Harlingen, McAllen, Laredo, Victoria. This is the way it would be for the next year, and Joe O'Neill . . . *Spider* . . . was watching from Midland. O'Neill was rangy and ready, always more open and—hell—unguarded than any of the old gang still strapped on that desert roller-coaster ride in the oil patch. O'Neill had known Bush in the wide-open days. He had seen him in the pre-Broadmoor days, when Bush could drink hard and curse like a roustabout with a scorched hand.

Spider knew, everyone knew, that Ann Richards could push buttons—she could hold her own, twisting the screws on just about everyone in the Petroleum Club. O'Neill had a pet theory about what was motivating Dubya. Surely he hadn't forgotten what Richards had said about his father choking on his own silver foot—it was the same thing people had said about George W. himself in West Texas in 1978, the same thing he had heard in the Northeast, in college. "I'm sure it was like acid on his stomach," said O'Neill.[19]

ISRAEL HERNANDEZ was one of the hundreds of well-groomed, hustling people in their early twenties who had scrambled from Texas universities into jobs as earnest aides, gofers, and interns for state lawmakers in Austin. But what he really wanted to do was work for Bush. Hernandez made some calls, found out who was handling the Bush campaign personnel, and kept pushing until he wangled an appointment. He traveled from Austin to Dallas the night before and followed the route to Bush's office so he wouldn't screw up and get lost when it was time for his appointment. The next day, he showed up for the interview an hour early. He was rehearsing what he was going to say, his pitch to become George W.'s aide-de-camp, his all-around personal assistant, the job that David Bates, the Houston childhood chum of Jeb Bush, had handled for so many years for President Bush. Hernandez could see George W. on the phone with his back turned. Finally, George W. came out to talk to his secretary. Hernandez was stunned; it almost seemed unbelievable. When George W. entered the room, Hernandez thought that he could almost be the president, the similarity was that striking.[20]

Bush waved him inside, and they talked for two hours. Hernandez was hired, and he became driver, scheduler, gofer, and, for a while, house guest—fetching another one of Bush's favorite Altoids mints, making sure someone got the candidate his favorite granola, egg-salad sandwiches, and the coconut macaroons, making sure there was time allotted every day for the three-mile jog, each mile requiring between seven and eight minutes.

On the day of the first official Bush for Governor campaign announcement and the start of the twenty-seven-city tour, Bush and Hernandez stepped off the King Air campaign plane dubbed *Accountability One* and began the drive through Houston to the hotel press conference. George W.'s father and mother were deliberately absent. And if anybody needed to be reminded why, it had all been spelled out the day before, when the *Houston Chronicle* had run a picture to go with a story about George W. speaking to the Texas Federation of Republican Women—and instead of using his picture they had mistakenly used one of his father. In Florida, forty-year-old Jeb was making his own campaign appearances and getting laughs by saying he was thinking of changing his name to Reagan or Eisenhower.

Now Bush was cackling as the limousine sped downtown and the striking Houston skyline, an Oz on the Gulf coast, began rising before them. Bush was trying to think of a nickname, something better than Israel. The new aide was worried, not saying the obvious: "Shouldn't you be thinking of your speech?" A satisfied sound to his voice, Bush announced it: "And your name is now . . . Izzy!"

The bewildered aide asked, "Isn't that the Olympic mascot?"

Bush roared back: "No, no, no, your name is Izzy!"

As the Team Bush caravan pulled closer to the Houston hotel and the horde of reporters, Bush suddenly burst into song: "Izzy Fuzzy? Wazzy Fuzzy? Izzy?" His aide began singing with him.[21]

Three hundred people were waiting at the hotel near the fabled Galleria shopping mall, only about a mile from his father's home. A still slightly bewildered Hernandez listened as Bush stepped to the microphone and began his campaign announcement: "I view Texas as a way of life, a state of mind, a way to think. . . . I don't want Texas to be like California. . . . I was a small businessman. . . . I believe everybody should be held responsible for their individual behavior. All public policy should revolve around the principle that individuals are responsible for what they say and do. . . . Our leaders should be judged by results, not by entertaining personalities or clever sound bites."[22]

As he was wrapping up, a Houston radio personality went on the air: "Former President George Bush kicked off his gubernatorial campaign today. . . ."[23]

MESSAGE DISCIPLINE was the mantra, the four food groups: The campaign would stick to tort reform, crime, education, welfare reform. "It's a simple formula," said Don Evans, the Midland oilman who had helped orchestrate George W.'s 1978 congressional race and was now emerging as one of his most important moneymen. "I'm going to get four issues, and I'm going to hammer on them, I'm going to hammer on them, I'm going to hammer on them."[24] Message Discipline, both the lack of it and the way the messages had been obscured, was what had killed George W.'s father. Maybe it was Darman's fault, who really knew, but the horrible way his father's "no new taxes" pledge had turned into a wicked boomerang was easily one of the biggest lessons that George W., his adviser Karl Rove . . . *Turd Blossom* . . . and everyone else had walked away with. The mistakes would not be repeated. Somehow Reagan's message hadn't been obscured, and the people who had been witnessing the evolution of George W. Bush personally all these years were coming to the same conclusion as stalwarts such as Jim Pinkerton and even Fred Malek: that if he hadn't been born a Bush he would have been a Reaganite. "He's been very good at learning a lot of things from his father to do—but I think he's also been very good at learning a lot of things from his father to do differently," said his father's pollster Bob Teeter.[25]

During the campaign, it wasn't just Al Hunt from *The Wall Street Journal* wondering if Bush had, as Hunt said, "matured." His sister,

Dorothy would say that it was "still very hard" for him to squelch his anger.[26] His cousin Elsie Walker wondered if there would be an explosion, an eruption—or some other form of discipline to accompany the Message Discipline. In the meetings in the Congress Avenue headquarters of Ann Richards's opposition research squads, it certainly came up as the easy-money bet: How do we play it when Bush breaks down, screaming and cursing? John Ellis, the cousin who studied the ebb and flow of the five Bush children more closely than anyone else, felt that the 1994 version of George W. Bush was a more disciplined tactician than almost anyone other than Mary Matalin allowed—maybe because so many other people were assuming that someone else, maybe Karl Rove, should be credited for his emergence in Texas. He was more skilled at the New Politics than his father; like his mother, he was better at being instantly likable and in-stantly able to inspire fear. "That's what people don't understand about him," said Ellis. "They don't understand how fucking tough he is."[27]

DURING A RALLY in Waco, George W. turned toward a college student who was insisting on having a one-on-one chat with him about his crimi-nal justice programs. The earnest man had a "Bush for Governor" button on, but Bush's voice screwed up with anger at being interrupted. "You don't need to hold a press conference. I'm the guy who holds a press con-ference," he snapped. During that campaign swing, he had a Washington-based reporter whom he suspected of helping derail his father's campaign erased from interview lists and denied access to the campaign plane.[28] In internal strategy sessions, Rove had distributed a memo outlining the need to curtail access to the media, and now he took on the task of ex-plaining why Bush wasn't going to talk to anybody from the national media: he had "battle scars" from his father's campaign, and there were too many reporters avoiding the issues and wanting to play their "East Coast gotchas" games.[29]

Meanwhile, Texas newspapers were reporting that at least two of Bush's four proposals—denting the regulatory powers of the state educa-tion agency and establishing more local control of schools; locking up ju-venile offenders—were in fact already being discussed by the state legislature. Team Bush eventually moved fractionally beyond the four food groups and released highlights of their candidate's extended plat-form: increasing state spending for education; locking up juvenile offend-ers and certifying them to be tried as adults at the age of fourteen; supporting an "anti-sodomy" statute that gay leaders were trying to repeal; being personally prolife but prochoice if that's what the law called for—while seeking parental consent for teenage abortions; making it legal to carry handguns; denying benefits to children born to welfare recipients who had already had at least two children; and building more anti-immigrant fences along the Texas-Mexico border.

At the end of the year, *The Wall Street Journal* issued a report card giving Richards an A for economic development—and for being the state's "premier salesperson." In the microscopic Texas Panhandle town of Canadian, Bush stood on a street corner, working the back roads of Texas and trying out his new campaign thread: "I don't want Texas to become like California."[30] He was never specific, but most people in Texas assumed he wasn't just talking about California's convoluted politics—who cares about that in Canadian, Texas?—but more about something distastefully liberal, some California lifestyle, some excessive, out-of-Texas thing that might be attached to Ann Richards's celebrity.

The reverse-geography strategy, making New Haven–born Bush seem more Texan and more All-American, making Ann Richards seem less Texan and more prone to California "excesses," would be emphasized until the final day of the campaign. There was now an encroaching, two-part dimension to the campaign: deflecting the tendencies of writers and critics to point to what they saw as the baronial tendencies of the Bush-Walker legacy, with its roots in a nineteenth-century plantation, corporate boards, Andover, Yale, and Wall Street; avoiding any mention of Bush's laborious efforts inside the Christian Right and the hard edge of the conservative movement. As he had told Alphonso Jackson, the problem was making him seem like a "real person"—something Prescott Bush had never worried about, something his father had struggled to do.

His advisers began the process: "He understands Bubba because there is more Bubba in him. He is clearly the wild son," Karl Rove had once insisted to reporters.[31] Now it was easier to make that pitch, especially when the first campaign contribution reports were released the week Bush was in Canadian. Seventeen of the twenty Bush donors who had written checks for $20,000 or more had also contributed to his father's presidential campaign. Bush's donors included legendary Dallas Cowboys quarterback Roger Staubach, Texas Rangers partner Rusty Rose, financier Richard Rainwater, Austin golf star Ben Crenshaw, football coach Mike Ditka, and Florida Marlins owner Wayne Huizenga.

Richards's donors included Steven Spielberg, Annie Leibovitz, Linda Ellerbee, Don Henley, Willie Nelson, Robert Redford, Sharon Stone,

Barbra Streisand, Farrah Fawcett, James Garner, Henry Winkler, and Roseanne Arnold.

IN A delicate dance, and almost by unspoken mutual consent, Richards and Bush had steered clear of the Drug Question. Stories had already run in 1990, during the last Texas gubernatorial campaign, about allegations of her drug use. Now, in 1994, if she and Bush lingered over substance abuse, it was about their mutual attraction to alcohol—and the very different ways they had stopped drinking. She and her friends talked about her recovery program for alcoholism, about the way the disease had developed and taken shape in that singularly unfettered period in the 1970s in Austin when Richards had spent time with "outlaw" country musicians such as Willie Nelson—the ones who had found some measure of peace in Austin and the Texas Hill Country. They talked, too, about the way Ann Richards had gone sober in 1980 after her best friends had intervened and said she needed to get help at a treatment center in Minnesota.

Bush, on the other hand, simply said he had willed himself to quit drinking that summer morning in 1986 at the vacation resort in Colorado Springs—and in Austin, around the State Capitol, cynical political wags agreed that the way the two candidates had abandoned alcohol was simply the difference between the Republicans and the Democrats: Richards had quit drinking by consensus, by committee; Bush had gone cold turkey, without any outside regulation.

But from the outset of the 1994 race and through the next several years, unsubstantiated rumors about George W.'s drug use and even his marital fidelity would continue to take hold, culminating in major media outlets across the nation writing about the existence of the unproved rumors as a sort of modern media phenomenon, a "consequence" of political life in the Clintonian and modern media age. There would be, five years after his race against Richards, exhaustive stories—stories that included denials and didn't otherwise prove any of the rumors but that explored the evolution of the unproved rumors. The pitch and pace of the rumors and how they evolved were intense, the sources of the rumors diverse.

An internal memorandum from the Richards campaign, sent from one "opposition" researcher to another, insisted that a staffer find Bush's records for driving while intoxicated—even though there had apparently never been any such arrest. Years later, a defense attorney was telling a Texas writer he had heard of someone who knew someone who had sold coke to the president's son but that no one really wanted to talk about it; a woman in Lubbock suggested to a reporter that she had heard a rumor about George W. Bush being arrested but that his record had been scrubbed clean; a West Texas resident said he had heard a rumor that an older woman had turned a corner and come upon George W. Bush with drugs. Well beyond 1994, beyond Texas, the unproved rumors about things that had allegedly happened in Texas kept multiplying. A former resident of the Davenport dormitory at Yale said he had heard unsubstantiated rumors about prostitutes being bought for the amusement of Bush and his West Texas oil friends.

Finally, almost exactly four years after his race with Richards, some members of the national media had succumbed to what they considered a solution: they would write about the existence of the rumors as, again, a sort of singular 1990s phenomenon of political life. That technique allowed several new unsubstantiated rumors to course into print and through Washington: he had been high at his father's inauguration, he was still drinking, he was having an affair with a GOP staffer, he had tried to buy coke on a city street corner. The rumors themselves, and the phenomenon of how the rumors were covered by the media, certainly outstripped anything his grandfather or even his father had experienced.

The elder George Bush had seemed alternately bewildered and angered by the way the new media had covered him, especially when his marital fidelity and his manhood had been questioned. But in Texas, the younger George Bush would come to constantly mention his self-described "young and irresponsible years" without cataloging what he had done in that time period. He would mention his "nomadic" period so often that finally some longtime political observers in Austin began to quietly theorize that the younger George Bush was again proving himself to be a more contemporary strategist than his father: the theory was that the younger Bush wanted to make his personal life a dead political issue by drawing attention early and often to his so-called, ill-defined "nomadic" years. The extended theory among political pundits in Austin was that doing so also somehow served to make Bush seem more like a million other baby boomers in the modern, "confessional" age—and that it even served to steer rumor-mongering reporters away from critiquing his policies and even his family's "gilded" history in American business and politics.

One thing was very clear in Texas in 1994: George W. Bush certainly seemed less bewildered and less flustered than his father when it came to countering rumors and questions about his personal life.

The first week of May, the *Houston Chronicle* had decided to openly grill him about whether he had experimented with illegal drugs: "Maybe I did, maybe I didn't. What's the relevance?" he had told the reporter.[32]

Now, the day after the story appeared, he had flown to Lubbock on the campaign plane, *Accountability One*, and there were still more questions. Standing on the steps of the Lubbock County Jail with an ominous string of prison guards behind him, he thought he was going to be talking about his controversial suggestion to warehouse more convicts in Texas by building some Spartan prison tent camps. No one wanted to know about the prison tent camp plan or the four food groups. He had crafted an answer to the Drug Question, one that he would repeat for years, and in Lubbock he also decided to invoke his opponent's name.

"What I did as a kid? I don't think it's relevant, nor do I think it's relevant what Ann Richards did as a kid," he said with those Lubbock, Texas, police officers in their crisp uniforms and mirrored sunglasses still standing behind him. "I just don't think it matters. Did I behave irresponsibly as a kid at times? Sure did. You bet."[33]

IN HOUSTON, Barbara Bush was working on her memoirs, reportedly having sold them for $1 million. Her adjustment to private life had been somewhat of a revelation; she hadn't realized, for instance, that you could call a pizza parlor and have pizza delivered to your home. Two of her sons were running for office, and she was telling people that her other two sons had "always hated politics," even though six years earlier she had told people that Neil was "dying" to run for office.[34] The attacks on her children had been relatively unrelenting throughout the Bush administration; in addition to the Harken questions, *The Nation* had suggested that George W. had been peddling influence by calling on Argentine energy officials; Jeb, who had served as chairman of the Dade County Republican Party, Florida's secretary of commerce, and chairman of Governor Bob Martinez's doomed reelection campaign, had been criticized for his connections to multimillion-dollar real estate loans that had defaulted; Neil had eventually paid a $50,000 fine after federal regulators had sued him in the spectacular billion-dollar collapse of the Silverado savings and loan.

An old Skull & Bonesman, ex-Congressman Lud Ashley, emerged to cobble together some fund-raising operations for him.[35] Neil had thought about moving back to Texas and finally accepted a job with an old family friend and campaign contributor who ran a Houston-based sports cable television company, Transmedia Communications. He later worked out of an office near where his father had set up his postpresidential clearinghouse for interview requests and speaking engagements. With Neil being faulted for embarrassing and undermining his father's presidency, Barbara was more openly bitter than anyone else in the family about his treatment at the hands of investigators and the media. He could have run for office: he had such an easy way with people, and he had been training as far back as 1978, when he had moved to Lubbock to work for his eldest brother in that doomed congressional race.

She and the elder Bush had avoided being seen with either Jeb or George W. for three months. Richards was already outraising the first son by almost $1.6 million. Over the course of two weeks in March, the parents finally agreed to show up at two high-priced Texas banquets, and exactly $1.6 million was raised quickly. When they were through, they flew to Florida for the first time to campaign and began a three-day, eleven-city fund-raising caravan for Jeb's campaign against the incumbent, Lawton Chiles. On his first day in Florida, the Old Man broke down in tears in Boca Raton when he started talking about how stirred he had been by the thought of his second eldest son running for governor. Heading outside, the members of Team Bush retired to the high-tech mobile home and bus that Jeb worked out of. The brand name of the rolling campaign office was *Dynasty*.[36]

THE RICHARDS CAMPAIGN had voted to attack Bush the same way Garry Trudeau had attacked the president in *Doonesbury:* "There is no there there." Bush had a phantom campaign, he hadn't announced any real initiatives, and the few ideas he had presented were already being weighed by state lawmakers. In Washington, operatives at the Democratic National Committee were watching, noting that he didn't rise to the bait. And they were coming to the understanding that Bush would never veer from his core food group of messages, that he was staging a Texas interpretation of a blithe Reaganesque campaign, his version of what Atwater had tried so hard to sell to his father, using Message Discipline to pry loose the vulnerable, dissatisfied baby boomers. His slogan, "If you're happy with the status quo, don't vote for me," sounded a lot like Reagan's slogan, "Ask yourself if you are better off today than you were four years ago."

In frustration, the Richards campaign began planning an all-out assault on Bush's business record, suggesting that his companies had been failures and kept alive only by the deep fortunes of the Bush-Walker family, and that his problems with the SEC had never been adequately addressed. While the Richards campaign waited for the SEC to release its files on any investigations into Bush's stock trade, its researchers delved deeper into the allegations that landowners had been seduced and had their property condemned, all in the name of a lavish, new, tax-subsidized ballpark for Bush and the other owners of the Texas Rangers.[37]

In Dallas, Team Bush had also been hoping for a letter from the SEC—"at this time, no enforcement action is contemplated with respect to him"—that they could produce to confront questions about the investigation into his stock sale.[38] People familiar with the investigation noted that the SEC often does not take action against insider traders who miss their first filing deadline for reporting stock sales. Dissatisfied Democrats would eventually suggest that the SEC was run by Bush appointees, including some who had worked with the family in the past, and that the SEC's investigation into Bush should itself be investigated. Bush was prepared to tell interviewers that if he had held on to the stock for a year the price would have rebounded, and, in fact, he had possibly lost revenue in the long run by selling.

GEORGE W.'s and Jeb's platforms, not just their quotes about their parents and their children, were uncannily similar, though Jeb was bolder about hawking his conservative wares. When he mentioned reducing government, he talked about "blowing up" state agencies, and he had carefully selected the Christian Coalition's Legislator of the Year as his running mate. Together, Jeb and George W. were moving away from some things that had roots in the paternal, patrician eastern wing of the GOP symbolized by Prescott Bush. They railed against control by big government, the know-it-all "welfare state," and regulatory controls on the environment and schools. Jeb, who had been a Phi Beta Kappa at the University of Texas, sometimes felt as out of place with the old, moderate, establishment wing as his brother had at Yale and Harvard. Now they were both running for office in the anti-big-government Sun Belt, doing exactly what Atwater always knew they would eventually have to do if they ever wanted to get elected. George W. and his father arrived at the hard fact that it was better that the elder Bush simply stay away from the first son; maybe he could make an appearance at two Dallas banquets, but certainly no speeches.

Barbara, though, agreed to write letters for and make appearances with her son; she obviously could never become a political liability, and she was a key to bridging the gender gap that Richards had benefited from in the last campaign. His mother still hadn't gotten over the moment, in the reassuring comfort of Kennebunkport, when she had watched the TV broadcast of Richards ridiculing her husband at the Democratic National Convention in 1988. She had felt that it was "ugly, devastating," and, after watching it for ten minutes, had snapped the TV off with a sick feeling in her stomach.[39]

Now Richards was essentially saying the same things she had back then. "It is really difficult to run against someone who doesn't have a clue," Richards had drolly told people in July.[40] She had started slowly at first and had then been calling George W. "Shrub" . . . "Junior" . . . "Prince George" and making references to "Some Jerk." Her staffers knew she really believed what she said, she wasn't just talking policy. She really thought he didn't have a clue about what it meant to run a wicked campaign in a state like Texas.

IN AUSTIN, George W. stepped out of the campaign van and into the thick of the August heat. By now, his troika of daily operational advisers was set: consigliere Karl Rove, uncompromising spokesman Karen Hughes, and the new campaign manager, Joe Allbaugh, who had been brought in from Oklahoma GOP circles to make the trains run on time. Allbaugh was "a Norman Schwarzkopf look-alike and sound-alike," said one observer. They were all in agreement: don't rise to the chum, and don't conform to expectations by blowing up—even when Richards staffers started making hay of the fact that Bush, on the requisite staged Texas hunting trip for reporters on the first day of dove season, had blown an endangered killdee out of the sky with a blast from his twenty-gauge shotgun. Almost immediately, he began openly making jokes at his own expense, and the incident eventually died.

Now, near his campaign van, just outside an Austin elementary school, he suddenly started flapping his arms wildly up and down and doing the Jerk. He knew she had people he would never get: Robin Williams was going to her fund-raisers. "Jerks for George!" he shouted merrily, still doing the Jerk, as the second-graders and the reporters stared at him.[41] By September he and Richards were dead even in the polls.

Three weeks before the election, the Texas Poll showed George W. in the lead for the first time.

At the strategy sessions, his staffers talked about the crucial TV ads and how they needed not to be perceived as attacks on Richards. An attack on Richards could be translated as a defense of his father, a revenge-seeking blitzkrieg, and maybe the underlying reason why the first son was running in the first place. According to one of Bush's oldest friends and fund-raisers in Midland, Rove worked hard to smooth out Bush's pugnacious tendencies. High-ranking Richards operatives were saying they knew of sessions at Bush's house alongside Rainbo Lake in East Texas, days of teaching Bush how to control his anger—to *feist out*—to communicate better, not to rise to the bait. Don Sipple, the leathery-looking, hardened GOP image maker who had worked on his father's campaign, was also brought to Texas to create TV ads and to tutor Bush on effective, nonconfrontational communication.

Bush and Rove had also decided that they would agree to only one debate, held eighteen days before the election in receptive, Republican Dallas. With the polls showing a scary erosion of Richards's support, her handlers urged her to attack Bush hard on his business record—on the lingering questions about his sale of Harken stock and on his being on the boards of Caterair International and other companies that Richards said were not the most efficient in Texas. Rove knew it was necessary to paint a picture of Bush the Longtime Businessman, Bush the Outsider—not the son who had thought about running for office as far back as 1971, not the one who had been coordinating regional, state, and national campaigns for years. The day of the debate, Bush went running, came back, and told Izzy he needed to be left alone. In the house, Izzy, peeking out the window, spotted nervous press secretary Karen Hughes . . . *the High Prophet* . . . circling the Bush house in her car, afraid to come in but calling Izzy from her car phone: "Is *now* a good time?"[42]

At the debate, Bush stuck to the script: "I have been in the business world all my adult life. . . . If Texans want someone who has spent her entire life in politics, they should not be for me."[43] And he maintained a muted tone accented by a thin smile. There were no surprises, no knockout punches by the capable Richards. The Washington operatives from the Democratic National Committee who studied the debate tapes said the same thing over and over: Message Discipline and delivery discipline. It was the last thing anyone had expected, he was supposed to have lost it, the way he had lost it with all those reporters in Washington. It was the same thing his startled, disbelieving cousin Elsie Walker said to herself as she watched Richards go after the first son: her cousin was like a dog with a bone, he must have gone through some sort of steely "transformation—he held his tongue, developed discipline." Still disbelieving, she immediately sent a telegram to her aunt Barbara Bush: "WHAT HAS . . . WHAT DID HE DO?"[44]

15

Giant Killer

On the day of his seventeenth wedding anniversary, George W. took a last low-tech, old-school barnstorming bus trip to central Texas hamlets that were definitely not California. The Bush bus moved through Burleson, Hillsboro, Corsicana, and Waxahachie—places where the Hill Country had finally given way to a smooth, endless expanse of farmland. He had deliberately worn his eel-skin boots and Texas Farm Bureau jacket, and he made sure to order the hubcap-sized chicken-fried steak at the Thunderbird Restaurant. To reinforce the idea, he had former Dallas Cowboys tight end Billy Joe Dupree and actor Chuck Norris . . . *Walker, Texas Ranger* . . . with him. Meanwhile, Ann Richards was stepping onto a stage in Dallas with Rosie O'Donnell to address a woman's right to abortion: "I don't think anybody ought to have control over my body but me and Tom Cruise," shouted O'Donnell. "Definitely not a guy named Bush."[1]

The two largest papers in Texas, *The Houston Chronicle* and *The Dallas Morning News*, had endorsed Bush. Richards's approval ratings in the weeks before the election were still in the 60 percent range, but he was, by all estimations, campaigning harder than Richards in the rural and suburban parts of Texas that never receive much publicity unless they are stricken by drought, tornado, flood, or some other enormous human tragedy; he was working diligently at dozens of luncheons and rallies on the outer rings of the cities, continually courting all the GOP women who had once been attracted to Richards. Some of her staffers were worried that she was tired—maybe not of running but of being a governor in a polarized state where her cult of personality was both her lifeblood and the thing that generated so much venom. She was, as one Texas writer had wisely put it, too popular for her own good.

Even now, up into the last day of the eighteen-month campaign, he had resolutely refused to elaborate or move much beyond the four basic food groups: giving local control to school districts, reducing frivolous lawsuits, cutting crime by refusing parole to sex offenders and imposing harsher penalties on juveniles, and slashing welfare rosters. The last item was the embodiment of his bedrock antigovernment, personal-responsibility, antitaxation philosophy. It was something that was sure to appeal to the voters who could flip the campaign for him: the dissatisfied white middle-class in Dallas and Houston; the farmers, ranchers and oil-men in smaller cities in West Texas; all those suburban women and in-dependents who were reluctant to follow the last-minute endorsement that Ross Perot, the man whose third-party efforts had turned him into a sworn enemy of the Bushes, had extended to Richards.

His selection of welfare reform as one of the four bedrocks of his platform also allowed Bush the opportunity to allay any lingering fears of the skeptical Christian Right that the New Haven–born, prep school, Ivy League son of former President Bush also had some slippery, inconsistent commitment to harder, faith-grounded, socially conservative principles rising up in America's heartland. Though both he and his father had flirted with the First Presbyterian Church in Midland and both had taught Sunday school there, they had eventually aligned themselves with other denominations. His father was famous for his Episcopalian allegiances in Houston; the first son had willingly joined his wife in the Methodist church, though he told a Houston reporter, "I'm sure there is some kind of heavy doctrinal difference, which I'm not sophisticated enough to ex-plain to you."[2]

In the late 1970s and with Don Evans, his financial supporter in Midland, Bush gravitated toward more of the ubiquitous men's church meetings and early-morning businessmen's prayer breakfasts that are the required hallmark of almost every small Texas city. And in 1985, at the exact time his father was keenly interested in asserting his credentials with the evangelical community and just before the first son gave up drinking, Bush began a series of conversations with Billy Graham after the evangelist was invited to one of the usual summertime retreats at Walker's Point. After having been in far West Texas, after working so closely with ex–Assembly of God minister Doug Wead, and serving as his father's constant arm to the hard Christian Right, Bush was also coming closer to the theory that only those who had personally accepted Jesus Christ were destined for heaven.[3]

Bush had debated the theory with his mother, and she had immediately called Graham and asked him to weigh in on her son's rigid understanding of the New Testament. "I happen to agree with what George says about the interpretations of the New Testament, but I want to remind both of you, never play God,' " said Graham. After the exchange between Bush and Graham was first revealed in a Houston newspaper, Richards's staffers seized the biblical dialogue as a possible campaign wedge and bought advertisements aimed at Jewish voters. Bush began to back away from his earlier insistence and frequently told reporters, "I believe God decides who goes to heaven, not George W. Bush."[4]

The episode served to reinforce the twin-faced political perception that Bush had intimate ties to the inflexible evangelical community but, at the same time, could move to a more moderate stance. The revelations also made it safer for Bush to use welfare as the one policy initiative where he could openly talk about his own personal belief system—and where he could more easily conform to the demands from the Christian Right that he be more muscular than his father when it came to injecting religion into public policy. By the end of the campaign and with Rove's guidance, Bush was beginning to craft a "personal responsibility" manifesto that suggested that Texans would be better served by turning to God, not government, to improve their social standing. His proposed welfare cuts would be wrapped in a velvet hammer called "Faith Based Programs"—a popular concept with Newt Gingrich, William Bennett, and other GOP policy shapers. Outlined by a Bush welfare adviser, an ex-Marxist University of Texas journalism professor and author named Marvin Olasky, the programs called for a wholesale rejection of 1960s-inspired health, welfare, and social services policies.

Olasky's book *Tragedy of American Compassion*, passed from Bennett to Gingrich and on to other stalwarts of the unfolding Republican Revolution of 1994, outlined how churches and the private sector—corporations and middle-class volunteers—would take control of food handouts, cash handouts, housing assistance, and health care. It was, according to the plan, a nineteenth-century concept from an era when "benevolent" industrialists and churches ostensibly provided the bulk of social services to American citizens. In many ways, it harked back to the period when George W.'s nineteenth-century role models George Herbert Walker and Samuel Prescott Bush had helped to define what it meant to be a "businessman-statesman." "Government doesn't have a monopoly on compassion," Bush was saying in almost every speech. And many observers in Texas began to suggest that if Bush was ultimately interested in crafting the way he was perceived nationally, he had found an all-purpose, easily translatable way to do it through his welfare and social services proposals. Some people who took the time to study the plans to dismantle the state and federal programs said it was a heavy moral nod to the Christian Right—and a more aggressive version of what his father had once proposed: using volunteers, reducing the role of government, cutting programs, and finding "a thousand points of light."

Bush would become enamored of the bearded, bespectacled Olasky and his theories; the latter's very résumé, the fact that he had been a dedicated Marxist in the 1960s but then had realized the error of his ways and become a Presbyterian elder, editor of Christian magazines, and devotee of right-wing causes, was perfectly symbolic. Olasky had turned his back on the same sort of guilt that Bush had seen at Harvard and Yale—everything, anything that might have led to the time that Yale students had tried to burn the Old Man in effigy.

Through Rove, Bush also became interested in David Horowitz and Myron Magnet, two other essayists and sociologists who had been deriding the 1960s as a period of moral decay and knee-jerk northeastern liberal policies that the country was still paying for. Each further served to convince Bush that the 1960s had been the root of the societal ills of the 1980s and 1990s: the welfare generation, the permanent underclass, the suffocating limitations of governmental regulations, the antibusiness climate that continually squelched visionary entrepreneurial activity. In Horowitz's book *Destructive Generation: Second Thought About the '60s* and Magnet's book *The Dream and the Nightmare*, Bush found the final ideological proof of what his gut had been telling him through all those years in the belly of the "arrogant," "cynical," "claustrophobic," and "guilty" worlds of Yale and Harvard—the worlds that stood in marked contrast to the way he viewed his father's arrival in Midland, his own arrival in West Texas.

He had always seen himself as a Texan, and he was still deriding William Sloane Coffin decades after he sensed that Coffin had attacked the Old Man—had attacked, really, the entire Bush legacy. For thirty years, Coffin had symbolized the essence of everything he hated about those people who had pierced holes in the certitudes of the world he inherited from Prescott Bush and his father. He couldn't wait to leave the Northeast and return to Texas, especially an isolated piece of the state where the things that defined the 1960s for many Americans seemed never to have occurred.

"The Sixties created the victim groups that now tear at the fabric of American enterprise," Horowitz once wrote. "That they could have so quickly acquired legitimacy in locales such as the university, and that their assault on the notion of e pluribus unum could continue to be so successful, are ominous developments requiring close surveillance at the very least . . . We saw Pandora's box being opened in the Sixties."[5] That perfectly encapsulated Bush's attitude about the political foment in the 1960s at Yale and the early 1970s at Harvard, and it was a welcome relief to read the reformed radical, the ebullient Horowitz—who had once been in the vanguard of the New Left as editor of *Ramparts* magazine before abruptly becoming the kind of unabashed new breed of Reaganite who could embrace pop culture just like P. J. O'Rourke and Rush Limbaugh while managing to serve as one of the leading professional critics of the 1960s.

GEORGE W. had asked his father to stay away right up until the last day before the election, and now the Old Man and his Secret Service detail had carefully driven through crowded traffic to the cordoned-off noon-time Monday rally in Houston at the Hyatt Regency. Just a few weeks earlier, he had been dwelling on his name, his father's name: Miami reporter Tom Fiedler had flown to Texas, doing a piece about the way George W. and his brother Jeb were carrying on the political legacy—and were poised, perhaps, to surpass the Kennedys, Tafts, Rockefellers, Adamses, and Roosevelts as the preeminent American political dynasty. The writer wondered if someone named George Bush would really rather exercise political control from a safe distance—by wielding the family's considerable power from offstage rather than in elected office. "I never looked at it that way, being kingmaker instead of king. I guess it doesn't fit my personality. When your name is George Bush, with the kind of personality I have, which is a very engaging personality, at least outgoing, in which my job is to sell tickets to baseball games, you're a public person," George W., self-described salesman, had replied.[6]

His father had been at Jeb's side in Florida for only four days, but those had been splashy, wide-open-visibility days. In Houston, his brief hotel appearance marked his first and only big-time, side-by-side public statement of support for his first son, and it came less than twenty hours before the election. It was muggy in the usual energy-sapping Houston way, and both of them looked tired. People watching the son and the father said that even if they hadn't been so drawn, they had never looked more alike. The elder Bush was casual and self-effacing in a surprisingly endearing way, mocking the way he himself had a tendency to drop nouns and pronouns—the thing that Dana Carvey had picked up on in *Saturday Night Live:* "It was suggested that I come up here and criticize the present governor. Not going to do it. Wouldn't be right. Wouldn't be prudent."[7]

Her numbers dwindling, Richards had been in full-frontal attack mode for the last eight weeks, strafing George W.'s business inadequacies, the alleged trading irregularities, the fact that you could count his key "issue" areas on fewer than five fingers. At the same time, her high-level staffers and advisers were warring with one another about whether she had focused too much on what he hadn't done as opposed to what else she could do. Over the last thirty days, her strategists had issued a blizzard of statements demanding that Bush release the contents of the report on the SEC investigation into his Harken stock trade and alleging that on three other occasions he had also failed to meet other SEC deadlines.

After his appearance with his father in Houston, he immediately flew *Accountability One* back to Dallas; he had a rule that he would always return to Dallas at night after each day's campaigning ended. He didn't sleep well, and he woke up early to do the going-to-vote photo opportunity at an elementary school in Dallas. At the polling station, he was still foggy, suddenly realizing that he had forgotten his wallet and his voter's ID card. Election officials let him go behind the curtain to vote anyway. Later in the day, he went to the Cooper Aerobics Center for a run, and in the afternoon, he, Laura, and the twelve-year-old twins prepared to fly to Austin and stay at the GOP campaign suite at the Capitol Marriott.[8]

In the suite, there was one phone call after another from his father in Houston, who called ten times that day. Rove, Hughes, college roommate Clay Johnson, and Midland oil buddy Don Evans were fidgeting into and out of the Bush circle. The lead was evident early, and it simply kept widening. At 10 P.M., Richards called and conceded; some people who saw her after she gave up said she looked almost strangely relieved. Izzy Hernandez, his personal aide, watched him closely and saw a massive smile spread across his face as he listened to Richards. Minutes later, Bush was told that his father was on the line again. Next, George W. called the two other most powerful elected officials in Texas, both of whom were old-school Democrats: dogged Speaker of the House Pete Laney and unbridled Lieutenant Governor Bob Bullock. At 10:30 P.M., the first son, Laura, and the twins began preparing for the heady walk down to the stage in the Marriott's Capitol Ballroom. It looked as if half the population of Midland were hanging in the hallways, threading into the ballroom, swilling long-necked beers and jockeying to be in his sight line. CNN was reporting him the winner, 54 percent to 45 percent—he had won by 335,504 votes, the biggest margin in twenty years.

In Washington, D.C., a Democratic National Committee "opposition researcher," whose primary mission was to quietly unleash investigative inquiries into GOP candidates around the country, had already begun thinking of the ramifications for the presidential race in the year 2000. Bush had gotten a bounce from the Newt Gingrich–fueled Republican Revolution in 1994, which had certainly whipsawed back against someone as vulnerably high-profile as Richards. But it wasn't all just him being gusted along by the armies of the Right. Richards wasn't supposed to lose. Before the final numbers were even in, the DNC operative was already jotting down notes about the Bush campaign's winning strategy and had broken it down into the same factors the DNC had been watching all year. First, there was the Message Discipline: staying on target with only three or four simple, key, core ideas. That was easy to understand, the obvious game plan from the outset of the campaign. But it was the personal discipline, the obvious campaign to reinvent himself, that no one had forecast. In Washington, the idea was that Richards was supposed to win the election—just as she had won in 1990—simply because he was supposed to lose. George W. Bush and no one else, none of the advisers left over from his Old Man's campaigns, none of the advisers scrambling to take credit for his upset of the best-known governor in America, could have done it. His blunt friend Mary Matalin had affectionately called him "a political terrorist"—by finally, at the age of forty-eight, understanding how to balance the modern curse and the modern benefit of the Bush-Walker legacy.

"I want to thank the rest of my family, scattered all over our country," George W., flanked by two Texas flags, told the election-night crowd. "But I particularly want to send my love to two Houstonians—in case you weren't sure who I was talking about, one of them has real gray hair and wears pearls."[9]

IN HOUSTON, the elder Bush and Barbara were watching him on TV. His father was already busy mentally preparing statements for both his sons. Earlier in the evening he had called Jeb. "Stay calm," he had said, even though Jeb could tell his father was unusually nervous.[10]

Minutes after he had also watched George W. claim victory, Jeb finally turned away from the computer screen and the four TV screens in his Miami hotel room and called Lawton Chiles to concede him a victory by 74,500 votes. All year long, the pundits, enchanted by the possibilities of a Bush dynasty, had been coming from everywhere, including Europe and Asia. They had wanted to define him and his brother, compare them to the Kennedys, and they had come to the oft-repeated conclusion that Jeb was more inclined to delve into the arcane, wonkish nuances of policy and restructuring government. Jeb was still the slower, steadier-burning one, the ideologue who felt obliged to underscore his hard, right-leaning conservative policies with bits of history, statistics, analysis. Even his older brother said as much: "Jeb is a very idealistic fellow. He absolutely has a philosophical grounding and he's got great faith in his ideas," George W. said to a writer that fall.[11]

But unlike George W., Jeb was willing to talk about the obvious political legacy in the family. "I want to be able to look my father in the eye and say, 'I continued the legacy,' " Jeb had said suddenly not long before the election.[11] Jeb had also told people that he had, thankfully, never been psychoanalyzed and measured against his father in the same way as George W. After he had excelled at tennis and graduated Phi Beta Kappa from the University of Texas, he had moved to Florida "to get out from under my Dad's shadow"[13] and begun a complex, often-criticized career in real estate. Unlike his brother, he wanted to be away from Texas. Jeb was seven years younger than his brother, but he liked to talk about the fact that he had grown right alongside the evolution of what he called the "therapeutic age of politics." He knew what was required of him and his brother, and that it was something his grandfather and father had loathed: "You've got to be an exhibitionist to be in this" is how he put it.[14]

After he called Chiles, then talked to his father in Houston, Jeb stayed awake deep into the morning hours, sipping on scotch, thinking about his political future, and weighing whether a round of golf might not be just the thing to clear his head. Tennis, golf—it was what his mother had always done when things went wrong.[15] Back in Houston, his father dutifully talked about his ambivalent feelings. "It's your own son, your own flesh and blood," he said, beginning to explain it. "The joy is in Texas but our hearts are in Florida." Jeb's loss was "hurtful to the family," and George W.'s win was "a great joy for us, seeing that flash on the screen. I can't tell you the emotion I feel and the pride in the way he conducted himself."[16]

George W.'s father added something else, one more thought about what he would do for his first son now that he had won an election, now that a Bush held elected office again: "My role will be to stay out of the way."[17] Which, of course, is what his first son had asked him to do as he tried to convince people that he could finally win something on his own.

THE DAY AFTER George W. was elected governor of Texas, a completely naked man loped past the alarmed pedestrians on the city's main artery, Congress Avenue, a long, broad, gently sloping boulevard that stretches for miles directly toward the front door of the largest state capitol in America. The stunning pink-granite palace is seven feet taller than the U.S. Capitol in Washington, D.C., and was constructed from hand-cut pieces of Granite Mountain in Marble Falls, Texas, and filled with seven miles of oak, pine, cherry, cedar, walnut, ash, and mahogany wainscoting, as well as an impressive painting of Alamo defender Davy Crockett.[18]

The sprinting man was dressed just in socks and sneakers. The words "BLACK TUESDAY" were carefully painted on his bare chest—and the words "I LOVE ANN" painted on his bare ass. Texas had lost its most prominent and nationally compelling Democrat, but not its most powerful.

Lost amid the campaign hype was the fact that the blustery Democrat most people said was channeling the ferocious, over-the-top spirits of both LBJ and Foghorn Leghorn—Lieutenant Governor Bob Bullock— had been saying nice things about Bush—"a surprisingly personable young man"—even before the election. With his ominous, road-hardened face, the combustible sixty-five-year-old Bullock was the single most feared Democrat in Texas. He had day-to-day command of the Texas Senate, but, more important, he had spent decades specializing in what people at the State Capitol quietly called "drive-by ass-chewing": flogging lobbyists and lawmakers in both private and public. Most state officials simply addressed him as "Governor."

Über-Texan Bullock, who had previously served as a state legislator, state comptroller, secretary of state, and assistant attorney general, was like an omnipresent figure from the lost chapters in the diaries of Louisiana's Huey and Earl Long: married five times, including twice to the same woman; a recovering alcoholic who bragged about how he had "enrolled in drunk school" and who also suffered from clinical depression; a man who had been stopped for driving 106 miles per hour; a prankster who had once sent a box jammed with cow shit to a columnist: "This is bullshit, and so is your column." For years, he had demanded that people swear proper allegiance to Texas. Also for years, he had literally seesawed between life and death as parts of his lung were removed, as he was treated for a heart attack, as depression took a grip on him, as a spinal disc ruptured. His aides began to use a few unsettling, black humor lines every time they sent out a press release: *"If alive, Comptroller Bob Bullock will be appearing . . ."*[19]

The stories people told about him and that he told about himself, were outrageous but often true in a peculiarly Texas way where the political truth is never what it seems: Wasn't it Bullock and his political pals who pulled out a pistol in the old barbecue joint in downtown Austin and began aiming it at the rat they saw slithering by? Wasn't it Bullock who firmly gripped the hand of a *Dallas Morning News* reporter he had met for the first time and said that what he really wanted to do was make love to one of the highest-ranking editors in Texas journalism—though he used a more colorful word to describe what he really wanted to do to her? Wasn't it Bullock who called up reporters in the Austin press corps and accused them of "smoking dope" in the State Capitol? Wasn't it Bullock who fearlessly called the leading Democratic operative in Texas an "amoeba with a pinhead"?

If Atwater had ever wanted to trot out a living history lesson, a Southern Democrat who knew more than anyone else about disarming enemies and reporters, it would have been class-conscious Bob Bullock: "You want a piece of fried chicken? Are you rich? You're a hippie, aren't you? Go on, you can tell me," Bullock would insist, all in one breath. Bullock loved the game more than anyone at the State Capitol could remember anyone else loving the game, and he was warlike in his open insistence on allegiance to all things Texan—a running joke was that if it had been 1836, Bullock would have been on the roof of the Alamo. He ended every speech and legislative session with his three favorite words, "God bless Texas." Bullock often defined people by their knowledge of Texas history and their ability to recite the nuances of all the battles that had led to the founding of the Republic of Texas.

He was the consummate backdoor man and Democratic kingmaker; some people said he had even more in common with Ann Richards than the telling lines on their faces. Richards, who had battled alcohol herself, had helped steer Bullock out of the alcoholic fog and somewhere toward sanity. But during her tenure as governor, the corrosive sides of their personalities had begun to eat away at each other. Bullock, Mr. Texas Democrat, felt that he was being ignored by Mrs. Texas Democrat—she wasn't working as hard as he was, she wasn't there half the time, and she was, as Bullock was saying, too popular for her own damned good: "Her heart's always been in the right place, it's just that the television camera took its place for a while."[20] Bullock knew that the governor's office in Texas was a bully pulpit, that it had been specifically created to be constitutionally weak, to defang any aspiring kings or queens. He knew that the governor of Texas didn't make law but urged law, cajoled law. The governor of Texas was a cheerleader, a salesman—who, if he or she was good at the job, could get the lieutenant governor in the Senate and the Speaker of the House to take care of the senators and representatives who were carrying bills on behalf of the governor. The governor of Texas could appoint committees, veto legislation, and call special sessions—and Bullock and the Speaker of the House could break up the committees, override the vetoes, and simply not show up for the special sessions.

In Texas, in the end, one of the rarely appreciated verities of political life was that the governor's function was often not the open, clear creation of bold, visionary legislation; often it had to do with getting along with and prodding the 31 members of the Senate and the 150 members of the House. The governor's office in Texas was really the ultimate extension for someone who had been a head cheerleader in high school, the stickball commissioner, the fraternity president, the agribusiness salesman, the land man, and the public face of a baseball team.

In many ways, Bullock was Bush's best chance at surviving his first term as governor of Texas. Lee Atwater would have known; Atwater had said it back in Washington when he had stolen that line from LBJ: "I'd rather have him inside the tent pissing out than outside the tent pissing in."

Now that Bush was governor, Bullock was also thinking about his first serious conversation with the former president's son. Just five weeks before the election, Bullock was at his limestone home a few blocks from the State Capitol, recovering from open-heart surgery and surrounded by pieces of parchment and yellowed photographs from his decades at the pinnacle of Texas politics. The phone rang, and one of his loyal foot soldiers in the Texas Senate was on the other end. The state senator said that GOP gubernatorial candidate George W. Bush wanted to pay a secret courtesy call to the lieutenant governor of Texas.

Rumors were coursing through Texas power circles that Richards and Bullock had finally ceased talking to each other. Bush wanted the meeting. It would be the culmination of all of the dozens of quiet meetings he had been arranging with key state lawmakers since he had moved back to Texas six years earlier. A few minutes later, Bush's car arrived in front of Bullock's tree-shaded home just a few blocks from the State Capitol. Bullock laughed when he saw Bush arrive. He thought Bush was "playing Dick Tracy," bustling out of the car and then ordering his driver to begin circling the block. Bullock thought it was "real *kin-dee-garten* stuff."[21]

Bullock instantly did what he and LBJ always did; he tried to disarm his visitor. Atwater would have been proud: "I still am an alcoholic, a recovering alcoholic," Bullock bluntly said to Bush.

Most people knew that Bullock was nearing the end of his political life and that he was thinking about his legacy in Texas, all his decades in service to the partisan machine. He had thought about trying for governor, but the timing had never been right. People said he didn't care about rising in the party anymore—but he did care about his legacy, maybe as a man who had done something truly bold in Texas political history.

Bullock listened as Bush told him about his years in Midland, "staying out too late and drinking." Bullock felt a bond—he had only one real friend who hadn't once made a habit of staying out late, and that was because that friend didn't drink in the first place.

Without hesitating, the Democratic lieutenant governor of Texas said, "I was very, very disappointed, and I still am, in Ann Richards. If you're going to be that kind of pussyfooting, headline-grabbing, television-grabbing governor, forget it."[22]

He waited. Finally, Bush said what the lifelong, ailing Texas politico wanted to hear as the final bits of his legacy were being written: "I'm going to work with you." It was all Bullock needed. It was all Bush really needed to win the crusty legend in Texas who cracked the whip and made the political beasts of burden move on time.

THE TEXAS LEGISLATURE meets for just 140 days every two years. In early 1995, at the outset of the seventy-fourth session, Bush called Bullock and Speaker of the House Pete Laney and asked them to join him every Wednesday morning for a series of closed-door power breakfasts. The meetings continued for months. Laney, less volatile than Bullock, could be just as vital to Bush's success in selling himself in the marble halls of the State Capitol as an effective first-term governor. Laney was a beak-nosed, unpretentious native of the cotton lands and sandy loam soil of Hale Center, Texas, a twenty-five-year veteran of state politics with a drawl as deep as the Palo Duro Canyon; he was a less tortured soul than Bullock but as good a student of Texas political history. He was a faithful Democrat from West Texas and as much of a Lone Star zealot as Richards or Bullock—"Laney will Texas you to death!" Bullock would bark. But, unlike Bullock, Richards, or Bush, he had never been saddled by anything even remotely approaching celebrity. He avoided it, leaving it to Bullock, Richards, and anyone else who wanted it. Laney was a party loyalist who had his hands full riding herd on a snorting, fractious group of 150 state representatives who descended on free-spirited Austin from every far-flung corner of Planet Texas every two years. Without fail, in almost every session, one of those esteemed lawmakers would do something to confirm everyone's worst fears. Laney had to explain how to write bills, introduce them, and vote on them. Truth be told, he wanted to be remembered as an efficient prairie parliamentarian, a traffic cop, someone who made sure the whole unfettered Texas thing didn't succumb to the level of a honking, sweaty institutional gridlock. He wanted lawmakers to show up, work, and not yell at one another; he was, more than anybody else at the highest elected levels in Texas, a pragmatist. And Laney had already thought hard about the new governor. "I don't think he thought he was going to win," he said. "I think he thought this was going to be his first attempt. He's still probably pinching himself."[23]

Laney knew that Bush had already studied the bills coursing through the Texas legislature, seen that education and crime were prominent, and jumped on board those issues even before the gubernatorial votes were cast. Laney never resented that; it was what anyone who wanted to get elected would have done. All of that just meant forging easy, early alliances with the people in Texas who mattered, and it created an image of Bush driving the train. "If you find four things that are already fixin' to happen that you can believe in, then you're politically naive or dumb not to utilize that," drawled Laney.[24]

Laney also realized something else about the Texas legislature, something that led to the demise of Ann Richards: "You know, you can make yourself politically vulnerable by saying what you think every time. Ann had already segregated herself with a cause and, well, she had a higher calling."

THE JANUARY INAUGURATION festivities stood in marked contrast to Richards's "march on the Capitol" with Kris Kristofferson and Willie Nelson. Bush's old oil patch buddy Dennis "Weemus" Grubb was put in charge of the entertainment, and the Oak Ridge Boys, Larry Gatlin, Chuck Norris, Nolan Ryan, the Dixie Chicks, and the Geezinslaws—an Austin novelty act whose defining song was "I'm White and I Can't Get Down"—were among the featured guests. Ann Richards was not in attendance; she was traveling in California.

All of his siblings were there under a gunmetal gray, overcast sky. "You know what? I'm not giving interviews," snapped Neil. "No advice," his father tersely replied when someone asked what he had told his first son about governing.[25] Billy Graham, of course, gave the invocation; for years, Bush had been crediting Graham with helping him grow closer to the Bible. Graham solemnly referred to the "moral and spiritual example his mother and father set for us all."[26] The night before, Bush had finished working on his ten-minute speech with Karl Rove and press secretary Karen Hughes. Unlike Ann Richards, who had announced a "new Texas," Bush was going to proclaim that this was the era of "the responsible Texas." It was a satisfying salve for the Christian conservatives, and it was also an attack on all the guilty losers from the 1960s, from the Northeast, as well as a subtle attack on Bill Clinton's personal shortcomings.

The speech could identify George W. as someone who had come of age in the 1960s, a baby boomer like Clinton, but one who exercised personal control: "For the last thirty years, our culture has steadily replaced personal responsibility with collective guilt. This must end. The new freedom Texas seeks must be matched with renewed personal responsibility."[27]

Rove, who had worked to have George W. capitalize on the family name but not have it transmute into a ball and chain, was nearby and beaming. The Atwater of Texas talked about the dynastic elements, the way it was all just like the Kennedys: "On this day, George W. Bush clearly comes into his own, and no one can dispute that. We really do have a generational passage here. Sort of like Joe Kennedy handing off to young John."[28]

As the final swearing-in oath was administered, the one making the elder Bush's son only the second Republican governor in Texas since Reconstruction, cameras whirred as the elder Bush was wiping away a tear from his eye and reaching to hug his thirteen-year-old granddaughter Jenna.

GEORGE W. put his shares of the Texas Rangers in a blind trust, and the family moved into the private, three thousand-square-foot second-floor quarters of the Governor's Mansion, where Texas Republic President Sam Houston had once slept. Jenna and Barbara, the twins, brought along their Green Day CDs. The parents talked about putting them in a private school in Austin, and political observers said Bush advisers wondered whether doing so would create political liabilities for a first-term governor who was pushing hard on disassembling state regulations on local school districts. Jenna, friends of the family said, was the volatile and feisty one, the cutup, the one more like her father; Barbara was quieter, more like her mother. In a perhaps unsubtle reference to Hillary Clinton, Bush once described

Laura to a Texas writer as "the perfect wife for a governor" and not some-one "trying to butt in and always, you know, compete. There's nothing worse in the political arena than spouses competing for public accolades or the limelight."[29] The campaign strategy had been to gradually place her in front of supportive, nonconfrontational GOP women's groups; by the end of the race, she had traveled to 30 of Texas's 254 counties.

The new governor ordered Richards's official Ford Crown Victoria to be retired and replaced by a Lincoln Town Car. Her old office walls were torn down, and the governor's office on the second floor was en-larged to three times the size it had been under her administration. And he moved in the chunky mahogany desk that had been passed down to him from his father.

He placed his 250 baseballs, many of them autographed by the game's stars, in a glass-paneled wooden cabinet at one end of the room. On a small oak table behind his desk he arranged several photographs: a framed shot of him being sworn in as his father and mother stood to his right; an-other shot of a toddling George W. Bush, his parents and Prescott Bush and Dorothy Walker Bush posing in front of a prop plane at the Midland airport in the 1950s; a faded black-and-white photograph of Prescott Bush waving to an audience at a 1952 victory rally.

According to officials with the State Preservation Board, Bush con-sidered several paintings to hang on his office wall, including some in the collection of the University of Texas. He eventually selected an 1830s por-trait of Texas founder Sam Houston, "Sam Houston as Marius Among the Ruins of Carthage." The painting, attributed to artist Washington Cooper, depicts the frontiersman and president of the Republic of Texas in a toga. It was, according to Texas legend, a portrait that Sam Houston, the old general and president, had come to regret.

Joe Allbaugh, the six-foot-four, 280-pound campaign manager who had started in politics at the age of twelve by working for Barry Gold-water, was named chief of staff. Karen Hughes, the ex–TV reporter from Fort Worth whose father was a major general in the Army and the last governor of the Panama Canal Zone, was named chief spokesman. Vance McMahon, a corporate finance attorney from Houston, was named direc-tor of policy and research. Clay Johnson, George W.'s lifelong friend from their days at Andover and his roommate at Yale, was designated to oversee the governor's appointments to state boards and agencies. Karl Rove, of course, remained his chief political adviser. During his tenure as governor, many of the people who had helped him and his father get elected would also receive state assignments: Fred McClure was given a seat on the Texas A&M board of regents; Don Evans received a similar post with the University of Texas; Chase Untermeyer, his father's director of White House personnel and the former assistant secretary of the Navy, would be named chairman of the State Education Board; and Michael Williams, a close Midland friend whom he had personally recommended to his father for a Bush administration post as assistant secretary with the Department of Education—and who had drawn the intense, national ire of civil rights and NAACP leaders for declaring race-based admissions policies at public schools "illegal"—would eventually be named to the Texas Railroad Commission. Nolan Ryan was made a state parks commissioner, as was Susan Howard, who had starred on *Dallas* and was on the board of directors of the National Rifle Association.

At the end of his first month as governor, he and Laura accepted an invitation to the annual White House dinner for the nation's governors. They flew to Washington, and after they arrived at the party, Bush said he was feeling "nostalgic" about being back in the White House for the first time since his father had been ousted. Mary Chapin Carpenter was scheduled to sing, and the menu included crab, lamb chops, sorbets, and a selection of American wines. "I look forward to seeing our friends who worked here in the White House—people who served from one administration to the next, the ushers and waiters," the younger Bush said.[30]

He and Laura mingled with some familiar GOP faces, including presidential possibilities Christine Todd Whitman from New Jersey and William Weld from Massachusetts, and when people asked him how Clinton was doing in his state, Bush announced that "he's in trouble in Texas." Then the couple stepped to the back of the slow-moving, lengthy receiving line. The march to shake hands with and pay homage to the tuxedoed President Clinton and Hillary Rodham Clinton, dressed in a black velvet Donna Karan gown and an antique, beaded necklace, seemed interminable.

"I've never had to stand in line here before," Bush said under his breath.[31]

BUSH STEPPED UP his courtesy calls and invitations to dozens of state lawmakers. Laney, along with Bullock, saw him every Wednesday morning. One wary Austin liberal lawmaker, a Jewish transplant from New York, described himself to Bush as a "New York Yankee in LBJ's court"; Bush, the Connecticut Yankee, instantly won him over by telling him he had the same problem. He worked hard selling himself the way he knew best, holding one-on-one meetings with high-powered Austin lobbyists, doing all the disarming things with reporters and staffers that his mother and Lee Atwater had mastered. His mother, he knew, was still a formidable political presence, and he decided to draw attention to her with a Senate resolution that every Texas senator approved: *"The most famous mother in Texas . . . beloved and admired throughout the nation, Barbara Bush is a special treasure to the citizens of Texas, and Mother's Day is an appropriate opportunity to express our gratitude to her for her many contributions to our state."*

By the end of the 74th Legislative Session, he had made no gaffes, and through more than a hundred backroom meetings he had succeeded in convincing a handful of senators and representatives to continue to carry his four main food groups forward. Texas had embarked on plans to return more control to local school districts; it had begun a sweeping—some called it onerous—series of welfare cuts; it had passed several bills imposing stricter penalties on juvenile criminals; it had taken measures toward reducing "frivolous" personal-injury lawsuits, as well as holding down the monetary awards in those lawsuits. For most Democrats and many moderates, it was a pro-business but relatively benign agenda.

For his many supporters in the State Capitol, it was a wholesale success and a testimony to his powers of persuasion. He was criticized for ignoring or avoiding other areas that Ann Richards had explored: the environment, AIDS, job programs for displaced welfare recipients, minority appointments to important state positions. Through his first year, Bush's approval ratings chugged forward from the 50 percent range and up into the 60s, and he joked that it was all because of a "case of low expectations. When I first came to Austin, I thought most legislators were drunks and philanderers. And they're not. They're extremely hard-working citizens of Texas," he said one Wednesday afternoon over lunch.[32]

Four months later, Clinton made a swing to Texas to visit his handful of longtime fund-raisers and supporters in Austin and Dallas. The Million Man March was unfolding in Washington, and Clinton also scheduled a forty-minute speech on racial harmony to ten thousand listeners at the University of Texas. Governor Bush told reporters he was pleased Clinton hadn't argued for a "new law or a new government program" to combat racial problems and that the solution was a matter of personal responsibility "in the hearts of individual Texans and Americans." When he returned to Washington, Clinton sent a handwritten letter on October 26 from the Oval Office: *Dear Governor—I enjoyed my visit to Texas and was pleased to get your note, and your comments about the importance of personal responsibility. A lot of Democrats have positive things to say about you. . . . Sincerely, Bill Clinton.*[33]

TIME, THE CHRISTIAN Science Monitor, The Boston Globe, and *The New York Times* all began taking note—not so much of the scope of his ideological vision as of his blossoming bipartisan numbers. They also couldn't help notice the excited, deferential way other national GOP leaders were beginning to behave around him, something that had started at the GOP training session for incoming governors, when people had congratulated him for toppling Ann Richards. As the honeymoon went into its second year, there were also some cautionary signs in the State Capitol of a slowly building resistance and even an emerging sense that he was only biding his time as he passed through Texas and flirted with a run for the presidency. Some initially swooning Democrats, baby boomers, and moderates began to register alarm when he defended big health maintenance organizations, said Texas might consider requiring children to pay their parents' nursing home bills now covered by Medicaid, opposed more environmental regulations, blasted proposals that would help minorities earn state contracts, and threw his political muscle behind Senator Phil Gramm's presidential bid before reluctantly supporting Bob Dole.

Bullock was already seeing Bush's national inclinations; he was there when Bush called Gingrich and "straightened" him out about something Gingrich had said about Texas public policy. Late into 1996, George W. was openly being discussed as Dole's vice presidential nominee. But his father said what he already knew: he would need at least two terms as an elected Texas official first. In a nod to his numbers, the flattering profiles in the press, and the unspoken but obvious ability of the Bush name to raise millions of dollars, he was asked to cochair the GOP National Convention in San Diego, where a special tribute to his father was planned.

"It'd be wonderful," his father told a reporter that summer, the idea of his first son becoming president, probably unseating Al Gore and the rest of the Clintonites, beginning to form in his head. "But it's not—I'm not like Joe Kennedy sitting there: 'Here's a couple of hundred thousand—go out and win the West Virginia primary.' I, you know, it's not a scheme. It's not a dynasty. It's not a legacy."[34]

GEORGE W. was clamping down on an unlit cigar, and his sagging staffers trailed after him—"The Energizer bunny" they whispered. The 1996 convention was like 1992's coming-out party all over again, with Karl

Rove and others orchestrating a nonstop series of profile-escalating interviews in San Diego. With Dole floundering in the same drowning pool of generational politics that his father had found so confusing and distasteful, the younger Bush was one of the few young, photogenic, quotable GOP luminaries around. And out on the convention floor, GOP consultants were gleefully telling glum fund-raisers and skeptical reporters that George W. Bush was "our Clinton." They were adding that he was perfectly situated in the party, able to cater to the real conservatives in a way that other rising, suspiciously moderate stars such as New Jersey Governor Christine Todd Whitman never could. Besides, he was a better modern politician than his grandfather and father: "He's of a different generation, he's a different person," said family adviser Bob Teeter.[35]

At the start of the next legislative session in 1997, he again began flirting with his father's legacy, with the one policy area that had, in a sense, helped destroy his father. Without fully informing Speaker of the House Pete Laney and Lieutenant Governor Bob Bullock—or key policy advisers on his staff—he decided to make a $3 billion cut in property taxes the centerpiece of his new legislative agenda. He had also come up with a complex budget package that some critics complained could come at the expense of the social services system in Texas. Almost completely ignored by the media and concurrent with his plan to cut property taxes, he was quietly dispatching his Health and Human Services czar to the White House to argue for fast-track federal approval of a plan to privatize Texas's multibillion-dollar system of administering health care, emergency cash, housing, and other necessities to the poor and the elderly. The plan, which would have affected up to twenty thousand state workers and hundreds of thousands of lower-income Texans, was to allow major international firms and defense contractors, including Electronic Data Systems (EDS), Lockheed Martin, and IBM, to bid for a computerization of the state's Health and Human Services network.

The privatization plan was being carefully monitored by dozens of states and even foreign countries where Lockheed and IBM were pushing for similar proposals. In Texas, unionized state workers and social workers quickly organized against the plan and began enlisting the aid of national labor leaders and the same political consulting firm that had handled the attack strategy for Ann Richards against Bush. Under enormous pressure from the AFL-CIO, the plan stalled in the White House. In response, Bush fired off a stream of angry letters to the Clinton administration, demanding federal approval to begin the privatization process. But mindful of the national labor union pressure, Clinton and Health and Human Services Secretary Donna Shalala rebuffed him and the episode evolved into his only definable defeat at the federal level. The ripple effect was immense—and not just because he had been slapped down by the White House.

Now in Texas, with no easy, clear money to make up for his property tax cuts, some state legislators were proposing their own tax solutions. The session ended in a puddle of muddled headlines—and with Bush claiming victory with a more modest property tax cut, a scaled-back privatization program, and a variety of cuts in welfare benefits.

The end of the session was a lesson: stick to simpler messages, less complex themes, and issues; stay attuned to more modest goals. There was one more lesson in store for Bush as he met with Rove and other GOP advisers and they tried to account for Bill Clinton's nagging popularity and how Bob Dole was dismissed by baby boomers—and how there seemed to be an increasingly virulent reaction to Newt Gingrich and the other spear-carriers for the Republican Revolution of 1994. The GOP, Bush told his Texas advisers, was still seen as the party of anti-empathy.

In a way, in the summer of 1997, he was deciding to come full circle and find his father—at the risk of being called a wimp himself. He would have to discipline himself one more time, to convince people that he had recast himself as a moderate, a politician who was ardent on "personal responsibility" but who walked with a caring, empathetic soul. Concurrent with the reshaping, there would still be an almost constant string of references and allusions—some of them even coming from himself, his brother, his closest advisers and friends—to those cloudy, ill-defined "nomadic" years. Some Austin insiders still suggested that it was all part of a broader strategy to personalize him, to support the belief that instead of having spent his life in carefully measured moments—almost every month structured and accounted for by a job or political campaign orchestrated by his father—he was really just like most baby boomers, all those people of the '60s who had been distracted before they found the right path.

To recast himself, of course, he would use the same phrase that doggedly loyal Ron Kaufman—a Good Man, an FOB—had used to describe his father. He had settled on the perfect phrase, the same perfect, ten-year-old phrase that the upper echelons of Team Bush had once decided to use when they were packaging his father for his run at the presidency: Compassionate Conservative.

THE 1997 session ended with furious storms, including one of the most devastating two-hundred-mile-an-hour tornadoes in the history of Texas, a howling black mass that killed dozens as it marched in the general direction of the State Capitol and the Governor's Mansion. The tornado finally stalled to the north of the city and almost took the small farming town of Jarrell and its four hundred citizens completely off the map. The tornado dissipated, and the devils in the statehouse were dispatched home. Rove instantly began spinning more gold, selling the legislative session as another victory. He also told reporters that his phone didn't stop ringing with calls from people volunteering to help Bush run for president.

Bush's father had always been reluctant to call his arrival in barren, unpaved West Texas in the 1940s a "Horatio Alger thing"—but Rove definitely saw something in the way the first son had arrived in 1975 from Harvard. "This is a guy who threw his life's possessions in the back of a car and drove to Midland. He lit out for the flat plains of West Texas. This is part of the American West. It is a throwback to an earlier era where people were judged by the content of their character and not their curriculum vitae," Rove insisted to a visiting reporter.[36]

Some Bush staffers were quietly envious of the relationship between Bush and Rove, a relationship that stretched back to the early days when they had both known Lee Atwater, who was writing the rules for the new brand of remorseless politics. Rove and Bush talked constantly, said one of Bush's special assistants, at least twenty times a day. Rove . . . *Turd Blossom* . . . was always there, working on the fringes, from the days of the Watergate-era dirty-tricks allegations, back to when he used to fetch the car keys for the first son after he arrived in Washington from Harvard.

Rove had only just quit his job as a paid consultant to Philip Morris in the wake of allegations that he had been working for Bush while also working with tobacco lobbyists to "discredit the Democratic attorney general and head off the state's tobacco lawsuit."[37] Rove had pitched in on every national presidential campaign back to 1980, but people presumed that he really wanted to *run* one—that he harbored hopes of finally escalating to the celebrity political operative status of Atwater, James Carville, Mary Matalin, and even Paul Begala, who lived in Austin when he wasn't working in the Clinton White House. Sometimes Rove, who still hadn't graduated from college, was invited to lecture at the University of Texas, and when he was once asked how it was possible for someone with only a high school diploma to take the place of the professors, he would say, "I'm very good at what I do."[38]

Rove still ran his national political consulting and direct-mail-political-advertising twelve-man shop out of a windowless office blocks from the Governor's Mansion, and he had masterminded almost every statewide election of every Republican in Texas. In Austin, more than a few people knew that he was unflinching about taking on anyone he thought had wronged him; he had once sued former U.S. Attorney General Dick Thornburgh for not paying him $175,000 for work he had done on Thornburgh's Pennsylvania Senate race.

If Atwater had survived his cancer, he would have been pleased. Rove had assumed Atwater's role in George W.'s life, and he wanted to make sure that the first son never took the same false steps as his father. Rove had been waiting for George W. Bush. He was, Rove said, "the kind of candidate and officeholder political hacks like me wait a lifetime to be associated with."[39]

16

Dynasty

The campaign for the presidency of the United States began in earnest on August 23, 1997, in Indianapolis. George W. had already asked an old friend of Team Bush to tackle the old question, maybe on a national level. Bob Teeter, the beleaguered member of the troika that had managed the Bush presidential campaign in 1992, had begun making quiet inquiries, checking into whether or not people were confused when they heard the name George Bush: was it George Herbert Walker Bush or George Walker Bush? "They know it's me," said George W. when people asked him what he was learning from Teeter about name recognition, about whether or not all the pre-presidential polls that had his name on top were actually recording a case of mistaken identity.[1]

Now, Bush was awarded the spotlight, the Saturday-evening showcase in front of the national media and the Republican heavyweights attending the GOP Midwestern Leadership Conference in Indianapolis. GOP insiders knew that the August cattle call was a good outside-the-Beltway showcase to remind people about the lingering power of the Bush name and to gauge how his track record as Texas governor would play at a national level. It was like a pre-championship-bout strut, a chance for chest thumping and righteous anger at the way Clinton continued to slip-slide away from political payback. It was also the obvious coming-out party for possible contenders: Dan Quayle, Steve Forbes, Lamar Alexander, Jack Kemp, and Senator Fred Thompson were going to appear. Bush had worked hard on his twenty-five-minute speech. He had decided to build it slowly, to concentrate on what Rove and Don Sipple had told him about holding an audience's or a camera's gaze, slowing down a little and introducing early jokes that would also serve as a reminder about the money-and-networking power still at his disposal: "I know there's all kinds of speculation and all kinds of rumors about future politics. The national media, many of whom are here today, are having a field day, wondering out loud whether I'm going to follow my father's footsteps. I want to confront that matter head-on tonight. I will not jump out any airplanes," he said with his slash of a grin, rocking his head from front to back. The GOP leaders nodded and applauded the reference to his father's recent, well-publicized adventures during a skydiving expedition.

"Speaking about Mother, I have learned that no matter how old you are or what your job is, you can never escape your mother," George W. continued, to more applause. He said his mother was still giving him advice, and cowboys in Texas told him he needed to listen to her. Laura, he said, was now an asset, a tried and tested campaigner who was serving willingly.[2] Then something went horribly wrong as he downshifted into his checklist of accomplishments, the ones that the Texas media had been lauding him for but that, in Indianapolis, didn't translate into anything even remotely resembling adrenaline or even Republican anger. When he mentioned his father, his mother, it seemed endearing.

But anyone could see that he was losing some GOP kingmakers and, worse, the national media, when he began talking about how he was a compassionate conservative trying to bring sense to a guilt-riddled age, how he was the champion of smaller government, how he had pushed through a $1 billion property tax cut in Texas, how he was making education his principal priority, how he was a Texas moderate with a record that was going to appeal to the fence-straddling Democrats waiting for some reason to switch allegiances. Sympathetic Republicans who listened to his speech said he wasn't the razor-edged Bush they had just met in the impromptu, one-on-one gabfests in the hallway. Away from the confines of Texas and giving a speech in a national forum, he was off his cocky rhythm, and he came off sounding as if he were offering the same bloated superlatives airlifted from Anybody's Moderate Campaign. Some of the underwhelmed Republicans went one more step by suggesting that even Forbes and Quayle had more pointed, righteous anger. They said that Bush could have been talking about himself, or even his father, that Saturday night when he said, "Our president is the classic president for a society that has come to believe everyone is entitled to something, because he will promise something to almost everyone."[3]

Bush flew back to Texas and weighed the negative press. His father had already told him that he needed to have his priorities in order: get re-elected, become a two-term governor. And make sure that you win big, really big, that you ride those reelection projections hard and make a dent where it counts—among Hispanic voters, baby boomers, suburbanites. Against Ann Richards, the edict had been to avoid even the semblance of a personal attack on Mrs. Texas. The new edict passed down through the reelection staff and among the inner circle was to avoid mention of a White House run in the year 2000.

All interview requests were going to be carefully scrutinized, especially ones coming from the national media. Selected reporters would get a few minutes on the airplane. He promised that a Texas-based writer from *GQ* would eventually get a rare, lengthy interview. And he promised that a Texas-based writer from *The New Yorker*—"What are they going to do—some Gail Sheehy kind of thing?" he asked[4]—would not. "He makes it a practice to avoid events that might tend to look beyond 1998 and toward 2000," press secretary Karen Hughes began saying.[5]

In his office, months later on a brutally hot summer day, Bush was railing against the northeastern media, for all the old reasons: they had savaged his father, mistaken his comportment for indecision, and cost him the election by attacking his character, promoting Clinton, and pinning the tax fiasco on him. Now they're going to want to know about George W.'s relationship with his father. They're going to want to know exactly what he has done to move beyond his father. He loved it when author Richard Ben Cramer had described him as an ass-kicking foot soldier, a quick-witted spy, "the Roman candle" in the family.[6] He had all of that memorized; you could see him perk up when he retold his favorite descriptions in Cramer's book about the 1988 presidential race. That part was simple, clean. It was the other part that he still loathed: the measurements against his father. "Psychobabble," he muttered in his office, the word coming out of his mouth like the most vile thing imaginable.

EVEN WITH his setback in Indianapolis, the last living Texas Democrats cursed and swore that they were being drowned out by the roar of a jet leaving the airport; somehow their message had been lost and swept up in all the Bush presidential backdraft—all the drum rolls about the Bush dynasty, the way Jeb was running for governor again in Florida and hoping to join his brother just as Nelson and Winthrop Rockefeller had once done. The gubernatorial campaign against the set-upon, diligent Democrat—Garry Mauro, a Richards supporter and a Texas land commissioner who had made the state's wretched environmental record one of his highest priorities—was really over before it had begun. Money and national media focus were already being directed toward Bush in unprecedented waves.

Rove was still telling the media that he was still being inundated with calls from GOPers who were interested in working on any bigger, future campaigns that Bush might be involved in. The effect was a Democratic gubernatorial campaign that began with a palpable sense of being the underdog and would finally dissolve under the frustrating, dispirited belief that it was being completely ignored. It was an open secret among the highest levels of Bush supporters that the gubernatorial campaign was really about refining Bush the candidate—spending months and millions of dollars redefining and packaging him as a more palatable, caring candidate to Hispanic voters, women, and baby boomers. Late into the night at the Austin Club, the Caucus Club, at Club DeVille, at all the watering holes where the spin doctors, legislative aides, and Bush staffers gathered in Austin to trade secrets and wait for someone to say something that could be turned into political capital, the prevalent thought was that Bush was using the election to experiment with that national image.

The fact that the election coincided with a non-legislative-session cycle was almost too perfect—there was no need to worry about spending undue time on a legislative agenda that could possibly get out of hand. If needed, there was plenty of time to pinpoint what else there was to do to avoid any unnecessary linkage to his father and the century-old Bush-Walker legacy.

"It's hard to believe, but—I don't have time to worry about being George Bush's son," Bush said to a reporter in July. "Maybe it's a result of being confident. I'm not sure how the psychoanalysts will analyze it, but I'm not worried about it. I'm really not. I'm a free guy."[7]

IT WAS A Lone Star betrayal that took on immediate, tragic proportions. By the end of the year, Democrat Bob Bullock grandly stated that he was writing a campaign contribution check to Republican George W. Bush even though he was godfather to Garry Mauro's daughter. It wasn't that the crafty dinosaur of the old Texas Democratic machinery was suddenly going to win Bush more voters, it was that the national media would fixate on the event as proof of Bush's bipartisan appeal. Bullock, whose health had been stumbling again, cornered reporters and insisted he was doing what was right for his beloved Texas, as if this were going to be his Alamo, his legacy. In the middle of his betrayal, Mauro's office returned a birthday gift that Bullock had sent to Mauro's daughter—the young girl who also happened to be Bullock's goddaughter. Bullock picked up the phone, called Mauro's office, and told them he was sending the gift back and they damned well better keep it. They did.[8]

Reeling, the Mauro campaign said that Bullock's defection had to do with the fact that Bush was stealing Democratic riffs: raising teachers' salaries, promoting literacy, supporting antistalking measures. "As governor, my number one priority for Texas is that every child learn to read," Bush announced at almost every major press event. Another Democratic breaking point came when Bush advisers spread word of a surprise "major" announcement by the governor; Bush announced a limited restoration of welfare benefits to legal immigrants, and Democrats immediately said it was a relatively inexpensive and politically safe way to begin the wholesale effort to lure Hispanic voters. The Mauro campaign also argued that Bush was still meeting with the disciples of the Christian Right, still committed to the death penalty, and bent on erasing the church-state separation through his welfare programs.

The polls kept gurgling upward, pushing his projected percentage of the votes into the 60s and then the 70s. Wary national reporters who were dispatched to see him came back to Washington saying that he was not as they remembered him in 1988 and 1992—and he certainly wasn't as old-fashioned as Dole, as preachy as Bennett, as ideologically fervid as Gingrich, as zealous as Kemp. He offered them cigars, peeks at the hundreds of baseballs in his office, flights in his King Air campaign plane, and tours of the governor's mansion. When they pressed him as to what his most important initiative, the one thing he would push harder than anything else during the race for reelection, would be, he repeated one word over and over again: education. But not dismantling state agencies that monitored local school districts, which he had advocated during his first year in office. This time he was pushing reading, literacy, the things his mother and wife were associated with. Laura's crowning achievement as first lady had been to institute the Texas Book Festival, a lauded, sweeping set of seminars and tributes to Texas authors, many of whom had once been unabashed supporters of Ann Richards and champion fund-raisers for liberal causes and issues.

In July, Bush invited Myron Magnet to fly to Austin to lecture his staff about the role of government. Magnet, the editor of *City Journal*, who was affiliated with the Manhattan Institute for Policy Research, served the same purpose as David Horowitz, Doug Wead, and Karl Rove: he was an unflinching proponent of the notion that the 1960s had introduced an epidemic of social ills. Magnet's book *The Dream and the Night-*

mare condemns a culture of victims, self-denial, reliance on government—all condemnations that resonated well in far West Texas, in the oil patch where an antiregulatory, antiwelfare culture had been in place for a half century. When he returned to New York, Magnet typed out a note: *Dear Governor Bush, I enjoyed our conversation enormously and came away with the greatest admiration for what you achieved and what you intend.*[9] A week later, Bush composed a handwritten note in his usual, almost illegible scrawl: *Dear Myron, Thanks for your time and sharing your thoughts with me and my staff. We were all fired up after you charged our intellectual batteries.*[10]

Other people were also charging his intellectual batteries, or at least keeping him in touch with valuable national allies for a possible run for the presidency. Christian Coalition Director and political consultant Ralph Reed had been regularly meeting and discussing strategy with Rove and Bush, and he had been invited to stay at the governor's mansion as an overnight guest. Meanwhile, Doug Wead quietly continued to serve as one of Bush's advisers on the Christian Right. Wead, who had moved to Arizona and launched a failed congressional bid after he was forced from the White House, spoke to Bush about writing his autobiography, maybe getting someone else, perhaps David Horowitz, to do it.

From his home in Apache Junction, Wead continued his affiliation with Amway and frequently called Bush or faxed memos to his office on matters that he thought might affect Bush's national standing among Christian Right leaders and any bid by Bush to win the GOP presidential nomination. The family's always delicate standing with the Christian Right reached a crisis point in January 1998, when Bush was presented with the most publicized event of his tenure as governor of Texas: the impending execution of Texas death row inmate Karla Faye Tucker.

The convicted pickax murderer's case was dominating international headlines; Bush was receiving clemency pleas from the pope; thousands of others called or wrote to claim that Tucker had undergone a true, profound spiritual conversion while on death row and didn't deserve to become the first woman in Texas executed since the Civil War. The case, of course, took on political overtones when Pat Robertson and other leading members of the Christian Right adopted her cause and said Tucker should be spared because she was a true repentant Christian. On February 2, 1998, ten months before the gubernatorial election, Wead and Bush communicated about how the whole incident might impact Bush's presidential aspirations against possible opponents such as Senator John Ashcroft. Wead, who had spent years preparing strategy reports for the elder Bush and George W., faxed over a careful outline on how the "SBC," the Southern Baptist Convention voters, would feel about Bush in a presidential contest.

Wead, anxious to remain George W. Bush's guide to the evangelical "movement," reminded his former boss of the potency of Christian voters and of Pat Robertson's shocking successes in the 1988 race. He also mentioned how the 1988 Bush campaign had tried to prove that the elder George Bush really wasn't a "wimp" by releasing political advertisements blaming Michael Dukakis for the furlough of Willie Horton, a black man who had been convicted of murder and rape. The Atwater-devised ads, critics said, had eventually backfired on Republicans because they had wildly inflamed racial fears and stereotypes.

In his memo, Wead also wanted George W. Bush to keep his eyes on Iowa, to focus on that state's key role in the early phases of a presidential campaign, to be prepared to "impact" Iowa and its evangelical voters—and to forget about trying to prove how "tough" the Bushes could be. When George W.'s father had tried to be tough by using the Willie Horton ads, it had backfired horribly; Wead thought that if George W. were trying to be tough by insisting on a Karla Faye Tucker execution, it could also backfire. Wead told George W. that the evangelical voters still followed Pat Robertson, and Pat Robertson wanted Karla Faye Tucker to have a reprieve.

Wead's February fax said, in part: *MEMORANDUM TO GOVERNOR GEORGE W. BUSH: You are losing the Robertson crowd over this. 'Is he trying to prove he is tough?' (We have all anticipated the ghost of Willie Horton but who would have thunk it, the return of the 'wimp factor'?) Republican politicians are always trading away the evangelical vote for some Democratic constituency that never votes for them anyway. It's easy to do. But just ask Colin Powell. You must have evangelicals to win the Republican nomination.*

Later in his lengthy memo, Wead had a suggestion: *Forget Willie Horton. You don't look tough, you look insensitive. Grant the 30-day reprieve. Gauge the reaction. Move on from there.*[11]

The day after the fax arrived, Bush called Wead.[12] He had already made up his mind by the time he had communicated with his Christian Right liaison. That afternoon, the clock ticking toward the scheduled 6 P.M. execution, Bush paced in his office and refused to grant a reprieve. Maybe he didn't need the Christian Right; maybe it was better to simply avoid bending the letter of the death penalty law. Clay Johnson, his old high school friend and loyal college roommate who was overseeing the governor's appointments to state boards, had gotten a call from his wife:

"Go see George, this isn't a time for him to be alone." Johnson walked up from his lair in the basement of the Capitol and joined him.

Bush had a special communications device hooked up that was giving him updates every five minutes from the Texas prison and death row chamber in Huntsville. Hundreds of phone calls, faxes, and e-mails were flooding in. Johnson had never seen Bush so serious.[13] They were both quiet when word came back that Tucker was dead. Karen Hughes had prepared a press release, and Bush approved it before she faxed it out: *May God bless Karla Faye Tucker, and God bless her victims and their families.*

BY APRIL 1998, the Bush campaign was unleashing its millions of dollars and attracting even more prepresidential attention from the national press, much of it also fueled by Jeb's reemergence as the gubernatorial candidate in electoral-vote-rich Florida. Columnist Robert Novak wrote that an Austin Democratic strategist had been speculating about asking Mauro to drop out of the campaign and let Bush run unopposed.

Garry Mauro was working, as one of his frustrated aides said while dragging on a cigarette, like a "goddamned mule." The gaggle of zealous Democrats and true believers was convinced that Bush was stealing issues from Mauro, and by extension the Clinton administration, especially when it came to concentrating on education and finding a way to raise teachers' salaries. Karen Hughes would eventually begin demanding, "What part don't they like? The conservative part or the compassionate part?" Texas Democrats were even more convinced that reporters were blinded by Bush presidential stardust: "Here is the guy with umpteen million dollars, and here is a guy with a million point five or whatever we had," complained John Hannah, one of Mauro's high-ranking advisers. "One guy is being touted by the national press corps as someone running for president."[14]

At the end of the month, Bush flew to Los Angeles, this time making an appearance in controlled confines, with the press forced to listen to him through keyholes of a ballroom door. David Horowitz had invited Bush to give a Wednesday-morning speech to Hollywood power brokers, including Oliver Stone, as well as possible contributors. This one was smoother, more convincing, smaller in scale, but bigger in impact than the speech he had given in Indianapolis. Bush keyed into his theme of "personal responsibility," and even some of the skeptical West Coast listeners felt that he had immeasurably improved his sales skills since the GOP Midwestern Leadership Conference. He returned to Texas and learned that his approval ratings were up to 80 percent.

In Florida, his brother was headed into double-digit leads in his race against Lieutenant Governor Ken MacKay. As always, George W.'s and Jeb's campaign teams were exchanging polling data and strategies. Any of those rivalries, those things that traced back to the impromptu races around the grounds of Walker's Point, the pick-up basketball games, the endless lists of who-was-better-at-golf-tennis-horseshoes-tiddlywinks were absent. If George W. was going to move forward, beyond Texas, he needed Jeb to win Florida. And of course, Texas money began flowing into Jeb's campaign—at least $1 million from the same people who had forked gobs of cash into George W.'s fund-raising network. Jeb ordered his campaign staffers to ship every new TV campaign clip to his father for approval. And, as in 1994, his father and Barbara were in Florida. "Vote early and vote often. That's the way we do it in Texas," Barbara slyly said in Sun City.[15]

Laura, who had been immersed into all that Dorothy Walker–inspired competition that was completely foreign to an only child, would develop a theory: "In many ways, the '92 defeat, as hard as it was on George and Jebbie—in a lot of ways it was the first time in their lives they were liberated from the shadow of their Dad. It was literally the first time they felt like they could say whatever they thought, without it reflecting on their father, without having to think: 'How would this sound?' "[16]

And in Florida, people who talked to Jeb were saying that he had worked to become more like his older brother and that his older brother had worked to become more like him. Jeb was trying to emerge as more gregarious, less cerebral, less the ideologue. He was also dancing across the Christian Right lines, moving away from his history as an Oliver North–and–Nicaraguan contra supporter, and he was also unabashedly campaigning as a compassionate conservative, working hard to lure both black voters in the inner cities and Jewish retirees in south Florida.

Meanwhile, with Karl Rove's guidance, George W. remained in touch with Horowitz, Magnet, and Olasky, trying to assemble something resembling a portfolio of ideas, something that would at least begin to measure up to the policy wonk tendencies of Al Gore, the man most people assumed he would run against in the year 2000 race for the White House. His friends said that George W. was defensive when people suggested he was still searching for a depth that people assumed his younger brother—the Phi Beta Kappa student who had graduated from the University of Texas in less than three years—had always possessed. For years, Rove had been in the habit of providing books for George W. Bush, some of which might appeal to their mutual disregard for the 1960s, ones that might also serve to offset the creeping notion and allegations, spread by Democrats in Texas, that George W. Bush never had the patience or the discipline to study policy, that he suffered from some sort of attention deficit, that he was the exact opposite of an ideologue, that he was a proficient master of delegation and so anti-introspective that he was bordering on being an outright anti-intellectual. Bush staffers openly began insisting to Texas reporters that they saw him reading mysteries and biographies of Teddy Roosevelt and Winston Churchill. He told people that *Austin Powers, International Man of Mystery* was a favorite film, he still preferred to listen to country-and-western singer George Jones, his favorite hymn was "Amazing Grace," he liked the Western oil painting by W. H. D. Koerner that Joe O'Neill III had loaned him and that he had hung on the eastern wall of his office. And he said he had surprised everyone, even himself, by fishing *alone* for bass at the East Texas lake house.

But there was frequently never any prevalent, easily agreed-upon answer from his closest friends or even his family as to whether there were any particular works of art or literature, music, maybe an aria or a melody, that had ever shaken him to his soul. Maybe it was the same thing his father felt, the way he was suspicious, almost accusatory, when people probed: "Don't stretch me out on the couch," his father would say.[17] In her office near the governor's suite, Karen Hughes once summoned one Austin reporter inside and angrily lectured him on how many books Bush was reading, how he read "even more books than Karl Rove, and Rove reads a lot of books."

As his always more boisterous brother inched closer to making his public declaration for the presidency, Jeb once searched his mind for it, for his brother's poetry, so to speak. After a long pause he decided that it was really only his brother's wife and twins, and maybe the religious beliefs that he had begun moving toward in the mid-1980s. One day when a writer suggested to the first son that his next youngest brother was the more intellectual one, George W.'s face cracked into a half smile. "I'm the smart one," he said. "He's the tall one."

IN TEXAS in June, Bush was in the campaign plane and bristling at the national reporters using the dreaded word, the imperial-sounding, Rockefeller-Kennedy word: dynasty. A May poll in *USA Today* showed him beating Al Gore in a presidential race. Now that Jeb was projected to win in Florida, the Bush-Walker progression to power that some journalists had first explored in 1994 was being extraordinarily amplified. By the end of the summer, a reporter from the British Broadcasting Corporation was in Texas, putting together a lengthy segment touching on the Bush-Walker connections to the English monarchy and how there was a very real possibility that, for the first time in American history since John Adams and John Quincy Adams, a son would follow his father into the White House.

The dynamics intensified when Bill Clinton, Hillary Rodham Clinton, and Al Gore began making the first of several appearances in Texas. They were old friends of Mauro, and Texas was an invaluable state with wealthy, Austin-based Clinton supporters. The Clintons and Gore collectively made fourteen trips to Texas. Bush told an adviser that he was pleased they were coming and that he was going to dent the Democratic base and take heavily Hispanic El Paso; no Republican candidate for statewide office had ever won more than 36 percent of Hispanic voters, and Bush made fourteen trips to El Paso, finally winning the endorsement of that city's Hispanic mayor, Carlos Ramirez.

The Clinton-Gore trips validated his national strength, but he would sometimes look away when people suggested that the Clinton-Gore team was trying to fracture the Bush dynasty before it completely unfolded. "Dynasty. In a dynasty, you don't have to earn anything. In a democracy, you've got to earn it," said Bush.[18]

By August, Clinton's personal travails had seeped into the Texas gubernatorial campaign. The lifestyle-and-vices questions that had been raised against him in 1993 and 1994, during George W.'s bitter campaign against Richards, were being asked again. "George is getting all the attention for his early childhood, thankfully . . . for his late childhood. I'm glad he is the pathfinder on that one. I don't have to relive all of my interesting days," said a grateful Jeb.[19]

In between stops in East Texas, George W. couldn't resist. The coming backlash against Newt Gingrich and all the other moralizing Republicans was impossible to forecast, and, this was a good time to reclaim some righteous authority, the thing that had been missing that miserable Saturday night in Indianapolis, the thing that would reveal some Christian backbone deep in the backwoods Bible Belt of Texas. It was the day after Clinton had testified to Ken Starr's grand jury and admitted in a national address that he had lied about the Monica Lewinsky affair.

It was his last stop of the day, it was pushing past 90 degrees, witheringly humid, and Bush had practically bounced out of a Texas sheriff's car, toured the Rusk County courthouse, and listened patiently as someone explained about the new roof. He loved this. It was "retail politics." A woman named Suzy gave him a batch of fresh Henderson cane syrup, and he nodded as she said, "If it turns to sugar there's nothing wrong with it, just heat it up"; someone else was playing "America" on the piano; he skipped to the side of some middle school children who had come over for pictures; he dropped into a chair next to an elderly woman, quickly grabbed her hand, and posed for more pictures. All day long, at several other East Texas appearances, he had occasionally offered lines alluding to the events unfolding in Washington: "First and foremost, I've got to tell you, my personal life is great," he repeated to the 150 people in the local community center.[20]

"People are going to want to ask the question: 'Will this person bring dignity or will this person embarrass?' " Bush also said that day, talking to a Texas reporter, "It doesn't do any good to inventory the mistakes I made when I was young. I think the way I'm going to answer questions about specific behavior is to remind people that when I was young and irresponsible, I was young and irresponsible. I changed when I married my wife and I changed when I had children."[21] Then he flew back to Austin and waited.

Former White House special counsel Lanny Davis, who had once been at Yale and the DKE house with him, had made the first move in an appearance on MSNBC. "I was in college with George Bush Jr., and if we start seeing smug, sanctimonious comments from public officials—especially Governor Bush—throwing stones in glass houses, I think everyone is going to be at risk." Davis received at least a hundred phone calls from the media, including one from a journalist in Japan, each of them wanting specifics. When pressed, Davis backed away from his statements and said that he had just "lashed out" without any information that could derail Bush's run for the presidency.

The few Bush insiders in Texas who had been naively clinging to the belief that the governor's race was really only about reelection began to realize that something bigger and more complex was in play. Democratic operatives were already attacking Bush, the national media were stacked up on the runway for interviews, and press secretary Karen Hughes mistakenly called a reporter she had been avoiding for weeks and months: "Hello, Paula Zahn, please!" she cheerfully trumpeted into the phone before realizing she had actually reached the unwanted newsperson.

Over the next few weeks, as the backlash took shape against Gingrich and the other soon-to-be-defrocked soldiers from the 1994 Republican Revolution, Bush steered clear of any other overt assaults on the Clinton White House. "I think all of us have a little sin in our system. Have I been faithful to my wife? Yes," he told reporters.[22] Instead, almost as if it were inevitable, he spoke in terms of his own concerns about moving into the Oval Office. "One of my concerns is about putting my family in the bubble. If you end up being the president, once you're in the bubble you're always in the bubble."[23]

In Florida, Jeb would once suggest that he had it figured out. Maybe foibles were what voters, reporters, were looking for in a therapeutic age. But their father was resolutely against it—against the confessional aura of politics, against the digging, even into Clinton, because it obviously would mean digging into his first son, his second son.

Again, it was obvious that the rules had changed since the Walkers and Bushes had first taken center stage in American business and politics before the turn of the century. Decades ago, George Herbert Walker and his daughter Dorothy Walker had instilled the ferocious sense of competition on one side of the family—their belief that life was essentially broken down into a constant series of competitions that needed to be won at all costs. And Samuel Prescott Bush and his son Prescott Bush had obviously moved their wing of the family toward that overriding sense of noblesse oblige and style, that sense of "prosperity with purpose"—the purpose being to serve as efficient, proper stewards rather than as insistent ideologues or visionary sculptors of policy.

For decades, the tendencies from both sides of the Bush-Walker clan had seemed to work in concert as dozens of family members moved from the most powerful academic settings, into the almost requisite military roles and then into the most influential positions in business and politics. But now there were obviously different demands, different rules, in the still evolving Clinton era. That history of competition and the willingness to serve, because those who can afford to serve are also obligated to do so, weren't immediate guarantees of elected office. And the elder George Bush once wondered what it all meant for his first son, especially for a first son who had inherited his name and, really, the sprawling Bush-Walker legacy that stretched from the seventeenth-century settlers in Maine, to the eighteenth-century settlers in Virginia, to the railroads and steel mills of the Midwest, to the investment firms on Wall Street, to Yale, to Kennebunkport, Maine, to Jupiter Island, Florida, and to Texas.

"Sometimes he did a lot of heavy lifting," George W.'s father had once said. "'Cause he could go to people and . . . save me the agony of having to break the bad news to people. And he did it. And that seasoned him. He probably passed a test there somewhere . . . and the test being, you know: 'Am I strong enough?' "[24]

One day in his second-floor suite in the gleaming Texas State Capitol, the first son pushed himself away from his desk and bounded energetically to his feet. His aides, peeking in the doorway as shafts of light spread from the towering, wood-louvered windows, watched him carefully as he shouted, "My father told me that if I went any further in political life, I would be like a cork in a raging river!"[25]

IN SEPTEMBER, new polls showed that 55 percent of the people in Texas wouldn't mind if George W. ran for president. By now, he was projected to win 70 percent of the vote in the gubernatorial reelection race. In the last several months, he had made trips to Indiana, New Mexico, Ohio, New York, California, Florida, Tennessee, South Carolina, North Carolina, Washington, D.C., Arizona, Kansas, Colorado, and Ohio. He had also raised more than $10 million almost effortlessly.

And by September, the final details were being worked out from the ownership group's decision to sell the Texas Rangers baseball team; he was going to earn $14.9 million from his initial $606,000 investment ten years earlier. It was the Big Elephant Field, "the liberator" that the wistful, hard-drinking men in the West Texas oil patch liked to talk about when they huddled together at the Petroleum Club and swapped stories in the Wildcatter's Room. It was the "liberator" that finally yielded more money than his father had ever made in all those years of investing the Bush-Walker fortune in far-flung oil rigs in the Midland desert and the unpredictable, cloudy waters of the Gulf of Mexico. It was something that George W. brought up frequently when people asked what was in his future, sometimes when he was slumping into the high-backed leather chair behind the massive desk his father had passed down to him.

"I don't need money," he said, letting his black boots drop onto his desktop.[26] He had two favorite things in his office, aside from his family photos: those baseballs in the burnished display case and the Western painting that Joe O'Neill III had loaned him. The painting was like dozens of others in the Petroleum Clubs dotting West Texas; it showed a horseman pushing himself and his mount along a jagged path. The image was based on the Charles Wesley hymn "A Charge to Keep": "To serve the present age, my calling to fulfill; O may it all my powers engage to do my Master's will."

Now, at the age of fifty-two, he told a visitor to his office that he had all the money he would ever need. He and O'Neill had also talked about it and though George W. disliked the term, O'Neill always felt that by the summer of 1998, it was now an official case of noblesse oblige that pushed

George W. closer to all the old-money motivations that had once gusted Prescott Bush into politics. At the very least, thought O'Neill, his friend's financial windfall lent a pretense of purity, of unfettered public service—maybe not so much a sense of being attracted to filling a high office because of a burning ideological fire but of being born to hold office because that is simply what Bushes do. His father had made money, had always had the family to rely on; there had always been Uncle Herbert Walker, and all the countless Texas oil millionaires ready to stand by. Now Bush had his own small fortune, and it was easier than it had been for his father to insist that he was in politics solely as a public servant.

"I think the universe of people that could serve is too narrow these days . . . and I think George would agree with that," said Jeb.[27]

In Austin, in September, Bush had been to a five-hundred-person fund-raiser in the stunning home of thirty-nine-year-old Texas software entrepreneur Steve Papermaster. Bush was the gregarious star amid the suddenly rich, usually apolitical techno-wizards, the talented twenty-somethings and thirty-somethings who had begun coming to Texas in droves from California when Ann Richards was governor and who had turned the belly of the state into a Silicon Prairie. The Bush campaign had specifically targeted the new wave of Internet-and-software impresarios as future GOP allies; start-up specialists such as Papermaster and the almost iconic entrepreneurs like thirty-four-year-old multi-billionaire Michael Dell in Austin were being courted. There was already an Internet site named Bush2000.com, even though visitors who logged on initially found no information on their computer screens other than the site's name.

At the fund-raiser, which reportedly netted Bush $200,000, a young mother approached Bush and said that her daughter wanted to grow up and go to work in the White House as president of the United States: "I think I'll be out of there before then," teased Bush.

In an Austin suburb that same month, he was preparing for a speech at the headquarters of one of the city's ubiquitous high-tech computer firms. As Bush supporters loped into the room, four men in E.T.-style "dust- and germ-free" suits silently insisted that people accept their company brochures. With Republican Senators Phil Gramm and Kay Bailey Hutchison standing to either side, he confidently began his speech about deconstructing government: "Save us from the federal government, Texans can run Texas, we don't need any help from the federal government." Suddenly, there was a commotion in front of the stage; someone screamed at him, "Sir! Shouldn't we abolish the Federal Reserve and the Council on Foreign Relations?" It was, of course, the same question people had shouted at him exactly twenty years before, when he had first run for office in Texas. It was the thing, of course, that had cost him the election—the notion that Prescott Bush, George W.'s father, and the children were part of an exclusive American fraternity beyond the ken of the ordinary voter. Bush froze and stared down at the accuser. His security detail was already moving in and pulling the well-dressed man out a doorway. A light rain sifted down as they pressed the man against an office window and yelled, "Trap him on the glass!"

Bush resumed his speech: "Isn't it wonderful to live in a country where you're able to express your opinions the way you feel like it? Frankly, that's the freedoms we're up here to uphold—freedom for people to express themselves, freedom for people to worship as they see fit. Texas is a free place. And we intend to keep it that way."[28]

Back in his office at the state capitol, he would still sometimes stare at the photographs taken on the day he had first taken office as governor. A favorite, as always, was the one of the moist-eyed Old Man listening to his first son being sworn in and reaching out to hug his first son's daughter. In one corner of that photograph was his brother Jeb. When George W. studied the picture, he thought that there was something almost unsettling about the way Jeb looked. His brother had let some sadness mix with his loyalty.[29]

"They're loyal to him," said cousin John Ellis. "If you're a member of the family, you're on the team and that's it. And it doesn't matter, nothing else matters."[30]

THE TEXAS ROUND of Speculation Days was finally over. George W. was on his way to pick up Laura at the back gate of the governor's mansion, he was hanging out the window of the Lincoln Town Car, grinning and yelling at all the reporters lingering in the circular driveway and huddled together under the gray, rainy skies: "Welcome to Reality Day!" Laura gingerly stepped outside the towering mansion doors to join him, they broke free of the media pack and walked briskly to the voting booths at the old Travis County Courthouse across the street and backdropped by the hills to the west. Tomorrow would be her birthday; the day after that would be their twenty-first wedding anniversary. The loyalists, half of Midland in all those dusty cars exiting off Highway 71 after the six-hour drive from the West Texas desert, were just now pulling alongside the black limousines at the Four Seasons Hotel. By late afternoon, he was there in the ninth-floor campaign suite, surrounded by bouquets of fragrant, swooning yellow roses.

He bolted from one end of the room to the other, his face close to almost everyone he talked to, shouting nicknames, doing two-minute-long interviews with each reporter who trooped into the room, ordering each of them to sit on what he was calling the "media couch." With a favored Dallas celebrity photographer circling the room, he flopped onto a bed and stared at the news channels, at CNN, waiting for the latest numbers from Florida in between the footage of devastating Hurricane Mitch. Suddenly, Dan Quayle was on the screen, staring back at him. In the Convention Center ballroom Quayle's image was beaming down from the projection screens and onto the assembling victory party. Bush slipped his hands behind his head, and then people in the room saw him instantly pop up. His brother was on the TV, in Florida, thanking everyone, including their parents.

At 9:30 P.M., Garry Mauro, who had worked almost anonymously in state government for sixteen years, called to concede. The security detail began rounding up the conga line for the move from the ninth floor down to the Austin Convention Center ballroom. The numbers were cresting: up to 67 percent of all the votes, close to 50 percent of the Hispanic votes. Every Republican running for state office was winning.

Don Evans had already left the suite to offer a few stilted comments to the three thousand people pressed into the hot ballroom with the soiled carpet. Chuck Norris was squeezing through the crowd, aiming for a cordoned-off area behind the main stage. After Evans finally stepped offstage, Fred McClure took his place, stepping sprightly to the microphone: "Are we excited yet?" In Dallas, all week long, they had already been disassembling the Bush campaign office.

From just behind the dark blue curtains, Bush was bouncing on his toes, peeking into the ballroom. He grinned, shrugged once, and the balloons began cascading as a security man flipped back the curtains and led the short walk to the stage. Bush shook hands with McClure, his father's loyal White House aide. He bounced to the microphone, and Laura stood to his right as he began speaking: "Tonight is an historic night. . . . This is an amazing victory . . . and I want to say something to the newly elected governor of Florida: good going, brother."[31]

For days he had been publicly insisting that he hadn't made up his mind yet about declaring his candidacy for the presidency: *"I don't think anybody knows what the deal is like . . . like I know what the deal is like."* Just that morning, he had been standing in the quiet damp side yard of the venerable governor's mansion as an occasional raindrop slipped off a tree limb, plopped onto his suit jacket, and blossomed in the fabric. He was talking about running for office, any kind of office.

"People who like me will like me, people who don't like me just won't like me. How's that for profundity?" he said, starting to rock, again, on his heels. "*Vamos a ver*—we're going to see."[32]

EXACTLY THREE months later, the just-retired Lieutenant Governor of Texas was in a small back bedroom of his home a few blocks from the state capitol . . . losing ground to his cancer and, really, to all the accumulated demons that had chased him during a lifetime in the mad forest of Lone Star politics. Bob Bullock, the craggy heir to LBJ's legacy, had already lived longer than most people in Texas thought he would. Ashen-faced, struggling to form his words, and sometimes slipping into rambling incoherence, Bullock was surrounded by a half-century of Texas totems and ciphers—the burnished gavels and the dusty, framed, editorial cartoons hanging crookedly on the walls.

For years, people had said that the demanding and crafty Bullock would be the next old-school Democratic governor of Texas. Instead, his last dramatic act was to embrace the Republican son of the former president—and to watch as the Republicans took every statewide office for the first time since Reconstruction. In the end, Bullock had lived long enough to see his own party crippled by something that Connecticut Yankee George Herbert Walker Bush had set in motion three decades ago and that New Haven–born George Walker Bush had capitalized on.

"Rosie O'Donnell . . . I can't stand that bitch," Bullock suddenly barked, sitting straight up in his bed. Without warning, he was thinking about O'Donnell, about the way Texas native Ann Richards had been friends with too many Hollywood types. Bullock instantly smiled, his tone abruptly bright: "Y'all want some coffee?" he drawled, pointing a bony finger at the gleaming sterling silver coffee service on his dresser. As the words settled, he fell back on the bed.

With his wife peering at him from a doorway, Bullock stared at the ceiling. Late in his life, the hardened Bullock had taken to occasionally talking about how he regretted not being closer to his family, to his own son. In Texas, some old political hands said Bullock even seemed to be adopting the young George Bush. Bullock had met the elder Bush in 1995, after being personally invited to a quiet lunch with the ex-president in Houston, and in a moment of spontaneity Bullock said that the elder Bush's first son was going to go to the White House one day. The elder

Bush listened carefully and then tears began streaming down his face. For months, Bullock and the elder Bush wrote each other letters, and the more Bullock wrote, the more he wondered if the first son "had been deprived of his father" when he was growing up.

"Only an idiot wouldn't believe that having a famous name benefits you. But, you know, the hardest thing in the world is trying to live up to the reputation of a famous father. President of the United States. How much more famous can you get?" muttered Bullock from his bed, his voice barely audible.

"I think any president's son begins to dream a little, daydreams a little," added Bullock, his thin right hand resting lightly on his forehead. "And some of them even begin to set a course."

Notes

1: REALITY DAY

1. Letter from George W. Bush to Michael Dell, January 5, 1998, Office of the Governor, State of Texas.
2. "Correction," *Houston Chronicle*, November 8, 1993.
3. Author interview with William "Bucky" Bush, February 18, 1999
4. Author interview with Elsie Walker, February 22, 1999.
5. Author interview with John Ellis, February 10, 1999.
6. Author interview with Texas Speaker of the House Pete Laney, February 12, 1999.
7. "The Heavyweight," *The Weekly Standard*, September 14, 1998.
8. "Bush Adviser: It's About 2000 Now," *Austin American-Statesman*, October 18, 1998.
9. Jack Shepherd and Christopher Wren, eds., *Quotations from Chairman LBJ* (New York: Simon and Schuster, 1968).
10. Phillips Academy at Andover Yearbook, 1964.
11. "George Bush: Where Does He Stand?," *Christian Herald*, June 1986.
12. Governor George W. Bush, press conference, Jubilee Center, Waco, Texas, October 18, 1998.
13. "Executive Profile," *The Dallas Morning News*, October 13, 1994.

2: DEEP MONEY

1. Herbert Parmet, *George Bush: The Life of a Lone Star Yankee* (New York: Scribner's, 1997), pp. 13–21.
2. Transcript of Oral History Interview with Prescott Bush Jr., 1992, Greenwich Library Oral History Project.
3. Ibid.; Parmet, *George Bush*, p. 25; "Samuel P. Bush, 83, A Steel Executive," *The New York Times*, February 9, 1949.
4. Transcript of Oral History Interview with Prescott Bush Jr., Greenwich Library Oral History Project.

5. Parmet, *George Bush*, p. 34; "George H. Walker, Donor of Golf Cup; Investment Banker Who Put Up British-American Amateur Trophy Is Dead at 79," *The New York Times*, June 25, 1953.

6. Donnie Radcliffe, *Simply Barbara Bush* (New York: Warner Books, 1989), p. 132.

7. Transcript of Oral History Interview with Prescott Bush Jr., Greenwich Library Oral History Project.

8. Transcript of Oral History Interview with Mary Walker, 1991, Greenwich Library Oral History Project.

9. Transcript of Oral History Interview with Prescott Bush Jr., Greenwich Library Oral History Project.

10. Ibid.

11. Author interview with Jonathan Bush, February 23, 1999.

12. Author interview with Florida Governor John Ellis "Jeb" Bush, January 26, 1999.

13. Ibid.

14. Parmet, *George Bush*, p. 17.

15. Ibid., pp. 43–45; Barbara Bush, *Barbara Bush: A Memoir* (New York: Scribner's, 1994); Radcliffe, *Simply Barbara Bush*, pp. 80–90.

16. Bush, *Barbara Bush*, p. 27.

17. Certificate of Birth, Connecticut State Department of Health, Bureau of Vital Statistics, certified by Carole Longobardi-Fortier, Deputy Registrar, July 15, 1998.

18. *New Haven Evening Register*, July 6, 1946.

19. Bush, *Barbara Bush*, p. 27.

20. Prescott Samuel Bush, Columbia University Oral History Project, 1966.

21. Richard Ben Cramer, "How Bush Made It," *Esquire*, June 1991.

22. Harry Hurt III, "George Bush, Plucky Lad," *Texas Monthly*, June 1983.

23. Bush, *Barbara Bush*, p. 33.

24. James Presley, *Saga of Wealth, The Rise of the Texas Oilmen* (Austin: Texas Monthly Press, 1983).

25. John Howard Griffin, *Land of the High Sky* (Midland, Tex.: First National Bank of Midland, 1959).

26. Samuel D. Myres, *The Permian Basin: Petroleum Empire of the Southwest* (El Paso: Permian Press, 1973).

27. Gus Clemens, *Legacy* (San Antonio, Tex.: Mulberry Avenue Books, 1983), p. 145.

28. Author interview with Randall Roden, September 14, 1998.

29. Bush, *Barbara Bush*, p. 34.

30. Pamela Killian, *Barbara Bush* (New York: St. Martin's Press, 1992), p. 51.

31. Advertising literature for Ideco, courtesy of the Permian Basin Petroleum Museum, Midland, Tex.

32. Cramer, "How Bush Made It"; George Bush, *Looking Forward* (New York: Doubleday, 1987).

33. Bush, *Barbara Bush*, p. 37.

34. Bush, *Looking Forward*, p. 58.

35. Author interviews with John Younger, July 1998.

36. Ibid.

37. Ibid.; Presley, *Saga of Wealth*, pp. 231–232.

38. Myres, *The Permian Basin*.

39. Author interview with Randall Roden, September 14, 1998.

40. Ibid.

41. Presley, *Saga of Wealth*, pp. 335–364; Permian Basin Petroleum Museum archives, Midland, Tex.; author interviews with independent oilmen in Midland, Texas, July 1998.

42. Interviews with independent oilmen in Midland, Texas, July 1998.

43. Presley, *Saga of Wealth*, p. 357; author interviews with independent oilmen in Midland, Texas, July 1998.

44. Author interviews with independent oilmen in Midland, Texas, July 1998.

45. Permian Basin Petroleum Museum archives, Midland, Texas.

46. Parmet, *George Bush*, p. 79.

47. Author interviews with Earle Craig, August 1998.

48. Bush, *Barbara Bush*, p. 32.

49. "A Well Worn Friend," *Dallas Morning News*, June 14, 1987.

3: THE CORE

1. Author interview with Jonathan Bush, February 23, 1999.

2. Ibid.

3. Harriet Hanna Caldwell, *A History of the First Presbyterian Church—Midland, Texas*, courtesy of Marty Burns, First Presbyterian Church.

4. Undated photograph described as "George Bush and his son, George Jr." at the "eight-year-old age division" electric train races at the YMCA, from the files of the Midland YMCA.

5. Samuel D. Myres, *The Permian Basin: Petroleum Empire of the Southwest* (El Paso: Permian Press, 1973), pp. 347–348.

6. George Bush with Vic Gold, *Looking Forward* (New York: Doubleday, 1987), p. 25.

7. "Ex-Senator Prescott Bush Dies; Connecticut Republican Was 77," *The New York Times*, October 9, 1972.

8. Ibid.

9. Transcript of Oral History Interview with Prescott Bush Jr., 1992, Greenwich Library Oral History Project.

10. Author interview with Bill Collyns, October 8, 1998.

11. Author interview with Rosenelle Cherry, October 15, 1998.

12. Herbert Parmet, *George Bush: The Life of a Lone Star Yankee* (New York; Scribner's, 1997), p. 34; "A Pair of Dominant Grandfathers Shape a Presidential Persona," *National Journal*, September 7, 1991.

13. "Permelia Reed's Disappearing Black Sweaters, Great Wealth in America," *Forbes*, October 22, 1990.

14. Bush, *Looking Forward*, p. 68.

15. David Maraniss, "The Bush Bunch," *Washington Post*, January 22, 1989.

16. Permian Basin Petroleum Museum archives, Midland, Texas.

17. Ibid.

18. Ibid.

19. Barbara Bush, *Barbara Bush: A Memoir* (New York: Scribner's, 1994), pp. 45–49.

20. "Good-bye to Robin," *Texas Monthly*, February 1988.

21. Author interview with Elsie Walker, February 22, 1989.

22. Author interview with William "Bucky" Bush, February 18, 1999.

23. Author interviews with Lud Ashley, January 26 and February 1, 1999.

24. Author interview with Randall Roden, September 14, 1998.

25. "George Bush: A Midland Scrapbook," *Midland Reporter-Telegram*, January 20, 1989.

26. "Don't Call Him Junior," *Texas Monthly*, April 1989.

27. Author interview with Earle Craig, August 1998.

28. Author interviews with Sue "Anna" Williams, February 1999.

29. Author interviews with Otha Fitzgerald Taylor, October 1998.

30. Ibid.

31. Author interviews with Austine Crosby, August 1998.

32. Author interview with John Bizilo, August 6, 1998.

33. Author interviews with Joseph O'Neill III, July 1998.

34. Donnie Radcliffe, *Simply Barbara Bush* (New York: Warner Books, 1989), p. 129.

35. Author interview with Jonathan Bush, February 3, 1999.

36. Author interviews with Joseph O'Neill III, July 1998.

37. Author interviews with Frank Ittner, October 1998.

38. Ibid.

39. "George Slept Here," *Life*, November 1988.

4: STYLE

1. Susan Hillebrandt Santangelo, *Kinkaid and Houston: 75 Years* (Houston: Gulf Publishing, 1981).

2. Ibid.

3. Ibid.

4. Author interview with Julian William "Tex" Robertson, August 12, 1998.

5. Texas Air National Guard Records of George Walker Bush.

6. Author interviews with Michelle Smith, former fashion writer with *Houston Chronicle*, October 1998.

7. Author interviews with Art Goddard, Barry Moss, Charles Sanders, August 1998.

8. Ibid.

9. Fitzhugh Green, *George Bush: An Intimate Portrait* (New York: Hippocrene Books, 1989), p. 73

10. Donnie Radcliffe, *Simply Barbara Bush* (New York: Warner Books, 1989), p. 128.

11. George Bush with Victor Gold, *Looking Forward: An Autobiography* (New York: Bantam Books, 1988), p. 26.

12. Author Interview with Doug Hannah, September 3, 1998.

13. Ibid.

14. Author interview with John Ellis, February 10, 1999.

15. Phillips Academy, *Guidebook to Andover,* 1997–1998.

16. Ibid.

17. James S. Kunen, Class of 1966, in Frederick S. Allis Jr., *Youth from Every Quarter: A Bicentennial History of Phillips Academy, Andover* (Hanover, N.H.: University Press of New England, 1979).

18. Author interviews with Steve Kroll, August 1998.

19. Author interview with Bill Semple, October 1998.

20. Ibid.

21. Author interview with Timothy Booth, September 21, 1998.

22. Author interview with Clay Johnson, July 1998.

23. Ibid.

24. Ibid.

25. "Excellence and Intensity in U.S. Prep Schools," *Time,* October 25, 1962.

26. Ibid.

27. Author interview with Bob Marshall, September 1998.

28. Author interview with James Lockhart III, September 1998.

29. Author interview with Henry Hobson III, September 1998.

30. 1964 Phillips Academy at Andover Yearbook.

31. Author interview with Doug Brown, September 1998.

32. "George Bush, Too," *D,* April 1992.

33. Author interview with Jeff Stripling, September 1998.

34. Author interview with Peter Neumann, September 1998.

35. Ibid.

36. Ibid.

37. Ibid.

38. Ibid.

39. "Go East, Young Man," *Texas Monthly,* June 1999.

40. Author interview with Frank DiClemente, August 29, 1998.

41. Author interview with Dr. Jose Gonzalez-Inclan, September 11, 1998.

42. Author interviews with Lacey Neuhaus, October 1998.

43. "Go East, Young Man."

44. Author interviews with Doug Hannah, September 3, 1998.

45. Author interview with Henry Hobson III, September 1998.

46. Author interview with George W. Bush's cousin Kevin Rafferty, August 31, 1998.

47. Author interview with Henry Hobson III, September 1998.

48. Author interview with Bob Marshall, September 1998.

49. Author interview with Tory Peterson, August 26, 1998.

50. Author interview with Randall Roden, September 14, 1998.

51. Phillips Academy at Andover Yearbook, 1964.

52. Ibid.

53. *Andover Bulletin,* Phillips Academy, Vol. 58, No. 2 (July 1964).

54. E-mail to author from Seth Mydans, October 9, 1998.

55. "Ex-Senator Prescott Bush Dies," *Washington Post,* October 9, 1972.

5: THE ARROGANCE

1. Lyndon Baines Johnson, commencement address to Johnson City High School, May 29, 1964.

2. Herbert Parmet, *George Bush: The Life of a Lone Star Yankee* (New York: Scribner's, 1997), pp. 109–111.

3. Ibid.

4. Ibid.

5. Ibid.

6. Barbara Bush, *Barbara Bush: A Memoir* (New York: Scribner's, 1994), p. 60.

7. Sally Helgesen, *Wildcatters: A Story of Texans, Oil, and Money* (New York: Doubleday, 1981).

8. Author interview with Robert Mosbacher, January 20, 1999.

9. Author interview with Lacey Neuhaus, October 1998.

10. George Bush with Doug Wead, *Man of Integrity* (Eugene, Oreg.: Harvest House, 1988), p. 120.

11. Author interview with Robert J. Dieter, September 15, 1998.

12. Ibid.

13. "LBJ, Salinger Win," *Yale Daily News*, October 30, 1964; "69 Percent for Johnson in New Survey," *Yale Daily News*, October 29, 1964; "Political Survey: New Data," *Yale Daily News*, October 30, 1964.

14. "24 Alumni to Appear on Ballots," *Yale Daily News*, November 3, 1964.

15. Parmet, *George Bush*, pp. 87–109.

16. Bush, *Barbara Bush*, p. 34.

17. *The Dallas Morning News*, October 24, 1964.

18. "Professors Feel GOP at Its Low," *Yale Daily News*, November 6, 1964.

19. "Born To Run," *Texas Monthly*, April 1994.

20. Ibid.

21. Letter from William Sloane Coffin to Texas Governor George W. Bush, September 15, 1998.

22. Letter from Texas Governor George W. Bush to William Sloane Coffin, September 30, 1998.

23. Author interview with Yale professor Bradford Westerfield, November 20, 1998.

24. Bush with Wead, *Man of Integrity*, p. 132.

25. Author interview with Robert Dieter, September 15, 1998.

26. Author interview with James Lockhart III, September 8, 1998.

27. Author interview with Clay Johnson, July 1998.

28. Secretary of State filings, State of Louisiana, Articles of Incorporation for Circle Drilling Co. and Ciroco Exploration, Inc., 1945–1988.

29. Author interview with Arn Smith, longtime friend of Lee Welch, August 19, 1998.

30. Author interviews with Shelby Prather, Bill Duhon, Drew Cornell, B. T. Wood, Marilyn Smith, Cleary Hinton, former employees and associates of Vincent & Welch, Circle Drilling or Ciroco Exploration, Inc., August and September 1998.

31. Author interview with Doug Hannah, September 3, 1998.

32. Bush with Wead, *Man of Integrity*, p. 118.

33. "Junior Is His Own Bush Now," *Time*, July 31, 1998.
34. Bush with Wead, *Man of Integrity*, p. 118.
35. Author interview with Clay Johnson, July 1998.
36. *The Felon's Head*, Vol 5, No. 2 (October 14, 1965).
37. Author interviews with Collister "Terry" Johnson, September 1998 and May 1999.
38. Author interview with Craig Bolles, November 11, 1998.
39. *Yale Daily News*, April 8, 1966.
40. Author interview with Lacey Neuhaus, October 1998.
41. Joe McGinnis, *The Selling of the President* (New York: Trident Press, 1969), p. 45; Parmet, *George Bush*, p. 119.
42. "From Party Boy to Party Leader," *Fort Worth Star-Telegram*, November 29, 1998.
43. Author interview with Robert Beebe, October 1, 1998.
44. *The Felon's Head*, Vol. 5, No. 16 (October 8, 1966).
45. Author interview with Edgar Cullman, September 23, 1998.
46. Yale transcript contained in Texas National Guard military records of George Walker Bush, released under the Freedom of Information Act.
47. Author interview with Bob Wei, September 11, 1998.
48. David Maraniss, "The Bush Bunch," *Washington Post*, January 22, 1989.
49. "Deficit at Yale," *The New York Times*, October 16, 1949. Author interview with David Heckler, January 1999.

6: THE HEAVINESS

1. Herbert Parmet, *George Bush: The Life of a Lone Star Yankee* (New York: Scribner's, 1997), p. 121.
2. Ibid., p. 119.
3. "George Bush, Too," *D*, April 1992.
4. "Bush Admits Being Caught with Wreath in '66 Prank," *The Dallas Morning News*, September 6, 1998.
5. Author interview with Elsie Walker, February 22, 1999.
6. Author interview with Doug Hannah, September 3, 1998.
7. Ibid.
8. Author interview with Jeb Bush, January 26, 1999.
9. Ibid.
10. "In the Fish Bowl with Little George," *Chicago Tribune*, May 1, 1992.
11. Author interview with Doug Hannah, September 3, 1998.
12. "Cupid Hitched a Ride on Santa's Sleigh," *Houston Chronicle*, January 1, 1967.
13. Ron Rosenbaum, "An Elegy for Mumbo Jumbo," *Esquire*, September 1977. Rosenbaum graduated with George W. Bush in the Yale Class of 1968.
14. Ibid.
15. Author interview with Robert Reisner, October 1998.
16. "Bones and Keys Rattle in the Night at Yale," *The New York Times*, April 29, 1967.
17. Author interview with Roy Austin, October 1998.
18. Author interview with Muhammed Saleh, October 1998.
19. Author interview with Britt Kolar, October 1998.

20. "Go East, Young Man," *Texas Monthly*, June 1999.

21. Author interview with Jeb Bush, January 26, 1999.

22. Author interview with Elsie Walker, February 22, 1999.

23. Ibid.

24. Author interview with Doug Hannah, September 3, 1998.

25. Donnie Radcliffe, *Simply Barbara Bush* (New York: Warner Books, 1989), p. 130.

26. Author interview with Doug Hannah, September 3, 1998.

27. Ibid.

28. *Yale Daily News*, October 1967.

29. Author interviews with Bob Wei, September 1998.

30. Author interview with J. P. Goldsmith, November 8, 1998.

31. Robert Draper, "Favorite Son," *GQ*, September 1998.

32. Author interview with Dan Begel, September 18, 1998.

33. Author interview with Franklin Levy, September 1998.

34. Author interviews with Collister "Terry" Johnson, September 1998 and May 1999.

35. *Yale Daily News*, November 3, 1967.

36. Ibid.

37. "Branding Rite Laid to Fraternity," *The New York Times*, November 8, 1967.

38. "No Intervention for Fraternities," *Yale Daily News*, November 7, 1967.

39. "Defends DKE," Letter to Editor, *Yale Daily News*, November 7, 1967.

40. Author interview with William Sloane Coffin, December 1998.

41. "Yale Topples Tigers," *Daily Princetonian*, November 20, 1967; "Charlie Loses Spirit; Library Loses Lights; Princeton Loses Big," *Daily Princetonian*, November 10, 1967.

42. Author interviews with Princeton police officials, June and July 1998.

43. Author interview with Donald Ensenat, September 14, 1998.

44. "Negro Group Boycotts Yale Classes," *The New York Times*, March 14, 1968.

45. "Class of '68: Time to Take Stock," *The New York Times*, May 30, 1993.

46. Author interview with J. P. Goldsmith, November 8, 1998.

47. Author interview with James Lockhart III, September 8, 1998.

48. Selective Service System Classification Records, Year of Birth 1946–Bush, George Walker Bush.

49. Author interview with Robert Beebe, October 1, 1998.

50. Author interview with Doug Hannah, September 3, 1998.

51. "Junior Is His Own Bush Now," *Time*, July 31, 1989.

52. "George W. Bush: Politics, Baseball and Life in the Shadow of the White House," *The Dallas Morning News*, February 25, 1990.

53. "Evidence Doesn't Indicate Bush Got Help Joining Guard," *Fort Worth Star-Telegram*, November 29, 1998.

54. "Brewster of Yale Says Draft Stirs 'Cynical Gamesmanship,' " *The New York Times*, June 10, 1968.

55. "Yale Awards 2,042 Degrees and Honors 14 at Commencement," *The New York Times*, June 11, 1968.

56. Draper, "Favorite Son."

57. Author interview with Clay Johnson, July 1998.

7: FLYING

1. "Another Bush?," *The New York Times*, September 13, 1998.
2. Author interview with Albert Barclay, December 2, 1998.
3. "George Bush, Too," *D*, April 1992.
4. "Richards, Bush Anticipate Focus on Personalities," *The Dallas Morning News*, September 11, 1994.
5. Joe Hyams, *Flight of The Avenger: George Bush at War* (New York: Harcourt Brace Jovanovich, 1991), p. 32.
6. Ibid., p. 131.
7. Author interviews with General Walter "Buck" Staudt, November 1998.
8. Remarks of Governor George W. Bush at Schreiner College, Kerrville, Texas, April 10, 1996.
9. "Understanding What the National Guard Is All About—An Interview with Governor George W. Bush," *National Guard Review*, Winter 1998.
10. Author interviews with General Walter "Buck" Staudt, November 1998.
11. "Like Father, Like Son," *Houston Post*, November 7, 1993.
12. Author interview with Joe Briggs, November 14, 1998.
13. "Evidence Doesn't Indicate Bush Got Help Joining Guard," *Fort Worth Star-Telegram*, November 29, 1998.
14. "Bill Clinton's Draft Critics Are Hypocrites," *Seattle Times*, September 21, 1992.
15. Author interviews with Lloyd Bentsen III, December 1998 and May 1999.
16. George Walker Bush, Texas Air National Guard Service Records.
17. Author interviews with John Adger, October 1998.
18. Author interviews with John Daugherty, October 1998.
19. George Bush, *Looking Forward* (New York: Doubleday, 1987), p. 108.
20. Donnie Radcliffe, *Simply Barbara Bush* (New York: Warner Books, 1989), p. 139.
21. Author interview with Doug Hannah, September 3, 1998.
22. Ibid.
23. "From Party Boy to Party Leader," *Fort Worth Star-Telegram*, November 29, 1998.
24. "Who Was the Washington Blonde Photographed Last April with Prime Minister Pierre Trudeau of Canada?," *Washington Post*, June 14, 1981.
25. "Life with Lace," Washington Post, May 31, 1982.
26. Gene Tierney with Mickey Herskowitz, *Self Portrait* (New York: Wyden Books, 1979).
27. Author interview with Doug Hannah, September 3, 1998.
28. Author interviews with John Daugherty, October 1998.
29. "Old Is New Again for London Vistors," *Houston Chronicle*, September 15, 1991.
30. "I Was Young and Irresponsible," *The Dallas Morning News*, November 15, 1998.
31. Author interviews with Tom Hail, aviation historian for the Texas Military Forces Museum, October, November, December 1998.
32. Author interview with Bernard Reynolds, February 1999.
33. Author interview with Roger Dahlberg, February 1999.
34. Author interview with Norman Dotti, December 1998.
35. Author interview with Joseph Chaney, December 1998.

36. Author interview with Jeffrey Kenyon, February 1999.

37. Fitzhugh Green, *George Bush: An Intimate Portrait* (New York: Hippocrene, 1989), p. 111.

38. Green, *George Bush*, p. 109; "George Bush, Plucky Lad," *Texas Monthly*, June 1983; Bush, *Looking Forward*, p. 101.

39. Parmet, *George Bush*. p. 140.

40. Ibid., p. 140.

41. "I Was Young and Irresponsible."

42. Author interview with Roger Dahlberg, February 1999.

43. Author interview with Jeffrey Kenyon, December 1998.

44. Author interview with Dean Roome, November 1998.

45. "From Party Boy to Party Leader."

46. Press Release, Office of Information, Texas Air National Guard, March 24, 1970.

47. Author interview with Donald Ensenat, September 14, 1998.

48. "I Was Young and Irresponsible."

49. Author interview with Doug Hannah, September 3, 1998.

50. Parmet, *George Bush*, p. 141.

51. Monica Crowley, *Nixon off the Record* (New York: Random House, 1996), p. 46.

52. Parmet, *George Bush*, p. 148.

53. Author interview with Doug Hannah, September 3, 1998.

54. Ibid.

55. Author interview with Jonathan Bush, February 23, 1999.

56. Gus Clemens, *Legacy* (San Antonio, Tex.: Mulberry Avenue Books, 1983), p. 153.

57. "Is There Room on a Republican Ticket for Another Bush?," *The New York Times*, September 13, 1998.

58. Author interview with Donald Ensenat, September 14, 1998.

59. "George W. Bush; Politics, Baseball and Life in the Shadow of the White House," *The Dallas Morning News*, February 25, 1990.

60. Author interviews with Lloyd Bentsen III, December 1998 and May 1999.

8: PRIMOGENITOR

1. Author interview with Andrew Clark, former attorney for Stratford of Texas, September 21, 1998.

2. Author interview with Robert Gow, September 23, 1998. At the time of the interview, Gow was residing in the Mexican Yucatán and overseeing a new business venture involving the commercial production of bamboo.

3. Author interview with William O. Turney, former Stratford vice president, September 22, 1998.

4. Author interview with Robert Gow, September 23, 1998.

5. Author interviews with Peter Knudtzon, October 1998.

6. Author interview with O. S. "Todd" Simpson Jr., October 13, 1998.

7. Author interviews with Gene Biddle, October 1998.

8. "Born to Run: What's in a Name?," *Texas Monthly*, May 1994.

9. Author interview with Robert Gow, September 23, 1998.

10. Ibid.

11. "Legislative Race Eyed by Bush Jr.," *Houston Post*, October 23, 1971.

12. "Bush Pays Tribute to 'The Aide,' " *Midland Reporter-Telegram*, January 20, 1989.

13. Author interviews with Winton Blount III, November and December 1998.

14. Winton M. "Red" Blount with Richard Blodgett, *Doing It My Way* (Lyme, Conn.: Greenwich Publishing, 1996), p. 119.

15. Ibid., p. 63.

16. George Walker Bush, Texas Air National Guard Service Records.

17. "I Was Young and Irresponsible," *The Dallas Morning News*, November 15, 1998.

18. Author interviews with Winton Blount III, November and December 1998.

19. Author interview with Robert Reisner, November 1998.

20. Donnie Radcliffe, *Simply Barbara Bush* (New York: Warner Books, 1989), p. 140.

21. "The Bush Bunch," *The Washington Post*, January 22, 1989.

22. Ibid.; "Junior Is His Own Bush Now," *Time*, July 31, 1989.

23. Robert Draper, "Favorite Son," *GQ*, September 1998.

24. "Junior Is His Own Bush Now."

25. Author interview with Doug Hannah, September 3, 1998.

26. Author interviews with Ernie Ladd, Edgar Arnold, and David Anderson, former PULL staffers, October, November, and December 1998.

27. Ibid.; "Junior Is His Own Bush Now."

28. Author interviews with Edgar Arnold, October 1998.

29. George Walker Bush, Texas Air National Guard Service Records.

30. Ibid.

9: DESPAIR AND CAPITAL SINS

1. Author interview with Nathaniel Butler, November 1998.

2. Ibid.

3. Author interview with Jonathan Bush, February 23, 1998.

4. Author interview with Nathaniel Butler, November 1998.

5. Ibid.

6. Author interview with Peter Gebhard, February 4, 1999.

7. Ibid.

8. "George W. Bush: Politics, Baseball and Life in the Shadow of the White House," *The Dallas Morning News*, February 25, 1990.

9. Robert Draper, "Favorite Son," *GQ*, September 1998.

10. Donnie Radcliffe, *Simply Barbara Bush* (New York: Warner Books, 1989), p. 139.

11. Author interview with Elsie Walker, February 22, 1989.

12. Author interview with Jonathan Bush, February 23, 1999.

13. Author interview with Jeb Bush, January 26, 1999.

14. Author interview with Peter Gebhard, February 4. 1999.

15. Author interviews with John Axelrod, October 1998.

16. Author interview with William Glass, president of the 1974 Harvard Republican Club, December 31, 1998.

17. David Maraniss, "The Bush Bunch," *The Washington Post*, January 22, 1989.

18. "Professor Muhammad Ali Delivers Lecture; Poems and Parables Fill Talk on Friendship," *The Harvard Crimson*, June 12, 1975.

19. "Class Day Speaker Gregory Tells Seniors: Something Must Be Wrong with America," *The Harvard Crimson*, June 12, 1975.

20. "A First Family That Just Won't Quit," *People*, January 30, 1989.

21. " 'Dark Horse' Candidate Had Promising Beginning," *Midland Reporter-Telegram*, July 2, 1978.

22. Barbara Bush, *Barbara Bush: A Memoir* (New York: Scribner's, 1994), pp. 123–125.

23. Author interview with William "Bucky" Bush, February 18, 1999.

24. Author interviews with Dr. Charles Younger, July 1998.

25. Ibid.

26. "In the Fish Bowl with Little 'Little George,' " *Chicago Tribune*, May 1, 1992.

27. "George W. Bush: Politics, Baseball and Life in the Shadow of the White House."

28. "GOP Probes Official as Teacher of 'Tricks,' " *The Washington Post*, August 10, 1973.

29. Deposition of Karl Rove, gathered during the 1996 State of Texas lawsuit against the tobacco industry. Rove, according to his deposition, worked for Philip Morris as a paid consultant, to "help them make wide use of their political dollars." In his deposition, he noted that at the time he was a Philip Morris consultant he was also the director of the Governor Bush Committee.

30. "Top Bush Aide Brings Aggressive Style to Effort," *The Dallas Morning News*, March 21, 1999.

31. Letter from George Walker Bush to Karl Rove, November 7, 1995.

32. Author interview with Ed Thompson, October 1998.

33. Ibid.

34. Author interviews with independent oilmen in Midland, Texas, July and August 1998.

35. Author interview with Dr. Charles Younger, July 1998.

36. Author interviews with Joseph O'Neill III, June 1998.

37. Author interview with Robert McCleskey, October 1998.

38. Author interviews with Walter Holton, December 1998.

39. Author interview with John Younger, July 1998.

40. Ibid.

41. Author interviews with independent oilmen, Midland, Texas, July and August 1998; author interviews with Charles Younger and Joe O'Neill III, July 1998.

10: SOMEONE REALLY POLITICAL

1. Author interview with Julia Reed, October 18, 1998.

2. Julia Reed, "The Son Also Rises," *The Weekly Standard*, February 10, 1997.

3. Ibid.

4. Author interview with Robert Reisner, October 1998.

5. Ibid.

6. Author interview with Don Evans, June 1998; David Maraniss, "The Bush Bunch," *The Washington Post*, January 22, 1989.

7. Herbert Parmet, *George Bush: The Life of a Lone Star Yankee* (New York: Scribner's, 1997), p. 209.

8. Ibid., p. 207.

9. Ibid.

10. "Born to Run: What's in a Name?," *Texas Monthly*, May 1994.

11. Deposition of Karl Rove during the 1996 State of Texas lawsuit against the tobacco industry.

12. "Midland Man Announces as First in House Race," *Lubbock Avalanche-Journal*, July 20, 1977.

13. Steven K. Wilmsen, *Silverado* (Washington: National Press Books, 1991), p. 65.

14. Author interviews with Ruth Schiermeyer, December 1998.

15. "First Lady," *The Houston Chronicle*, July 20, 1997.

16. Ibid.; "Bush Stumps for Husband on Home Turf," *Midland Reporter-Telegram*, May 12, 1994: "She said she met her husband at a party in August 1977 in Midland and a few months later they were married."

17. "Laura Bush, Adjusting to the Spotlight," *The Dallas Morning News*, September 24, 1995.

18. Author interview with William "Bucky" Bush, February 18, 1999.

19. "Born to Run: What's in a Name?," *Texas Monthly*, May 1994.

20. "Laura Bush, Adjusting to the Spotlight."

21. "Born to Run: What's in a Name?," *Texas Monthly*, May 1994.

22. "Newlyweds Seeking Government Posts," *Lubbock Avalanche-Journal*, March 13, 1978.

23. Ibid.

24. Author interview with Charles Black, January 26, 1999.

25. "Texas Runoff Strains GOP Relations; Some Sour Feelings in Bush Camp over Reagan's Role," *The Washington Post*, June 3, 1978.

26. Ibid.

27. Author interview with Doug Hannah, September 3, 1998.

28. "Bush (of Connecticut) Reveals His Single Regret," *Midland Reporter-Telegram*, June 2, 1978.

29. "President's Son Emerges as a Likely Candidate for Next Year's Gubernatorial Race in Texas," *The Wall Street Journal*, April 3, 1989.

30. "Sign's Advice Gladly Heeded," *Midland Reporter-Telegram*, June 4, 1978.

31. Author interview with Jim Reese, October 2, 1998.

32. Author interview with Kent Hance, October 8, 1998.

33. Ibid.; author interview with C. R. Hutcheson, October 6, 1998.

34. Author interview with C. R. Hutcheson, October 6, 1998.

35. "Bush Not Making Issue of Father in Campaign," *Lubbock Avalanche-Journal*, March 30, 1978.

36. "Congressional Candidates Swap Blows in City Debate," *Odessa American*, October 25, 1978.

37. "GOP Candidate Bush Under Fire from Hance Camp," *Midland Reporter-Telegram*, November 3, 1978.

38. Author interview with Mel Turner, October 4, 1998.

39. Ibid.

40. "Bush and Sons," *Miami Herald*, September 25, 1994.

41. "Hance Raps Foe's Contribution List," *Lubbock Avalanche-Journal*, October 13, 1978.

42. "George W. Bush: Politics, Baseball and Life in the Shadow of the White House," *The Dallas Morning News*, February 25, 1990.

11: THE BIG ELEPHANT FIELD

1. Author interview with Joseph O'Neill III, July 1998.

2. George W. Bush, in an unpublished portion of interview with Texas journalist Charlotte Anne Lucas, May 1994.

3. "Bush Cites Reagan Stamina, Class," *Midland Reporter-Telegram*, February 15, 1981.

4. "Younger Bush Wasn't Surprised," *Midland Reporter-Telegram*, May 27, 1980.

5. George W. Bush, in an unpublished portion of an interview with Texas journalist Charlotte Anne Lucas, May 1994.

6. Author interviews with independent Texas oilmen, Midland, Texas, June, July, and August 1998.

7. Author interview with Jonathan Bush, February 23, 1999.

8. Author interview with Kim Dyches, October 14, 1998.

9. Author interview with Becky Ferguson, September 1998.

10. Author interview with Mark Owen, October 12, 1998.

11. Ibid.; author interview with Charles Prather, former trustee and general manager of Waggoner Ranch, October 19, 1998.

12. George W. Bush, in an unpublished interview with Texas journalist Charlotte Anne Lucas, May 1994.

13. "What Laura Wants: Why Texas' First Wife Has Thought Twice About the Chance to Become the Nation's First Lady, Keeping a Focus on Kids," *Austin American-Statesman*, April 18, 1999.

14. "Bush Grandchildren," United Press International, November 28, 1981.

15. "What Laura Wants."

16. "Bush Has Fared Well Despite Firms' Troubles," *The Dallas Morning News*, May 7, 1994.

17. "Bush Abandons Connecticut Bid for Senate Seat," *The New York Times*, July 28, 1982.

18. "Bush Has Fared Well Despite Firms' Troubles."

19. "Vice President George Bush's Son Says He Hopes His Father Will Run in 1988," Associated Press, September 6, 1984.

20. John Brady, *Bad Boy* (New York: Addison-Wesley, 1996), pp. 138–139.

21. "The Wackiest Rig in Texas," *Time*, October 28, 1991.

22. "The Color of Money," *U.S. News and World Report*, March 16, 1992.

23. Author interviews with Phil Kendrick, founder of Harken Oil and Gas, December 1998.

24. Paul Rea, unpublished interview with Texas journalist Charlotte Anne Lucas, 1994.

25. "Who's Going to Make It in '88? Here's What the Insiders Say," *Washingtonian*, April 1986.

26. Author interview with Al Hunt, April 8, 1999.

27. Author interview with Joseph O'Neill III, July 1998; "Governor George W. Bush as Well as Other Members of His Family on His Life, Career and Political Ambitions," NBC News, July 30, 1997.

28. "Jerry Dumps George: Falwell's Vanishing Endorsement," *The New Republic*, November 24, 1986.

29. "Righting Reagan's Revolution," *The Washington Post*, March 22, 1983.

30. "Wead, Bakker Close, Ex-PTL Officials Say District 6 Candidate Downplays Ties," *Phoenix Gazette*, September 3, 1992.

31. Doug Wead Files, George Bush Presidential Library, College Station, Tex.

32. "A Study of the 1988 Presidential Campaign," oral history transcript of interview with Doug Wead, University of Texas, Center for American History.

33. Doug Wead Files, George Bush Presidential Library, College Station, Tex.

34. "George Bush: Where Does He Stand?," *The Christian Herald*, June 1986.

12: BEHAVIOR MODIFICATION

1. "Why Is Lee Atwater So Hungry?," *Esquire*, December 1986.

2. John Brady, *Bad Boy* (New York: Addison-Wesley, 1997), p. 153.

3. Ann Grimes, *Running Mates* (New York: Morrow, 1990), pp. 186–194.

4. Ibid.

5. "George W. Bush, Politics, Baseball and Life in the Shadow of the White House," *The Dallas Morning News*, February 25, 1990.

6. Author interview with Jim Pinkerton, February 17, 1999.

7. Author interview with Fred Malek, February 16, 1999.

8. "George Bush Is Mr. Nice Guy," *Chicago Tribune*, June 19, 1988.

9. Author interview with Jim Pinkerton, February 17, 1999.

10. "Junior Is His Own Bush Now," *Time*, July 31, 1989.

11. George Bush with Doug Wead, *Man of Integrity* (Eugene, Oreg.: Harvest House, 1988), p. 42.

12. Brady, *Bad Boy*, p. 157.

13. Author interview with David Hoffman via e-mail from Moscow Bureau of *The Washington Post*, March 31, 1999.

14. Ibid.

15. Author interview with Margaret Warner, May 17, 1999.

16. "George Bush Jr. Likely to Seek Elective Office—One Day," *The Dallas Morning News*, August 2, 1987.

17. Author interview with Charles Black, January 26, 1999.

18. Author interview with Robert Mosbacher, January 29, 1999.

19. Author interview with Roger Ailes, January 29, 1999.

20. Author interviews with David Bates, former assistant to President George Bush, January 1999.

21. "George, Washington," *Texas Monthly*, June 1999.

22. "Personal History: Delicate Relations," *Newsweek*, February 10, 1997.

23. Author interview with John Ellis, February 10, 1999; Richard Ben Cramer, *What It Takes* (New York: Vintage Books, 1993), p. ix.

24. Author interviews with John Mashek, January 1999.

25. Author interviews with Collister "Terry" Johnson, September 1998 and May 1999.

26. "A Study of the 1988 Presidential Campaign," oral history transcript of interview with Doug Wead, University of Texas, Center for American History.

27. "Notable Quotes," Associated Press, February 9, 1988.

28. "Vice President Bush's Son and Spokesperson Hold Press Conference," *Southwest News Wire*, July 21, 1988.

29. Author's observation at 1988 GOP National Convention in New Orleans.

30. Peter Goldman and Tom Mathews, *Quest for the Presidency* (New York: Touchstone, 1989), p. 323.

31. "Asleep at the Wheel," *Chicago Tribune*, August 19, 1988.

32. "It's a Dog's Life," *The New York Times*, August 10, 1997.

33. Author interview with Fred Malek, February 16, 1999.

34. "Bush's Eldest Son Relishes Role as a Texas Delegate," *Houston Chronicle*, August 16, 1988.

35. Ibid.

36. Author interview with Bob Teeter, February 3, 1999.

37. "Team Player," *Texas Monthly*, June 1999.

38. "Bush and Bentsen Sons Say No Strings Pulled in Their Guard Sign-ups," Associated Press, August 24, 1988.

39. Joan Mower, Associated Press, August 18, 1988.

40. Jack W. Germond and Jules Witcover, *Mad as Hell: Revolt at the Ballot Box, 1992* (New York: Warner Books, 1993), p. 400.

41. "Sore Winners," *New Republic*, December 5, 1988.

42. Barbara Bush, *Barbara Bush: A Memoir* (New York: Scribner's, 1994), p. 249.

43. Author interviews with David Bates, January 1999.

44. "As Operative for His Father, Loyalty Was the Foremost Watchword," *Houston Chronicle*, May 8, 1994.

45. "Bush, Texas, Both Face Change as Day of Inauguration Arrives," *The Dallas Morning News*, January 17, 1995.

46. George W. Bush Files, George Bush Presidential Library, College Station, Tex.

47. Ibid.

48. Ibid.

49. "All the President's Children," *U.S. News and World Report*, February 12, 1990.

50. "Prince George of Texas," *The San Diego Union-Tribune*, December 30, 1988.

51. Author interview conducted April 2, 1999; interviewee asked to remain anonymous.

52. "Don't Call Him Junior," *Texas Monthly*, April 1989.

53. Associated Press, March 18, 1989.

54. "Team Player."

55. "Rose Burying 'Mortician' Image,' " *Dallas Business Journal*, January 24, 1992.

56. Ibid.

57. "Other People's Money," *U.S. News and World Report*, March 16, 1992.

58. Bob Woodward and Carl Bernstein, *The Final Days* (New York: Simon & Schuster, 1976), p. 169.

59. Author interview with Fred Malek, February 16, 1999.

60. "Sports News," Associated Press, March 22, 1989.
61. "Younger Bush and Partners Purchase Majority Ownership in Rangers," United Press International, March 18, 1989.
62. "First Lady Advises Son Against Texas Governor's Race," United Press International, April 28, 1989.
63. "Baseball Thrusts Bush into Spotlight," *The Bergen Record*, May 5, 1989.
64. "The Face Is Familiar, the Resume Eerily So," *Newsday*, May 8, 1989.

13: AMAZING GRACE

1. Author interview with Kent Hance, October 8, 1998.
2. "Major Production," *Adweek*, June 5, 1989.
3. "Bush, Texas, Both Face Change as Day of Inauguration Arrives," *The Dallas Morning News*, January 17, 1995.
4. "Island Long on List of Filthy-Rich Towns," *New York Post*, May 14, 1999.
5. "Clements Says Bush Decision Will Have No Effect on GOP Primary," United Press International, August 2, 1989.
6. "Bush Makes Global Relations a Family Affair," Associated Press, December 1, 1991.
7. "There Will Be Lots of Activity," United Press International, August 17, 1989.
8. "A Crisis in the First Family," *Newsweek*, July 23, 1990.
9. "Bush Has Fared Well Despite Firms' Troubles," *The Dallas Morning News*, May 7, 1994.
10. "The Wackiest Rig in Texas," *Time*, October 28, 1991.
11. Mike Shropshire and Frank Schaefer, *The Thorny Rose of Texas* (New York: Birch Lane, 1994), p. 210.
12. Ibid.
13. "Shadow and Substance," *Washington Times*, August 13, 1990.
14. Author interview with and correspondence from Douglas Wead, February 22, 1999.
15. Letter from Doug Wead to Jerry Falwell, June 30, 1989, Doug Wead Files, George Bush Presidential Library, College Station, Tex.
16. Author interview with and correspondence from Douglas Wead, February 22, 1999.
17. Ibid.
18. "Wead's History, Agenda Are the Issues," *The Arizona Republic*, October 27, 1992.
19. Author interview with Fay Vincent, December 1998.
20. "In Land of Big, Ryan's Biggest," *The New York Times*, July 18, 1990.
21. "Bush's Son Cuts Harken Stake," *USA Today*, April 8, 1991.
22. "From Family Black Sheep to National Political Heavy," *The Atlanta Constitution*, April 4, 1992.
23. Peter Goldman, Thomas M. DeFrank, Mark Miller, Andrew Murr, and Tom Mathews, *Quest for the Presidency 1992* (College Station: Texas A&M University Press, 1994), pp. 303–307.
24. Ibid.
25. "George W. Bush: An Operative for His Father," *Houston Chronicle*, May 8, 1994.
26. Author interview with Fred Malek, February 16, 1999.
27. Ibid.

28. Author interview with Mark Langdale, September 15, 1998.

29. Author interview with Lawson Pedigo, September 15, 1998.

30. "Queen Elizabeth and the Bush Black Sheep," *The Washington Post*, May 21, 1991.

31. Author interview with Jette Campbell, November 1998.

32. Author interviews with Comer Cottrell, December 1998.

33. Author interviews with Harry Gugder, former president of NAACP Arlington, Texas, branch, December 1998.

34. Author interviews with Comer Cottrell, December 1998.

35. Author interviews with Harry Gugder, former President of NAACP Arlington, Texas branch, December 1998.

36. Author interviews with Comer Cottrell, December 1998.

37. Goldman et al., *Quest for the Presidency 1992*, p. 390.

38. Ann Grimes, *Running Mates* (New York: Morrow, 1990), p. 194.

39. Marlin Fitzwater, *Call the Briefing* (Holbrook, Mass.: Adams, 1995), p. 328.

40. Goldman et al., *Quest for the Presidency 1992*, p. 394.

41. Mary Matalin and James Carville, *All's Fair* (New York: Random House and Simon & Schuster, 1994), p. 335.

42. Author interview with Mary Matalin, March 9, 1999.

43. Ibid.

44. "The 1992 Campaign; A Bush by Another Name Runs in Missouri," *The New York Times*, August 2, 1992.

45. Author interview with Fred Malek, February 16, 1999.

46. "George W. Bush Discusses His Father's Campaign," CBS News, August 17, 1992.

47. Author interview with Brian Mullahy, April 7, 1999.

48. Goldman et al., *Quest for the Presidency 1992*, p. 586.

49. "Read Her Lips," *The Boston Globe*, October 25, 1992.

50. "Reliable Source," *The Washington Post*, October 27, 1992.

51. "The Two George W.'s: A Fiercely Loyal Son or a Peevish Prince?," *Austin American-Statesman*, February 21, 1999.

52. George W. Bush Files, George Bush Presidential Library, College Station, Texas.

14: A DOG WITH A BONE

1. Author interview with Alphonso Jackson, September 15, 1998.

2. "Bush and Aides Attend Funeral for His Mother," *The New York Times*, November 24, 1992; "Dorothy W. Bush, Mother of President, Dies at 91," *The New York Times*, November 20, 1992.

3. Ibid.

4. Barbara Bush, *Barbara Bush: A Memoir* (New York: Scribner's, 1994), p. 517.

5. "Baseball Misses a Chance with Bush," *The Dallas Morning News*, November 13, 1994.

6. Author interview with Alphonso Jackson, September 15, 1998.

7. Author interview with Mark Langdale, September 15, 1998.

8. Author interview with Fred McClure, December 1998.

9. "Born to Run: What's in a Name?," *Texas Monthly*, May 1994.

10. "Laura Bush," *The Dallas Morning News*, September 24, 1995.

11. Author interview with Alphonso Jackson, September 15, 1998.

12. Mike Kingston, Sam Attlesey, and Mary G. Crawford, *Political History of Texas* (Austin: Eakin Press, 1992), p. 194.

13. Author interviews with Collister "Terry" Johnson, September 1998 and May 1999.

14. "Richards on Solid Ground," *The Dallas Morning News*, July 26, 1993.

15. "Born to Run: What's in a Name?"

16. "Path Clear for Bush to Run for Governor," *The Dallas Morning News*, August 31, 1993.

17. "Bush Brothers," *Odessa American*, October 31, 1993.

18. Author interview with Jeb Bush, February 26, 1999.

19. Author interview with Joe O'Neill III, July 1998.

20. Author interviews with Israel Hernandez, November 28 and December 4, 1998.

21. Ibid.

22. "Bush Eldest Son to Run for Texas Governor," United Press International, November 8, 1993.

23. "First, Get Specific About Which George Bush," *Houston Chronicle*, November 13, 1993.

24. Author interview with Don Evans, July 1998.

25. Author interview with Bob Teeter, February 3, 1999.

26. "Executive Profile," *The Dallas Morning News*, November 13, 1994.

27. Author interview with John Ellis, February 19, 1999.

28. "New Campaigns for Bush Sons: Their Own," *The New York Times*, November 30, 1993.

29. "Bush's Son: Talking Only to Texans," *The Washington Post*, February 13, 1994.

30. Jim Hudson, "George W. Bush," "Ochiltree Observer" column *Perryton Herald*, January 13, 1994.

31. "In the Fish Bowl with Little George," *Chicago Tribune*, May 1, 1992.

32. "Drugs Irrelevant to Race," *Houston Chronicle*, May 3, 1994.

33. "Counterattack: Past Use of Illegal Drugs Irrelevant to Race," *Texarkana Gazette*, May 4, 1994.

34. "Bush's Pillows, Bed Will Go Along with Them, as Usual," Associated Press, November 15, 1988.

35. Herbert Parmet, *George Bush: The Life of a Lone Star Yankee* (New York: Scribner's, 1997), p. 428.

36. "Name Opens Doors, Shuts Some for Campaiging Bush Brothers," *The Dallas Morning News*, September 7, 1994.

37. "Team Player," *Texas Monthly*, June 1999.

38. Securities and Exchange Commission, Division of Enforcement, letter to Robert Jordan, "Re: In the Matter of Trading in the Securities of Harken Energy Corporation," October 18, 1993.

39. Bush, *Barbara Bush*, p. 225.

40. "Bush Criticizes Education Data; Richards Say Opponent Doesn't Know What He Is Talking About," *The Dallas Morning News*, July 16, 1994.

41. "Meanwhile, Back on The Campaign Trail," *Houston Chronicle*, August 20, 1994.

42. Author interviews with Israel Hernandez, November 28 and December 4, 1998.

43. "Richards, Bush Clash in Dallas Debate," Associated Press, October 22, 1994.

44. Author interview with Elsie Walker, February 22, 1989.

15: GIANT KILLER

1. "Governor's Race, a Battle to the End," *The Dallas Morning News*, November 6, 1994.

2. "The Candidates and the Higher Authority," *Houston Post*, October 2, 1994.

3. Ibid.

4. "The Gospel According to George W. Bush," *The Weekly Standard*, March 22, 1999.

5. Peter Collier and David Horowitz, *Destructive Generation* (New York: Free Press, 1996), p. 373.

6. "Bush and Sons," *Miami Herald*, September 25, 1994.

7. "Bush Makes Last Dash Across State for Votes," *San Antonio Express-News*, November 8, 1994.

8. "A Bit Absent-Minded," *The Dallas Morning News*, November 9, 1994.

9. George W. Bush, remarks from victory speech, November 8, 1994.

10. "Jeb Bush Can't Match Big Brother's Feat," *The Dallas Morning News*, November 9, 1994.

11. "Bush and Sons," *The Miami Herald*, September 25, 1994.

12. Ibid.

13. "After Getting Out from Under Shadow of Famous Dad, Jeb Bush Seeks Help," Associated Press, November 1, 1994.

14. Author interview with Jeb Bush, January 22, 1999.

15. "Jeb Bush Pushes Forward with His Life Following Defeat," *The Orlando Sentinel*, November 10, 1994.

16. "Election '94: Governor," *Houston Chronicle*, November 9, 1994.

17. Ibid.

18. Richard Zelade, *Austin* (Houston: Gulf Publishing Company, 1992), p. 174.

19. "Position of Power," *The Dallas Morning News*, December 27, 1998.

20. Author interview with Bob Bullock, February 15, 1999.

21. Ibid.

22. Ibid.

23. Author interview with Pete Laney, February 12, 1999.

24. Ibid.

25. "The Bush Inaugural," *Houston Chronicle*, January 18, 1995.

26. Ibid.

27. Inaugural speech of Texas Governor George W. Bush, Austin, Texas, January 18, 1995.

28. "Bush, Texas Both Face Change as Day of Inauguration Arrives," *The Dallas Morning News*, January 17, 1995.

29. "Laura Bush; Adjusting to the Spotlight," *The Dallas Morning News*, September 24, 1995.

30. "Putting on a Happy Face," *The Washington Post*, January 30, 1995.

31. Ibid.

32. "Capitol Notebook," *Houston Chronicle*, April 27, 1995.

33. Letter from Bill Clinton to George W. Bush, October 26, 1995.

34. "Father and Son, George and George W. Bush Share Political Views from Walker's Point," CBS News, August 11, 1996.

35. Interview with Bob Teeter, February 3, 1999.

36. "The Eyes of the Nation Are upon You, Gov. Bush," *St. Petersburg Times*, May 17, 1997.

37. "Top Bush Aide Brings Aggressive Style to Effort," *The Dallas Morning News*, March 21, 1999.

38. Deposition of Karl Rove during the 1996 State of Texas lawsuit against the tobacco industry.

39. "The Eyes of the Nation Are upon You, Gov. Bush."

16: DYNASTY

1. "Filling the Shoes," *Texas Monthly*, August 1997.

2. George W. Bush, remarks at Republican Midwestern Leadership Conference, August 23, 1997.

3. Ibid.

4. George W. Bush, conversation with author, May 13, 1998.

5. "Bush Misses GOP Presidential Event that Underscores Divisions," Associated Press, March 28, 1998.

6. Richard Ben Cramer, *What It Takes* (New York: Vintage Books, 1993).

7. "Governor Bush as Well as Other Members of His Family on His Life, Career and Political Ambitions," NBC News, July 30, 1997.

8. Author interview with Bob Bullock, February 15, 1999.

9. Letter from Myron Magnet to George W. Bush, July 10, 1997.

10. Letter from George W. Bush to Myron Magnet, July 17, 1997.

11. Memorandum from Doug Wead to Gov. George W. Bush, February 2, 1998.

12. Ibid., marked "Gov. called 2-3-98."

13. Author interview with Clay Johnson, June 1998.

14. Author interview with John Hannah, April 17, 1999.

15. "Jeb Brings Out the Big Gun, Mom, as Race Nears Finish," *The Tampa Tribune*, October 22, 1998.

16. "Brothers Bush: All in the Political Family," *Austin American-Statesman*, October 25, 1998.

17. "Day of the Dauphins," *The New York Times*, November 4, 1998.

18. "George W. and Jeb Bush Are Easily Elected Governors in Texas and Florida," *The New York Times*, November 4, 1998.

19. Author interview with Jeb Bush, January 26, 1999.

20. "Bush: 'My Personal Life Is Great,' " *Henderson Daily News*, August 19, 1999; author interview with Joanna Tucker, August 20, 1998.

21. "Bush Touts Character as an Election Issue," *Austin American-Statesman*, August 19, 1998.

22. "Bush: Family Considerations Weigh Heavily in Any Presidential Thinking," Associated Press, September 17, 1998.

23. Ibid.

24. "Governor George W. Bush on His Life, Career and Political Ambitions," NBC News, July 10, 1997.

25. George W. Bush, conversation with author, June 23, 1998.

26. Ibid.

27. Author interview with Jeb Bush, January 22, 1999.

28. George W. Bush, remarks made at press conference at DuPont Photomasks, Round Rock, Texas, September 12, 1998.

29. "George W. and Jeb Bush Are Easily Elected Governors in Texas and Florida."

30. Author interview with John Ellis, February 10, 1999.

31. George W. Bush, remarks made November 3, 1998.

32. Ibid.

Acknowledgments

AT THE *Dallas Morning News*, editors Ralph Langer and Gilbert Bailon quickly set the wheels in motion for my sabbatical. Next, Texas journalist and public affairs expert Patrick Graves joined the project early and performed invaluable and precise research in an endless variety of complicated areas. The support of his family as well as his humor, diligence, and knowledge of the usually unfathomable ways of Texas always carried this work forward. W. Michael Smith joined the project in midflight and became a brilliant copilot who helped steer the final product onto the runway. He was a fearless fact checker and researcher, a most valued editor, and an extraordinarily intuitive sounding board on everything from the history of the Republic of Texas to the legacy of the 1960s. Given the enormous hurdles involving time and access on this project, these colleagues regularly performed miracles.

A note of appreciation must go to other veteran Texas and Washington journalists. Jordan Smith brought unflagging energy, idealism, and intelligence; Vanessa Valencia spent hours helping; Stacey Freedenthal never stopped accumulating documents; Stephen Power, among the most conscientious journalists I know, has my respect for volunteering to work at night and on weekends. Tracy Everbach and Al Brumley, savvy reporters and writers, arrived to help with very important research. Rebecca Christie, Lisa Falkenberg, and Wendy Smith took valuable time out from their studies at the University of Texas and they deserve enormous credit. Several *Dallas Morning News* journalists should be thanked for advice and friendship: the entire staff of the Austin bureau (in particular Sam Attlesey, Christy Hoppe, Wayne Slater, Christopher Lee, Pete Slover, Terrence Stutz, George Kuempel, and Richard Oppel Jr., now with *The New York Times*), Gayle Reaves, Steve McGonigle, Bill Lodge, Laura Jacobus, Thomas Huang, Todd J. Gillman, Lori Stahl, Diane Jennings, Mike Weiss, Harriet Blake, Lennox Samuels, Rodger Jones, Mark Edgar, Stu Wilk, Carl Leubsdorf, Kathy Lewis, and Howard Swindle.

The Wall Street Journal's Robert Tomsho, a best friend, had especially sage advice on this project; the fearless and knowledgeable CNN correspondent Charles Zewe was always kind when I met him on the press conference trail; Sam Gwynne, the savvy

Time correspondent in Texas, willingly shared ideas; Charlotte Anne Lucas with the *San Antonio Express-News* was immensely generous with her time and knowledge; Laura Tolley, also of the *San Antonio Express-News*, is to be thanked for her friendship; R. G. Ratcliffe and Polly Ross Hughes of the *Houston Chronicle* offered important insights; Jay Root of *The Fort Worth Star-Telegram* was exceedingly kind to share his knowledge; Ken Herman of the *Austin American-Statesman* and Michael Holmes of the Associated Press were helpful. Veteran Austin reporter Sam Kinch shared lunch and history with me. Texas journalist Ross Ramsey, who offered me the opportunity to write my first book many years ago, was kind. Three more old friends and skilled journalists must be mentioned: John Branch, the talented political cartoonist of the *San Antonio Express-News*; Jeff Franks of Reuters; John Burnett of National Public Radio. Each of them, over the years, has proved to be rock-steady, even through my unevenness. Too, I have been the beneficiary of unbridled support from my colleagues at *The Sporting News*, including Mike Nahrstedt, John Rawlings, and Joe Hoppel. Nick Newton, my coauthor on another book, is thanked for his patience. Three people from Dallas should be mentioned for their inspiration over the years: the Right Reverend R. L. Griffin from south Dallas, Ruben Guanajuato from Oak Cliff, and Dinh Phuong from east Dallas. Others to be thanked for conversation and insights are Shermakaye Bass, Michelle Stanush, Chuck Nevitt, Robert Draper of *GQ* magazine, Joe Nick Patoski of *Texas Monthly*, and Michael P. Geffner of *Details* magazine in New York. Louie Canelakes and Bette Ahern must be thanked for repeatedly offering their home and restaurant (Louie's) as sanctuaries on my research trips. Mr. Canelakes is one of the most intelligent social observers in Dallas, and (here's a free plug offered without a hesitation) anyone who wishes to understand that city should seek an audience with him.

Herbert Parmet, the Distinguished Professor of History Emeritus at City University of New York, was most generous with his wisdom. His definitive biography of President George Herbert Walker Bush, *George Bush: The Life of a Lone Star Yankee*, was a constant Rosetta stone for my research, and to him and his important work I am deeply indebted. Several other people have been prompt and courteous with their help: William Leon, the Texas National Guard officer who handles Freedom of Information Act requests; Tom Hail, the National Guard historian; Clay Johnson, Douglas Wead, Don Evans, Reggie Bashur, Tony Garza, and the other Bush staffers and advisers who were willing to spend hours with me; Lyda Molanphy and Patrick Woodson, who generously pointed me to important documents; Bill Miller, who offered observations on Texas politics; Kim Black, the ever-patient and pleasant staffer in Texas Governor George W. Bush's office, who endured hundreds of phone calls from me; Betty Orbeck, the archivist at the Permian Basin Petroleum Museum in Midland, who was kind enough to spend the day driving me around the city and who made available her exhaustive files; Doug Hannah, the longtime Bush family friend who proved to be an invaluable source of information from Houston; Michelle Smith, an old colleague from the *Houston Chronicle* who pointed me in the right direction.

There are many authors who have done groundbreaking reporting on Bush's life and whose work was the source of much information in this book: Ann Grimes, Mike Shropshire, Frank Schaefer, Donnie Radcliffe, John Brady, and Pamela Killian are the ones who immediately come to mind. Mention should go to my treasured friend Claudia Feldman of the *Houston Chronicle* for her excellent coverage of Texas First Lady Laura Bush. The staffs at several libraries were very helpful: the Midland County Library, the New Haven Library, the Greenwich Library, the libraries of Columbia University, the George Bush Presidential Library, the Houston Library, the Austin Library, and the University of Texas Library. At Andover, archivist Ruth Quattlebaum and Michael Wall were more than cooperative. The legendary lieutenant governor of Texas, Bob Bullock, should be thanked for seeing me on a day when he was battling life-threatening health problems; he passed away five months after granting me what would turn out to be his final, extensive interview.

My hardworking agent, David Hale Smith, brought me to this project, and to him and his capable staff I am completely, enormously indebted. David was also the one who introduced me to Jonathan Karp, easily one of the finest editors to ever wield a pen and a measured opinion. Jon showed enormous faith and patience as this project unfolded and then he displayed his brilliant editing skills; I am fortunate to have worked with him. At Random House and Times Books, there are several others who should be recognized: Carie Freimuth, Monica Gomez, the brilliant copy editor Lynn Anderson, the equally brilliant copy editor Nancy Inglis, Rose Pena, Will Weisser, and Sabrina Hicks.

My late father, born in 1905, was a master printer for more than four decades. He labored with ink, trays of type, and bars of lead at an inner-city printing plant and also at the ancient printing press in our cramped basement. This book, in some way, is about the importance of family, and I felt my father's presence as the book took shape. My mother, born the year World War I ended, has worked harder than anyone I know, and she has always been an inspiration to me. My wife's extended family has been supportive with encouragement and baby-sitting. Finally, Holly was there for the late-night trips to the copy shop, to the express delivery service, and to everywhere in between. She, Rose, and Nicholas never complained about the way I seemed to be disappearing into a writing cave for weeks on end. They were and are the loving reminders that friends and family are sometimes all that really matter.

Index

Note: In subheadings, George W. Bush is referred to as "Bush." His father is referred to as "George Bush."

About the Author

BILL MINUTAGLIO has distinguished himself as one of the top journalists in Texas, with the *Abilene Reporter-News*, the *San Antonio Express-News*, *The Houston Chronicle*, and *The Dallas Morning News*, where he has worked since 1983 as a special writer. His work has been recognized by the National Headliners, the Texas Headliners, the National Association of Black Journalists, the National Conference of Christians and Jews, the University of Missouri-Columbia School of Journalism and the American Association of Sunday and Feature Editors. His work has appeared in many national magazines and newspapers; he has coauthored two books and served as a contributing author to three other books. He lives in Austin with his two children and his wife, Holly. He can be reached at BMinutag@aol.com.